TRANSPARENCY IN GLOBAL CHANGE

TRANSPARENCY IN GLOBAL CHANGE

THE VANGUARD OF THE OPEN SOCIETY

Burkart Holzner and Leslie Holzner

UNIVERSITY OF PITTSBURGH PRESS

Published by the University of Pittsburgh Press,
Pittsburgh, PA 15260

Copyright © 2006, University of Pittsburgh Press
All rights reserved
Manufactured in the United States of America
Printed on acid-free paper
10 9 8 7 6 5 4 3 2 1

Library of Congress Cataloging-in-Publication Data
Holzner, Burkart.
 Transparency in global change: the vanguard of the open
society / Burkart Holzner and Leslie Holzner.
     p. cm.
 Includes bibliographical references and index.
 ISBN 0-8229-5895-3 (pbk.: alk. paper)
 1. Transparency in government. 2. Freedom of information.
3. Social change. I. Holzner, Leslie. II. Title.
 JC598.H65 2006
 352.8'8—dc22
                        2005028767

CONTENTS

ACKNOWLEDGMENTS

We had a good time writing this book. We have learned a lot that we didn't know before we started and the actual work needed to prepare for it was a joyful shared adventure. We were helped along the way by a number of people. Many of these people are noted in the list of consultations, which notes our many and far-flung consultants.

A few people need to be singled out for special mention. First and foremost is Professor John Marx. John, of the University of Pittsburgh's Sociology Department and the Graduate School of Public Health, spent time, patience, and considerable intelligence reviewing every word in this book, and his help has been profound. We are very grateful. In Europe, our colleague Dr. Heinrich Schneider, professor emeritus of the University of Vienna, also read each chapter very carefully and gave us copious and useful critique. Professor Schneider is a prominent expert on the European Union and the process of European integration generally. He was for many years the representative of the Vatican in the Organization for Security and Cooperation in Europe. Our book is better because of his reading.

Finally, at the University of Pittsburgh Press, Nathan MacBrien worked with us in early days and was both enthusiastic and helpful. Cynthia Miller and Deborah Meade shepherded us through the late stages of finishing and producing this work in a manner that was both animated and consummately professional. Jane Flanders, our editor, worked hard, with care and intelligence. Our thanks go to all of these people.

We have learned in the work that produced this book that the path to a world in which transparency is ascendant is neither straight nor without obstacles. However, we retain the hope that the future we desire is the one we shall all see come to fruition. We dedicate this book, and the cautiously optimistic message that we trust it sends, to the next generation: Steven, Daniel, Weir, Claire, and Sara. Most especially, we offer our work and this book to those on the front lines everywhere, working for the furtherance of transparency. Our wish is for their success.

TRANSPARENCY IN GLOBAL CHANGE

THE CULTURE SHIFT TO TRANSPARENCY

In the title of this book we combine two intersecting themes: transparency in global change and the vanguard of the open society. The first means that the demand for trust based on transparency increases in the context of global transformations. The second means that transparency, the value of openness in the flow of information, is at the forefront of the movements to create the open society. These linked circumstances bring about dramatic changes in social structures, in the behavior of centers of power, and in the emerging transnational groupings. This book explores new ground both in the changes of information values and rules, and in the new alignments of social bonds and institutions. These changes do deeply affect centers of power, whether they are governments, corporations, or professions, for success or failure. The consequences are serious for health, markets, governance, and security.

The idea of the open society is a democratic society, with alert and engaged citizens able to understand and use the information that is accessible to them. Henri Bergson may have been the first to use the term in *The Two Sources of Morality and Religion,* in which he spoke of the concept in terms of a religious, mystical relation between the closed and the open, between closing and opening. But the open society is not an inevitable new phase of history. As Karl Popper says, one must make it happen:

> Instead of posing as prophets we must become the makers of our fate. We must learn to do things as well as we can, and to look out for our mistakes. And when we have dropped the idea that the history of power will be our judge, when we have given up worrying whether or not history will justify us, then one day perhaps we may succeed in getting power under control. In this way we may even justify history, in our turn. It badly needs such justification.[1]

The idea of the open society has matured since Popper's time, and there is reason for some optimism. However, it is buffeted by attacks of ideologues from both right and left and by criminal dictators.

Popper's work was a clean break with much of earlier historical philosophy: Plato, Hegel, Marx, all were enemies of the open society. Popper did admire Karl Marx's empirical work and his description of nineteenth-century capitalism, but he concluded that Marx's predictions were dramatically wrong: "The reason for his failure as a prophet lies entirely in the poverty of historicism as such, in the simple fact that even if we observe today what appears to be a historical tendency or trend, we cannot know whether it will have the same appearance tomorrow."[2] A turn to pragmatism seems to be indicated in lieu of further attempts at prophecy and its totalitarian enforcement.

The idea of the open society was implicit in Immanuel Kant's essay of 1795, *Perpetual Peace: a Philosophical Sketch*. It was also a vision of global, peaceful change. Indeed, the open society became an inspiration that led to the United Nations. The practical, political work in defining democracies and the creation of constitutions has moved toward openness. The U.S. Constitution and its Bill of Rights guaranteed the freedom of citizens. Other legal advances protecting freedom of speech and expression occurred early in Sweden and later in many other countries.

The United Nations' Universal Declaration of Human Rights of 1948 was a giant step toward the values of individual dignity, openness, and freedom. Its famous Article 19 anchors the freedom of information: "Everyone has the right to freedom of opinion and expression; this right includes freedom to hold opinions without interference and to seek, receive and impart information and ideas through any media and regardless of frontiers." Seven treaties on specific human rights have been adopted by the UN. Even though treaties may be violated, they establish landmarks by asserting values in international law that are signposts on the way toward human rights and transparency.

All open societies reserve some form of protection from complete openness. In this sense Bergson was right. No single, uniform model for transforming the idea of the open society into local reality will ever exist. Sweden, Costa Rica, Canada, the United States are only imperfect approximations, like the member states of the European Union. They are all electoral democracies, they guarantee certain rights to all their citizens, but they have different value profiles. The United States cherishes individual freedom over equality; Sweden sees this constellation in very different terms. France is a mainly centralized state, while Germany is a federal one. All of these countries subscribe to the values of freedom of expression, albeit with somewhat different limitations. Nevertheless, they are far from being closed societies.

The defense of closed societies, religions, and ideologies is vigorous in today's world. Even in democracies, many fear openness, since it means the flow of ideas and people across borders, thus respect for human rights and tolerance. Mastering openness requires learning and adaptation. The open information society is necessarily a learning society, and that is a condition for success, even survival, in this era of global transformations. To be sure, all societies protect their boundaries. Immigration societies like Canada and the United States are relatively open, and yet they control the inflow of new citizens, and all liberal economies control the flow of goods and capital. This concept is now espoused by global civil society on a grand scale. Major examples are the Open Society Institute and the Soros Foundation Network, established by the millionaire George Soros, who has donated funds and mobilized thousands of people in the service of democracy, freedom, and transparency.

Transparency in Global Change

Transparency is valued by people who seek freedom, but it is not the open society; it is a value in information culture. The open society is vastly more complex. It stands for human rights and balanced values that include autonomy, accountability, privacy, and, yes, responsible secrecy. Transparency is increasingly demanded in the context of global change because of the need to create trust across vast cultural and geographic distances. Business requires valid information about markets and their risks and opportunities; political relations demand probes of valid information about intentions and strategies among countries; protection of public health needs global information sources to deal with possible epidemics; global institutions like the United Nations or the World Bank are beginning to adapt to openness.

The work that went into the creation of this book spanned several years, but its themes are as current as the morning newspaper. We are writing about the rise of new information cultures, a secular process that started many centuries ago but is reaching a new culmination. Instead of focusing on specific, immediate events, we trace the major currents in the changing values of information. In the United States, founded on the ideals of the Enlightenment, there is still ambivalence about openness and privacy, secrecy and transparency, information disclosure and civil rights.

Clashing Views of America in Global Change

Recent years have seen major setbacks for transparency and openness in the United States because of fears roused by the terrorist attacks of September 2001. As we anticipate the threat of terrorism becoming part of the world we live in for decades to come, we also observe and anticipate further constraints on transparency in America as politicians manipulate those fears for their own ends. Conservatives on the political right talk about "empire." They assume that the world's most powerful country should command an empire based on unilateral, direct military power. One expression of this idea was the Committee on the Present Danger established during the cold war. William Kristol and Robert Kagan write:

> A little over twenty years ago, a group of concerned Americans formed the Committee on the Present Danger. The danger they feared, and sought to rally Americans to confront, was the Soviet Union. It is easy to forget these days in the mid- to late 1970s that the Soviet Union was really a danger, much less one that should be challenged by the United States. This was hardly the dominant view of the American policy establishment. Quite the contrary: prevailing wisdom from the Nixon through the Carter administrations held that the United States should do its outmost to coexist peaceably with the USSR. . . . It would take a revolution in American foreign policy, the fall of the Berlin Wall and the disintegration of the Soviet empire to prove just how right they were. . . . Does this Cold War tale have any relevance today as Americans grapple with the uncertainties of the post–Cold War era? . . . But there *is* a "present danger." It has no name. It is not to be found in any single strategic adversary. It does not fit neatly under the heading of "international terrorism" or "rogue states" or "ethnic hatred."[3]

These writers worried that the United States would neglect its responsibilities as the world's dominant power and outlined a strategy for greater military preparedness. They compared the United States to ancient Rome because of "its war-fighting capabilities and its ability to intervene in conflicts anywhere in the world on short notice."[4] Most of those who share these views believe in policy pursued by secret means, by stealth as well as by confrontation.

Another voice on this topic is Chalmers Johnson, for whom stealth and secrecy inevitably produce distrust and enmity. Johnson opens the introduction to *Blowback* (2004): "In a speech to Congress on September 20, 2001, shortly after the terrorist attacks of September 11, President George W. Bush posed this question: 'Why do they hate us?' His answer: 'They hate our freedoms—our freedom of religion, our freedom of speech, our freedom to vote.' He commented later that he was amazed 'that there is such misunderstanding of what our country is about that people would hate us . . . I just can't believe it because I know how good we are.'" Johnson then asks:

> But how "good" are we, really? If we're so good, why do we inspire such hatred abroad? What have we done to bring so much "blowback" upon ourselves? This book is a guide to some of the policies during and after the Cold War that generated, and continue to generate, blowback—a term the CIA invented to describe the likelihood that our covert operations in other people's countries would result in retaliations against Americans, civilian and military, at home and abroad.[5]

In *The Sorrows of Empire* (2004), Johnson claims that the American "empire" has already become a dangerous and destructive reality:

> There is plenty in the world to occupy our military radicals and empire enthusiasts for the time being. But there can be no doubt that the course on which we are launched will lead us into new versions of the Bay of Pigs and updated, speeded-up replays of Vietnam War scenarios. When such disasters occur, as they—or as-yet-unknown versions of them—certainly will, a world disgusted by the betrayal of the idealism associated with the United States will welcome them, just as most people did when the former USSR came apart. Like other empires of the past century, the United States has chosen to live not prudently, in peace and prosperity, but as a massive military power athwart an angry, resistant globe.[6]

Johnson hopes that the American people will awaken and regain control over the Congress and carry out major reforms, especially at the Pentagon and in the secret agencies. He concludes, "Failing such reform, Nemesis, the goddess of retribution and vengeance, the punisher of pride and hubris, waits impatiently for her meeting with us."[7]

Transparency Does Not Stand Alone

We state in this book the fact of the rise of transparency. Sociologists call it a "social fact" (in the meaning of Durkheim). While our focus is on the wave of transparency, secrecy also has a place in a mature society. It is at certain times a necessity. Georg Simmel regarded secrecy as one of society's most important achievements. However, it is often a destructive evil, as Max Weber observes:

> This superiority of the professional insider every bureaucracy seeks further to increase through the means of *keeping secret* its knowledge and intentions.

Bureaucratic administration always tends to exclude the public, to hide its knowledge and action from criticism as well as it can. . . . However, the pure power interests of bureaucracy exert their effects far beyond these areas of functionally motivated secrecy. The concept of the "office secret" is the specific invention of bureaucracy and few things it defends so fanatically as this.[8]

Even though the member states of the European Union are moving toward transparency and openness, they too all have their own traditions of secrecy.

Transparency and openness are the vanguard of the future, but it would be naive not to acknowledge that the cancer of excessive secrecy developing in the current administration could lead toward an "illiberal democracy." The demand for information about the risks of the changing environment, of man-made and natural catastrophes, of disease, of corruption and oppression, of corporate or governmental malfeasance, is growing rapidly. That demand culminates in a cry for historical transparency: calling to account the perpetrators of past crimes committed by governments. We have reason to believe that the current government's cult of secrecy will in retrospect be considered an aberration from the historic legacy of openness anchored in the U.S. Constitution and traditionally embraced by the American people.

The Culture Shift to Transparency

The beginning of a new century holds the promise of freedom and progress, but also the threat of catastrophic breakdowns. The ideal of the open society is within reach in this era of advancing democracy, of information technology, and of growing global links and expanding civil society. But there are enemies of openness, and they are not only the obsessed fanatics defending misguided traditions. The culture shift to transparency, to the open flow of information and to accountability, has advanced worldwide in spite of fierce resistance. In a new global world, people are forced to interact across boundaries. They require new norms and new solidarities beyond national boundaries. Information cultures are at the center of these changes.

The last decades of the twentieth century saw a dramatic change in the values, norms, and cultures of information. Our work deals with the emerging set of values and norms for public information access about and from centers of power and their accountability. The public's "right to know" and the "duty to disclose" are expanding.

The norms of transparency, properly applied, make it possible to understand information, but this understanding is subject to the cognitive capacity of its recipients. People interpret or ignore information to fit into their frames of reference because the effort of reconciling new information with cherished views can be difficult. It is part of the social construction of reality.[9] The sources of information also have their own interests and perspectives. Transparency is effective to the extent that centers of authority, citizens, customers, and clients construct valid information and achieve understanding. Nevertheless, transparency now vastly increases the flow of new information. It will lead to an open society if an alert and critical citizenry can assess the quality of information and understand it.

The vastness of the value change itself arouses resistance. Secrecy (hiding information intentionally) and opacity (absence of information, sometimes manipulated) are still powerfully entrenched and are even increasing in some domains, especially in response to security threats or for the protection of illicit gains and privileges of special interests. This tumult in changing information cultures is part of the transparency phenomenon.

Much has been written about the new technology of information and its revolutionary impact. This book, by contrast, is sociological, not technological, though we respect the social impact of the information technology revolution. Our work is about change in the values, norms, and expectations for information disclosure by centers of power. Most are going through major changes in response to demands for transparency that create new patterns of power and influence, the adoption of explicit codes of conduct and new rules for dealing with information. The information technology revolution opens opportunities for surveillance and "information security."

For sociologists the "transparency phenomenon" is becoming increasingly critical. It is a powerful tide of culture changes for accountability and open information, new information rights and duties, formalization, and altered power relations. These changes entail moral, political, and legal innovations and alter the structure and functioning of institutions and communities. They are controversial and are often resisted.

Early sociology was motivated by the industrial revolution and the social and structural changes it brought about. People moved beyond their tribes and small villages, and even beyond simple urban areas. Division of labor, complex role structures, and sophisticated nation-states became the norm for industrial societies. In those times of radical change, a major question for social scientists, and especially for sociologists, was "What will hold everything together? What is the nature of solidarity in these conditions? What is the social glue?" And from these questions flowed the analyses of *Gemeinschaft* and *Gesellschaft*.

The current era is witnessing changes of just such a radical nature. The

7

industrialized world, the entire world in fact, is moving from being a collection of nation-states to recognizing the global environment shared by all. Modern economies require trust at a distance, relationships among people who may never meet face to face—who have no need to—and who may never inhabit the same space. Increasingly, international and global political organizations adopt forms of behavior that differ from indigenous ones. Again, the questions arise, "What will hold everything together? What is the nature of solidarity in these conditions? What is the social glue?" A large part of the answer is a demand for transparency. The disclosure of valid information by centers of authority makes possible global interactions and relationships.

The cultural shift in favor of transparency is a complex matter. It has come to be one of the most powerful contemporary cultural changes, even though ours is a time of terrorism, wars, widespread official corruption, crime, and government secrecy. And battles for and against transparency are raging, as are battles for and against secrecy. Calling for transparency is perceived by many as an onslaught against tradition, identity, security, as well as against established authority and privilege. At the same time, it is a cause energetically advanced by reformers fighting against inequity, corruption, and authoritarianism, and for freedom, openness, civil rights, and personal autonomy. Many of the great social movements of our time for human rights, for women's rights, for a sustainable global and local environment, for accountability and against corruption, use the demand for transparency even more as a strategy to expose evils and mobilize public outrage against those responsible.

Very powerful forces in the shift toward transparency, however, are the requirements of the marketplace, of competitive politics, and of technology. Scientists and engineers continue to improve devices for generating, storing, and distributing information. The spread of communications technology worldwide means that people can try new projects, can probe the limits of what previously was impossible or impermissible. The technical capacity for bringing transparency to business, government, and professional activities has increased greatly, as has the range of social choices. This, of course, has played a large role in commerce. Markets have always required information. Today it is even more obvious: those that operate without transparency are expensive and at risk. The same is true of governments: those that lack transparency are also costly and even dangerous. Certainly this is true of democratic countries. Credibility and legitimacy are at stake.

Even though secrecy is on the defensive on many fronts, it remains essential and grows on several others. Business competitors must be transparent about their accounting practices, their corporate governance, and the quality of their products, but there always will remain a reserve of secrecy about new products that they hope will surprise the competition or about new ideas they might pursue. Similarly, there remains a domain of secrecy for governments on issues of security and criminal investigation. Even further, there are information values at work competing more generally with the value of transparency, such as protection of privacy, informational property, surveillance, monitoring, and indeed secrecy. Transparency cannot be a stand-alone value; it is part of an interdependent cluster of values which we call the "transparency/secrecy syndrome."

Nevertheless, even though transparency is assuming a growing role in transnational affairs, it occurs in a world still dominated by opacity and many domains of secrecy, especially in many developing countries and military states. Not only governments, but also corporations and professions that try to evade the rising norms of transparency lose the trust of the public and pay dearly in attempts to regain it. Centers of power must deal with the fact that many of the information norms regarding public access to knowledge are changing away from secrecy toward transparency. It is not a tranquil phenomenon: it is a contentious social force.

Above all, the right to know, and the duty to disclose, are grounded in trust. The transparency movement is a response to uncertainty and distrust. Like all social transformations, this one creates instability and takes place on a cultural battlefield. Therefore, it is important to understand its dynamics. The purpose of this book is to sketch the broad outlines of the vast, global panorama of the transparency shift and to illustrate its complexities and consequences.

What We Did to Learn About Transparency

In addition to reviewing scholarly resources, we consulted active professionals dealing personally with global change, and specifically with the impact of changing information norms, needs, and demands. We conducted about ninety consultations in the United States, Japan, China, Belgium, Britain, Germany, Greece, France, Italy, and Luxembourg.

Our consultants were knowledgeable professionals directly engaged in activities and projects that exhibit and illuminate the transparency phenomenon. Our purpose was to trace the phenomenon in many different domains, drawing on the hands-on experience of those in the field. Many of these interviews opened new perspectives to us. All of our interview partners conveyed a sense of urgency about addressing the problems brought by current changes in the world. Sometimes the pace of change seemed too fast for the people to whom we talked; others were impatient, feeling that change was occurring too slowly for what they wanted to see happen. From our personal contacts we have created a sociological frame of reference in which to make sense of the transparency shift, its causes, and consequences.

The Plan of This Book

The true scope of the recent impetus toward transparency is not fully known. Chapter 2 sketches some historical markers in the evolution of information cultures and documents the dramatic increase in information disclosure, access, and availability in the last decades of the twentieth century. It has not been an easy process. Several historical episodes illustrate the intensity of struggles against freedom of information. After all, freedom of thought and speech, freedom of expression, and the idea that there is a right to know and a duty to disclose information about the workings of power, are values that developed during the Enlightenment and its descendants in democracies, free markets, and human rights. Until recently secrecy and opacity were the dominant conditions in human societies. In many places they continue to be so, although they are shrinking.

The spread of democracy raises questions about the nature and the historical stage of specific modern states, some of which are democracies in name only, or "illiberal democracies."[10] Chapter 3, which addresses global change and transparency across many domains of social life, presents a sociological approach to this social fact and defines the path to understanding its causes and consequences. A key concept is the value/countervalue syndrome. Transparency is not a stand-alone value. There are powerful countervalues such as secrecy, opacity, and privacy. The transparency syndrome of values is dominated by openness of information and individual autonomy. By contrast, in the secrecy syndrome, hierarchy, loyalty, and obedience are dominant. This is the architecture of an information culture.

Especially in an era of armed conflict in a dangerous world, we need to examine the shifts in and across these structures and how changes in one value affect other values. The information cultures in different world regions move along different paths. Further, increased concerns with security do not lessen the significance of transparency in all domains; in fact, as documented in chapters 3 and 4, in some domains the pressure for transparency is increasing.

Chapter 5 compares the information cultures of the world's major centers of power: the United States, the European Union, and Japan. These are, after all, the major drivers of information technology and (often ambivalently) of the transparency phenomenon. They have both similar and divergent views.

Chapter 6 surveys the various and growing roles of transparency in civil society both in developing countries and in the rich industrial ones. The coalescence of global civil society is very much a part of the transparency phenomenon and a major new feature in global change, as is the world-circling shadow of crime and terrorism. We examine the dynamics underlying governance structures in global civil society, of competition and cooperation among its organizations, with the crystallization of institutions. We describe several of these organizations, with a major emphasis on Transparency International, the leader in the global fight against corruption.

Chapter 7 deals with new scrutiny and control over corporate governance, showing how corrupt business practices lead to scandals and demands for reform. In recent decades the accounting profession, as well as certain branches of the legal profession, were also involved in business scandals. Reform is under way, indicating how transparency forces beneficial change.

Chapter 8, on transparency in the health professions, covers the evils of Nazi medical practices during World War II. The war crimes tribunal at Nuremberg defined standards for medical experiments with human subjects, but much more evolved, leading to remarkable transformations in the ethics of health care worldwide. Chapter 9 deals with historical transparency, the disclosure of crimes committed by past governments. This is an explosive issue in countries emerging from dictatorship and striving toward democracy and the rule of law. The establishment of special tribunals charged with finding the truth has now led to transnational efforts to establish universal jurisdiction that transcends national boundaries. As part of our examination of how transparency plays a role in changing a society's moral framework, chapter 9 again describes the emergence of transparency as a force for reform. In our conclusion, we summarize the sources of energy for expanding the global demand for transparency and against secrecy, and the preconditions for a future open society.

2

THE RISE OF TRANSPARENCY

Some Historical Turning Points

Transparency may seem a straightforward matter: it means the open flow of information. However, in fact it is not so simple: many cultural, social, and economic conditions are necessary for it to happen. Transparency is not synonymous with knowledge, but both intersect. Knowledge is validated information that can lead to action. Transparency depends upon access to information held by authorities who are presumed to tell the truth—although, of course, sometimes this presumption is wrong. This summary of the relation between transparency and knowledge only hints at the complexities of transparency as a concept.

In this chapter we present sketches of the cultural changes that allowed the emergence of a demand for transparency. This will take us far back in history. Each historical turning point added a new dimension to information cultures and capabilities—new forms of knowledge, measurement, communication, freedom, and information technology. Most important, many of these turbulent and often very contentious events created new standards of truth, a new ethos for information culture. Some occurred during intercivilizational encounters that created conditions conducive to value changes. These are dialectical processes, and they frequently appear to be chaotic or even violent to the actors involved. Yet their resolution yielded change, frequently progress, not least in the area of our interest: the push to support the conditions for, and the actual presence of, greater transparency.

With the extension of democracy around the world in the late twentieth century came an unparalleled rise in transparency and a substantial increase in the complexity of information cultures. Note, however, that while transparency and democracy are linked, they are not the same. The demand for information freedom and a belief in the value of transparency are long-term outcomes of the eighteenth-century wave of democratic aspirations, but it

12

would be a mistake to identify transparency with democracy. There are uses of transparency in surveillance, for example, that may not have democratic purposes, and there are forms of transparency in economic matters that may be compatible with some level of authoritarian rule. Thus some forms of transparency in accounting rose in the nineteenth century, while the idea of openness in governments languished.

The enormous complexity of information cultures needs to be clearly understood. In fact, it is part of our definition of transparency: *it is the social value of open, public, and/or individual access to information held and disclosed by centers of authority.* These centers include governments, corporations, professions, or other influential agencies such as civil society organizations, foundations, regulatory agencies, transnational, supranational, or global authorities such as the United Nations, the European Union, the OECD, and other such entities of power. This value is a component of the transparency syndrome of values that encompasses transparency and its kindred values such as accountability and its countervalues such as secrecy. These values create a context for the expansion or limitation of transparency.

The achievement of transparency requires the establishment of norms for transparency. These may be compulsory and legal, as in freedom of information legislation, or other laws that force disclosure under penalty of law. Or such norms may be self-imposed programs, as in the case of codes of conduct or professional codes of ethics. Voluntary disclosures may, in fact, be coerced by strategic efforts to expose various misdeeds that cause scandals. And then, disclosures may be individual, spontaneous actions.

Transparency norms tend to be contested by various interested parties in encouraging or discouraging information disclosure. The institutionalization of transparency norms depends on the broader cultural-social context and the political and legal system. Shifts in social values will alter the normative requirements for transparency, just as the implementation of norms depends on the social and technological capacity for transparency, or the *transparency infrastructure.* For example, the introduction of money made business accounting possible; the erection of bureaucracy entailed the establishment of information and control systems; the invention of the printing press led eventually to wider literacy among the populace; the computer and the Internet represented quantum leaps in the movement toward transparency. These are the historical turning points without which the demand for transparency would be impossible.

The transparency infrastructure has an economic and political impact. Collecting information for disclosure can be expensive. A particular infrastructure may actually become dysfunctional, as we will see in our study of transparency in corporate business. A badly designed infrastructure may damage other values in the transparency syndrome, as in calling for transparency at a cost to privacy, confidentiality, and security. This is especially problematic in health care.

The social and technological capacity for transparency requires cultural changes that make the social construction of knowledge systems possible. Such changes occurred with the historical movement toward rationality over dogma, causality versus belief in miracles, precision in measurement versus estimates based on intuition, logical and mathematical reasoning instead of allegorical thinking. These developments help us to understand the historical dynamics leading toward transparency and the cultural and knowledge systems that make the open society possible.

Four historical periods of change in the evolution of transparency were early medieval Europe, late medieval Europe and the Reformation, the late-eighteenth-century and mid-nineteenth-century eras of revolutions, and the twentieth century and up to the present. Lack of information freedom, opacity, and secrecy were the dominant facts of life in traditional societies, as well as in many early modern nation-states. These conditions continue in dictatorial states today. Even in democracies, freedom of information is controversial when it clashes with the countervalues of security and secrecy, or with historical myths and the hard facts of historical transparency.

In the past the idea of the open society had more enemies than friends. Today the balance is shifting, but there are still pressures to maintain close control over information. This is painfully true in the era of global terrorism and especially in the United States' military response to threats to its security. Authorities typically prefer surveillance of the public to the disclosure of information about themselves. There continue to be enemies of all freedoms and especially freedom of information, even in this era of rising democracies. Yet, it is very intriguing that many centers of power today feel a need to become more transparent and do so voluntarily. In spite of all obstacles, transparency is spreading and is a notable characteristic of our era.

In the historical move toward freedom of information, the values of freedom of speech, freedom of expression, and transparency were formed in a slow, painful series of conflicts over centuries. We obviously cannot write a complete history of culture changes in information norms for centers of power. However, most accounts of world history or of the various country histories ignore the emergence of transparency as a cultural value; only recently has it come under scrutiny. Nevertheless, courageous thinkers and reformers, scientists and revolutionaries rose at special historical moments to break the walls of oppression, secrecy, and opacity and to create openings for freedom of information—that is, transparency.

Historical studies, for example, of freedom of the press and freedom of speech written in English are generally limited to America and Britain. However, some of the groundbreaking events in the history of these freedoms occurred elsewhere, for instance, in Sweden and other parts of northern Europe. A general history of transparency as a cultural value would require a new historical perspective. The historical currents that have changed information norms and cultures form the antecedents of what today we call transparency.

Historical episodes involving scandals and conflicts reveal a long-standing resistance to information freedom and yet they helped to drive it forward. There is an immense cultural complexity in this process. We hope to learn by examining these turning points more about the major forces that changed information cultures in the past, as well as the spread of information rights in more recent times. Data on legislation for freedom of the press, freedom of expression, or information disclosure by governments serve as rough indicators for this social fact of global change.

Some Historical Turning Points Toward Freedom of Information

Roots in Antiquity, Progress in the Middle Ages

The idea of freedom defined by citizens' legal rights had its origin in ancient Greece, where it was ultimately lost, and in the formal rights of Roman citizens. Rights to special freedoms became important issues again in medieval times as in the culture change creating limited but real "free spaces" in cities and changing conceptions of the nature of knowledge in the twelfth and thirteenth centuries. Europe's medieval idea of liberty was severely limited by boundaries in many ways, but it was liberty nevertheless and existed in social islands within societies of severe inequality. Max Weber drew attention to this fact in *The City (Non-Legitimate Domination).*[1] This title caused some consternation among readers: from a modern perspective, there is nothing illegitimate about the self-rule of cities. However, Weber was following the customary usage in his time, using the term *legitimacy* to mean the rule of traditional lords. Rights bestowed on or usurped by cities were an exception to feudal rule, an exception of bounded geographic scope. A social structure different from feudalism emerged in the cities, especially after 1347 and the plague years that followed. There began to emerge some cultural diversity and a new information culture in Europe.

Weber observed that cities welcomed immigration because it increased opportunities for everyone:

> For the same reason the burghers had a common interest in the elimination of the possibility that a serf, once he had become prosperous in the city, would be requisitioned for house and stable service by his lord, if for no other reason than to extort a ransom from him. . . . The urban citizenry therefore usurped the right to dissolve the bonds of seigneurial domination; this was the great—in fact, the *revolutionary*—innovation which differentiated the medieval Occidental cities from all the others. In the central and northern European cities appeared the well-known principle that *Stadtluft macht frei* [city air makes one free], which meant that after a varying but always relatively short time the master of a slave or serf lost the right to reclaim him.[2]

The gradual differentiation of city dwellers into powerful status groups and the emergence of relatively autonomous city authorities created special rights for urban citizens. Political and economic competition became possible through this autonomy and favored the city's development. Many early medieval cities exercised considerable political power in self-rule. These rights included the power to create their own laws. Thus they were able to legally establish specific market rights and pursue an autonomous urban economic policy. These cities became powerful elements in the early phases of capitalism and rational administration.[3]

In a few medieval urban centers, the early universities were created. Although the new institution of the university certainly changed patterns of information and communication among the elite, freedom of expression remained limited to certain free spaces and had to be guarded within them. Medieval societies had not only geographic but also sociocultural boundaries around these free spaces. Freedom of speech was permitted under limited conditions. Domains of sacred or political power were sensitive domains in which circumspection and respect were required. Fierce battles were fought about just where the boundaries of freedom were to be drawn. Nevertheless, these limited free spaces made the advancement of scholarship and philosophy possible. They were bounded enclaves tolerating inquiry and debate on certain terms. However, medieval society did not tolerate such freedoms anywhere else. The special freedom granted to a university, the grant of limited self-government to a city, the grant of legal rights to a guild, all were freedom-producing innovations, but with restrictive boundaries.

Such early roots of liberty grew in the twelfth and thirteenth centuries in Europe. Scholarly inquiry that raised questions about the bases of faith and knowledge did become possible in the new free spaces and in encounters with different cultures. This was the period of the Crusades, which introduced intercivilizational encounters and great political turmoil. Translations of Arabic, Hebrew, and Greek texts into Latin were now produced. Benjamin Nelson, a pioneer in the sociology of civilizations and their encounters, speaks of the rise of "moralities of thought" and "logics of action" when analyzing the "rationalization of intelligence" in these centuries. Thus the interactions and conflicts among civilizations that occurred a millennium ago created transformations in the pursuit of knowledge and its distribution in Europe.

Nelson points to the "giant strides which Europe achieved during the twelfth and thirteenth centuries. The years between the first crusade and the Council of Vienne of 1311 were extraordinarily eventful for Western Europe."[4] He emphasized five major developments in this period. The first point concerns the consequences of the conflict between Christians and Muslims and the end of Islamic hegemony in the Mediterranean that gave European powers control of the area. Intense intercivilizational encounters occurred in that period, and not only between Islam and Christianity. European society began to see a rapid increase in internal differentiation of society and the contentious establishment of various liberties. Competing centers of power crystallized. Cities were linked by networks of trade and thus became hubs of communication, leading to "the spread of liberties in the several senses of both liberties *from* and liberties *to*. In the present instance the critical liberties are the liberties *from* the control of territorial powers and liberties *to* employ one's own abilities in the 'public's' or one's own behalf."[5]

The rise of centers of learning, mostly in the cities, added another dimension of change. Nelson recognized the critical importance of the new liberty to "philosophize on matters not dogmatically established." The bitter clash between Peter Abelard, theologian and logician, and Bernard of Clairvaux, the founder of the Cistercian Order of White Monks and defender of the faith, was a momentous event in the struggle to understand the nature of reality and the way to know God. In Nelson's words, a "systematic concordance of knowledge and learning" was worked on, creating systematic bodies of knowledge, "summing up 'scientific' theology, natural philosophy, political philosophy, moral philosophy, and law—Roman, canon, common, municipal."[6] The idea of logical proof, on which Abelard insisted, gained ground, in spite of enraged attacks against his thoughts by the defenders of the faith. This demand for proof is, of course, an essential element in the quest for truth.

Europe exploited the newly learned techniques and skills that came from the Chinese, Hindu, and Muslim cultures. The development of mathematics advanced beyond the Hindu-Arabic numeral system and, most significantly, added the concept of the zero. These innovations had enormous consequences for the development of science, commerce, administration, and civilization in general. "In these centuries," Nelson writes, "the West was entirely to restructure the rationales of thought and action, knowledge, opinion, and conscience."[7] The period that saw the beginning of several forms of liberty in Western Europe also was a period of intercivilizational encounters, giving rise to, among other things, new information norms and the building of complex systems of knowledge.

Competition among centers of power played a major role in this process. In Nelson's words,

> The more we come to know the European cultural and social transformations of the crusading era the more we find ourselves having to conclude that they represent a watershed in the international history of civilizations. . . . Eager appropriations and sifting of critical traditions and texts are the hallmark of the time. Not only did the men of this era recover neglected Greek and Roman texts—notably, Greek philosophical and scientific writings and the Roman law—they also labored to translate Arabic, Hebrew, and classical works which had become part of the Islamic and Hebraic corpus.[8]

Changes in the Early Modern Age

Dramatic changes in information norms and capacities occurred simultaneously with the discovery of America, the invention of the printing press, the Reformation in Europe, the subsequent wars of religion, and the scientific revolution, from the late fifteenth century to the end of the seventeenth century. The greatest innovation in information technology and the spread of knowledge of the world was the printing press, which created markets for books and newspapers and made it possible to distribute translations of the Bible in the vernacular. This was also a period of secular conflicts caused by attempts to enlarge and build monarchic, absolutist states—with frequent warfare. By the end of the period, major changes had occurred in the practice, social organization, and communication norms of science.

The Protestant Reformation was a cluster of major movements of intense religious awakening and revulsion against corruption and misrule by the Catholic Church hierarchy. In an impassioned way the Protestants rose against corruption and called for a form of "prototransparency." Martin Luther, a dominant figure in this struggle, demanded stern reforms of a corrupt and oppressive Church and unleashed dramatic theological reforms, basing salvation on faith alone. The idea of the sanctity of conscience and of humanity's direct, personal bond to God had already appeared in some movements in the Middle Ages. But the Protestant movement spread these ideas as a main source of faith to very large populations of central and northern Europe. Indeed, the Protestant ethic posited a direct communication between the individual believer and God. Individual conscience, the sense of sin and guilt, and the anxiety over one's salvation were personal matters of great intensity. The religious cauldron that Luther, Calvin, and the other reformers had created boiled over into the political domain and revealed the fragility of the Holy Roman Empire of the German Nation. Protestantism grew in a field of intersecting and conflicting political and cultural movements and alliances. And, as happens time and again, scandal accompanied the birth of reform. Lutheranism and the stern Calvinist reforms brought about fundamental changes in what Nelson calls the "rationales of conscience." The Protestant message could be spread through the new technology of print and the new information infrastructures it had created. The Reformation and the Catholic Counter-Reformation had lasting effects on many domains of culture, and this period indeed transformed the world.

David Brin characterizes the changes brought by the new technology of print in this way:

> History certainly does warn us to be wary whenever a new communication technology arrives on the scene. While some seek to uplift humanity, others skillfully seize on the innovation, applying it to the oldest of all magical arts—manipulating others. Take the introduction of Gutenberg's working printing press, which ended the medieval control over literacy long held by the church and nobility.

The invention of printing liberated large publics—indeed, it created "publics." It eliminated old restrictions and enabled the circulation of new ideas. Brin continues,

It also freed demagogues to cajole with new slanders, spread effectively via the printed word. According to James Burke, author of *Connections,* the chief short-term beneficiaries of printing turned out to be religious factionalism and nationalism. The following two centuries illustrated this, as Europe drifted into waves of unprecedented savage violence.[9]

The period of the religious wars, which were at the same time wars about the emerging structures of domination in Europe, ended with the conclusion of the Thirty Years' War by the Peace of Westphalia in 1648. This was the peace treaty that created the system of sovereign states with the principle of autonomy and of noninterference in each other's internal affairs. It also stabilized the division of Europe into Protestant and Catholic regions. As explained by R. R. Palmer and Joel Colton,

> Neither side any longer expected to make territorial gains at the expense of the other. Both the Protestant and the Catholic Reformations were accomplished facts. Seen in the long view, each had succeeded, but each also had failed, for Protestants had not freed the whole Christian world of "idolatry," nor had Catholics been able to exterminate "heresy." A compromise was in the end accepted. Latin Christendom was partitioned. The breaking up of the medieval church, with the accompanying breakup of the medieval view of life and the world—a process that may be said to have lasted from 1300 to 1650, and was as slow and deeply disrupting as a geological upheaval—perhaps came as near as anything in European history to breaking up Europe itself; but after about 1650 such troubles became past history, and Europe entered upon a new age.[10]

The legacy of the Reformation, the subsequent wars, and the redrawing of Europe's political and cultural map led to significant differences in European information cultures that are visible to this day. The Protestant regions of Europe, especially the Scandinavian countries, developed new normative structures regarding authority. These, in turn, shaped their own sense of conscience about keeping records of personal data, documenting transactions and contracts, and having access to government information. The Catholic countries in the South took a different path after the Counter-Reformation. Openness was not highly valued among those in authority. In a different way, countries under the Greek and Russian Orthodox churches also preserved a culture of secrecy and mysticism. Their information cultures were least affected by developments in northern Europe. (The current pressures for transparency are now arriving in these regions.) Early modern times saw the growth of capitalism in Europe and America. The linkage between the Protestant ethic and the spirit of capitalism observed by Weber also holds for the link between Protestantism and early support for transparency (but always in what we have called "bounded" ways).

The scientific revolution, another development of this period, received a strong impetus from the values inherent in Protestantism. Robert K. Merton concludes that the Protestant ethic

> was at once a direct expression of dominant values and an independent source of new motivation. It not only led men into particular paths of activity; it exerted a constant pressure for unswerving devotion to this activity. Its ascetic imperatives established a broad base for scientific inquiry, dignifying, exalting, consecrating such inquiry. If the scientist had hitherto found the search for truth its own reward, he now had further grounds for disinterested zeal in this pursuit. And those once dubious of the merits of men who devoted themselves to investigation of the "petty, insignificant details of a boundless Nature now confronted a developing rationale for such inquiry."[11]

Just as Puritanism held to the view that God's law is awesome and immutable, the scientific revolution established the idea that the laws of nature are binding necessities. This gave rise to a shared conviction of immutable law, both in religion and science. Merton writes:

> The significance of this fundamental similarity is profound though it could hardly have been consciously recognized by those whom it influenced: religion had, for whatever reasons, adopted a cast of thought which was essentially that of science and so reinforced the typically scientific attitudes of the period. The society was permeated with attitudes toward natural phenomena that, derived from both science and religion, unwittingly helped maintain conceptions characteristic of the new science.[12]

Scientists adopted standards of precision in their observations that had not been known in previous periods of history, and technology soon followed. These standards of precision in observation and experiment also required standards of precision in the developing information system of science. Regarding this "universe of precision," H. Floris Cohen writes:

> The dynamics of the extraordinarily complex chain of events that ensued may in broad terms be thought of as follows. Almost from the day of its effective emergence at the hands of Kepler and Galileo, the universe of precision has proved to possess an unheard-of transformative power, which nothing in the world can escape once touched by it (which is what justifies its being called a "universe").[13]

21

The mathematization of experimental science had begun and was well under way by Newton's time. Science now required accurate observation and precise communication.

> On the social level, practitioners of the new mode of doing science began to organize their communications by means of informal meetings and exchanges of letters, yielding in the end formalized societies and regular journals. The societies, in particular, provided the means by which something of a scientific community came into being and by which the confident *mores* of that increasingly self-confident community were gradually worked out in practice.[14]

The basic forms of scientific precision, experiment, and communication had been invented and laid the foundation for the competitive mode of rigorously reviewing experimental, observational findings and theoretical arguments by the community of scientists. Cohen's "universe of precision" had found its way into the information norms of science. The competitive structure of science is what Donald T. Campbell calls the internal social system of science. He sees it as a community of quarreling and competing "truth seekers." Campbell pursues the idea of a "sociology of scientific validity." The disciplined, focused scientific debate among competing researchers increases the probability of discovering errors and falsifications. This competitive arena of disciplined inquiry has norms that require disputatious, skeptical inquiry.[15] This internal social system of science is *in principle* egalitarian.[16]

The Eighteenth Century and the Beginnings of Modern Democracy

The rise of democracy was accompanied by crucial changes in information norms. Democratic ideas burst on the scene in the era of the great revolutions of the late eighteenth century, although there had been earlier movements for protodemocratic legitimation of government. The concept of liberty became a prominent part of English law early, building on old cultural traditions. It became a formal rule in the Magna Carta of 1215. Over the following centuries, English history saw a step-by-step, struggle-by-struggle transition to a democracy under a constitutional monarchy. The Glorious Revolution of 1688 culminated in the English Bill of Rights of 1689. This document raised several serious accusations against the abdicated Catholic King James II that included arbitrary taxation, discrimination against Protestants, maintenance of a standing army, and violating the freedom of elections to Parliament, and it established the new Protestant monarchs William and Mary as guardians of the religion, laws, and liberties of the land. The Bill of Rights became part of a political tradition that, enlarged by the political philosophies of the Enlightenment, played an important role in the American Revolution and the U.S. Bill of Rights.

In the great revolutions of the eighteenth century in America and France, several historical currents converged. Despite their differences, they both occurred in a context of widespread demands for democratic legitimation of political rule. The philosophers of the Enlightenment had prepared the way. There was, John Markoff writes, a "transnational democratic revolution with powerful upheavals in Holland, Belgium, Switzerland, Italy, Poland, England, Ireland as well as France and the United States—and one whose repercussions were world-wide and enduring."[17] The American and French Revolutions were inspired by similar values and were linked by leaders like Lafayette and the French war alliance with the American colonies against Britain. However, these revolutions left very different legacies with regard to freedom of information, with enduring effects on the information cultures of America and Europe even today.

America: A New Political Culture

After the Revolution, American leaders created a new federal state and literally invented a new political culture. The framers of that culture had to find solutions to problems that had never before occurred in this form. The crucial documents were the Declaration of Independence, the Constitution, and especially of the Bill of Rights, the ten amendments to the Constitution adopted in 1791.[18] These documents did not primarily address information norms, even though some were included. They were designed to limit the powers of the federal government over the states, a limitation demanded by the Antifederalists, who were concerned with what came to be known as states' rights.[19] In addition to a concern with limiting federal power, there was also an awareness of the need for public knowledge that went beyond the European common sense of the time: the census was mandated by the Constitution, as well as a State of the Union Address by the president to the Congress. Both were innovations in the information culture.

Creating the Constitution was neither simple nor always a glorious effort. Compromises had to be negotiated to make the whole enterprise acceptable to all the states. Deals had to be made, some in secrecy. The great regional cleavage was caused by the issue of slavery that divided North and South. For all practical purposes, the issue was set aside for the time being. However, the issue of representation in national elections was clouded by the bargain made about how the population of states that maintained the system of slavery should be calculated to determine their representation in Congress. Garry Wills describes the controversy in in his study of the election of Thomas Jefferson in 1800:

> If real votes had been counted, Adams would have been returned to office. But, of course, the "vote" did not depend solely on voters. Though Jefferson, admittedly, received eight more votes than Adams in the Electoral College, at least twelve of his votes were not based on the citizenry that could express its will but on the blacks owned by southern masters. A bargain had been struck at the Constitutional Convention—one of the famous compromises on which the document was formed, this one intended to secure ratification in the South. The negotiated agreement decreed that each slave held in the United States would count as three-fifths of a person—the so-called federal ratio—for establishing the representation of a state in the House of Representatives (and consequently in the Electoral College, which was based on the House and Senate numbers for each state in Congress).[20]

The "three-fifths clause" did not receive much attention in American history books until fairly recently. The reason for this silence may be that in the nineteenth century slavery remained a topic to be avoided until, of course, the period of the Civil War. The Thirteenth Amendment abolished slavery in 1865, and the three-fifths clause disappeared. However, it was part of what allowed the states of the American South to have a powerful role in a wide array of negotiations. Wills writes: "On crucial matters, when several factions were contending, the federal ratio gave the South a voting majority. Without the federal ratio as the deciding factor in House votes, slavery would have been excluded from Missouri, Jackson's Indian removal policy would have failed, the 1840 gag rule would not have been imposed, the Wilmot Proviso would have banned slavery in territories won from Mexico, the Kansas Nebraska Bill would have failed."[21] The compromise on slavery held until the Civil War.

Garry Wills documents antigovernment attitudes in the United States in *A Necessary Evil: A History of American Distrust of Government.*[22] His outline of the contrasting value constellations about trust and distrust of government inspired us to develop the concept of the transparency value syndrome. He details the compromises that allowed the approval of the Bill of Rights, which was mainly designed to reduce the Antifederalists' fears of an overpowering central state, not primarily to defend individual rights. It provided for restraints on federal powers. For example, the federal government could not infringe on the citizens' freedom of speech or religion, although the states could do so. The conflict between the Federalists and the Antifederalists was not primarily about information freedom and its values, but about the balance of power between the states and the federal government.

James Madison, who was an advocate of freedom at all levels, proposed an amendment that he considered to be especially important: "No state shall violate the equal rights of conscience, or the freedom of the press, or the trial by jury in criminal cases."[23] It failed. Madison's purpose was to limit all levels of government abuse. In the course of time, however, his purpose became reality. Gradually, over the nineteenth century judges began to apply the Bill of Rights also to the states. In the end, the Federalist interpretation of the Bill of Rights prevailed as Madison had intended, even though his most important amendment was rejected. The spirit of the Bill of Rights was universal, even if it restrained only the federal government until court interpretations broadened its power.

Wills uses this example of the legislative battle about the Bill of Rights as one of many illustrations of the pervasive American distrust of government. He documents the cluster of antigovernment values in American culture that has been a strong force throughout the nation's history. These values found powerful expression in the disputatious politics surrounding the adoption of the Bill of Rights. These attitudes, however, led to the emergence of myths and distortions of the historical reality of the drafting of the Constitution and of its meaning. Wills, for example, debunks the myth that citizens' militias and amateur soldiers were decisive in bringing victory over the British in the Revolution. In fact, the conflict could not have been won without the regulars of the Continental Army and French military support. Similarly, Wills places the notions of the amateur politician, the Minuteman, and the Short-Term Man into the same category of myths based on antigovernmental values rather than facts.[24] History shows them to be false. All were constructed to support the idea that "rugged individuals," private persons, not organized government and disciplined professionals, were the real, positive forces in American history. These myths evolved from the widespread American belief that government is a "necessary evil."

However, there is also a cluster of government-oriented values that play a strong role in American history. The conflicts between these two value sets have given American information culture its peculiar, historical openness. The often antigovernment views held by some segments of the public rarely, if ever, were totally dominant. Countervalues supported government authority, confidentiality, indeed secrecy and orientation to duties. The in-

terplay between these values and countervalues that Wills describes provides a useful approach to studying the dynamics of value syndromes.

Abiding, Contradictory American Values

Wills lists the antigovernmental values that surface again and again in
American history, along with corresponding progovernment values. Table 1
provides an overview of what we call a value syndrome, showing two conflicting value constellations in a dialectic relationship. As one of these values
rises or falls, it affects the structure of the entire syndrome. We will return
later to this useful concept.

Table 1. An American Value Syndrome of Two Value Constellations

Antigovernmental Values	Governmental Values
Provincial	Cosmopolitan
Amateur	Expert
Authentic	Authoritative
Spontaneous	Efficient
Candid	Confidential
Homogeneous	Articulated
Traditional	Progressive
Populist	Elite
Organic	Mechanical
Rights-oriented	Duty-oriented
Religious	Secular
Voluntary	Regulatory
Participatory	Delegative
Rotating labor	Dividing labor

Source: Garry Wills, *A Necessary Evil: A History of American Distrust of Government*
(New York: Simon and Schuster, 1999), 38.

Some explication of the polarities in Wills's table may be needed, although the overall pattern is quite clear. The left side of the table describes the value beliefs of populists and traditionalists defending the culture of a village society. For example, in such a society rotation of labor would be natural because of the variation of the seasons. On the right side are the values of the modernizers for whom a division of labor is a matter of course, like the image of society as articulated rather than homogeneous.

This value syndrome resembles in sociological terms what Talcott Parsons called "pattern variables" of particularism and diffuseness (on the left side of table 1) and universalism and specificity (on the right). Particular values entail commitment to and preference for one's own group, family, religion, or race. Universal values are in principle valid across all social categories. They embrace universal rules of reasoning and conduct that are applicable everywhere and can be used equitably, without preference on the basis of ethnicity, race, or religion.[25] The tension between particularism and universalism is, of course, not just a characteristic of American society—it is a general phenomenon. It is a major problem complicating global change. Somehow worldwide norms need to be universal and yet linked to the particular cultures where they are applied.

In the United States, however, the tension between the universal and the particular takes the form of a cultural conflict between government values and their antigovernment opposites. This powerful strain of antigovernment feeling helped to shape the unique historical profile of the United States. Certain constellations of value syndromes in dialectic tension will emerge when we explore the dynamics of transparency and its countervalues. It is important to emphasize here that the distrust of government that Wills identifies in his critical history has had a major influence on the U.S. information culture, a legacy that has added a special, sometimes positive but often destructive, twist to American democracy. In chapter 5 we will discuss the historical roots and the contemporary, very complex configuration of American information culture.

The Legacy of the French Revolution

The French Revolution had an outcome quite different from the American War of Independence and therefore left a different legacy. The commitment to liberty, equality, and brotherhood led to the abolition of feudalism in France and eventually in all of Europe. The dramatic events of 1789 reached their epitome in the statement adopted on August 11: "The National Assembly destroys the feudal regime in its entirety!"[26] The Declaration of the

Rights of Man and Citizen, issued on August 26, 1789, became a symbolic inauguration of a new era of freedom. The event gave a major impetus to the demand for democratic legitimation of governments in other European nations. Indeed, the Declaration of Rights became an illustrious beacon for democracy and liberty throughout the world.[27]

However, the long-term outcome of the tumultuous revolutionary period was the evolution of France as the model of the modern, military European nation-state and only ultimately a mature democracy. The Revolution included the Reign of Terror under Robespierre, the Directory, and the era of Napoleon Bonaparte, who crowned himself emperor. French imperialism led at first to enormous conquests but ended in disastrous defeats, ultimately at the Battle of Waterloo. France then was returned to a monarchy under Louis XVIII, an event followed by a period of revolts and coups and a reestablished empire under Napoleon III, who declared war on Prussia in 1870. The French defeat in 1871 lead to the Peace of Frankfurt and France again became a republic. French history after the Revolution of 1789 was turbulent and the ideological conflicts opened long-term cleavages. The specter of violent revolution surfaced again and again. Nevertheless, there are good reasons to claim that the French Revolution ultimately created the prototype of the modern, highly rationalized, administrative and military national state that emerged in the nineteenth century.[28]

One important step toward transparency was a direct result of the American and French Revolutions. John Markoff points out how the demand to make state archives publicly accessible arose in the course of the French Revolution.[29] As mentioned earlier, the U.S. Constitution included information norms that went even farther. Clearly, the framers of the Constitution were aware of the need for credible public information. At the time, the idea of publicly accessible census results, or of state (or princely) archives, was a radical innovation. Census results in most feudal regimes were treated as state secrets.

Europe engaged indeed in "nation building" in the nineteenth century, and in many ways the new nations continued the state culture of secrecy. An uneasy balance of power arose among its nation-states. "Ancient regimes" continued to exist even past the end of the century in eastern Europe, and even the new nation-states of Italy and Germany retained influential relics of the feudal era. Partisan struggles and virulent social movements surfaced and were suppressed. The revolutions of 1848 failed all over Europe, perhaps most spectacularly in Germany. The democratic freedoms to which these revolutions aspired had been curtailed under repressive governments and cultures. Nationalism was most certainly the dominant ideology of the time, along with the competing ideologies of socialism, communism, and the forerunners of fascism, as well as laissez-faire liberalism. The need to find explanations for the vast changes that had transformed Europe and to present strategies for mastering the future strengthened the creation of these ideologies. Marxist communisms and socialisms gained a foothold in most European countries. The fear of revolution was pervasive on the Continent.

The Mirage of World Domination

In the colonial era, the struggle for dominance in Europe had escalated into a struggle for empire and ultimately a pursuit of the fantastic mirage of world domination. European nationalism and imperialism, the wars of the nineteenth century, and internal political volatility in many European countries—especially the fear of revolution—were not conditions particularly friendly to freedom of expression. There were audacious advocates of liberty, nonetheless. The rising profession of journalism became important. Newspapers and journals became powerful cultural influences. Karl Marx's work was published in the *Neue Rheinische Zeitung*. However, the European states of the nineteenth century were far from embracing transparency. Secrecy was the dominant value in statecraft and diplomacy. In fact, the secrecy syndrome that prevailed in the modern nation-state grew in the highly institutionalized, large-scale bureaucratic states of nationalist Europe. State structures and military establishments were wedded to the secrecy and loyalty syndrome. This syndrome evolved into cultural traditions that generated a morality of social closure and loyalty, engendering great disgust for the idea of criticizing government and fear of the crime of treason. The hierarchical secrecy syndrome was one of the cultural tools for building the absolutely sovereign, modern military nation-state. Except in Sweden, the idea of freedom of access to information was no doubt considered a strange notion.

Because of these developments leading toward nationalism and militarism, the legal framework upholding freedom of information in Europe took a different turn from the course it followed in America. The establishment of the French civil code in 1804 was the most important influence on the civil codes all across continental Europe, even spreading to Latin America and parts of Asia. This tradition was modified in the civil codes of Germany and Switzerland early in the twentieth century and again later. These traditions left their mark on Europe's government-oriented and government-based information culture, indeed, on the early stages of the European

29

Union. Today the EU is still an ambivalent but on certain special issues even a vigorous advocate of transparency, still struggling with the historical legacy of secrecy that once prevailed in Europe's nation-states.

The idea of democracy continued to grow in Europe, even though it had multiple enemies. It came about as a result of major political battles and remained a continuing force after the revolutionary eighteenth century, even though so many aspects of what constituted democracy remained unclear. Certainly this was true of the ideas of democratic inclusiveness in suffrage and civil rights. Markoff writes:

> In the long period from the 1780s to about 1910, very important battles were fought whose outcomes gradually came to specify what we understand as *democracy:*
>
> • Struggles for the authority of elected parliaments over decision makers (the struggle for parliamentary control over ministers in Britain, for example)
>
> • Struggles over the expansion of the suffrage (elimination of property qualifications, for example)
>
> • Struggles to make power holders subject to the will of electorates (as in Great Britain, where the unelected House of Lords exercised significant power until 1911)
>
> • Struggles for honest electoral counts (as in France, where as late as 1913 politicians provided already-marked ballots to villagers, who, visible to all, placed them in ballot boxes)
>
> • Struggles for acceptance of organized political parties as legitimate social actors and contestants in elections
>
> • Struggles to emancipate populations from ties of personal dependence that made a mockery of any claims that the entire people were freely choosing their government (as in the slave emancipations in the Western hemisphere and the gradual ending of "feudal rights" over rural majorities in Europe).[30]

Gradually, and in international discourse of movements not necessarily involving governments, the conceptual shape of what constituted a "democratic state" began to crystallize, even though many states did not represent it in reality. Transparency for the most part was not even on the agenda.

A Special Kind of Knowledge Creation

Another development in the history of transparency was the purposeful creation of knowledge about public affairs by government-sponsored investigations and the emergence of empirical social science. Writing on "Social Knowledge and Public Policy," Robert K. Merton examines the role of commissions charged with inquiring into social conditions and problems. He began with the royal commissions of inquiry in Britain and quoted Karl Marx's tribute to them in *Capital:*

> The social statistics of Germany and the rest of Continental Western Europe are, by comparison with those of England, wretchedly compiled. But they raise the veil just enough to let us catch a glimpse of the Medusa behind it. We should be appalled at the state of things at home, if, as in England, our governments and parliaments appointed periodically commissions of inquiry into economic conditions; if these commissions were armed with the same plenary powers to get at the truth; if it was possible to find for this purpose men as competent, as free from partisanship and respect of persons as are the English factory inspectors, her medical reporters on public health, her commissioners of inquiry into the exploitation of women and children, into housing and food.[31]

The early efforts at systematic reflection on governance on the European continent took the form of "cameralistics," still far from empirical social science. With the emergence of the disciplines of scientific historiography, political economy, economics, and sociology in the second half of the nineteenth century, the quest to create information about society began in earnest. Scholars like Auguste Comte, Herbert Spencer, Emile Durkheim, Georg Simmel, Max Weber, and Ferdinand Toennies laid the conceptual and empirical foundations for systematic social inquiry. The penetration of social opacity through social research had begun in systematic ways. Only a few of these early social scientists were specifically concerned with the role of information as we see it. Georg Simmel was an exception and gave much attention to the role of knowledge in social life.

Sweden: A Special Case

Transparency norms have spread slowly since their emergence in the eighteenth century, but even before the great revolutions of that era, Sweden moved to the forefront of innovation about transparency. It was a period of great turmoil following wars, hardships, political struggles, and the transition from a major military power to a small nation-state on the northern rim of Europe. It is worthwhile to attend to the old roots of a transparent information culture in Sweden. It is a special historical and cultural milepost.[32] It also illustrates the point that path- breaking innovations in information cultures occur at times outside the political arenas of the major powers.

In the late Middle Ages, at the end of the Viking era, Sweden had a culture different from that of most European countries. It had a strong commitment to egalitarianism and placed a high value on the rule of law. In Sweden, serfdom and slavery were abolished in 1335—an astounding fact when one considers the long history of serfdom in, for example, Austria and Russia, and the abolition of slavery in the Americas in the nineteenth century. For much of Sweden's earlier history, it had an elective kingship. A thirteenth-century Swedish law demonstrates this tradition, Becker writes, with this statement: "The Swedes take a king but may also depose him." The Swedish monarchy did not become hereditary until the mid-sixteenth century.[33]

The disastrous Great Northern War of 1700–21 pitted Russia, Poland, and Denmark against Sweden's assertion of supremacy in the Baltic region, causing heavy losses of life. Sweden lost about one-third of its people. The war was followed by a period of internal conflicts and turbulent change. The Age of Freedom (1719–22) saw the establishment of a constitution. It did not last long. Again, warfare against Russia (1741–43) caused hardship, provoked dissent, and incited a peasant uprising. The power struggles between the parties (the Hats and the Caps) and with the king and the estates continued.

The establishment of freedom of the press in 1766 was not purely motivated by the ideals of freedom: it was a partisan move by the Caps. Nevertheless, it was also a step in the direction of information freedom, since it provided for both freedom of the press and access to government documents such as Riksdag debates and administrative records (with some restrictions on the latter). The first daily newspaper started publication just one year later (Peter Momma's *Dagligt Allehanda*) and other newspapers appeared soon. The reestablishment of an "enlightened despotism" under King Gustavus III led to serious revisions and limitations of the freedom of the press act in 1774. A new constitution was created in 1809, the year of the establishment of the office of ombudsman—another Swedish innovation.[34] Both these innovations were created in turbulent times as strategic and partisan moves in political struggles. As we have said, power struggles, scandals, and political motives frequently provide the context for innovations in transparency. Sweden is justifiably proud of its early institutions of freedom of the press and the office of ombudsman, integral parts of its culture much earlier than in any other Western country.

After the World Wars: A Historical Watershed

We now move closer to recent events. The system of European nation-states was shaken by the two world wars and the enormous changes that followed.

The global transformations of the later twentieth century fundamentally changed the cultures of information. However, much occurred in the turbulent earlier decades. There was a period of hope in the interwar years. Germany made strides toward democracy in the Weimar Republic. In an episode of great historical irony and sadness, the German government even established in 1931 formal rules for the conduct of research on human subjects that were more specific and advanced than those that followed the Nuremberg war crimes trials after the war. When the Nazi party came to power with Hitler at the helm, these rules were abandoned, even though they remained technically in legal force throughout the Nazi regime.

Faden and Beauchamp write:

> The extreme disregard of ethics in the Nazis' exploitation and abuse of subjects is all the more remarkable in light of the fact that in 1931 Germany had enacted, on moral grounds, strict "Richtlinien" [regulations or guidelines] to control both human experimentation and the use of innovative therapies in medicine, issued by the Reich's Health Department. These regulations remained binding law throughout the period of the Third Reich. Consent requirements formed two of fourteen major provisions in the guidelines, one dealing with "New Therapy" and the other with "Human Experimentation." It was demanded in both cases that consent (first party or proxy consent, as appropriate) must always be given "in a clear and undebatable manner."
>
> Questions of the nature of appropriate information, bona fide consent, careful research design, and special protections for vulnerable subjects were all carefully delineated in these guidelines. Human experimentation was declared to be impermissible without consent, and absolutely impermissible with dying patients. A special irony is that no other nation appears to have had such morally and legally advanced regulation at the time of the Nazi abuses and during the Nuremberg Trials. A second irony is that although the Nuremberg Code is widely assumed to be the first major document in the history of research ethics to deal with consent in a detailed manner, the 1931 regulations contain no less adequate provisions than those in the Code itself.[35]

The Great Depression engulfed the world for ten years, creating extreme economic hardship. In Germany the sense of injured pride and the clamor for revenge for the lost war and the harsh period of reparations and inflation fed the fervor of those favoring totalitarianism and defeated the forces of democracy. After the democratic period of the Weimar Republic, the Nazi party succeeded in 1933 in establishing its dictatorship and rapidly consolidated its power. Around Central Europe and in what had been the Austro-Hungarian Empire, nationalism and fascism flared. Authoritarian regimes

33

rose in Poland under Pilsudski, Salazar in Portugal, Franco in Spain, and Dollfuß in Austria. Fascist-type regimes also spread in Latin America and elsewhere. The utterly catastrophic collapse of Russia at the end of World War I and its revolution and civil war created the climate for the rise of totalitarian Bolshevism and the murderous reign of Stalin. Totalitarianism existed in its destructive extremes both in parties of the far right and in the Leninist-Stalinist forces of the far left.

These dictatorships were the terror and blight of the twentieth century. The Soviet dictatorship had no use for democracy or transparency. The Nazi movement and its government in Germany had designs for "racial purity," embarked on the 1939–45 war of ethnic cleansing, and expropriated whole territories to create a German *Lebensraum*. The Nazis hated democracy and considered it to be for "weaklings." Harsh leadership and violent authoritarianism were considered to be strong. Democracy, they believed, was harmful to Germany. Nazi policies were pursued with violence, hatred, and blatant distortions of truth.

There were beliefs in power, loyalty to the leader, obedience, and secrecy. Indeed, secrecy was given a high value and it was a tool of both corruption and oppression. The secrecy syndrome was brought to extremes and protected by both loyalty cults and threats of violence and death. The ideology of Nazism cherished the notion of a Nordic master race that had to be cultivated by eugenics for the purity of the Volksgemeinschaft—the people's commune. Impure races were to be cleansed from the Fatherland. (See chapter 8.)

The Nazi regime enslaved laborers from occupied countries for the German war effort, but the persecution and genocide of Jews and other "enemies of the people" were its ultimate crimes. Nazi totalitarianism fostered a culture of blindness to evil among the people of Germany and Austria and, in fact, among many who admired fascism elsewhere in Europe and even on other continents in the 1930s. All the totalitarian regimes of the twentieth century, including the militaristic regimes of Italy and Japan, were violent, haughty enemies of both democracy and transparency. In the end, they all collapsed. World War II was the epitome of the European national drives for dominance and its end opened a new era.

After the military collapse of Nazi Germany and of Japan, the historical facts of mass murder, the Holocaust, oppression, and exploitation by new forms of slavery came to light. In the West and in much of the world, the sense of horror and revulsion produced long-term effects. In sharp distinction to the policies adopted by the victorious powers after World War I, the

Allies of World War II, led by the United States, chose a stance of reconstruction and of striving for a new world order. The creation of the United Nations, the U.S. Marshall Plan, and the establishment of global financial institutions were motivated by hopes that new foundations could be laid for a better future.

These measures were intended to create a framework for overcoming and transcending the violence that had dominated centuries of European history. Not only Germany, but also much of the European state system was destroyed by the catastrophe of the two world wars. With a major role played by the United States, a new system of states was constructed in Western Europe after the end of World War II: the European Community that became the European Union.

The Postwar Intellectual Shift

Remarkable intellectual developments of this era gave rise to the forceful slogan, "Never again!" Karl R. Popper's wartime book, *The Open Society and Its Enemies* (referred to in chapter 1), is very relevant to our theme. It examines critically the social philosophies that are the enemies of democracy and rationality. It is written with a passion for the open society and for the philosophy of science that emphasizes the limits of science. It attacks the misconception that science yields absolute and ultimate knowledge about the end of history. Popper attacks those who claim to have discovered the "laws of history which enable them to prophecy the course of historical events."[36] These claims, shared by many of history's great philosophers, became pillars in the faith-based ideologies of totalitarianism. Admittedly, not everything in Popper's book survives criticism today. A much more cautious conception of the limits of science has emerged, as well as a careful and fruitful use of the probabilistic models of cultural evolution that do shed light on directions of history, after all.[37]

While most of the period after 1945 in the West was characterized by a new and constructive spirit, the world was dominated by the cold war from 1945 until 1989. For many years, democracy and certainly transparency seemed to be in peril. In the cold war the contending superpowers placed enormous emphasis on secrecy, intelligence, and covert operations. In fact, the secrecy syndrome became a powerful cultural and political force, in often quite different forms in many parts of the world and with mostly negative consequences.[38]

The Beginnings of the Cold War

From the 1950s to the mid-1970s, the United States played an ambivalent role in the efforts to encourage democracy in the world. It focused on the power competition with the Soviet Union during that period and pursued the cold war vigorously and often ruthlessly. Alliances with anticommunist rulers were believed to be necessary, even if they were authoritarians. Nevertheless, there developed a transnational legitimation of democracy. Markoff writes:

> Following World War II, political forces reshaped their own countries in ways that made considerable use of the transnational legitimation of democracy. But consider the situation of lesser players on the world stage a few years later and the specific sorts of appeals represented by the two rival superpowers. Eastern Europe was under the domination of the Soviet Union, and the countries of the region were hardly likely to suddenly transform themselves. Many other states in Asia, Africa, and Latin America depended on the United States or the Soviet Union both for military and economic support and were thereby likely to please their patrons. Not surprisingly, the post–World War II democratization wave was succeeded by a new countercurrent.[39]

But the idea of the open society and of democracy did gain ground, especially after the collapse of the Soviet Union and the dissolution of its empire. In the late 1980s and 1990s a new, global wave of democratization occurred and continues today in spite of the resistance of remaining autocratic and corrupt regimes in several parts of the globe.

Transnational Developments

Important elements in this spread of democracy and freedom of information were transnational developments. Very early in its existence, during its first session, the United Nations adopted in December 1946 a resolution declaring freedom of information to be a "fundamental human right" and the "touchstone of all the freedoms to which the UN is consecrated."[40] This was followed by several further actions. In 1966 the UN adopted a legally binding treaty establishing the International Covenant on Civil and Political Rights (ICCPR). Article 19 in this treaty states:

> 1. Everyone shall have the right of freedom of opinion. 2. Everyone shall have the right to freedom of expression; this right shall include freedom to seek, receive and impart information of all kinds, regardless of frontiers, either orally, in writing or in print, in the form of art or through any media of his choice. 3.

The exercise of the rights provided for in paragraph 2 of this article carries with it special duties and responsibilities. It may therefore be subject to certain restrictions, but these shall only be such as are provided by law and are necessary: (a) For respect of the rights and reputation of others; (b) for the protection of national security or of public order, or of public health or morals.[41]

These kinds of transnational and international pronouncements include also the famous Helsinki Accords of the Conference on Security and Cooperation of 1975. While these acccords have not had the effect of abolishing violations of human rights, including violations of information rights, they have become focal points of public debate in many countries, and they have been effective instruments in the hands of transnational movements. The Organization for Security and Cooperation in Europe (OSCE) has played a quiet but persistent role in attempting to moderate tensions and providing suggestions—for example, to promote the institution of ombudsmen.[42] The European Union is today an especially important transnational actor and is in certain ways a supranational authority. In the EU human rights are generally protected, as is the general principle of freedom of information and other rights of citizens.

In the period following World War II, and accelerating after the end of the cold war, democracy grew and transparency norms spread across many nations. The collapse of the Soviet Union and the transition of most central European nations to democracy and market economies (at least of sorts) was another major turning point in the emergence of transparency values. However, not all the countries that adopted the formal characteristics of democracies created genuine liberal democratic institutions. Many became "illiberal democracies." In later chapters we will discuss the complex dynamics of the recent rise of transparency in various domains.

The Rapid Spread of the Transparency Phenomenon Today

The extraordinary scope of the transparency phenomenon may be seen in the growth of democracy and the gradual diffusion of the norms of transparency. A Freedom House publication informs us:

> At the end of 2001, there were 121 electoral democracies among the world's 192 states (63%). The 1987–88 survey found just 66 of 167 countries (40%) were electoral democracies. In short, the number of new democratically elected governments has increased by 55 over the space of 14 years, an average of nearly four per year. This gradual, sustained expansion of electoral democracy has helped to create a framework for improvements in basic human rights.

37

Freedom House categorizes nations as "free," "partly free," and "not free" and notes significant regional patterns:

Democracy and freedom are the dominant trends in Western and East-Central Europe, in the Americas, and increasingly in the Asia-Pacific Region. In the former Soviet Union, the picture remains mixed, with progress toward freedom stalled and a number of countries consolidating into dictatorships. In Africa, too, free societies and electoral democracies remain a distinct minority. There are no democracies or free countries within the Arab world, and there is a low proportion of free and democratic Muslim states.[43]

Figure 1 presents the spread of world democracy in 2003, as charted by Freedom House. The results are very similar to the 2001–02 Freedom House survey. The number of electoral democracies has grown, as has the percentage of states that are electoral democracies, up to 64%. Clearly, a substantial number of states are still not democracies. We must also remember that not all electoral democracies are liberal democracies in the true sense of that concept. In fact, all democracies are different from each other in at least some characteristics. The Freedom House survey applies a number of variables for measuring political rights and civil liberties. It defines democracy as "a political system in which the people choose their authoritative leaders freely from among competing groups and individuals who were not designated by the government. Freedom represents the opportunity to act spontaneously in a variety of fields outside the control of the government and other centers of political domination."[44]

Some electoral democratic states are "illiberal democracies," as defined by Daniel Bell et al. in *Toward Illiberal Democracy in Pacific Asia*. The thesis of this work is that liberal, Western democracy is a cultural particularity. The two main ideals underlying liberal democracy are equality, meaning equal respect for personhood and dignity, and freedom in the sense of autonomy and self-determination for the individual. These ideas are based on three principles: legal recognition of pluralism, the state's respect for civil rights, and the state's obligation to protect minorities in a neutral way. Bell writes, "The principle of keeping the government out of the business of judging the good life is known as state neutrality, a principle that explains the uneasiness liberals feel when, for example, democratic majorities enact policies favoring a certain conception of family life as against the preferences of an unpopular minority."[45] These ideas arose in the West under very special circumstances and are not easily accepted in other cultures. However traditionally Confucian societies can move toward liberal democracy, just as illiberal democracies can develop in Western countries.

Fareed Zakaria discusses the tension between liberty and democracy in general historical and contemporary terms. He presents a trenchant analysis of the problematic relationship between democracy—seen as the rule of the majority—and liberty, seen as the protection of individuality, dissent, and the rights of minorities. He notes the existence of a wide spectrum of illiberal democracies, "ranging from modest offenders such as Argentina to near-

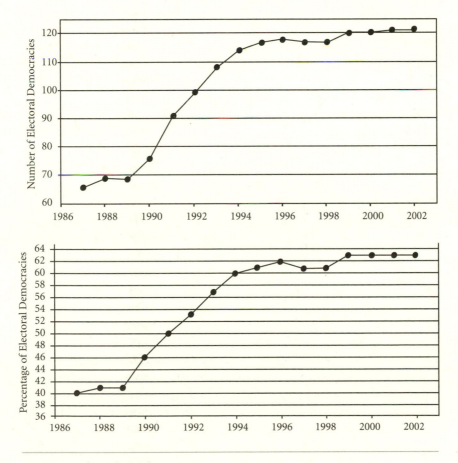

Figure 1. Tracking Electoral Democracy

Source: Freedom House, *Freedom in the World 2003*, www.freedomhouse.org/research/freeworld/2001/ methodology3.htm.

tyrannies such as Kazakhstan, with countries such as Ukraine and Venezuela in between."[46] In fact, Zakaria observes that of all the electoral democracies in the world, nearly half are today illiberal democracies. These are not just countries "in transition." The tension between democracy, which may degenerate into majoritarian populism, and liberalism, which requires constitutionality, exists also in the West: "The tension between democracy and liberalism is one that flourishes in the West's own past. It is most widely prevalent in one country in particular: the United States of America." Zakaria's observations also apply to the information cultures in America, the EU, and Japan.

Democracy and Transparency

Democracy is a form of government by the people and for the people. It is not to be equated with transparency, which is an information value, a set of norms and practices that serves the right to know. However, in democracies competitive politics and the pressure for accountability make democratic governments much more inclined to yield to demands for the open flow of information. Thus we regard the rising number of democracies as a secular trend in the world that also encourages the spread of transparency itself. The listing of democratic states we have presented shows the spread of electoral democracy in its often flawed form.

A more specific indicator of transparency is the date by which nations have granted legal access to government-held information.[47] Creating a freedom of information act does not guarantee that it will be well administered and will fulfill its purpose. However, such legislative action is a significant marker. Everywhere, governments are ambivalent about transparency versus secrecy. However, for our purposes here—with all due reservations—we rely on the historical markers of legislative action. The data show an extraordinary rise in freedom of information laws, especially in the last few years.

Sweden is, again, the leader in transparency with its Freedom of the Press Act of 1766, which included access to government documents. The United States adopted its Freedom of Information Act in 1966–67. It was a significant step, even though the exact boundaries of the right to access government information are frequently contested.[48] In 1980 the Law Ministers of the British Commonwealth (a voluntary association of fifty-four countries based on historical links) stated that "public participation in the democratic and governmental process was at its most meaningful when citizens had adequate access to official information."[49] From the early 1980s on, nation-states have adopted freedom of information laws with increasing frequency.[50] Australia, Canada, and New Zealand acted in 1982–83. In Asia the Philippines (1987), Hong Kong (1995), Thailand (1997), South Korea (1998), and Japan (2001) have passed such laws. In Africa, the Republic of South Africa implemented freedom of information legislation in 2001. In the Middle East, only Israel has such a law (1999). Almost all European countries (with the exception of Switzerland and Germany)[51] have now freedom of information access laws, as does the European Union itself (access to documents, 2000). Peru passed this legislation in 1994 under the formula *habeas data*. In the same year Belize, and in 1999 Trinidad and Tobago passed freedom of information legislation. However, full implementation of the UK freedom of information act was delayed until 2005. Scotland adopted its law in 2002. Eastern European countries are rushing to adopt them. They include Albania (1999), Armenia (2003), Bosnia and Herzegovina (2002), Bulgaria (2000), the Czech Republic (2000), Estonia (2001), Finland (1999), Georgia (1999), Hungary (1992), Latvia (1998), Lithuania (2000), Moldova (2000), Poland (2002), Romania (2001), Slovakia (2001), Slovenia (2003), Russia and Ukraine (1992). Figure 2 summarizes these developments, with data from other world regions as well, such as Iceland (1996), Pakistan (2002), Panama (2002), Peru (2003), South Africa (2001), India (2003), Mexico (2003), and Uzbekistan (2003). Zimbabwe also passed a Freedom of Information Act in 2002, but it is so distorted we cannot list it as such.[52]

Ombudsmen

As a third indicator, figure 3 summarizes the spread of the office of ombudsman. This office is an invention in governance created and adopted by Sweden in 1809 (when Finland was a part of Sweden). It was intended to be an office providing assistance to individual citizens when they encountered difficulties in dealing with their government. It gradually became a globally recognized institution.

The office of ombudsman plays a crucial role as a link between the citizenry and their government in 111 countries. The three functions of the ombudsman are: (1) to investigate citizen complaints about the government and determine whether it had acted according to law or had been unfair; (2) to make recommendations to the government for redressing wrongs and for the improvement of administration and laws; and (3) to report findings to the government and the legislature as well as the general public. On occasion, the ombudsman may propose new legislation if it is clear that legal action is necessary to deal with frequently encountered difficulties in government service.[53] By now, the ombudsmen of the world have become a pro-

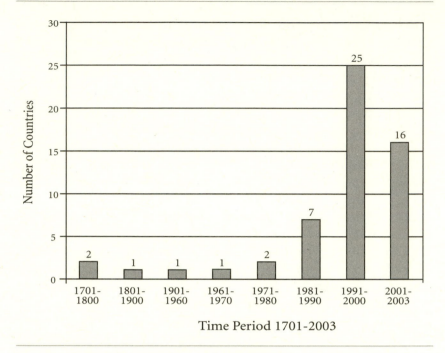

Figure 2. Freedom of Information Legislation, 1701–2003

Source: David Banisar, ed., *Freedom of Information and Access to Government Records Around the World,* July 2002, www.freedominfo.org.

Note: 1981–1990, 7 countries adopted legislation; 1991–2000, 25 countries adopted legislation; 2001–2002, 8 countries adopted legislation.

fession with a special ethos of nonconfrontational but critical service. They are part of government, but independent. Many ombudsmen are selected by unanimous consent of the entire parliament. Many of their functions deal with information access for citizens, information norms for the government, and the empowerment of citizens. The International Ombudsman Institute at the University of Alberta in Canada now helps to develop this profession that is a new force for transparency.

Sir Brian Elwood, former chief ombudsman of New Zealand and a global leader of the rising ombudsman movement and profession, regards the adoption of the ombudsman office by governments as an extraordinary event.[54] In his words:

The time was right for the growth of this institution that had been proven credible by history. It creates mediation between the institutions of government and individual citizens. The time in history was right. There had been a growing concentration of power in government, post–WWII, that escalated. In 1809, Scandinavia instituted the ombudsman. Four thousand years ago the emperor of China had one. It was a necessary counteraction to the growth of governments. Most governments have now agreed.

When asked if he sees the spread of the profession, he replied:

It is a movement. In the last seven to eight years it developed momentum. It had much to do with limiting the might of government and with the increased education of people after World War II. Now, everyone wants to jump on board. This is nowhere more pronounced than in the United States—but they have gone in the wrong direction. There, the title is used by anyone who wants to review complaints, but they are not independent. Also, the U.S. does not have a federal or state ombudsman. It is a strange phenomenon. . . . Ombudsmen are really not seeking winners or losers; they are not confrontational but inquisitive.

Elwood believes that the ombudsman is an institution that advances the transparency phenomenon. When asked if he saw a relation, he replied:

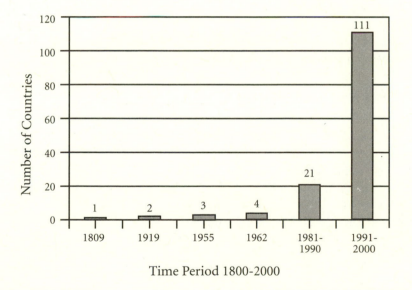

Figure 3. Number of Countries with Office of the Ombudsman, 1800–2000
Source: International Ombudsman Institute at the University of Alberta, Canada,
www.law.alberta.ca/centre/ioi.

Yes. I was invited by the Bertelsmann Foundation to North Rhine Westphalia in Germany and found there a philosophical commitment to "This is government information." That is a fundamental misunderstanding of the role of government to serve people. There are elsewhere also official secrets acts. The role of the ombudsman is to be a mediator, to open information access. The ombudsman must be independent, nonadversarial, not adopting an advocacy role. There is a distinction between a human rights advocate and an ombudsman. We must not see an ombudsman as a cure-all. It is better to have an advocacy institution *and* an ombudsman. We don't stand on a soap box.

When asked about the ombudsman as a profession, he responded:

We do training. The International Ombudsman Institute is a professional body and we have standards for the profession. I have been invited to China twice, but never to the United States. In China there are eleven million bureaucrats who feel they must act honestly for their government. I am hopeful about China—I told them about the ancient Chinese idea that your citizens must know that you are looking out for them. Outside the royal palace a bell would ring, and someone would come out to listen to the citizen. There is a commonly held ethos among ombudsmen. There is cohesion among ombudsmen for whatever is good for individuals, a need to balance and fairness. The ombudsman has influence, not power. You can be an influence for the good of others. That permeates the behavior of people genuinely appointed as independent officials. There is something magical about it all. It works.

The New Role of Evaluation Research

Something else was at work toward the end of the twentieth century: the role of the social sciences and the demand for accountability as well as for transparency to be measured. This brought the entry of evaluation research and evaluation science as aspects of transparency. Karl Marx had noted, much earlier, the superior efforts to provide knowledge about social conditions in Britain through the commissions of inquiry. Social science in Europe and America expanded these efforts in the later nineteenth and twentieth centuries. The study of social problems and the field of policy studies did bring new light into understanding the evils of many social conditions. However it was not until the late twentieth century that evaluation research grew into a set of professions that are now beginning to form a global network.

Evaluations of organizations, projects, and policies are efforts at increasing transparency through gathering relevant and valid information about how well they are fulfilling their purposes, their legal mandates, or their aspirations. The idea that scientific methods can both illuminate social conditions and measure value-relevant outcomes evolved from applied social research. A great pioneer in building institutions and creating methodologies for the field was Paul F. Lazarsfeld, the Viennese mathematician who became an American sociologist at Columbia University and later the University of Pittsburgh. He created the Bureau of Applied Social Research at Columbia University in 1939 and led it for many years. His latest work dealt with applied social research and its uses for evaluation.[55] Edward Allen Suchman also became an innovator of evaluation research, which he helped to make a discipline. His first contributions to this thematic were made in the field of public health and its relations to sociology, and his book, *Evaluative Research,* became the guidebook for the emerging field.[56]

The growing profession established the American Evaluation Association in 1972, from the beginning seeing itself as an international professional society. Now it has 3,700 members from across the United States and from fifty countries. Evaluation has grown into a set of disciplines in public health, education, social action programs, and organizations. Evaluations are conducted in development projects on a global basis, in the field of NGOs, in business policies and practices, and in government and even military operations. In 1995 the first International Evaluation Conference was held in Vancouver, Canada, with 1,600 evaluators from 66 countries and five continents in attendance. This huge meeting set ambitious goals for the profession in the global context, signaling to the profession that something very big had occurred. The intellectual outcome was a handbook for the evaluation profession edited by Eleanor Chelimsky and William R. Shadish.[57] There was also an organizational outcome in that evaluators formed an extensive global network.

Many new evaluation organizations have been founded in most parts of the world in connection with development projects and policies. The OECD set up a Development Co-operation Directorate (DAC) with links to evaluation network participants in Australia, Canada, Denmark, the European Union, Finland, France, Germany, Ireland, Japan, the Netherlands, Norway, Spain, Sweden, the United Kingdom, United States, and the Asian Development Bank. Its links reach out to a network of global NGOs and international agencies.

Evaluation societies with an even broader scope include the African, American, Australasian, and Italian evaluation associations, the Brazilian Evaluation Network, the Canadian Evaluation Society, the United Kingdom,

French, German, and European evaluation societies (the latter extending throughout and beyond the EU), and the International Development Evaluation Association. By now the evaluation profession is an important factor in the rising demand for transparency. A veritable industry has grown up in a sprawling and bewildering landscape of evaluators and their institutions.[58] There are, of course, discrepancies between hopes and realities in these armies of evaluators. Their ethos is that of valid transparency and the service to evaluation science that must connect values and purposes to relevant facts in a scientific way.

Some Preliminary Conclusions

The end of the twentieth century was a time of vast expansion of democracy and of transparency in government activities in many parts of the world. Later chapters will show that the transparency shift has also occurred in many professions, corporations, international agencies, and nongovernmental organizations. It is a phenomenon of vast scope. Further, we have been able to make the point that this current phase of history is unique in the speed and scope in the change of information cultures toward transparency. Although information cultures are changing toward transparency with great speed, cultures of secrecy continue in today's world. The conflicts with transparency are lively.

This chapter has sketched significant historical turning points toward liberty and transparency, showing how changes in information norms and information capacities are intimately linked to contests of power and deep cultural values. These turning points in information and communication cultures have been eras of turbulence, conflict, and intense intercivilizational encounters. We therefore will pursue the hypothesis that the current era of advanced globalization and changes in information norms and capacities will generate far-reaching and turbulent culture movements in the dialectic of reform and reaction. Ours is an era of accelerated value changes that move in the general direction of at least formal democracy and human rights and—our focus here—information rights and duties. The demands for accountability and the need for valid information have created many growth areas for transparency, with evaluation a recent addition. Information norms are linked to very basic cultural forces and their changes.

3

PERSPECTIVES ON TRANSPARENCY

Linking Several Fields of Knowledge to One Social Fact

The *transparency phenomenon* is the term we use to describe the growing value placed on openness of information. It has led to special arrangements for information disclosure by those at the centers of power. The new respect for transparency proceeds through the creation of norms and infrastructures for access to information held by authorities. While the phenomenon occurs in many cultural domains, in diverse institutions and political arenas, their norms and infrastructures take similar forms. Yet they are not readily recognized as one macrosociological social fact. They may have similar causes but varying effects in diverse domains of social life.

Our task, then, is to shine light from different directions on the causes of change in information values and norms, to illuminate the transparency phenomenon from varied points of view. What we call *transparency* will emerge as a strategic factor in global change as well as in the formation of social solidarities in cohesion and conflict. We first explore the global contexts of the transparency phenomenon, then review the research literature on transparency. Finally, we analyze how sociology has grappled with earlier fundamental social transformations, with implications for the changes we are experiencing today.

First, since transparency is a global as well as local phenomenon, we describe the multiple dimensions of globalization as reflected in current scholarship—a vast literature covering a range of often contradictory opinions. We then describe ten major dimensions of global change. Next we turn to research on the transparency phenomenon, to outline its impact on many diverse institutions has produced broader social and cultural changes that in turn introduce new pressures for transparency. We conclude that the transparency phenomenon is based on the interaction between the information technology revolution and value changes favoring autonomy and the "right to know." Transparency is now a major factor in the information revolution's impact on modernity, and it will likely produce far-reaching social and political challenges.

Third, to understand the impact of changes in information cultures, we examine how the classical sociologists interpreted social change in their own era. The founders of sociology encountered forces of colossal import: the industrial revolution, political revolution, what Max Weber identified as rationalization, and the rise of the bureaucratic and military nation-state. Like sociologists today, they sought to identify and understand the emergence of entirely new social forms.

Because recent centuries have seen such profound transformations, we look at the significant, shared perspectives that emerged in the sociological literature of the nineteenth and early twentieth centuries. We examine how the early sociologists dealt with the entirely new, basic transformational influences in their times. They grappled with the social consequences of the industrial revolution, the new division of labor, rising individualism, and the dominance of the modern, military national state, as well as the impact of all these developments on solidarities and changing patterns of trust. Trust is a source of confidence. In the industrial age the importance of legal contracts increased as a source of confidence in business (and other) transactions. This development opened the possibility of trust beyond closely knit communities.

The far-reaching changes in information cultures we see today are as important in changing the fundamental social fabric as the transformations brought by the industrial revolution. To understand this impact, we look for insights in how sociological theory evolved in this period. The central themes of classical sociology, especially solidarity, rationalization, and their counterparts, are reemerging today in new forms that in turn create new relations between individuals and authority, as well as new sources of social cohesion and conflict.

What Is Globalization?

A worldwide debate about economic globalization is under way, and its elements are becoming clearer. The term *globalization* is used in a variety of ways, often referring either to the economic dimension of global interdependence or primarily to U.S. global policies and their impact. Discussions of globalization are frequently charged with strong feelings about the positive or negative consequences of the phenomenon. They range from the exuberantly optimistic *A Future Perfect* (2000) by John Micklethwait and

Adrian Wooldridge to Zygmunt Bauman's *In Search of Politics* (1999), which takes a pessimistic view of the future in general and of globalization in particular.

However, the polarized extremes of the "antiglobalizers" and supporters of the "free-market gospel" are receding in the scholarly debate. The focus has recently shifted to understanding empirical realities and assessing new policies. An important step forward is the articulate polemic opened up by Joseph E. Stiglitz in *Globalization and Its Discontents* (2002), a work that calls for a reevaluation of the policies undergirding the global financial system and economic development.

The wider scholarly literature, however, ranges from the conservative and stringent historical assessment found in Landes's *The Wealth and Poverty of Nations* (1998) to the nostalgic and misty socialism of Burbach, Nunez, and Kagarlitsky in *Globalization and Its Discontents: The Rise of Postmodern Socialisms* (1997) and the decidedly "postmodern" *Empire* (2000) by Hardt and Negri. By coincidence, both Stiglitz and Burbach and his colleagues chose the same title for their books, but they had very different things in mind.

The concept of *globalization* as we use it refers to the expansion and interdependence of the human population and the growing impact of human actions on the planet as a whole. We are beginning to realize that humanity inhabits a planet and with finite resources. The long history of interdependence is the subject of Jared Diamond's *Guns, Germs and Steel* (1997), Robert P. Clark's *Global Life Systems: Population, Food and Disease in the Process of Globalization* (2001), William McNeil's *Plagues and Peoples* (1998), and Robert Wright's *Nonzero: The Logic of Human Destiny* (2000). According to these books, globalization began as a slow process of migration that extended human settlements from region to region and ultimately across the globe. The growth of major world empires greatly expanded organized human activities. A significant acceleration began about five hundred years ago with European exploration and conquest of far distant lands. Globalization has since moved through several stages and epochs.[1] Recent decades have seen the arrival of a new constellation of forces in the global era. Martin Albrow discusses this epochal shift in *The Global Age: State and Society Beyond Modernity*.[2]

An authoritative assessment of the current phase of globalization is the work of David Held, Anthony McGrew, David Goldblatt, and Jonathan Perraton, in *Global Transformations* (1999). These scholars are careful to distance themselves from the "hyperglobalist" thesis that traditional nation-states have become impossible in the global era. They also dispute the skeptical

49

thesis that current economic globalization is nothing new. Instead, they build on the "transformationalist" thesis. They use the term *global transformations* to refer to specific, observed structural changes in the institutions of politics, economics, and culture. It is their conviction that "globalization is a central driving force behind the rapid social, political and economic changes that are reshaping modern societies and world order . . . a long-term historical process."[3] Their analytical framework emphasizes that global change consists of processes and structures that intersect in complex and not predetermined ways, owing to often unanticipated processes that can produce novel developments. They apply this analytical framework to changes in politics, the military, economics, financial patterns, corporate power and production networks, migration, cultures, and the environment. Held et al. conclude with the normative challenges for "civilizing and democratizing globalization." There is a need for new norms in a finite world, and the study of transparency can contribute to the need to "civilize" the tumult of global change.[4] There is now a growing awareness that the planet Earth is the unique and only habitat of all humanity, a fact that has important ethical implications.[5]

Ten Dimensions of Global Transformation

To emphasize the multidimensionality of globalization, we present a classification of the phenomenon that includes ten dimensions of change. Each is a current in the turbulence of global change that directly affects the transparency phenomenon. We add several currents not explicitly listed by Held et al.—globalization as it affects inequality, education, terrorism, forms of civil society, information technology, and the impact of history.

Global Inequalities

Today's world has an enormous diversity of cultures and vast inequalities in power, wealth, and capabilities among regions and countries. While social inequality and poverty have been endemic throughout history, today the discrepancy between great riches in the industrial countries and great poverty in the undeveloped countries has become much larger. Further, the awareness of the gulf between the rich and the poor continues to grow. As a consequence, any one of the global transformations we mention has to be seen in the context of global inequality. In this information age, knowledge of the deadly threats imposed by poverty and powerlessness is broadcast daily in all parts of the world. The technological revolutions in information gathering, communication, and travel make inequality, poverty, and despair visible everywhere. This is a form of transparency that informs citizens of rich countries of the humanitarian cost of poverty, but even more about the threats to their own health, environment, and security arising from poverty somewhere far away. In turn, transparency has become a powerful weapon used by reformers in poor countries to curb corruption and to demonstrate failures as well as successes in development efforts.

Inequality was considered an inevitable world condition in the colonial era, but it is no longer generally accepted. Transnational civil society is no longer based only in rich Western countries, but has formed influential, indigenous movements in poor countries as well. Efforts to reduce poverty are no longer just a matter of development aid sent by rich countries, but also have been taken up by civic and by some political leaders in very poor countries. Nevertheless, huge inequalities persist, as do incompetent and corrupt regimes.[6] Inequalities between rich and poor also pose cultural and political dangers. Educated people in poor countries inevitably resent the degradations of their culture and religion, which are causes of extreme frustration, rage, and misguided choices for revenge, often in the name of religion and ideology. Terrorism flourishes in this environment.

The *World Development Report 2000/2001* summarizes recent conditions:

> The world has deep poverty amid plenty. Of the world's 6 billion people, 2.8 billion—almost half—live on less than $2 a day, and 1.2 billion—a fifth—live on less than $1 a day, with 44% living in South Asia. In rich countries fewer than 1 child in 100 does not reach its fifth birthday, while in the poorest countries as many as a fifth of children do not. And while in rich countries fewer than 5% of children under five are malnourished, in poor countries as many as 50 percent are. This destitution persists even though human conditions have improved more in the past century than in the rest of history—global wealth, global connections, and technological capabilities have never been greater.[7]

The *World Development Report* contains ambitious plans for fighting poverty. Inequality, however, is not limited to economic poverty only, nor are its causes readily remedied solely by economic development policies. There are cultural and political dimensions that virtually isolate many countries from the positive aspects of global change—notably, cultures of racial and ethnic exclusion and of discrimination against women. Dictatorships like Iran, North Korea, Burma, and too many others, with their efforts to maintain control over information and their virulent methods of oppression, are today failed but dangerous countries. There are many more volatile regimes in the world. Incompetent leaders and their fear of democracy and

51

citizen empowerment, as well as civil wars and political instability, are widespread even beyond these states.[8] These are the failing states in which national government controls have failed entirely in all domains of institutional and social life.

Many poor countries are unable to marshal their resources because they are victims of drastic failures by the state, corruption, kleptocracy, and bribery. The world's inability to deal effectively with devastating epidemics like HIV/AIDS has much to do with local government incompetence and denial, as well as with the economic problems of stark poverty and the high cost of pharmaceuticals. Inequality is a matter of international power and an aspect of the global structure of power. Political instability, civil war, and government corruption are among the factors determining international powerlessness. However, the fundamental problem is that the United States, as the only superpower, and the other great powers—prominent among them the European Union—are dominant in shaping global policies and often pursue their own interests without taking into account the effect of their decisions on world poverty. The scope of inequality is a reflection of the global power structure and the interest constellations of the great powers. Joseph Stiglitz, the 2001 Nobel Prize winner in economics, has launched a passionate critique of the role of the U.S. Treasury and the market liberalization policies pursued by the IMF in the 1990s.[9]

Economic and Technological Globalization

The rapid expansion of transport, communication, and markets in trade, finance, production networks, and the rising role of transnational corporations around the globe are major forces behind the growth of transparency—as well as certain domains of secrecy. The quest for transparency in economic globalization has intensified worldwide at the beginning of the twenty-first century. This is in part a political phenomenon, in the poor as well as rich countries, intended to curb opacity and malfeasance in the conduct of corporations as well as international institutions. In part, a new awareness of the value of transparency is inherent to the dynamics of markets themselves, since markets in the global era extend across vast distances. Both buyers and sellers, and especially investors, have to rely on "trust at a distance," that is, institutional guarantors of valid information and honest transactions.

Economic globalization is also intimately linked to technological revolutions in transport, communication, information gathering, manufacturing, and services. These changes in technology also affect policies for economic development. The major policy institutions in this domain are the International Monetary Fund, the World Bank, and the World Trade Organization, all created in an era when states were virtually, and officially, the only actors in international economic affairs. Since then, economic globalization has transformed the world and brought many other actors into the arena. It has undoubtedly caused some of the most visible and consequential structural changes within countries and in global relations by opening new markets, promoting the rise of transnational corporations, enabling the relocation of entire industries, and raising new worries about global economic crises.

The quest for free trade as pursued by the great powers and the international financial institutions has shaped the recent patterns of economic globalization. It has led to global trade agreements and the creation of frameworks for regulating and deregulating markets, financial transactions, and property rights. World trade has reached unprecedented levels, and there has been exponential growth in global financial markets—also of unprecedented scope. Held and his colleagues state:

> Compared with the era of the classical Gold Standard, or that of Bretton Woods, contemporary financial globalization has many distinctive attributes. Chief among these is the sheer magnitude, complexity and speed of financial transactions and flows. . . . The sheer magnitude of capital movements, relative to either global or national output and trade is unique. . . . Contemporary financial globalization represents a distinctive new stage in the organization and management of credit and money in the world economy; it is transforming the conditions under which the immediate and long-term prosperity of states and peoples across the globe is determined.[10]

The same must be said of the growth of multinational corporations and their networks of production: globalized production is organized predominantly by multinational corporations. They have achieved a controlling position in world output, trade, investment, and transfer of technology.[11]

The global economic domain is immensely complex, thus vulnerable to economic crises, mistaken policies, and what Thomas L. Friedman calls the "electronic herd" of investors in the global marketplace. In stampedes of the "electronic herd," great harm can result, but there is "no one to call"—there are few effective controls.[12] Economic globalization is now a major arena of debate and conflict that has led to a search for new approaches, including an appeal to political institutions. There is an intense demand for creating accessible political channels capable of influencing the economic policies of the international institutions. Such demands have been pressed not only by developing countries, but also by social movements and nongovernmental organizations in the West.[13] Political articulation of issues and interests requires institutional avenues, but very few exist today. As a consequence, the economic globalization debate is a major driver of the transparency phenomenon, with all its ambiguities.

Furthermore, economic transparency is a necessary basis for transactions across great geographic and cultural distances, and therefore a need for transparency is built into functioning market systems. It is a condition of trust. Because economic transactions require relevant information, corporations have responded to this necessity, but also have made efforts to preserve some domains of secrecy.[14] The recent movement in the business communities and in civil society for corporate codes of conduct indicates an increasing recognition of the importance of accountability and transparency in transactions and decisions. Transparency is a rising concern in corporate accounting and regulating national and global financial systems. As a consequence, international institutions such as the Organization for Economic Cooperation and Development (OECD), the WTO, the World Bank, and others have pursued certain (limited and ambivalent) transparency strategies, especially in recent years, in response to financial crises and challenges to their legitimacy. Thus for transitional countries like China, membership in the WTO has become a powerful force for transparency in those countries' internal markets.

Political Globalization

Transparency has become a requirement in many aspects of political globalization in a complex and often not symmetrical way. Today, politics extends beyond national and even regional boundaries to deal with global issues that are often also matters of significant local concern. A major aspect of political globalization is the effective spread of at least nominal democracy, as described in chapter 2. In particular, transitional countries try to enact democratic constitutions. There is extensive documentation of the role of transparency in global diplomacy and in the functioning of treaties and of specialized regimes.[15] The level of trust among nation-states, global corporations, international institutions, and powerful movements is generally low. There is a strong demand for proof before power centers will make a commitment or form an agreement. Providing proof is a necessary step for building confidence and creating trust across distances.

Nation-states have become enmeshed in transnational and often global networks that are essential for their own functions. The internationalization of normal state functions has become routine. Democratic states clearly find international cooperation easier than authoritarian ones. Even for some authoritarian states like the People's Republic of China, normal state functions are taking on international dimensions. They may include such functions as collection of taxes or regulation of immigration and police cooperation, which now require the establishment of cooperative working networks among states. Many more routine state functions are being internationalized, such as the protection of public health, promoting clean air and water, defending property rights, the fighting international crime, and fostering transportation and communication systems. The war against terror expands this need for internationalization further.

Given the close connections between many local issues and global concerns and global actors, scholars have invented a number of terms to describe the phenomenon. Roland Robertson speaks of "glocalization" and James N. Rosenau has created the term "fragmegration" for the paradox that certain issues require global integration as well as political fragmentation at the same time.[16] However described, globalization has now reached the point where global politics is a reality not only for states and their political structures, but also for communities, corporations, civic organizations, and individuals. It has become particularly visible in the protest movement against global economic policies as pursued by the great powers and the major international economic and financial institutions. These protest actions remain politically chaotic, but they express an articulate demand for new political norms in the global arena and for allowing all parties affected by global change to be heard. The current phase of political globalization has created a "quasi-market"[17] of competition for global solutions offered by social movements, nongovernmental organizations, international agencies like the World Bank, and by state governments. Again, the demand for transparency is advanced by these movements.

Hence, the demand for publicly accessible information is rising—as well as the supply. The expansion of global politics and governance is well under way in domains as diverse as trade policies and negotiations, fishing rights, control of epidemics, agricultural subsidies, extradition of criminals, property rights, human rights, and the fight against terror. However, there is no institutional forum for global politics, in spite of the important role played by the United Nations and its agencies.

One response to this demand for global politics has been the creation of a system of treaties among nations. Examples include the Law of the Sea, the United Nations Convention, and the Kyoto Accord on Climate Change, the treaty to ban land mines, the verification protocol for the biological weapons convention, and the International Criminal Court. Under President George W. Bush, the United States has withdrawn from most of these treaties in a policy swing meant to protect U.S. sovereignty. However, the effect has been to return to the anarchy and precarious "balance of power" among sovereign states characteristic of the so-called Westphalian states system. This posture of the United States has been condemned by virtually all its allies and much of the world. Yet the demand for institutions and norms governing global politics does not abate and is inexorable. The demand for transparency in global matters is rising, albeit in complex ways. In many cases treaties are avoided, but "regimes" are arranged to avoid the binding obligations of international treaties. Such international regimes may be based on pragmatic arrangements, but they can function only when the participating states perceive that the regime will be followed. Even in this condition, transparency is needed.[18]

Legitimacy of Transnational and Supranational Authorities

A major part of transnational political globalization concerns the legitimacy of those in authority. Such legitimacy is a special dimension of globalization because it relies increasingly on transparency in the creation of new norms. The central global political forum and political instrument is the United Nations system. Its legal framework is that of a community of sovereign states, represented in the General Assembly, but with special privileges given to the permanent members of the Security Council. With the power to make final decisions that cannot be appealed, the Security Council indeed does claim supranational powers in various global emergencies. During the cold war, the United Nations was virtually deadlocked. Nevertheless, it served as an important forum for political discussion. The specialized agencies set up by the United Nations have produced advanced understandings of global conditions and problems that need attention. Today, the United Nations has become increasingly important both as a political forum and as a source of concerted action, difficult though its structures and procedures remain. The progress of international law continues, albeit slowly and with odd twists. In the words of David Held and his colleagues:

> The UN has provided a vision, valuable in spite of all its limitations, of alternative principles of global governance to those of traditional geopolitics, principles based on collective decision-making between governments and nongovernmental organizations, and, under appropriate circumstances, of a supra-

national presence in world affairs championing human rights. Indeed, this vision, if carried to its logical extreme, challenges the whole principle that humankind can or should be organized as a society of sovereign states above all else.[19]

The European Union is generally regarded as the only political entity with legally defined supranational powers over its member states. It has become the first large, new community of nations agreeing to drastic limitations of their sovereignty in favor of a supranational political, communal institution. After the devastation of two world wars, originating in Europe, the EU has been an outstanding success, creating permanent peace among its members and establishing a democratically governed domain of states subscribing to shared principles of human rights, openness, and the rule of law. The expansion of the European Union to include many nations of the former Soviet bloc has created new challenges and opportunities. Today there is a vigorous debate in the EU about the nature of a future European constitution. While there are certainly important disagreements as to the content of such a constitution, there is now a consensus that something like a constitution is needed—but the debate continues. Transparency in the EU has become a powerful demand and expectation, as well as a topic of concern and entrenched resistance. (The European Union will be further discussed in chapter 5.)

In addition to the EU, there are global institutions with specialized and limited authority that wield de facto supranational power. Many were established as a result of or support by U.S. foreign policy initiatives, building upon the Bretton Woods agreement of 1944 and its evolution into a world financial system. For example, the World Trade Organization (WTO) was established in 1994 as a permanent institution with real powers to oversee trade agreements, enforce rules, and settle disputes. The World Bank was designed not as a supranational, but an international authority; however, it certainly wields such power over developing countries that seek to borrow from it. Economic transparency is what these agencies have asked of their clients for some time. Similarly, the International Monetary Fund (IMF) is a transnational organization designed to promote global financial stability. As a result of criticism of some of their policies, transparency has been demanded of these institutions themselves. International organizations have learned much about the needs for disclosure in negotiations with each other, with states, and civil society. As a consequence, transparency is emerging as an essential, if contested ingredient in this domain.[20] For example, the IMF has officially established a transparency policy for its own activities—a change from its past practice of demanding transparency from its client countries, but much less from itself. The policy shift is clearly the result of criticism by civil society movements as well as experts like Joseph Stiglitz. The creation of the Independent Evaluation Office (IEO)—operating at "arm's length from IMF management" and following a well-publicized agenda, is one step designed to rely on transparency to gain legitimacy.[21] (The turn to transparency had much to do with the then president of the IMF, Horst Köhler, who later became president of Germany.) Many other global and regional agencies form a vast web of regulations, consultative networks, and international treaty–based regimes such as the special agencies of the United Nations. They, too, are aware of the demand for transparency.

Military Globalization

A global set of competing and conflicting, but partly interconnected networks in military matters has emerged, leading to major changes in the role of war and peace in global affairs. The concept of "military globalization" may appear strange at first glance, but our definition of globalization refers to the expansion of human activities to encompass the entire world—it is not synonymous with global integration. By military globalization we mean what Held et al. refer to as "the expanding reach of organized violence." This includes not only state-organized military forces, but also privatized military organizations, warlords, and plundering by armed gangs in civil wars or other conflicts. Held et al. describe the evolution of a "world military order" from 1492 to the present, stretching from Europe to embrace the world.[22]

Today, military globalization has taken historically unprecedented forms. First, the United States has emerged as the world's most powerful unrivaled military force. Second, weak and failing states have become breeding grounds for "privatized violence." Stefan Mair points out that since the end of the cold war "European and American decision makers have tended to consider conflicts in apparently unimportant countries as none of their business. This was partly changed by September 11—just as it changed many other things in world politics. Suddenly, the North realized that state failure, authoritarianism, cultural disintegration, social deprivation, and economic hopelessness not only are tragic developments for the have-nots in the South but also affect the haves in the North."[23]

Third, there is a massive outbreak of privatized violence by criminals, terrorists, warlords, and rebels in many parts of the world. Much of Africa, the

Middle East, parts of Asia and Latin America, southern Europe, and parts of the former Soviet Union are seriously affected. There are distinctions to be made between terrorists, warlords, and rebels, as each category acts for different motives. However, their networks can, and do, connect with each other. Because they all depend on international money and resources, major world states and international agencies take an interest in systematically monitoring the flow of support from outside. A specialized demand for transparency arises. Fourth, the world is awash in weapons—mostly conventional weapons, but also weapons of mass destruction. This means that the demands for disclosure (like the motives for secrecy) become very urgent. One problem for international security is to have the technological capacity for verifying military capabilities of various powers and states. Satellite information plays a crucial role in global surveillance, another impetus behind the need for global transparency.[24] Paradoxically, military globalization is a major force strengthening the demand for transparency, while also increasing pressures for secrecy, an area of constantly changing concern.

Michael Mandelbaum describes peace, democracy, and free markets as the three ideas that conquered the world. In military affairs, he takes an optimistic view of the future. He compares the gradual construction of strategies for long-term peace to the slow progress in the struggle to cure cancer: "The fight against cancer advances in small steps rather than great leaps. Research produces new therapies by modifying existing ones. So it was with common security. The treaties at its heart took years to conclude, they were not the first treaties ever signed, and in important ways they resembled others already in place."[25] These security treaties—the Anti-Ballistic Missile (ABM) Treaty of 1972, the Intermediate-range Nuclear Forces (INF) Treaty of 1987, the START I Treaty of 1991, the START II Treaty of 1993, and the Treaty on Conventional Forces in Europe (CFE) of 1990—have established a framework for peace. In Mandelbaum's words:

> Together these agreements reshaped the armed forces of the opposing sides in the Cold War according to two principles that together define common security. The first principle is defense dominance, according to which armed forces are organized and deployed for defending territory but not for attacking and seizing it. The second principle is transparency, meaning that all countries are able to see for themselves just what armed forces all others have and how and where they are deployed. . . . This common security order is for war and peace what democracy is for politics and the free market is for economics: a formula for achieving a universally desired goal. The liberal approaches to politics and eco-

nomics are vehicles for freedom and prosperity; common security is a mechanism for securing peace. Like democracy and free markets it is a system of voluntary association, albeit of sovereign states rather than individuals.[26]

Mandelbaum's argument reinforces the major role of transparency in military affairs in the era of globalization. However, there is a serious negative side to the increasing reliance of states on commercial "private security enterprises," as they are used in the war in Iraq. These organizations are not accountable to the public and typically operate in secrecy.

Military globalization has affected transparency as well as secrecy in sometimes paradoxical ways. In fact, transparency has itself played a major role in global military activity, albeit in conjunction with efforts at international or mutual surveillance. Certainly, military interests have forced advances in information and surveillance technology. Both the Internet and satellite information technologies had military origins, and their military as well as civilian significance continues to grow.

Global Terrorism

Terrorism as a weapon is not a new phenomenon in world history. However, in a global context it has taken on new forms and causes. The increasing awareness of powerful cultural changes sweeping the world poses threats to many cultural traditions and their entrenched elites. Those who are threatened by these changes may cultivate rage fueled by damaged pride and fear of loss of identity. Cultural changes that are threats to the belief in "revealed truths" of any form can rarely be settled by arguments alone—they involve cultural protests and reforms. Non-negotiable identity claims to territories and to uncompromising demands for power can make terrorism endemic for long periods of time. In the context of global inequality, defensive elites find fertile recruiting grounds for terrorist activists.

The spread of military technology, the use of dangerous but commonplace devices such as airplanes, cars, and trucks for terror attacks, the technical empowerment enabling dangerous and even suicidal individuals to wreak havoc on a large scale have created new and dangerous global threats. The "war against terror" today inevitably blurs the lines between interstate warfare and global surveillance and transnational police actions. As grievances multiply, the means of using terror as a weapon abound as well. The international responses to the threats of terrorism are led by the United States and are at once, offensive, defensive, and aggressively interventionist. Protective measures require increased attention to security, including surveillance, secret plans for defense and prevention, police cooperation, and new international security policies. Secrecy, limitations of privacy, and infringements of civil rights have increased. Paradoxically, transparency continues to be an essential ingredient in the war against terror. The demands for information among states create new challenges for both transparency and secrecy.

Globalization of Education

An important aspect of global transformations, education, has not been sufficiently studied from the point of view we espouse. There is actually a trend toward convergence of educational standards and even curricula in the world, even though it is vigorously opposed by some religious extremists and nationalists.[27] The migration of university students, especially from developing countries to the developed world (predominantly to the United States, Canada, Britain, Australia, and the European Union) has increased impressively in the last few decades. The cultural effects are complex, but there is a possibility that new generations of international students will create both an important diaspora for their countries abroad and will become professionals and potential political leaders back home.

Higher education is in transformation in many parts of the world. In Europe the reform process involves all universities in the EU and in the countries of the wider European circle that participated in the Bologna Declaration of 1999. This accord established the European Area for High Education (EAHE), which introduced "transparent" rules for academic degrees and curricula, thus making universities accessible to students across borders.[28] The introduction of the bachelor's degree has become part of this system. Further, the World Bank is seriously engaged in building tertiary education institutions in the developing countries.[29] While there continue to be large differences and inequalities in higher education systems across the world, there is a global process toward some convergence and improved standards.

However, beyond higher education, which has long had an international aspect, international efforts at improving elementary and secondary education in developing countries are beginning to have an impact. Comparative studies of educational attainment across many countries have become a routine element in international competition. "Global competence" has become a slogan (no matter how vague) for setting educational goals. There is a very significant "transparency" aspect in this development for educational institutions themselves. Further, it provides greater exposure to the facts about historical transparency and historical accountability in international education.

The globalization of education also produces a globalization of occupational competence. The assumption that technical professionalism is the monopoly of the mature and rich industrial countries has to be questioned today. Highly educated professionals in developing countries like India and China are willing and eager to work for global corporate network systems at a far lower wage than might be commanded in the United States or Europe. A major shift in economic competence and labor power seems to be in the offing.

Globalization of Information Technology

The development of information technology is certainly one of the most important direct and indirect drivers of global transformations. It is also responsible for the emergence of complex technical infrastructures for creating and storing information and making it accessible.

There is also a great effort under way to refine technologies for protecting information security. The development of information technology also provides techniques for keeping secrets. This fact needs to be kept in mind when we discuss the transparency/secrecy value syndrome. Communication systems today reduce dramatically the costs of communications and increase their speed worldwide. The development of satellite-based surveillance and mapping technologies can bring about an entirely new set of challenges to what can be kept secret, not only from government surveillance efforts, but from private inquiries as well. We return to this theme in our look at the literature on transparency.

Globalization of Civil Society

Concerns with human rights, environmental risks, poverty, and a wide array of social movements have reached global dimensions. Global civil society consists of nongovernmental organizations, networks of concerned persons, and professional organizations, at times joined by governments and government agencies. It is empowered by the information technology revolution, by the globalization of education, and the professionalization of journalism. The field includes health organizations, human rights groups like Amnesty International, fighters against corruption such as Transparency International, the International Organization of Ombudsmen, and the influential environmental organizations. For the most part, these groups have close ties to universities and relevant research institutes. Major foundations, often based in the United States, provide important financial and professional support and guidance. The preferred strategy of all these organizations and movements is transparency. (This phenomenon is discussed in greater depth in chapter 6.)

Historical Transparency

Certain dimensions of global dynamics affect cultures and cultural identities, with deep roots in the past. Many nations must struggle with painful historical truths, such as war crimes, racial suppression, and genocide, and continue to ask who is to be held accountable. These national, transnational—and in many cases global—debates on historical truth impinge on cultural identity and the moral stigma touching the pride of nations. International critiques not only of past deeds but also of national memories occur today in a global arena. Historical transparency can transform national cultures, as happened in Germany, South Africa, and Argentina. These countries also stubbornly resisted moral responsibility for a time, and such resistance continued until recently in Austria and Japan.

A global network of institutions and organizations has emerged, creating an infrastructure of support for "universal jurisdiction," for the International Criminal Court of the United Nations, and for local campaigns to unearth the historical truth about a nation's painful past. The pursuit of historical transparency has had a major impact not only on former victims and perpetrators, but also on politicians, journalists, judges, historians, political scientists, anthropologists, and sociologists. Historical transparency is a major and effective element in global cultural change.

What Does the Literature on Transparency Say?

How is transparency defined? And how is it explained and assessed? What are its consequences? Studies of transparency have appeared in many distinct domains of social life, and initially scholars treated it as if it were limited to, say, the domain of finance, or antibribery efforts, or the disclosure terms of arms control treaties. Seeking answers to these questions, we will look at the current scholarly literature. As an example of the narrow view, one colleague on a business school faculty insisted in conversation that the term transparency refers exclusively to certain information disclosure requirements imposed on publicly owned companies by the New York Stock Exchange. Ann Florini defined it in this way:

Just what is transparency? Put simply, transparency is the opposite of secrecy. Secrecy means deliberately hiding your actions; transparency means deliberately revealing them. This element of volition makes the growing acceptance of transparency much more than a resigned surrender to the technologically facilitated intrusiveness of the Information Age. Transparency is a choice, encouraged by changing attitudes about what constitutes appropriate behavior. . . . Transparency and secrecy are not either/or conditions. As ideals, they represent two ends of a continuum. What we are seeing now is a rapidly evolving shift of consensus among observers and actors worldwide about where states and corporations should be on that continuum.[30]

Whereas Florini emphasizes volition and the cultural change involved in shifting standards of behavior, transparency is not always voluntary. There are also legal requirements for disclosure that come under the heading of transparency. Florini notes the relationship between secrecy and transparency. However, transparency is not necessarily the "end of secrecy," nor is the relationship between these concepts a polar continuum—it is much more complex than that, as we demonstrate in chapter 4.

In *The Coming Democracy: New Rules for Running a New World*, Florini envisions a global future based on democracy created by transparency. She believes that some form of global governance has become a necessity. However, she fears that traditional solutions to this challenge, such as a world government, or a retreat to national borders, or trust in free-market forces will not work. Her purpose is to find a new approach to the problem of global governance in a democratic manner. She writes: "This is where hard thinking is needed about what constitutes 'democracy' in the context of global governance. It is important not to confuse the form with the function. Democracy requires two things: a system for providing people with a voice in the making of decisions that affect them and a mechanism for holding representatives accountable to those whom they represent."[31] To deal with this challenge, Florini offers transparency as "the most important concept for global democracy in the twenty-first century."

Although the movement toward transparency is often voluntary, there are circumstances where external pressures from the centers of power demand transparency. Coerced disclosure of information—as in the attempt to avoid a scandal, or imposed by an investigation, or by a new law—can also lead to the institutionalization of transparency. Florini explores the possibility of global solidarities, which she takes as a condition for the feasibility of global governance: "Thus, it is reasonable to think of this era of globalization as a time of searching for ways to create groups and networks able to handle global collective action problems, rather than assuming an inevitable splintering into hate-filled and violent rivalries."[32]

Florini examines the limited capabilities of states to deal effectively with global issues by themselves or even in international arrangements. Other actors such as transnational corporations and civil institutions have entered the picture. Corporations are increasingly adopting codes of conduct and actually, in a number of cases, opting for "certification" of their compliance with the code. There is a need for public regulation of corporate conduct: transparency. Similarly, civil organizations are recognizing a need for disclosing their activities. Applying these transformations to complex issues like economic globalization is not easy, but for Florini, "it is clearly possible. And it is essential. Secretive decision making by small groups of elites cannot and should not continue. Without broad and informed participation, policy decisions will fail to incorporate essential perspectives and will lack the legitimacy that only a public voice can bring. Good public policy, in economics as in other issue areas, has to be truly public."[33]

Florini calls this transformation of governance "the fourth revolution." (The first revolution was the invention of writing; the second, the alphabet; and the third, Gutenberg's printing press.) Today it is the Internet that makes transparency possible. She foresees a "messy" but workable democratic future based on transparency and wide participation:

> There will still be plenty of questions about the effectiveness of the resulting system, and indeed about the extent to which it is truly or fully democratic. But that is true today about governance at the national level. . . . The challenge is to take account of the scale of global problems and the diversity of the world's cultures while taking advantage of the new possibilities opened up by information technology in ways that will maximize the rule of the people. That, after all, is the literal meaning of democracy.[34]

Bernard Finel and Kristin Lord present a broad definition of political transparency: "In our view, transparency in the political realm is a condition in which information about governmental preferences, intentions, and capabilities is made available either to the public or other outsiders. It is a condition of openness that is enhanced by any mechanism that leads to public disclosure of information, such as a free press, open government hearings, the Internet, and reporting requirements in international regimes."[35] The emphasis on institutional mechanisms for openness appropriately broadens the concept further and embeds it in a systemic context. This is an insight endorsed by James N. Rosenau, who sees a "nascent norm" in the increasing importance of scientific proof in knowledge claims. "The provision of evidence and proof goes to the heart of the transparency issue. The more effectively it can be provided, the greater will be the transparency of diplomatic claims and, thus, the greater will be the power of knowledge as a source of statecraft."[36]

Finel and Lord close with this assessment:

Transparency is a rapidly spreading phenomenon that may be transforming world politics as we know it. This phenomenon—caused by the spread of democracy, the information revolution, the rise of the global media, international institutions, and international norms—is often portrayed as a boon to international cooperation, a solution to numerous global problems, and, indeed, morally desirable. The authors in this volume have painted a more complex portrait of transparency, however, arguing that it is often a mixed blessing.

There are gainers and losers in changes of transparency in international politics, and competing values play an important role. Yet, Finel and Lord conclude:

Although we are concerned about some possible implications of transparency—such as the potential of increased conflict due to miscommunication, contests over relative power, or political instability—we believe that transparency may ultimately prove extremely beneficial. Whereas the Industrial Revolution helped to spawn hierarchical, even totalitarian, states able to harness mass industrial power and drastically increased the power of states to wage war, we believe the transparency revolution will encourage the formation of open, decentralized and rule-bound societies. If our predictions are correct, the "winners" of the transparency revolution are those nations that make institutions more accountable to their people, empower them to challenge distasteful policies on both a national and international level, and educate them to excel in the information age. Governments that heed this advice will not only enhance their power, but further welcome an age of transparency that holds the promise to significantly improve human lives.[37]

Thomas Blanton points out, "History may well remember the era that spanned the collapse of the Soviet Union and the collapse of the World Trade Center as the Decade of Openness. Social movements around the world seized on the demise of communism and the decay of dictatorships to demand more open, democratic, responsive governments. And those governments did respond."[38] In that time twenty-six countries adopted laws establishing the right to free access of information. In the United States, the "U.S. Freedom of Information Act (FOIA) ranks as the most heavily invoked access law in the world. In 2000, the U.S. federal government received more than 2 million FOIA requests from citizens, corporations, and foreigners." In multilateral institutions such as the European Union, the demand for information freedom is also felt.

In spite of the war against terror, worldwide restrictions of information have been relatively few, Blanton notes. "Ironically, secrecy has made the most dramatic comeback in the country that purports to be the most democratic." The Bush administration has created an umbrella of secrecy concerning its activities. While some may be justified for strategic reasons, many have become habits. Blanton concludes, "The Bush administration's secrecy obsession will likely prove self-defeating, because like markets, governments don't work well in secret." Scandals play a special role in stimulating demands for transparency. Freedom of information acts (FOIA), typically driven by political partisanship, have been energized by scandals. The U.S. FOIA was certainly reinforced by the scandal of Watergate.

The widespread demand for freedom of information is a consequence of globalization. It is frequently seen as a form of market regulation, a spur to efficient government, and thus a contribution to economic progress. International public opinion tends to support these efforts toward openness and censures the scandalous conduct of irresponsible governments. Blanton concludes, "Making good use of both moral and efficiency claims, the international freedom-of-information movement stands on the verge of changing the definition of democratic governance. The movement is creating a new norm, a new expectation, and a new threshold requirement for any government to be considered a democracy. Yet at the same time, the disclosure movement does not even know it is a movement; its members are constantly reinventing the wheel and searching for relevant models." Blanton lists five fundamental criteria for freedom-of-information statutes: (1) they should be built on the presumption of openness; (2) any exception to openness should be as narrowly defined as possible; (3) exceptions should be made only when information release can be shown to create identifiable harm to a legitimate government cause; (4) even then, the harm to the state interest must be shown to outweigh the public interest served by making the information public; (5) there should be an independent authority that resolves any disputes on freedom of information cases, such as an ombudsman or a court. Finally,

Perhaps the ultimate challenge for the freedom-of-information movement will be to adapt to a new cultural and psychological climate. In colloquial Japanese,

67

for example, the term *okami* (god) is commonly used to refer to government officials. "You can't complain against the gods," one Japanese activist told a newspaper, summarizing the difficulty felt by ordinary people confronting the government. Or in the words of the Bulgarian activist Gergana Jouleva, "Democracy is not an easy task neither for the authorities nor for the citizens."

This feeling is also well known in America as in the saying, "You can't fight city hall." However, in reality you can.

In a very different vein, David Brin writes in *The Transparent Society* about transparency and openness of information from a technological and moral perspective. He raises an alarm about the risks inherent in information and surveillance technologies that make so many aspects of our public and private lives "transparent." There are moral choices to be made. Brin's passionate defense of the open society is dedicated "To Popper, Pericles, Franklin, and countless others who helped fight for an open society . . . and to their heirs who have enough courage to stand in the light and live unmasked."[39] Brin's moral message about transparency is conveyed in its subtitle, "Will Technology Force Us to Choose Between Privacy and Freedom?" This awareness of value dilemmas is very much part of our concern with the transparency syndrome. Brin discusses the great differences among political information cultures. Because dictators do try to enforce secrecy, Western institutions are at a disadvantage in undemocratic regimes. "Western corporations will need to use sophisticated encryption in many foreign lands for some time to come, because transparency works best when it is truly reciprocal. The open society may ultimately be a far better game for humanity, but it can be difficult to manage when the other side insists on playing by older rules. Clearly, common sense is essential during a time of transition."[40] Brin has major, justified concerns with surveillance and its potential pervasiveness and multiple forms. He discusses four dystopian scenarios: surveillance elites, surveillance obsession, surveillance acceptance, and surveillance overload. In the end, however, he remains optimistic: "These four scenarios were radical extrapolations of what might happen if we are stupid and let some malign trend reach its ultimate conclusion. In fact, though, I have faith that citizens of the neo-West will notice and correct such dismal tendencies before they get that far."[41] Yet Brin ends with a somewhat skeptical remark: "Transparency is not about eliminating privacy. It is about giving us the power to hold accountable those who would *violate* it. Privacy implies serenity at home and the right to be left alone. . . . We all have a right to some place where we can feel safe. After all these pages of playing the contrarian, I actually retain a fair amount of pragmatic skepticism aimed in all directions. Until I see that it really works as advertised, I'd be happy to have transparency move ahead in baby steps."[42]

There are common themes in this literature on transparency. The age of information freedom is relatively young, but its power is growing in the current era. Transparency was initially seen to apply only in very select arenas, but its comprehensiveness is by now understood. Specific applications of transparency, especially in conflict situations, are likely to have differential impacts, creating advantages for some and disadvantages for others. Transparency may have unanticipated outcomes. The information technology revolution increases the volume of information and its rapid communication; it creates new opportunities as well as threats such as loss of privacy and increased surveillance. There are also problems of credibility: how truthful is the information gained by transparency? Transparency has important effects on social structures and on cultures, and the path its evolution takes will determine the fate of the open society and of democracy.

Globalization and Transparency: Reflections Suggested by Two Indexes

Two major and widely noted indexes relating to different aspects of transparency in global change call for some reflections. They pursue quite different purposes: one attempts to measure the openness of countries to global linkages, and the other measures the transparency of countries by focusing on their levels of corruption. When compared, they suggest an interesting connection between transparency within a country on the one hand and openness to global connections on the other. Both indexes show that the relatively democratic and economically productive countries are at the top. Both place the poor countries at the bottom of both transparency and global openness. One may well think that a country's openness to global linkages increases its transparency—and its transparency in turn may well strengthen its global openness.

But there are also other forces involved in either supporting or hindering that connection between transparency and global links: these are the different use of power in a country. Many rich countries, including many small ones, are both transparent and globally open, as distinct from the struggling countries with high corruption and dictatorial regimes. Power with accountability is one thing, but power without it is free to block openness and transparency.

69

The first index is the A. T. Kearney/Foreign Policy Globalization Index (GI). It is a product of A. T. Kearney, Inc., and the Carnegie Endowment for International Peace and published in *Foreign Policy,* its journal.[43] It is a complex effort to measure the degree to which a country is "globalized."[44] The concept of this index includes four categories of globalization:

1. Economic integration into the global economy through "trade, foreign direct investments, portfolio capital flows, and investment income."

2. Personal contact: "International travel and tourism, international telephone traffic, and remittances and personal transfers (including remittances, compensation to employees, and other person-to-person and nongovernmental transfers)."

3. Technological connectivity: "Internet users, Internet hosts, and secure servers."

4. Political engagement: "Membership in international organizations, personnel and financial contributions to the U.N. Security Council missions, international treaties ratified, and governmental transfers."[45]

The resulting rank list of the globalization of countries does not include by any means all countries of the world—only sixty-two are rated. Nevertheless, this index is a rough but plausible measure of the degree to which a country is integrated into global linkages and transformations. And it raises intriguing questions.

The other index is the Transparency International Corruption Perceptions Index (CPI). It measures the levels of corruption in the public sector and in the politics of a country as perceived by business persons, academics, and risk analysts. While this index relies on subjective perceptions, albeit by knowledgeable people, it has become a widely used assessment of the level of corruption. Many countries attend very carefully to their CPI rankings. Obviously, the focus of this index is not on global openness, but on corruption. Many poor countries suffer exceedingly from corruption, while many of the rich countries are relatively low in corruption. Some European countries like Italy (CPI rank 35) and Greece (CPI rank 50) do present worrisome intensities of corruption, but generally the advanced Western countries try—increasingly in recent history—to reduce the scourge of corruption, and they are succeeding.[46]

Here are the rank lists on this matter. First, there is the Globalization Index (GI) of 2004, which lists the twenty most globalized countries. They are as follows:

1. Ireland	11. Sweden
2. Singapore	12. United Kingdom
3. Switzerland	13. Australia
4. Netherlands	14. Czech Republic
5. Finland	15. France
6. Canada	16. Portugal
7. United States	17. Norway
8. New Zealand	18. Germany
9. Austria	19. Slovenia
10. Denmark	20. Malaysia

Interestingly, many of these countries are quite small. Only the United States, the United Kingdom, France, and Germany are large countries in this top category. Of course, this is the result of the selection of the sixty-two countries included in the GI. Ireland, Singapore, Switzerland, Netherlands, Finland, New Zealand, Austria, Denmark, Sweden, Czech Republic, Portugal, Norway, Slovenia, and Malaysia are small countries, with Canada and Australia in between.[47] Most on this list, small or large, are relatively rich.

The TI Corruption Perceptions Index includes many more countries (133) than the Globalization Index. For example, the CPI includes Hong Kong as a country—it is almost free of corruption—in contrast to mainland China, which is properly ranked very low in the GI as well as in the CPI. The twenty countries judged least corrupt according to the 2003 CPI are as follows:[48]

1. Finland	11. Canada, Luxembourg, and
2. Iceland	United Kingdom
3. Denmark and New Zealand	14. Austria and Hong Kong
5. Singapore	16. Germany
6. Sweden	17. Belgium
7. Netherlands	18. Ireland and United States
8. Australia, Norway, and	20. Chile
Switzerland	

The top-rated countries in both indexes are fairly wealthy, they practice electoral democracy (not quite yet in Hong Kong), and they are also open to transparency. By contrast, most of the deeply corrupt countries listed in the CPI are not even included in the GI. It is obvious that those very poor countries would also have a very low rating in the GI, if all were included. The poorest countries and those with the least transparency, according to the TI Corruption Perception Index in 2003 are as follows:[49]

113. Republic of Congo, Ecuador, Iraq, Sierra Leone, and Uganda
118. Côte d'Ivoire, Kyrgyzstan, Libya, and Papua New Guinea
122. Indonesia and Kenya
124. Angola, Azerbaijan, Cameroon, Georgia, and Tajikistan
129. Myanmar and Paraguay
131. Haiti
132. Nigeria
133. Bangladesh

The lower end of the Globalization Index lists twenty countries low in globalization that are also poor and rank low in transparency. The lowest ranking countries in both indexes are poor and high in corruption, and low in openness. Several are struggling with the rule of law and may be striving to become electoral democracies. Several are listed as having relatively closed ideologies, such as Iran, the last named country. The inclusion of China, Turkey, and Brazil as not open to global links seems to reflect their large populations without resources that would enable them to be active in global links. However, we have observed that these nations are in fact beginning to play a global role. Turkey's position just above Bangladesh seems curious.

The following nations are listed by the GI as least open to globalization:[50]

42. Nigeria	53. Brazil
43. Ukraine	54. Kenya
44. Russian Federation	55. Turkey
45. Mexico	56. Bangladesh
46. Pakistan	57. China
47. Morocco	58. Venezuela
48. Thailand	59. Indonesia
49. South Africa	60. Egypt
50. Colombia	61. India
51. Sri Lanka	62. Iran
52. Peru	

Some of these poor countries also suffer from colossal megacorruption among their past and current leaders. Some of their names are published by Transparency International's Global Corruption Report 2004.[51] (This is different from the CPI.) President Mohamed Suharto of Indonesia is alleged to have embezzled $15–35 billion between 1967 and 1998. President Ferdinand Marcos of the Philippines is claimed to have grasped $5–10 billion between 1972 and 1986. Other amounts in the billions of dollars were accumulated by the president of Zaire (Mobutu Seso Seka, 1965–1997) and the president of Serbia/Yugoslovia (Slobodan Milosevic, 1989–2000), and there are other cases.[52] There are of course other problematic cases, especially in poor countries with important extractive resources of metals, oil, and gas. The poor countries suffer not only from poverty but also from misuse of power and limited connectedness to globalization.

The two indexes present two different objectives: measuring the global linkages of countries and measuring the level of corruption. There is an inherent connection between their findings and rankings: the single-minded focus on corruption in one index and the focus on open global linkages in the other, taken together, point to an underlying social force: namely, the reality of power, governance, and accountability. The power of rulers to profit from criminal megacorruption depends on the political helplessness of their citizens. Certain external power links support such exploitation. Ideologies that enforce the closing of a country also block transparency and foster corruption as well. The nature of a country's political power can hinder the forces for transparency and openness. However, where transparency and global openness rule, they support each other and empower citizens and thus move toward democracy. In the long term, the world can move in that direction.

Global Transformation in the Light of Classical Sociology

The Industrial Revolution and the Nation-State

Transparency has played a major role in each dimension of global transformation we have identified. The changes in the cultures of information today are as pervasive and significant as the great upheavals caused by industrialism, and they have had large consequences for the fabric of society. We are now at the point of placing our work into a context of sociological and even broader social scientific analysis for an important reason. More than one hundred years ago, sociologists began to grapple with the social causes and consequences of the industrial revolution, attempting to explain the creation of new solidarities that were transforming their societies. The changes produced by the values emerging under industrialization were creating new forms of social relations caused by the new technology and by the newly powerful nation-state. These changes wrought by new technology were engendering new values, elaborating new norms, and stimulating new forms of action.

Just as the new means of production, housed in factories, produced divisions of labor previously unknown, so the transparency phenomenon of the current information era is making possible relationships heretofore unknown and even, for transnational movements, previously unthinkable. The single most important challenge today for sociology—and for social science in general—is to understand how transnational solidarities are emerging, what they are and how they function, and how they might contribute to the global solidarities so urgently needed in the face of such enormous diversity and global inequality.

Although today's transparency phenomenon was unknown to the early sociologists, they did have to grapple with the realities of their times that were entirely new. They too had to deal with the shock of the unprecedented. Modernity was being born before their eyes. The industrial revolution, advanced capitalism, and the construction of the modern military and bureaucratic nation-state brought about drastic social transformations. The forces of their times strained the social fabric, increased productivity at great human and environmental cost, and engendered great crises in the international system of states. The changes in our time may seem similarly drastic, but they represent continuations of the trends that the early sociologists identified long ago.

Transparency is now a new social fact, a part of the social domain of reality as the founders of sociology understood it. According to Durkheim, "A social fact is every way of acting, fixed or not, capable of exercising on the individual an external constraint; or again, every way of acting which is general throughout a given society, while at the same time existing in its own right independent of individual manifestations."[53] As a social fact, transparency is a present condition as well as an emerging norm. Like Durkheim's social facts, it appears in three domains of social reality simultaneously: as a given, often taken for granted circumstance in societies and institutions; as a set of valid norms defining recognized rights and duties; and as the object of a social movement (with opponents), pressing for its further establishment and extension. In some societies, it has already become an objective condition, and it certainly is a constraint on actors. In this sense it exists between facticity and norm. It plays in important role in the new emerging forms of solidarities, while changing the old ones.

Solidarities Can Take More Than One Form

From the beginning, sociologists have focused on the changes brought by modernity. Social change came in many successive shifts and transformations, often arousing fears as well as hopes of progress. The sociologists' concern with solidarity was closely linked to their strong interest in ethics and morality. This is certainly true of Durkheim, Weber, Simmel, and Ferdinand

Toennies, whose *Gemeinschaft und Gesellschaft* (1887) bore the subtitle *Grundbegriffe der reinen Soziologie* (Basic concepts of pure sociology). With its emphasis on community and society, it was both a book of analysis and of somewhat nostalgic suggested remedies for the ills of capitalist society. Toennies was profoundly worried about the corrosive effects of individualistic *Gesellschaft,* based on "arbitrary will," with its contractual, rationally designed relationships in complex organizations and impersonal urban society. He mourned the decline of *Gemeinschaft,* which he characterized as based on "essential will," and cherished its form of solidarity. He advocated the establishment of voluntary *cooperatives,* or communal mutual assistance organizations, outside the capitalist profit-oriented economy. His hope was to create what we could call communitarianism to bring the virtues of *Gemeinschaft* into the capitalist era of *Gesellschaft.* He believed that sociology could show the way to a viable new form of German national solidarity.

Toennies's book epitomized a major theme of classical sociology: the transformation of Western societies from traditional forms of domination and a rural economy to new forms of power in the industrial, capitalist, urban era under the bureaucratic national state. In the third edition of his book, published in 1922, Toennies added a comment about the "terrible fractures caused by the capitalist-social world system, now even more ruthlessly displaying its disintegrative powers; giving rise to louder and louder calls for 'community.'"[54] This book was a work of distinctly national, indeed nationalist German sociology. Toennies dedicated its fourth edition to "the working German youth, in order to show that I do not despair of the German future, and that I trust in the meaningful concord of a new generation to understand the need for a social architecture so urgently required for the people's community." The creation of a national community and a sense of justice for citizens were high on Toennies's agenda, as they were also guiding principles of the German Youth Movement of the early twentieth century.

If Toennies's bipolar typology of social structures focused on solidarities and identities, Durkheim emphasized mechanical and organic solidarity. Durkheim's typology, though similar to Toennies's, was formed with a marked difference in its value accent on the productivity of organic solidarity in the division of labor. Mechanical solidarity as a type was quite similar to *Gemeinschaft.* However, Durkheim saw the transition to organic solidarity as a progressive move in the advancing division of labor.

While sociology was concerned with solidarity in the new industrial, military, and bureaucratic nation-states of Europe, it remained focused on the national domain. An important discovery was that solidarity could take more than one form. Today, sociology in the global era must be alert to the new forms that solidarities can take as they extend beyond national boundaries. A current example of this effort is *The Problem of Solidarity,* edited by Patrick Doreian and Thomas Fararo, which regards solidarity as a key problem for the world and for sociology. "At present, the world is undergoing some sort of transformation we barely understand. Social systems thought to be secure have broken down. Old hostilities based on ethnic identities have been renewed. On the other hand, globalization of the economy seems to be driving a process of integration at the world level."[55] The book examines the multiple possibilities of solidarities, including those in the global context.

The work of Karl Marx was fueled by the industrial revolution, the new forms of work resulting from the division of labor, the emergence of new solidarities in national states, and, Marx hoped, a new consciousness in the revolutionary classes. The social promises and threats of capitalist industrialism, the division of labor, and system differentiation were central, overarching concerns of the early sociologists as well. All persistently dwelt on the theme of the industrial revolution—it was, after all, the dominant force of social change at the time. Karl Marx's ideological conviction that capitalism would inevitably be followed by its own self-destruction, the workers' revolution, and the transition to communism was a major question faced by nineteenth- and twentieth-century sociology, and of course a powerful stimulus to ideological and political movements.

There are many lessons to be learned from the founders of sociology about the rise of capitalism in the West and its consequences in social inequality and new solidarities. Emile Durkheim's life work addressed not only the division of labor, but especially the integration of individuals into the solidarity of society (and its failures in anomie and "egotism"). He gave great attention to the problems of religion and morality and thus to the roots of social cohesion.[56] The high point of the study of societies and their internal organization was the concept of the social system and its differentiation. This conceptual tool of sociology remained focused entirely on the nation as an entity.

Therefore, understanding how systems function and examining the structure of the state became a matter of urgent concern. Functionalist theory built on the biological analogy that societies and groups may somehow be similar to organisms ("wholes") and that there is a need for the discharge of functions if the "whole" is to survive.[57] The functional necessities must adapt to changes in the environment. Herbert Spencer, in *Principles of Sociol-*

ogy (1885), was much concerned with these relationships—for example, the differences between war and peace, and how they result in different internal system structures. The modern state and the earlier forms of political authority became a major focus of attention. Max Weber's *Economy and Society* (19) includes a most comprehensive historical and sociological analysis of types of authority (*Herrschaft*) and the forms of legitimacy prevailing in that period. System functions are also a focus of modern sociological theory. The transparency phenomenon challenges classical ideas about system functions and the state, as well as phenomena such as social stratification, since it occurs in global as well as local contexts.

All of the classical theorists contributed to an understanding of social stratification and the massive changes occurring in their time. Weber systematized the concepts of classes, status groups, and political power structures (that is, political parties). The concept of the dynamics of power received a different treatment by Vilifredo Pareto in his theory of the circulation of ruling elites, elaborated in *The Mind and Society* (1935). However, it was Weber who pointed to the increasingly fluid forms of social stratification and inequality, arguing that it was the power of *rationalization* that generated the modern forms of social and economic inequality. This phenomenon of pervasive rationalization is one of Max Weber's most important themes.

Weber saw rationalization as a comprehensive, thorough transformation of society, economy, and culture. Rationalization takes many forms. There are purposefully rational acts as well as value-rational acts. Beyond that, there is "rationalization of music," the idea of the systematization, coherent structuring, and instrumentalization of an entire domain of cultural production. Rationalization of religion, of law, and of political administration are all processes of greater systematization, the logical structuring of various fields of society with special knowledge and skill. There is a further distinction between formal or procedural and substantive rationality.

Weber was ambivalent about the growth of rationalization in society and culture. He feared that the rationalized, bureaucratic German nation would become an "iron cage" that would suppress the spontaneity and creativity of its people. As a countermeasure he suggested to Germany's Constitutional Assembly charged with creating the Weimar Constitution that some form of charismatic authority be embodied in the presidency of the nation. He saw charisma as a creative, but also dangerous force. He had little idea of the disastrous future that lay ahead for Germany with a charismatic leader, Hitler, at its helm.

Much of current thought about rationalization identifies the concept only with the "instrumental rationality" exercised in the pursuit of specific interests. Bureaucracy is often used to illustrate such rationality in the domain of the state and in capitalist enterprises. Weber's multiple conceptions of rationalizations span a much greater spectrum and involve subtle distinctions. For him, rationalization is closely related to the "disenchantment" of the modern world, the rise of secularism and the disappearance of "magic gardens." The transparency phenomenon can be seen as an advanced part of the process of rationalization—a new element in the continuing phenomenon of historical rationalization.

Unequal access to information, a modern problem, was also a concern of early sociologists such as Georg Simmel, who focused much of his work on the role of information in the construction of the social fabric. He recognized that what people know (and don't know) about each other is crucial for maintaining structures of power and the viability of groups. Those in power depend on secrecy and loyalty as necessary for pursuing strategies and actions both in cooperation and conflict. The channels of information access as well as the denial of access were for him important sociological phenomena.

Simmel builds a subtle and complex argument on the necessity of discretion and secrecy for social life. He examines how the patterns of "knowledge, truth, and falsehood" in social interactions (that is, information norms in action) lie at the very core of social structures and solidarities. Indeed, he sees the conceptions of personal rights and of property as embedded in these patterns. In his brief essay, "The Lie," Simmel writes: "Truthfulness and lies are of the most far-reaching significance for relations among men. Sociological structures differ profoundly according to the measure of lying which operates in them." As societies become more complex, the greater the harm done by lies. Hence penalties for lying are much more lenient in simple societies, and more severe in complex ones. "We base our gravest decisions on a complex system of conceptions, most of which presuppose the confidence that they will not be betrayed. Under modern conditions, the lie, therefore, becomes something much more devastating than it was earlier, something which questions the very foundations of our life."[58]

Another major contribution by Georg Simmel was his work on money as a symbolic medium of exchange. *The Philosophy of Money* (1920) was far ahead of its time. In recognizing money as a symbolic medium of exchange, Simmel focused on effects of money on interactions and the relationship between individuals and society, as well as on solidarity. Money changes social relationships among individuals and enables people to consider many options and to make many choices, thus promoting opportunities to establish many social relationships. It is an efficient instrument in calculating value and encourages efficient exchange, thus increasing value. Since money as a medium of exchange requires a central authority to safeguard its stability and value, it becomes also an instrument for enhancing solidarity. There is a negative side to this phenomenon: since money lifts many constraints on the behavior of individuals, it becomes also a source of anomie. Money is one of the most powerful components of the historical process of rationalization. It establishes rational criteria of trust.

We agree that changes in norms for information disclosure, especially among those in power centers and between leaders and their publics, are likely to have significant consequences for social relations and for modern culture. In this we follow in the footsteps of Georg Simmel, especially his attention to secrecy. However, in the information society of the globalization era, the emphasis has changed to include a more complex constellation of information values, with a focus on its other pole, transparency.

We have said that changes in the current period are quite as profound as those that occurred in the transition to the industrial, national state. While the classical sociologists focused their attention on changes from traditional to modern forms of solidarity, we must attend to global transformations, the restructuring of networks and identities, and power systems that are increasingly shaped by access to vital information and control over information. Solidarities do matter in this new era of transparency as well; however, their significance today differs from how they mattered to the German Tönnies and the Frenchman Durkheim.

Solidarity, Differentiation, and Rationalization

Since the 1960s, sociology diversified—or we might say, splintered—into many subfields, some of which merged into other disciplines. Much of that diversification has caused sociologists to be concerned with new cultural issues, social problems, and the rise of social movements. There have also been disputes about the merits of alternative theories. However, in spite of the diversity of views and the declaration of many meanings of "postmodernity," the thematic legacy of the classical era of sociology endures, albeit in new forms. The era of global sociology is arriving.

Talcott Parsons undertook a synthesis of the achievements of classical sociology as his life work. *The Structure of Social Action* (1937) was an analysis of classical sociology (omitting Simmel, however) in which he presented a general theory of action as the foundation of sociology. This was followed by *The Social System* (1951) and *Toward a General Theory of Action,* edited with Edward A. Shils (1954), intended to create a comprehensive conceptual frame of reference for the field of social relations. It did not reach this ambitious goal, but Parsons' work awakened the interest of sociologists in the classical theories and in the possibility of building on their work. After the 1960s Parsons was neglected for many years and often criticized for his alleged conservative bent. There is today a renewed interest in Parsons' work and what it may offer for the emerging sociological issues of the global era. A recent volume of essays edited by Javier Trevino, *Talcott Parsons Today* (2001), is a welcome beginning in this direction.[59]

Both classical sociologists and Talcott Parsons used the concept of *society* as a synonym for the nation-state. Parsons was primarily, but not exclusively, concerned with American society. By attending to structures and relationships, which he held to be static phenomena, Parsons appeared not to acknowledge the important role played by change, development, and evolution. Yet, especially in his later work, he refined and modified his conceptual apparatus in ways that are useful for the emerging global sociology. His focus on the idea of the *societal community* allowed him to progress far beyond the concepts of the earlier works, permitting greater fluidity and flexibility in his analysis of society.

In *Talcott Parsons Today,* Uta Gerhardt introduces Parsons' concept of the societal community and suggests how this theoretical advance may be applied to the global expansion of sociological concerns.[60] The societal community is a conception of a moral framework guaranteeing the inclusion of diversities in ethnicity, race, and religion, as illustrated by U.S. policies devoted to affirmative action. Neal Smelser claims that affirmative action was "one of the most daring institutional innovations in the United States in the second half of the twentieth century." Affirmative action was a development that changed the unresolved "tugs-of-war between the poles of universalism-particularism and achievement-ascription."[61] For Smelser, the other two major developments in recent American history are the dispersal of the traditional nuclear family and the rapid emergence of globalization.

A more general characteristic of the advanced societal community is a moral consensus on the principle of inclusion of all citizens. The equal rights doctrine becomes the basis of the modern democracy characterized by social diversity. Such a democracy also adheres to procedural rules for settling disputes with an equal application of the law. It is a societal community that generates an active civil society. This conception of the societal community opens the possibility of forms of solidarity that extend beyond the nation-state. It may point the way toward the multiple forms and networks of solidarity and legitimacy required in the global era.

A central feature of Parsons' conception of the societal community is his recognition of four symbolic media of exchange: money, power, influence, and value commitments. All are crucially dependent on information. Of the four, money is the medium that most obviously reaches beyond a specific society's boundaries, and it is the most codified and regulated medium. Power also reaches across political, economic, and social boundaries as well, but rarely in the codified normative way of assuring democratic elections and the institutions that undergird democratic nation-states. The medium of influence is that of civil society, and it is indeed of global reach today. Transparency is one component. Transparency norms define the public's right to know and the duty to disclose by those at the centers of power. These norms derive from the values of citizen autonomy, responsibility, and authority; that is, they define citizens' rights. Those at the centers of power have corresponding duties. In transparent systems, both information rights and duties contribute to the value of informed public debate. Similarly, the value of autonomy for citizens legitimizes the norms of rights and duties of power holders and citizens alike. These frameworks of law protecting citizen's rights while enabling the functioning of the state, the emerging media of exchange of global reach, the growing idea of a transnational societal community, the forming of global networks and solidarities, and the complex effects of transparency may become the sociological components of future forms of solidarities of global reach.

Conclusions

Global transformations are creating pressures toward transparency, as well as counterpressures. On the whole, the pressures toward transparency tend to exceed the counterpressures, but the process is characterized by "informational ambivalence." Scholars agree that the transparency phenomenon now stretches across institutional domains and cultures. The role of truthfulness is a pivotal matter, since transparency is valued in light of its trustworthiness. As we have seen, at times proof is demanded to validate the truth claims made by authorities. The open society faces the dangers of secrecy, the erosion of privacy, and the spread of surveillance, some of the darker forms of change in information cultures.

The role of transparency in global change is tied to trust and may help us to bridge universal and particular values. It may also generate new forms of solidarity in a newly inclusive, transnational civil society. These ideas grow out of the theories of the classical sociologists and their struggle to comprehend the transformations of their era—the industrial revolution and the creation of the modern, bureaucratic, militaristic, industrial nation-state. Solidarities that are based purely on ethnicity, tribal loyalties, and religions will need to adapt to the requirements of civil and human rights in more diverse social systems. Parsons' dynamic, inclusive, and flexible concept of the societal community and of symbolic media of exchange may help us to understand the multiple solidarities and procedural norms required of humanity in the global information era. The outcome remains uncertain, however; transcending the tension between particularism and universalism is a daunting task.

4

INFORMATION CULTURES
IN TRANSFORMATION

The Secrecy and the Transparency Syndromes in Global Change

This chapter presents core concepts and thoughts about the dynamic of transparency and secrecy and their respective countervalues in the modern world. This dynamic is often messy, turbulent, and scandalous. Global transformations create both culture change and expanded social relationships across the world. This means the global expansion of solidarities as well as of lines of conflict. The long process of creating nation-states in Europe and North America was just such an expansion of solidarities, which could not have been achieved without civil wars and revolutions to determine what the new national solidarity and identity should—and should not—be.

Likewise, today's extension of solidarities to become global in scope occurs in a context of great diversity and inequality. It is again a very turbulent process, affecting struggles for identity and standards of morality, struggles for what not merely a nation but the world should become. The stakes are high and violence abounds. Moral (and immoral) frameworks collide with each other. What may have been normal one year may well become a crime in the next. Often that is the context for scandal.

The changing values of information cultures are linked to changes in identity and morality. We noted this link in our overview of historical turning points toward freedom of information. The encounters and the transformations of the rationales of conscience and knowledge that occurred in medieval Europe are relevant to our time as well. Similar changes affect the dynamics of transparency and secrecy in the global era. Changes in information cultures reflect changes in "the rationales of conscience" and in the frameworks of morality. These are not merely effects of advances in technology, even though technology vastly enlarges our range of choices to be made. These value choices are matters of strong emotions and ideological convictions.

To define our concepts: secrecy is most vigilant about guarding, protecting, withholding information that, if disclosed, could or would endanger the important, even sacred, bonds of loyalty and identity, of strategy as well as self-interest. Changing the scope and nature of a group's solidarities can be a grave threat to secrecy as traditionally established. Transparency, by contrast, is most vigilant about the widest scope of accountability for authorities of any kind. It is based on the values of autonomy and individuality and is a necessity in expanding solidarities. As noted, transparency is essential for trust among strangers and across cultural boundaries. There are other forms of trust that are based on ethnic or clan loyalties, but they do not work among strangers and with formal contractual relations.

The relationship in the dominance of secrecy and transparency is energized by progressive changes in morality, changes in "the rationales of conscience" that inevitably accompany the expansion of solidarities. This expansion can threaten old solidarities and their boundaries. Resentment by those excluded from rising solidarities can trigger an identity crisis and a turn to violence. The effect of progressive changes of morality in expanding solidarities is a powerful force for transparency and a challenge for secrecy because each is linked to essential core values. Secret activity previously taken for granted may become public and be viewed as questionable or even criminal. Conversely, the transparency demands and activities of one era may be labeled treason after a shift of the dominant moral framework. However, the evolution of the global era is leading to greater transparency in the extension of morality and responsibility.

Opacity and secrecy have long been ancient tools of authority in most, if not all, societies. The battles for information freedom and against secrecy have been bitterly fought. Transparency is new, and the struggle continues to make it ubiquitous even in an era plagued by fear of terrorism, security concerns, and rising government secrecy. Why is that so? To explain why this is happening, we outline the conceptual tools needed to study the dialectic relations between the information cultures of transparency and secrecy. We treat both not as single values, but as constellations which we call value syndromes. They are linked to even more basic values, and they spawn specific norms as well as their social support systems. We call this the "conceptual architecture of information value syndromes." Second, we analyze what a secrecy syndrome consists of and how it works. We focus on the growth of secrecy in America, while presenting a generic picture of the nature of secrecy. Third, we analyze the transparency syndrome and the "transparency process." Fourth, we explore the protectors of validity in transparency and its sources of energy. We comment on the power of transparency as a force in global change, about the role of markets and technology, about changing moral bases for transparency and secrecy, and about historical shifts in perspectives. This conceptual architecture will prepare us to examine transparency in action.

Secrecy and Transparency

There is no such thing as a stand-alone, absolute value paramount to all others, one value that is not linked to cognate values and countervalues. Thus, all values are constrained. Further, they carry different weights in different domains of society. Secrecy may be strong in matters of national security, while transparency may be preferred in markets and matters of legitimacy. Such complexity, but also moral flexibility and depth, is part of the strength of a free society. Unique dominant values exist only in the imagination of single-issue fanatics and in nondemocratic, theocratic, or totalitarian systems. Insistence on a single value is typically enforced by totalitarian rulers with the threat of draconian punishment, often death, for offenders. The global shift to democracy is a move away from such enforced obedience. It recognizes the autonomy of citizens and fundamentally alters the structures of power. Our analysis of information values focuses on the cultures of democracies and societies making the transition toward democracy. Even then, the shift from obedience to autonomy is not a shift from one single value to another.

The demand for transparency, like a preference for secrecy, defines an ideal. Similarly, norms based on the values of privacy, accountability, property, freedom of speech, and obedience, to mention a few examples, define citizens' rights and duties. They always exist in relation to other values and their rights and duties: protecting the privacy of one's home may have to yield to public intrusion in case of a catastrophe such as a fire; defense of property rights may have to yield to the greater good of the community in the case of threats to public health. Not only do all values have such limitations, they come in interdependent clusters at the core of a cultural domain—in our case, information cultures. We will call these clusters value syndromes, or patterns of symptoms that characterize or indicate a particular societal condition.

In democratic value systems, openness of information and freedom of expression—that is, transparency—and civil rights must be predominant in the general cultural value system. If they are not, the culture is outside the domain of democratic systems. However, transparency and secrecy both remain parts of democratic information value syndromes, albeit on limited terms, with priority given to the transparency of the system. A secret society cannot be a democracy. While the definition of an open, democratic society may take quite different forms, it always strikes some kind of equilibrium between transparency and secrecy, between individual freedom and duty to the state, between confident openness and defensive protection of security. How they are balanced differs in each political system and culture—depending on fundamental constitutional rules and parliamentary laws, plebiscites, or informal norms guaranteeing liberty and security. The search for the right balance is precarious and risky at times and requires vigilance by the defenders of transparency.[1] For each value, there is a complex system of (sometimes conflicting) norms that guide the interplay between rights and duties. These may be integrated with institutions, as for example, government departments, major organizations such as labor unions, and political parties or social movements that keep the system in flux.

The system of norms and their change or maintenance is the supportive infrastructure for the value syndrome. The infrastructure assures that the information for transparency or secrecy, respectively, actually exists, that it can be stored and accessed—in the case of transparency, by individuals and/or the public, in the case of secrecy, by authorized persons. Remember: opacity is a social condition without available information. For there to be information cultures, there has to be information in the first place. The creation and maintenance of such information systems and resources are, of course, crucial to information cultures. Without them, in the extreme case, there is no information flow, processing, protecting, or channeling. Finally, there is need for an infrastructure for adjudicating the relevance and validity of information as knowledge of acceptable quality. There are various types of intermediate linkage agencies between the creation of information, its processing and evaluation, its distribution and use.[2]

Table 2 provides a summary of the architecture of information value syndromes to show the connections among values, norms, technical and organizational infrastructures, support systems, larger contexts of social morality or rationales of conscience, and the dialectics of value shifts. There is a dynamic to these structures. The term *architecture* emphasizes that these cultural constellations have a certain robustness, but like built structures they can be rebuilt, renovated, or added to. These syndromes react to both inter-

Table 2. The Conceptual Architecture of Information Value Syndromes

Values and Countervalues

• An information value syndrome includes different but interdependent values (desiderata) such as transparency, privacy, autonomy, accountability, secrecy, and loyalty.

• Different cultures rank these values differently, as in the high rank of transparency in Sweden versus the dominant rank of secrecy in North Korea.

• Transparency is a rising value, often in conflict with secrecy and privacy.

Information Norms

• Information norms (rules) specify rights and duties of authorities and citizens, corporations, and customers or professions and clients on the disclosure and use of information.

• Information rules may be legally required and binding or voluntary.

Information Infrastructures

• Information flows can be possible only if information is created, stored, distributed, and understood; this requires knowledge capacity and technical, regulatory, and legal frameworks.

• Opacity (absence of information) is also an absence of information infrastructures.

• Technical infrastructures (from the creation of printing to the emergence of digital data banks and more) are rapidly increasing.

• Regulatory frameworks provide standards such as in accounting, informed consent, and settling disputes.

• Legal frameworks protect and enforce both information values and norms and infrastructures.

General Moral Frames: Contexts of the Information Value Syndromes

• Conceptions of power, authority, justice, human rights, freedom, as well as obedience and conformity, are often contested general moral frames of particular social communities; they shape the priorities of the architectures of information values.

• The transformations of globalization often create pressures for universal information values and rules and create conflicts between particular cultures and universal change.

nal and external pressures. The different hierarchies of values involved all have their own "constituencies" that may conflict or exist in equilibrium.

Those who handle the various infrastructures mentioned in table 2 develop their own agenda and dynamics, leading to change. Political forces may react to threats and challenges such as wars and economic crises, and thus alter the value rank order; for example, they may move secrecy up a notch or press for more transparency in particular sectors, such as accounting and banking. Most powerful forces of change have a basis in morality and conscience. They may result from conflicts about social values and intercivilizational encounters in the global extension of solidarities. Global pressures may cause change, reform, and adaptation, although these changes may be almost unnoticed at first. They may burst into the limelight through scandals or the discovery of illegal deeds covered by secrecy, such as the Watergate scandal. Even more often, they involve a shift in moral expectations, as in situations where a previously routine activity is defined in a new era as a violation of ethics or even a crime. As an illustration, Germany's former Chancellor Kohl still resolutely refuses to reveal the sources of campaign donations to his Christian Democratic party in the 1990s. (Such donations have been a common practice for all parties since the 1970s.)

Table 2 identifies the structural forces at work as values persist and change regarding the use of information in society. Institutions such as governments, corporations, and their markets, the health professions, religious institutions, labor unions—all have their own value syndromes, with different commitments to transparency or secrecy. Further, these values may change at different rates in various domains. For example, transparency in research with human subjects through the introduction of informed consent in the United States only began in the 1970s—decades after the Nuremberg principles called for this reform. Other kinds of transparency—such as freedom of the press in the United States—is two centuries old. For another example, Singapore is renowned for its high level of transparency in the business sector, while it has a much less transparent authoritarian government. Similarly, Hong Kong has achieved remarkable transparency in curbing corruption, while its government maintains a strong attachment to secrecy. Secrecy is, of course, an asymmetrical weapon: the holder of a secret protects it against inquiries by outsiders. Transparency may also be demanded in an asymmetrical way: governments often demand transparency in the conduct of corporations, but they may refuse to disclose information themselves. Similarly asymmetric information flows occur between corporations and their customers or clients, long a characteristic of economic development organizations and recipients of their aid.

Value changes and continuities are very complex, and we present them here in very abstract terms. Nevertheless, there are overall value profiles that characterize solidarities connecting nations or even civilizations. Such value constellations and their claims of moral validity may be contested, but they generally are the source of broad identities and solidarities. The European Union is a transnational community of more or less shared values with still fragile, but growing cohesion. The value differences and similarities between Europe and the United States is another issue for discussion.

The Structure of the Secrecy Syndrome

Secrecy is the deliberate withholding of information actually or potentially desired by others. As an information value, secrecy has long been a means of gaining and keeping power. It is certainly older than transparency, and to some extent has been a feature of all social structures ranging from the family to state officialdom. In the words of Georg Simmel:

> The secret of a given individual is acknowledged by another; that which is intentionally or unintentionally hidden is intentionally or unintentionally respected. The intention of hiding however, takes on a much greater intensity when it clashes with the intention of revealing. In this situation emerges that purposive hiding and masking, that aggressive defensive, so to speak, against the third person, which alone is usually designated as secret. . . . *The secret in this sense, the hiding of realities by negative or positive means, is one of man's greatest achievements.* In comparison with the childish stage in which every conception is expressed at once, and every undertaking is accessible to the eyes of all, the secret produces an immense enlargement of life: numerous contents of life cannot even emerge in the presence of full publicity. The secret offers, so to speak, the possibility of a second world alongside the manifest world; and the latter is decisively influenced by the former.[3]

Simmel goes on to say that secrecy may absorb the highest values. However, "on the other hand, although the secret has no immediate connection with evil, evil has an immediate connection with secrecy: the immoral hides itself for obvious reasons."[4] In any case, the ability to create and keep secrets is an ancient human practice. Many secrets are kept out of shame, while others may provide a hidden core for personal identity. Secrecy kept by a group establishes the solidarity and identity of a clandestine society in need of disguise and protection.

Secrecy differs from opacity, the absence of information. In many past societies and in most developing countries today, there is an absence of records about such things as legal definitions of property, commercial transactions, and even government actions. Indeed, there may be large lacunae in data about land use and about economic activity. Weak or broken communication channels can result in local opacity. Failing to record data about social life may be a deliberate effort to sustain opacity and assure social ignorance, but it is not targeted, planned secrecy. However, it can be costly. The PricewaterhouseCoopers Opacity Index estimates the economic costs of the absence of transparent information in thirty-five countries. While opacity can be a tool for maintaining power, it is very different from secrecy.

Stanton K. Tefft states: "At all levels of social organization . . . secrecy enables individuals and groups to manipulate and control their environments by denying outsiders vital information about themselves. In the arena of economic and political conflict this basic function of secrecy becomes even more important."[5] In the era of military nation-states and industrial economies, secrecy took a very different form from protecting the intimacy of family life or tribal lore from the awareness of outsiders. "Dark secrets" in business or government are those that would cause condemnation and punishment if revealed. Secrecy becomes formalized. Tefft proposes the concept of the "secrecy process," similar to our notion of the infrastructure of value syndromes, to define a process of acting and organizing that becomes necessary whenever secrets are kept. In his words:

> The secrecy process consists of a series of interrelated subprocesses that reinforce each other. Once information is concealed by individuals or groups, they must establish a security system to protect their secrets. This security system, in turn, necessitates the development of espionage operations by outsiders who, if they are to gain access to the secrets, must subvert the security system. To counteract the effects of espionage, the secret holders not only use counterespionage but also persuasive techniques by which they spread false information to delude outsiders about the true nature of their secrets. The secret holders also divulge some secrets to outside parties for strategic or political reasons. In turn the outsiders must develop ways to evaluate the information they gain from espionage as well as regulated disclosures offered by their opponents. Adequate evaluation of existing intelligence data may necessitate further espionage to establish its reliability and validity. . . . However, secret holders seem to use certain elementary security procedures. For example, the dissemination of false information is one such tactic. Through lies, propaganda, and other deceptive information the secret sharers attempt to distort the real significance of their hidden activities.[6]

The "secrecy process" leads to social consequences; the effort to keep the secret from the espionage efforts of enemies requires counteraction. These actions in turn require further actions, and they lead to the establishment of more layers of protection. This certainly is true of the secrecy syndrome in fully developed modern nation-states. In all European nations, secrecy has been a hallmark of diplomacy and public administration, and the secrecy syndrome has been institutionalized within a large system of values, norms, bureaucracies, and legal structures.

The secrecy syndrome in the United States is relatively recent; scholars argue that in the first century of the new republic, openness was largely treated as a matter of course. Yes, there were secrets in the process of creating the Constitution and selecting the site of the nation's capital. Without secret deals, these processes may well have faltered. Nevertheless, Clark R. Mollenhoff insists that in the first century of the United States there was little withholding of information. From its beginning, U.S. leaders enthusiastically embraced the value of openness. Mollenhoff describes how President Washington dealt with information about a major military debacle in 1791 when General St. Clair and 1,400 American soldiers were surprised by an attack by Miami Indians led by Little Turtle. More than 600 officers and men were killed and the others forced to retreat. When Congress inquired about the humiliating defeat, Washington called a meeting of his cabinet. Hamilton initially resisted disclosure, but Washington decided to disclose all the facts.[7]

The importance of secrecy grew more urgent, and more contentious, in the experience of wars. The world wars led to the development of major intelligence and homeland protection efforts. Much of this was justified by the conditions of warfare, but it took an emotional toll. The quest for secrecy increased during the cold war. Mollenhoff emphasizes that what he calls the "claim of secrecy unlimited" was first made in a very specific context, but then became a generalized instrument of executive power. The concept of executive privilege was articulated by President Eisenhower in the context of the Army-McCarthy hearings. Whereas Mollenhoff emphasizes the dangers of this presidential prerogative, Mark J. Rozell argues that this "is not an unfettered presidential prerogative. Although the president has the right to assert executive privilege, he can do so only for the most compelling reasons. In a liberal democracy, the presumption generally is in favor of openness and freedom of information. Nonetheless, liberal democratic republics, like all governments, have secrecy needs."[8] The debate about this point continues, of course, illustrating the dynamics of value syndromes.

Richard Gid Powers's biography of J. Edgar Hoover contains a fascinating account of secrecy exercised unchecked by the U.S. government. Powers writes:

> The massive FBI headquarters is a concrete monument to the man who ran the Federal Bureau of Investigation for forty-eight years. . . . As chief of federal law enforcement and guardian of domestic security, Hoover moved within the innermost rings of the most powerful circles of government, with critical responsibilities during the greatest political crises and national emergencies of the century. The Bureau he led, powerful, efficient, completely subordinate to his will, was a resource presidents and the public came to depend on for decisive, effective performance under the most sensitive and difficult circumstances. . . . The man and his Bureau were cloaked in a selective secrecy and protected by power so formidable that few dared to pry. The secrets—the files on Communists, on spies, the hundreds of millions of fingerprints, the dossiers on the great and the famous—were whispered to have silenced his critics and destroyed his enemies. To those who saw it as a threat to political freedom, Hoover's power was a frightening specter that haunted the nation. . . .
>
> Paradoxically, that secrecy and power, so terrifying to some, were what made him a hero to many more, perhaps even most, Americans. Hoover's imposing presence gave much of the country a sense of stability and safety as he gathered to himself the strands of permanence that connected Americans to their past: religion, patriotism, a belief in progress, and a rational moral order. To attack him was to attack Americanism itself. Millions were sure that Hoover's secret power was all that stood between them and sinister forces that aimed to destroy their way of life.[9]

Hoover crusaded against Communists. He grew up with—and never lost —the convictions of old morality. He valued family ties, preached about the importance of faith and church, and demanded deference to established authority. Richard Nixon eulogized Hoover at his funeral as "one of the nation's leaders of morals and manners and opinion."[10] His myth vanished when after his death the reality of the secret programs of Hoover's FBI became known. He fought civil libertarians, hated Martin Luther King, attacked unpopular speech, and waged a dirty war against black radicals. The public perception of his rule after his death became that of excessive, uncontrolled secrecy run amok. Powers states succinctly one of the facts in value change that reveals the dynamics of transparency and secrecy:

> In all nations, people truly live in different centuries and different cities of the mind, even when they seem to be contemporaries. Hoover had, all his life, even

as he lived and worked at the epicenter of the capital of the world's most powerful nation, a turn-of-the-century vision of America as a small community of like-minded neighbors, proud of their achievements, resentful of criticism, fiercely opposed to change. As twentieth-century standards of the mass society swept over traditional America, subverting old values, disrupting old customs, and dislodging old leaders, Americans who were frightened by the loss of their community saw in Hoover a man who understood their concerns and shared their anger, a powerful defender who would guard their America of memory against a world of alien forces, strange peoples, and dangerous ideas.[11]

J. Edgar Hoover died in 1972 and left the FBI in disarray. It became clear that while Hoover had superior leadership qualities and organizational ability, later in his career he no longer served the nation, but merely his own and the FBI's needs for protection in secrecy. By the end of his life, he was isolated and embittered.[12]

Secret establishments have continued to operate and grow in the United States, even though secrecy since the cold war era is regarded with growing skepticism. David Weir notes, "It is sad and ironic that in the final years of the century, as the formerly closed societies of the Eastern Bloc have opened their borders and exhumed the secrets of the cold war era, the United States has been unwilling to examine the damage a half century of official secrecy has done to our society."[13] In the era of worldwide threats of terrorism, the further expansion of secrecy is readily understandable. However, secrecy is also risky. As Daniel Patrick Moynihan warned, it can protect agencies, governmental or corporate, from public knowledge of their errors, cause public distrust, and create a climate for the formation of paranoid conspiracy ideologies. According to Moynihan, government secrecy in America during the cold war caused great harm to the United States. It created excessive and uncontrolled secret projects; it harmed realistic discussion of policy. Nevertheless, because some valued role for secrecy remains, recurrent efforts will be made to limit, subvert, or distort information.[14] Even in open societies like the United States, secrecy remains a major institutional factor.

Angus Mackenzie praises the effect of the Freedom of Information Act (FOIA) of 1966, championed by Rep. John Emerson Moss of California in the 1950s, as an instrument that made it possible to discover the enormous extent of U.S. government secrecy. The Freedom of Information Act was a breakthrough in democratic institutions—it came much later than the pioneering Swedish legislation, but as we have seen, many countries followed America's example in the last decade of the twentieth century. Yet despite the act's global significance, the battle between the FOIA and secrecy continued and even intensified over subsequent decades. Mackenzie describes the struggle:

> The 1947 National Security Act has become the Pandora's box that Ambassador Kirkpatrick and Congressman Hoffman had feared. Placing a legal barrier between foreign intelligence operations and domestic politics in the National Security Act has proved ineffectual. In the decades that followed 1947, the CIA not only became increasingly involved in domestic politics but abridged the First Amendment guarantees of free speech and free press in a conspiracy to keep this intrusion from the American people. The intelligence and military secrecy of the 1940s had broadened in the 1960s to covering up the suppression of domestic dissent. The 1980s registered a further, more fundamental change, as the suppression of unpopular opinions was supplemented by systematic and institutionalized peacetime censorship for the first time in U.S. history. The repressive machinery developed by the CIA has spread secrecy like oil on water.

He continues:

> The U.S. government has always danced with the devil of secrecy during wartime. By attaching the word "war" to the economic and ideological race for world supremacy between the Soviet Union and the United States, a string of administrations continued this dance for fifty years. The cold war provided the foreign threat to justify the pervasive Washington belief that secrecy should have the greatest possible latitude and openness should be restricted as much as possible—constitutional liberties be damned.

And finally:

> With the collapse of the Soviet Union as a world power in 1990, even the pseudo-war rationale evaporated. But the partisans of secrecy have not been willing to accept the usual terms of peacetime. The have made clear their intentions to preserve and extend the wartime system. They will find a rationalization: if not the threat of the Soviet Union, then the goal of economic hegemony. Thus the U.S. government now needs to keep secrets to give an advantage to American corporate interests. Yet it is entrepreneurs who have been making the most use of FOIA—not journalists, not lawyers. As of 1994, the great preponderance of all FOIA requests have been for business purposes.[15]

In 1999 Daniel Patrick Moynihan presented a blistering indictment of secrecy in America. About the 1997 Report of the Commission on Protecting and Reducing Government Secrecy, he commented: "Secrecy is a form of government regulation. Americans are familiar with the tendency to over-regulate in other areas. What is different with secrecy is that the public cannot know the extent or the content of regulation."[16] Moynihan likened U.S. government secrecy to "a hidden, humongous, metastasizing mass within government itself."[17] He cited the words of economist Joseph Stiglitz:

> There is, in democratic societies, a basic right to know, be to informed about what the government is doing and why. To put it baldly, I will argue that there should be a strong presumption in favor of transparency and openness in government. The scourges of secrecy during the past seventy years are well known—in country after country, it is the secret police that has engaged in the most egregious violations of human rights. I want to talk today about the kind of secrecy that is pervasive today in many democratic societies. Let me be clear: this secrecy is a far cry from that pursued by the totalitarian states that have marred the century that is drawing to a close. Yet this secrecy is corrosive: it is antithetical to democratic values, and it undermines democratic processes. It is based on mistrust between those governing and those governed; and at the same time, it exacerbates that mistrust.[18]

One strategy in the defense of dark secrets is deception. In *The Politics of Lying: Implications for Democracy,* about the United Kingdom and the United States, Lionel Cliffe and his colleagues examine an impressive array of cases obviously involving deception. The work disputes the claim by political "realists" that deceptions in state affairs are sometimes ethically defensible and even necessary. The large number of case studies and the systematic patterns of lying and secrecy they uncover in both the United States and the UK make a convincing argument to the contrary. In all cases there was no justification for deception based on national or public interest. The wish to deny gross government errors, to protect the personal interests of particular politicians, to undermine the credibility of critics, to hide conflicts of interest or outright corruption, these are by far the predominant reasons for political deception and therefore secrecy. Cliffe et al. demonstrate the destructive effects of government secrecy in encouraging this form of behavior that damages the institutions of democracy.[19]

The secrecy syndrome, as an elementary and pervasive phenomenon in all societies, has reached different degrees and scopes in modern states. The totalitarian systems, of course, were dedicated to secrecy and surveillance to a stifling and disastrous extent. However, democratic societies have also built their own defensive and offensive secret apparatus. There is a social structure of secrecy that is inescapably tied to its value syndrome: its central values are the protection of the community (whether this means the state or an organization), loyalty, exclusion, guardianship over boundaries, hierarchy, and obedience. The secret must be kept from others—whether this means an enemy or the unguarded public (who might unwittingly spill a secret to the enemy or to voters). Keeping secrets is necessary in antagonistic relationships, but it also may be chosen as an instrument of strategy in interactions among friends or partners: to make surprises possible, to prevent premature public debate about incomplete project plans, to time a revelation purposefully "at the appropriate moment."

Protection of the community, of a nation, or of an organization, is the central ostensible reason for secrecy. The relevant community may, however, often shrink to an immediate secret network of agents. Loyalty comes next in the hierarchy of values—treachery is the greatest offence against the secrecy syndrome. Exclusion of outsiders is an obvious necessity for the secrecy process. It requires boundaries and their vigilant protection; but boundaries are often blurred in the murky world of espionage and counterespionage. Hierarchy may not be the dominant feature of all secretive groups, but obedience to authority is certainly required in formal state organizations.

In the secrecy process, constraints arise from the need to create new information while protecting it from discovery. This necessitates strategies to keep inquisitive opponents at bay—which require surveillance, espionage, and counterespionage, and misleading the inquirer by spreading misinformation or misleading partial information. The major values of the secrecy syndrome are thus the protection of cherished information, exclusion of outsiders and the public, loyalty to the "cause" and to insiders, authority and obedience in service of the "cause." In a democratic order, this syndrome must be balanced with the transparency syndrome of openness, and there must be legally defined boundaries between them. But promoting transparency by others, for example, for the purpose of easier surveillance, is often a component of the secrecy syndrome. The secrecy syndrome is linked to its countervalues: transparency, inclusion, freedom of information, and autonomy, posing important ethical challenges.

Because espionage and surveillance do create new information, they may in the long run reduce opacity. Secrets are hard to keep hidden in the global era; after a period of time, revelation of the truth is virtually a certainty. The costs of secrecy can be very high. Secrecy practically invites corruption even in systems that have active supervisory structures. It offers attractive opportunities for hiding mistakes, for taking private advantage, or for undermining political opponents in devious ways. Given a sufficiently large organization, even if only a small number of people yield to temptation, some form of corruption will become a virtual certainty. Secret agencies often mislead the public and create distrust in the political system. With these costs, democratic societies must carefully circumscribe the domains of secrecy and vigilantly guard these boundaries.

There are powerful drivers of secrecy. The quest for security, the fear of attack by enemies, and the apparent need for defense are the most salient reasons offered for keeping secrets. But there are others: to avoid shame, to maintain information taboos, to seek political dominance, and to line one's pockets. These abuses are among the risks of adhering to the loyalty and authority ethic of the secrecy syndrome.

The Structure of the Transparency Syndrome

We now turn to the transparency syndrome. Its focus is the citizen's right to know and the duty of authorities of all kinds to disclose information. Primacy in the rank orders of values in this syndrome goes to information freedom and disclosure. It stands for the autonomy of individuals as well as for diversity, inclusion, and reduced hierarchy. The cluster of values in the transparency syndrome include the following: general human rights, freedom of speech and expression, free inquiry, privacy, the rights of persons, the rights of property, accountability, and necessary secrecy. The core values fostered by transparency are freedom of information and expression, as stated in Article 19 of the International Covenant on Civil and Political Rights, adopted by the UN General Assembly in December 1966, and enacted on March 23, 1976.[20] Privacy is another value protected by transparency: it protects individuals from intrusion by the state or by others and prohibits the unauthorized use of personal information. Some of these values conflict. How does privacy limit transparency? Where are the legitimate boundaries of secrecy? And how does the entire secrecy syndrome fit with transparency? How does honoring accountability require a balance of several complex value relations?

This complexity gives rise to informational ambivalence, or the tensions created by the attempt to reconcile these values. The concept is derived from Robert K. Merton's idea of sociological ambivalence, a term defined as "incompatible normative expectations incorporated in a single role of a single social status."[21] Informational ambivalence arises from tensions among the values of the transparency syndrome in relation to the secrecy syndrome.

The values underlying transparency need some explication. They continue to change because of rapid changes in information technology and the challenges brought by other global transformations. Transparency is linked to the value of respect for individual autonomy. Autonomy requires access to needed information—as in the case of informed consent in medical decisions. Clearly, the obvious countervalue to transparency is secrecy. While openness is a governing value in a democracy, secrecy is less so. By closing off information, secrecy limits autonomy. The contest between freedom of information and secrecy is a major cultural and political battle in the current era of expanding democracies amid global change.

While secrecy is not an unambiguous virtue in modern democracies, privacy is widely considered a right and indeed a virtue, even as it is eroded by technology. Information about our private lives, our medical and financial records, or our correspondence is to be given special protection. The challenges to privacy brought by new communications and new surveillance technology raise new legal and ethical questions. Privacy concerns have also entered the political arena almost everywhere.[22]

A respect for privacy may be found in the Bible and in the sayings of Mohammed. Legal protections guarding the sanctity of the home have long existed in England. However, while honored as an abstract value, even in the West privacy was an almost unimaginable luxury, given the practical conditions of life, even as late as the eighteenth century. While it has ancient roots, a concern with privacy rose in importance with the increase in the differentiation and specialization of social domains. Georg Simmel refers to it as "discretion." Erwin Scheuch puts it this way:

> Differentiation leads to the specification of life spheres, and privacy as a new norm allows us to function in such an area largely regardless of what we are in other areas. We are used to a life where work and the private residences are separated, where we are able to function differently with bureaucratic organizations and a leisure group of our choice. Managing the differences between the various spheres becomes a necessary social skill. Totalitarianism is the attempt to negate this kind of differentiation by enforcing the same ultimate meaning across all life spheres.[23]

Relationships between the state and individuals, between individuals and the public, are regulated by a fabric of laws and cultural conventions. These rules determine the strength or the weakness of civil society as well as the scope of free markets, the domain of free speech, and the degree to which the state can try to regulate the beliefs of its citizens. In a democracy, these rights are matters of law. An entire complex of laws govern the rights of property, since ownership of property is one major limitation to the power of the state. Private ownership of the means of production, which under-lies the concept of the private sector as well as the domain of market activi-ties, is a contested concept that has received widely divergent definitions in different legal systems. Moreover, the notion of private property has limits, as, for example, in the concept of eminent domain. However, where the institution of private property does not exist, or where it is assailed as detri-mental to the public welfare, as in the former Soviet Union, relations between individuals and the state are fundamentally different from those in democratic, market-based societies.

Ronald A. Brand examines the roles of property law in the relationship between the state and the individual.[24] He distinguishes between the "pri-vate function of property and the social function of property." On this basis he constructs "a private rights model and a social rights model of property law." While the former predominates in Western market-oriented societies, the latter characterized the welfare states of the former Soviet domain. Brand focuses less on the common concept of ownership than on entitle-ments to benefits provided by the state. The transition from the social rights (or entitlement) model of property law to the private rights model involves a fundamental change in relations between persons and the state. In the social rights model, all property is owned by the state, but the individual "owns" the rights to work, income, housing, health care, education, and so on. However, such social entitlements do not define a zone of personal autonomy, but rather constitute bonds of dependency—especially in closed, authoritarian societies. One could argue that the private rights model is more conducive to transparency than the social rights model. It draws the boundary of privacy as well as of autonomy around the property-owning person. In some communities, neither of these ideas makes sense. Many tribal cultures have neither a formal institution of property nor the idea of state-provided entitlements. Premodern, underdeveloped societies lack the legal concepts of property and the infrastructure for state support of proper-ty (through registers of title to real estate, or automobiles, or certificates of sales). In the diversity of cultures in the global age, conflicts over the legal nature and ethical underpinnings of property rights are intensifying. Often demands for transparency are wielded as weapons in the struggle. Pharma-ceutical companies that register patents and ownership of the medicinal use of tropical plants that have long been used in tribal cultures are now being charged with seizing tribal property. There are innumerable other conflicts over the definition and legitimacy of property rights asserted across cultural boundaries and into novel domains.

However, the legal institutions defining the rights of persons are far broader than those defining property rights. They cover the right of persons to negotiate contracts, as for example in labor-management relations or in commercial transactions. They include further rights to free inquiry, free speech, and freedom of assembly. In other words, these cultural value orientations provide the constitutional framework for the open society and make the formation of civil society possible.

Transparency also depends upon accountability, or taking responsibility for one's actions and their consequences. Transparency on the part of those in power clearly requires accountability to the public at large. In secret organizations, the hierarchy of authority demands accountability and obedience from those below. Accountability may involve conditional secrecy, as in the case of fiduciary responsibilities of a trustee or in the protection of property and privacy. The trustee is accountable to a client, a person, or legal entity. This entails the responsibility to protect information about the client's property rights. Intellectual property—as in the case of patents, for example—and business plans are examples of such rights. In fact, privacy rights and upholding the transparency of a system may well go hand in hand, as these different values are balanced against each other.

Accountability for authorities thus is closely linked to transparency. It is the responsibility of public actors to justify their actions, their motives, and their consequences. Being responsible in some cases means being liable for damages caused, as outlined in law. We discussed accountability with the ombudsman of the European Union, Professor Nikiforos Diamandorous. He observed:

> When the ombudsman enters a dispute about accountability, there are inevitable frictions. The system does wish to be seen in essence, as honest as Caesar's wife. When the ombudsman does come in, there is inevitable conflict. I'm very interested in that from the point of view of transparency and accountability in modern democracy. Accountability is very important in a situation; increasingly as democracy becomes more complex, the sense and feelings of people must be bridged. There is a gradual shift from the traditional concept of democracy, primarily equality, to liberal democracy, which requires different types of accountability and creation of checks and balances. I am making a distinction between vertical and horizontal accountability. Vertical accountability is through elections, held at intervals. Horizontal accountability implies willingness of modern mechanisms to develop, to hold officials accountable on a day-to-day basis, leading to auditors, independent commissions (for example, in the United States, the FCC). The state must be self-restraining, which alien-

ates parts of its sovereignty. The trend of the last fifty years is to complement egalitarianism with accountability.[25]

The European Union is committed to transparency, as shown by the creation of the office of ombudsman. To make information public requires quite an apparatus for creating and disseminating the information, considering the limits imposed by countervalues such as the rights of privacy or property ownership. Information support structures must be built or strengthened, if they do not exist or are insufficient, as in most developing countries. These structures, their norms and cultures, and the interests and incentives of those working in them or affected by them, constitute an important part of the dynamics of the system. Local or organizational politics and competitions may play surprising roles.

For example, when the government of Greece established the office of ombudsman and defined its legal obligations, rights, privileges, staff, and budget, it created a new force for transparency in Greece. The ombudsman discovered massive lacunae in Greece's policies toward immigration. Greece has not had to deal with these topics, since until recently it had very few immigrants. Now, after it joined the European Union and with the end of the cold war, immigration has become a major issue. Greece needed not only an information structure, but also an apparatus of law.[26] Similarly, when the European Union's preparation for the euro currency compelled the European Central Bank, the European Commission, and the central banks of the member states to introduce new transparency standards for banking systems, most members needed to change their information structures.

Thus, analogous to the secrecy process, there is a transparency process. Once a government agency, a corporation, or a profession has taken the step toward transparency, specific consequences follow. Decisions have to be made about what to disclose, to whom, and how. The boundaries of competing values need to be defined, learned, understood, and defended. There has to be an information infrastructure of a technical and professional kind. It costs money and manpower. A political force field of supporters, critics, skeptics, competitors will emerge. Relations with the media, contacts with professional journalists, will become more formalized. This may actually divert transparency into a morass of bureaucracy. Politics can confuse the process. Nevertheless, formalization of the process is inevitable.

Once steps toward transparency have been taken, it becomes difficult, if not impossible, to withdraw from it. Internal norms and procedures of the government or of organizations will have to be formalized to assure reliable records and data. Grievances formerly ignored will command attention. Planning processes will be different. Accountability will be a matter of routine, with complex consequences of its own. The transparency process is transformative and it points toward diversity, inclusion, and veracity. Understandably, initiating the transparency process often generates conflict. Attempts at concealment become very costly. As George Washington said in his Farewell Address of 1796: "Honesty is always the best policy."

The Dynamics of Transparency and Secrecy: What Drives and What Limits Transparency?

The need for transparency, of course, does not apply to all kinds of information, but information about knowledge held and actions taken by authorities in centers of power. Such information matters greatly to some people, and on occasion to the public at large. Transparency makes it possible to challenge the truth claims attached to the information made available. These claims have consequences. Since this information may influence decisions of significant import, there are compelling reasons for interested parties to be skeptical and to question the relevance, accuracy, and indeed veracity of the claims made. This gives transparency a very considerable force. However, information gained through the new channels opened by transparency must be examined with care. A senior official of the European Union said: "The impression of transparency is that it is a straight ray of light. But it can be simulated by a thousand mirrors." There are complex issues at stake, and skepticism is warranted. Certainly, authorities disclosing information to the public are likely to put the best spin on it, select the most favorable methodology for measuring their successes or disguising their failures, or even divulge mountains of information that hide the important facts. Skepticism that provokes debate is necessary to test the validity of truth claims. The sociology of knowledge becomes important here.[27] It is well known that what is accepted as knowledge in a political or commercial context cannot necessarily be empirically proved. Even scientifically unfounded information that rests on revealed faith or other unproved and unprovable convictions may subjectively be experienced as knowledge. What people accept as credible depends on culturally established epistemic criteria for judging truth claims. Nevertheless, a respect for scientific proof may be gaining among these epistemic criteria.[28]

The public is capable of making common-sense assessments of truth claims. Nicholas Rescher describes this as communicative pragmatism, guided by "general principles that govern how efficiently informative communication can function anywhere and everywhere."[29] He also discusses the conditions under which effective communication cannot happen, illuminating the circumstances in which effective communication is possible. For Rescher, effective communication is possible and reasonably efficient only if certain conditions are met. The sender must make an effort to be clear and not misunderstood. This might be accomplished by providing more elaborate information and context, enabling the recipient to comprehend the message. But there is a cost to this effort. It takes more time, work, and imagination. The receiver also has to make an effort to understand, which takes time and patience. These efforts are costs to the receiver. Thus Rescher takes an economic approach: "Effective communication is throughout a matter of maintaining proper cost-benefit coordination." The considerations on both sides—sender and receiver—are economic principles of balance. "They all turn on finding a point after which the benefit of further gain in information falls below the cost demanded for its process of acquisition."[30]

This pragmatic approach to communication can be useful in assessing how transparency might work in the context of everyday life and common sense. A message containing information may originate in a distant country and come from a different culture. The receiver's political and economic interests may be very different from the sender's, and there may even be deep canyons of distrust between them. In the context of globalization, truth claims based on information gained through transparency are tested in diverse cultures as to their universal validity. Skeptics in India or in Nigeria or in Canada may examine the same claims about the effectiveness of a pharmaceutical drug or an economic development policy of the World Bank. Cultural relativism as a doctrine is not tenable in this context—but in transnational communicative actions of transparency, bridges are being built (or at least attempted) to link universal truth claims to the realities of a specific culture.

This makes the demand for transparency an especially serious matter in global-era communications: relativism must yield to the truth and normative validity claims and verification procedures offered by such communications. This means that relativistic cultural views are threatened by the claimed universalism that comes with transparency. And yet, universally agreed standards for establishing "facts" are often not accepted and may be debated. Standards of the normative validity of values may differ significantly, causing cognitive clashes that may block effective communication and shared discourse. In *Between Facts and Norms,* Jürgen Habermas draws on multiple sources, including C. S. Peirce's pragmatism, the philosophy of language, and the idea of communicative reason. He describes how an "interpretation community" sharing an intersubjectively shared life world, can reach common understandings.

Habermas turns to a rational procedure whereby democratic discourse can link the universal claims of reason with the particular realities of diverse communities. This idea of accepting or rejecting claims of truth on the basis of facts and/or claims of validity of norms expands Max Weber's concept of formal rationality as well as Kant's practical reason. Habermas writes: "Discourse theory reckons with the *higher-level intersubjectivity* of processes of reaching understanding through democratic procedures or in the communicative network of public spheres."[31] Elsewhere Habermas discusses the difficulties and promise of such discourse across national boundaries as European nations entered into a union. This illustrates our concern with how truth claims are received across diverse cultures. Habermas refers to the inclusiveness of universal standards in this connection. His emphasis is on the rationality of procedure creating a sense of legitimacy. His title, *Between Facts and Norms*, indicates Habermas's effort to link particular conditions with universal standards, thereby to open an avenue to understand the growth of transnational solidarities.[32]

All this means that under "normal" conditions of life for most people in democracies and in aspiring states, information released by authorities is presumed to be credible, even though their claims could be questioned by those who are most concerned with the matter at hand and by permanent skeptics. Generally, most consider such information as contributing to "common sense," and given the added scrutiny provided by transparency policies, its legitimacy can be assumed. However, these conditions do not necessarily prevail across cultural or ideological boundaries—as in ethnic wars, religious conflicts, terrorist movements, or more routinely in democratic election campaigns. Special efforts to bolster credibility are then demanded. One way to accomplish this is to carefully present how the truth claims of the sender have been established by making these procedures transparent as well. This is seen as reasonable among democratic publics with a culture that respects knowledge criteria and information procedures.

However, there are conditions under which even these efforts can be frustrated. Totalitarian regimes will block efforts at transparency, incurring serious costs to themselves in the process. Charismatic movements with major emotional commitments to single values and "revealed truths" may be beyond the reach of rational argument. Under these conditions, the power of transparency and rationality are limited and precarious. The power of transparency has potential limits. What is assumed to be normal everyday life in a democracy certainly does not prevail everywhere in the world today. The pursuit of transparency functions only under the presumption of reasonable assessments of truth claims by the public.

Since the quest for transparency necessarily entails very complex matters of truth claims and their assessment as well as the need to bridge cultural boundaries or even hostile frontiers, this creates a serious educational challenge for the citizens of democracies. The flow of information opened by the transparency process may be too complex, too incredible, too demanding to be intelligently received.

What Drives Transparency?

The boundaries between transparency, secrecy, and other values can be a battlefield. The tactics of hiding versus revealing, committing fraud and outright lying versus telling the truth, may invite illicit or even criminal behavior. Many seek to avoid transparency, but countermeasures to fight deceit, fraud, and misleading propaganda campaigns have been created and are growing in sophistication. Of course, the frauds and liars are also becoming more sophisticated; there is a continuous battle, for both transparency and secrecy are concerned with trust and confidence. And, we believe, the forces of transparency will gain the upper hand in the long run. Transparency has to rely on public information that can be debated and tested. The confidence and trust needed to take action based on such information can reach across many cultural and political boundaries. It is trust at a distance that can generate new credibility and thus legitimacy. Secrecy also depends on loyalties and closures. This is trust in a closed circle. This form of trust depends on an existing surplus of legitimacy, or credibility. It is unlikely that the battle over these values will ever completely end.

Effective strategies to guard against deceit and just plain error include a reliance on creditable "brokers" of truthfulness, validity, and accountability; the powerful threats of legal penalties against fraudulent truth claims; and evaluation studies to assess the validity and relevance of claims for accountability and truthfulness. Brokers of credibility, law enforcement, and evaluation may in fact be interlinked, as in the fights that arise from scandals.

Brokers of credibility must themselves have a high level of legitimacy. "Blue-ribbon" commissions that investigate alleged wrongdoing must be of this quality to be credible. Political disagreements over disputed facts—as in the case of scientific knowledge about global warming—may be addressed by the Academy of Science. International agencies are increasingly called in to assess the state of human rights in particular countries, such as the International Red Cross investigating the treatment of detainees by U.S. soldiers in the "war on terrorism." These highly esteemed, prestigious institutions are held to a strict code of conduct and circumspection.

The threat of legal penalties may be the most direct and powerful guards against distortions of truth. They tend to require audits by qualified professionals and, increasingly, evaluations. The law known as the Sarbanes-Oxley Act of 2002 is designed to enforce accurate financial statements from corporate executives and chief financial officers, who are threatened with severe penalties if they fail to comply. Such penalties are direct legal devices to enforce transparency. U.S. tort law can impose serious sanctions against companies that sell dangerous products without revealing their risks. When customers are harmed, such as when automobiles are prone to roll over or otherwise spin out of control, there can be serious financial costs and loss of reputation to the manufacturer. Outright devious acts, however, may also cause damage to a corporation's reputation and incur large financial losses, once discovered. Transparency then can become a strategy for risk reduction.

The growing commitment to transparency and accountability has stimulated a demand for evaluation research. It is, however, a very diverse and multidimensional movement. The idea that there will emerge an "evaluation science" resulted in part from the "experimenting society" that Donald T. Campbell sketched and advocated.[33] Campbell's work in epistemology and methodology for the social sciences laid the foundation for a new understanding of the "open society" as an effective learning environment. However, evaluation research emerged in more pragmatic terms to meet the demands for effectiveness and accountability of public programs. As mentioned before, Edward Suchman created such a program for evaluation based on his experiences in public health, a profession that must increasingly deal with global as well as local issues. It necessarily encounters all the varied issues on truth claims we discuss as a central concern for creating valid transparency.

For Eleanor Chelimsky and William R. Shadish, the evaluation profession and movement, as they see it emerging in the twenty-first century, will increasingly deal with global as well as local issues. It must necessarily be diverse in its concepts, theories, and methodologies. They recognize three evaluation perspectives: the accountability perspective, the knowledge perspective, and the development perspective.[34] These views are quite different, though they can intersect. The accountability perspective requires measuring results as objectively as possible. It is related to—but can be broader than—an audit. Such an evaluation is often externally mandated. It can play a strong role in policy debates, not as an advocate but in a fact-finding role. Evaluation through the knowledge perspective seeks new insights and new methods. It tends to be critical but is wary of playing the role of advocate. Like the accountability perspective, the knowledge perspective values objectivity. Evaluation from the development perspective pursues the goal of strengthening institutions and may encourage the client being evaluated to engage in self-evaluation and cooperative work. Advocacy from this perspective may itself need an external review.

Clearly, the evaluation profession, with its different perspectives and its international and therefore intercultural branches, is central to the rise of transparency in the process of global transformation. It cannot be only a science of evaluation, but it must also come to an understanding of its own ethical and value frameworks. As Chelimsky and Shadish state at the beginning of their book:

> Evaluators, in whatever field of evaluation they may be, are likely to find themselves, at least at times, at odds with the political actors, systems, and processes in their countries that militate against the free flow of information required for evaluation. This means that as the world becomes more politically diverse and complex in the 21st century, evaluators will be called upon to exhibit considerable courage in the normal pursuit of their work. Because they are examples of admirable courage to speak truth to power, we want to dedicate this book to six men of the 20th century: Vaclav Havel, C. Everett Koop, Jean Monnet, Daniel Patrick Moynihan, Gunnar Myrdal, and Elliot Richardson. Their strength and vision have paved the way for the next generations.[35]

Transparency is not only pursued in a defensive mode. It is also powered by strong forces that thrust it into the foreground. This can be in bounded domains without necessarily becoming comprehensive across an entire system. In certain forms of government activity, transparency is threatened by the turn toward security and secrecy, but it continues to be a powerful force in other areas. Under normal democratic conditions, and given the increase in the number of democratic states, transparency practices and policies are becoming more and more routine. Freedom-of-information movements are a new but very sturdy phenomenon of global scope.

The sources of energy that power the transparency phenomenon fall into several groups, each with its own bounded domain. First, there are emerging historical forces that drive toward comprehensive transparency. Information technology is enabling transparency and also secrecy by presenting new choices for information cultures. Trustworthy information is needed in many sectors by interest groups and their political and economic constellations. Then we deal with the value-rational factors of constituents of the most salient values within the transparency/secrecy syndromes, such as the supporters of privacy, government accountability, environmental transparency, national security, and so on. We further examine the power of moral outrage and scandals and the shifts in frameworks of judgment; this leads to the powerful effects of shifts in historical values and time perspectives in historical transparency.

Choosing to adopt freedom of information policies can be the result of internal, voluntary decisions, but may also be the result of external constraints, such as the risk of lawsuits. In many cases, transparency rules are derived from freedom of information laws. In the rapid changes of governance—for example, in countries that join the European Union—transparency policies may be imposed by external pressures. This is also a possible result of policies imposed by global financial or trade institutions. Further, there are organized forces pressing for transparency, such as Transparency International, the INGO fighting corruption. There can also be serious unintended consequences caused by actions that are meant to be hidden from the light of transparency. Scandals such as the discovery of the secret agenda pursued by Enron executives have actually contributed to new transparency legislation.

Information technology has become more ubiquitous, inexpensive, and efficient, owing to a continuous stream of innovations. Its scope is expanding worldwide, and both the technology and its uses are changing. Information management has become sophisticated, as have communication and surveillance systems. The Internet has created global networks of communication and information that for a time seemed to be impervious even to government interference. Global social movements and aspirations for unconstrained freedom on the Internet felt very much empowered. Civil society benefited and grew even in unlikely places. However, political entities are finding ways to limit the freedom of the Internet. Individual privacy is being threatened because of the technological means of state surveillance and intrusion by private enterprises. It is becoming increasingly clear that "the biggest decisions about the internet's future will be political and social, not technological," a survey of the Internet society by the *Economist* concludes.[36] Political and social decisions, according to the *Economist,* will define the culture of information norms we are discussing. This is also the view of David Brin expressed in *The Transparent Society*: societies will have to deal with difficult and important choices to protect (or gain) their freedom. Nevertheless, the campaign for transparency on the whole will continue to benefit from the advance of information technology. This derives especially from the growing demands for government accountability and the intensifying cultural battles between the pressures for transparency and for secrecy.[37]

A very different set of factors increasing the scope of transparency are driven by the technological innovations that make information that previously did not exist available and accessible. The expansion of information today is simply enormous. For example, satellite surveillance and mapping technologies create knowledge about activities on the surface of the earth that is now widely available even to private persons. These technologies and other surveillance devices were originally developed for military purposes, but their uses have expanded greatly, producing changes of wide-ranging import. Information gathering about the activities of governments, organizations, or even individuals has become vastly easier, threatening both secrecy and privacy.[38] One consequence is that surveillance is no longer available just to governments. On the other hand, as Brin notes, the technologies have also vastly enhanced the ability to exercise surveillance and monitor the activities of "persons or organizations of interest."

In the normal functioning of advanced industrial states, many transactions of daily routine are recorded. This is true of all kinds of public bureaucracies.[39] It is also true in other sectors for purchases and sales, credit records, medical records, academic attainments, driving violations, criminal records, and many other things. There is a substantial concern with the role of privacy in these matters, but the simple fact is that much more detailed information about all sorts of activity does exist today than even in the recent past.

What is known can be communicated and broadcast, maybe even worldwide. It can, of course, be hidden by encryption and barriers of secrecy. However, the spread of existing information—of interest to at least someone—remains difficult to stop. The Internet is, of course, the primary factor in this development. The spread of computer networks and the ease of communication they bring about drastically transform the general information environment. Television and worldwide news broadcasting by CNN, BBC, and a few other networks bring knowledge of economic and political conditions to audiences virtually anywhere. This is a main factor in ending the isolation of remote communities from the external world. Simple isolation used to be a powerful force in maintaining power and loyalty in many cultures. It is no longer as effective as it once was. Secretive regimes will try their best to create a technological equivalent to simple isolation, although this is unlikely to succeed in the long run.

The growth of transparency norms also is likely to expand the domains about which information exists. That is, it shrinks the domain of social opacity. Transparency, of course, requires substantial infrastructures and information systems that gear into the routine transactions mentioned above. They store such information as land values, land ownership, and transfers of property, income data and tax records, health data, information on water quality, and multiple other domains of public concern. Government surveillance systems also store vast quantities of information. How it will be used will depend on the norms of information cultures and the strength of the values of the open society.

Instrumental factors in the pragmatic uses of transparency include the very practical needs of markets, democratic governments, and professions for information about what they do, about their goods or services, and how legitimate their authority is. Markets cannot function without a reasonable level of transparency between sellers and buyers. A pension fund manager, say, in Denmark, should want to know about the accounting practices and the disclosure rules under which firms in Hong Kong operate if he is considering doing business there. It seems reasonable to expect that the demand for transparency will increase as the cultural distance or "otherness" increases between partners in financial transactions. This generates a demand for standards or norms. For example, international organizations like the World Bank or the World Trade Organization encourage certain standards of transparency in financial matters (while in other respects transparency remains limited). In this domain the pressures for transparency have begun to function through a worldwide network. Consumer protection is a field of growing importance for transparency and legislation requiring it. Labeling food products to inform consumers of their actual content has become a nearly universal expectation, even though frequently resisted. Informing the public of environmental hazards and other risks is another source of transparency pressures.

New demands for transparency are also being felt by those in the professions. The transparency syndrome is clearly visible in the insistence on informed consent in medical practice and especially in research on human subjects.[40] There are efforts in all professions involving the education of clients about the responsibilities, practices (and their limitations) of those who offer professional services. The professions of accounting, management consulting, and law are all debating the rules (and in part defensively protecting them) to establish new bases of trust by means of transparency measures. Professional codes of ethics often emphasize the need to disclose information. The medical profession has moved toward transparency since the days of concealing bad news from patients, such as keeping a diagnosis of cancer from a patient.

These trends are amplified by the political and legal burdens imposed by disputes about risks and the liabilities for disasters. Recent examples may be observed in the European Union's concern with the responsibilities of governments, farmers, veterinarians, scientists, and still others regarding the spread of "mad cow disease." The calamitous experience of biotechnology firms with genetically modified plants, creating a deep crisis in public trust, especially in Europe, is another. In both instances, those involved emphasize that full transparency about these issues might have averted the breakdown of trust.[41]

Interest groups and their political and economic constellations often take a vital role in legislative battles about information norms. While many of them have a stake in limiting transparency, at times their efforts have the long-term result of advancing it. One illustration is the vigorous fight by U.S. auditing firms, by CEOs and board members of major corporations, and by some law firms to prevent the "expensing" of stock options for executives as part of their compensation. The argument is that giving the stock options to corporate leaders provided an important incentive for CEOs to increase the value of the shares of their companies and did not need to be included in corporate financial reports. However, common sense says, of course, that since stock options have monetary value, their disclosure should be required. The result was that senior executives grossly enriched themselves at the expense of the shareholders. The ensuing scandals led to drastic legislation adopted by Congress requiring improved transparency of corporate financial reports. New accounting rules moving toward harmonizing the U.S. system with new International Accounting Standards brought more transparency. However, many groups such as auditors, tax advisors, consultants, and corporate analysts continue to fight for ways to hide their questionable doings by contesting every rule change. Prosecutors, regulators, and oversight boards are now busily at work drafting new information norms. There is no doubt that the battles of accounting by major corporations will continue. Overall, they have thus far opened many windows of transparency.

111

There are value-rational influences pushing for transparency in the many volunteer organizations of civil society. Examples include Transparency International and Amnesty International, among a large array of other organized movements seeking to alleviate evils such as global inequality, corruption, repression, torture, and environmental degradation. They all share the basic strategy of exposing abuses, inviting shame, and demanding constructive reform. The worldwide movement to establish corporate codes of conduct illustrates the value-rational impact of these efforts: the people in these movements pursue specific values by means of well-formulated strategic plans and alliances. They are very different from the interest constellations just referred to. Value-rational advocates of transparency may make alliances with the pragmatic leaders of business or government and may undertake with them long-term, strategic campaigns for reform.

Moral outrage and scandals are probably the most visible and dramatic forces propelling the demand for transparency. Scandals about exploitative and fraudulent business conduct played a major role in creating modern oversight systems and rules of accountability. Scandals have led to reform in election financing and rules about the conduct of campaigns. Scandals have brought about the reform of informed consent norms for the health professions. As mentioned above, such scandals often reflect changes in widely shared moral frameworks. The most potent movements for information freedom are the global efforts at achieving transparency about historical facts, notably the past crimes of oppressive regimes. Today a global network of local and global movements is dedicated to bringing such crimes into the open and bringing to light the sufferings of the victims. Energetic activists are determined not only to address the past but also to prevent tyranny in the future.

Our review of the driving forces behind the demand for transparency started with the motives of people dealing with everyday life, but escalated to value-rational actions and finally to the passionate forces of moral outrage and the effort to transcend historical evils. The decisions to adopt transparency norms are quite diverse, ranging from the voluntary adoption of disclosure simply as sensible practice, to external imposition as in the case of countries wishing to become members of the European Union that must embrace openness as a condition of accession. External constraints, such as fear of liability suits for a manufacturing company may motivate disclosures of information up front. And, by now of course, many countries have a rich body of laws about disclosure norms that must be obeyed.

112

Summary

In this chapter we have laid out the conceptual tools of the value syndromes of information cultures, exploring their "architecture," their social benefits and risks, the defenses as well as the sources of energy for transparency. Secrecy is here to stay in some clearly defined and controlled domains. Openness of information will be the rule because the pressures for transparency are strong in the process of globalization.

5

TRANSPARENCY IN THE WORLD

Transparency is a value likely to change the relation between citizens and authorities, between professionals and their clients or patients, and between corporations and their workers, customers, investors, and communities. Transparency is linked with the values of accountability and autonomy. The values structuring information cultures determine which information values are of primary importance, and which may be subordinated. They may be anchored in nationalism or in transnational solidarities, religion, or in political ideology. They may also be anchored by racism, moral intolerance, and faith in authoritarianism. The same facts presented as "transparent" may appear to have very different meanings in different cultures.

The importance of transparency in the global context can serve as a new strategy for governance, capable of establishing trust at a distance, and thus potentially supporting extended solidarities by civil society. Civil society, once the set of voluntary organizations and movements within a state, now describes large transnational networks with considerable influence beyond states. Movements supporting women's rights, environmental protection, freedom of expression, and public health concerns address global as well as local issues. They form global networks and create forums of worldwide visibility and influence.

Nevertheless, opacity and secrecy continue in force, sustaining suspicion and mistrust in global affairs if not counterbalanced by a demand for transparency. The extreme inequalities between the poor countries and the rich industrial societies, and the special roles of the latter, have spawned the need for transparency in the information age. The fact of economic and social inequality among world nations is a constant factor to be kept in mind. Persistent poverty is a source of despair, leading to the fatalism of powerless millions. Exploitative dictatorships and overwhelming external powers pur-

114

suing their own advantage—including supporting corrupt rulers elsewhere — are sources of deep humiliation for many, creating rage and resentment. This rage fuels the deeds of extremists, who turn to terrorism to vent their hatred of the big powers of the world, especially the United States. Poverty, inequality, and a sense of humiliation are now recognized as the most dangerous challenges to successful globalization. They affect risks to health, environmental degradation, political instability, and violence. The United Nations and the World Bank have formally recognized the malignant effects of extreme inequality.[1] The entire international development aid community underscores the challenge of economic inequality. These problems are not only matters of economics. They are also problems of antimodern cultures and religions, incompetent leaders, and corruption in high office. The tyranny of dictators and their corruption and crimes are often the causes of poverty.

The culture changes needed to achieve peace, security, and sustainable economic growth in the world require large-scale improvements in education worldwide. Education on a mass scale is necessary to make democracy possible. It is already showing results: major developing countries like China and India have invested in public education, with positive results. Yet more economic policy changes must be made to reduce poverty. In fact, some development policies in this direction are now under way.

The paradigms governing development assistance from the rich industrial powers are now being reassessed. Intensive criticism of secretive practices and ineffective policies by professionals, civil society movements, and accumulated evaluative research have led to a process of reorientation. Major changes have already occurred in certain international agencies such as the World Bank. Still, many of the ways in which the rich countries provide financial aid are influenced by powerful domestic interests. The stubborn insistence by the United States, the EU, and Japan on providing lavish agricultural subsidies to their farmers is one example. The lack of access to pharmaceutical drugs in the poor countries is another. The policy demand for giving "free market access" to developing countries, chiefly a U.S. policy, further illustrates the types of strategies pursued by the great powers that are partly in their own interest. But change is occurring in the global arena. The unilateral U.S. strategies under the George W. Bush presidency have aroused noticeable and to some extent effective resistance to the economic policies of the major powers. Certain developing countries, notably China, India, and Brazil, are becoming significant powers in their regions. The development policies of the 1990s, with their emphasis on free markets and "economic globalization," are beginning to change.

115

International agencies and those offering development assistance can help to promote cultural changes leading toward modernity. They have a responsibility to advance and nurture the capacity for self-governance and the rule of democracy in the developing world. At this point, developing countries themselves have become more assertive in pursuing modernization and furthering their own interests. Educational, economic, and political advances in the major developing countries have made them significant powers. A new era has opened in debates about global development. Calls for greater transparency are among the reforms pursued by the development community, by global civil society in developing countries, and especially by many educated political leaders themselves.

This chapter concerns the transparency-versus-secrecy profiles of the three major centers of power and wealth, the United States, the EU, and Japan. These great industrial powers are the main sources of development aid, all with great influence on world events. They are the predominant sources of global economic policies, defending rigorously open markets, the free flow of investments, and privileges for global corporations. All three protect their domestic interests with little concern for their impact on other countries. For example, they pay huge subsidies to their farmers, which has a highly destructive effect on agriculture in developing countries.

Of course, the three major powers have to reckon with many other actors, and a shift in global power structures is under way. The developing countries of the South have established a front of resistance against the global policies of the three major powers. A coalition of twenty-one nations developed and solidified after their sharp protest against the major economic powers at the World Trade Organization (WTO) meeting in Cancun in 2003. They rebelled against the one-sided "free-market" policies being imposed on them. This action may be a sign of shifts to come in the global constellation of power.

Further, the United States, the EU, and Japan have to deal not only with nation-states, but also with rising transnational, indeed global, civil society,[2] much of it having its origin and its supporters within their borders, but acting worldwide. Social movements such as campaigns for human rights, women's rights, more humane corporate conduct, and transnational civil society are important energizers demanding transparency. We focus on the institutions that define the structure of the information cultures, as anchored in law. The United States has a Constitution, but in the European Union supranational institutions are based on treaty law and court judgments. There is great diversity among its member states, even though EU laws affect them all. Nevertheless, an overall framework of information values has emerged in the EU. Japan has a framework of law as well as cultural continuity that limits transparency.

While we focus on the institutionalized information cultures, legally anchored values differ from popular opinion, which can shape government policies. For example, while the constitutions of the United States, the EU, and Japan guarantee freedom of speech, popular outbreaks of intolerance and attacks on critics of popular views frequently occur, becoming more intense in the era of global terrorism.

The Transparency/Secrecy Syndromes in America, Europe, and Japan

The U.S. Information Culture

The United States has unambiguously cherished openness and freedom from the very beginning, when its Constitution and especially the Bill of Rights created the fundamental framework for citizens' rights. The founding of the republic marked a dramatic cultural turning point in the evolution of democracy and freedom of information. Freedom of the individual espoused by democracy also implies the imposition of limits on the state's power. The strength of civil liberties and the limits to government authority are preconditions that enable transparency to function. The legal right of citizens to obtain information from government officials of course means that officials have a duty to disclose information. It is not to be assumed that bureaucracies and governments carry out this duty with great joy. The revelations brought by transparency can expose scandalous events that powerful officials may wish to conceal. In America, civil liberties have flourished, even though many are ambivalent about such freedoms, especially in times of war.

By the twentieth century, the United States' strategic posture as a great military and economic power transformed American democracy. Still further changes are occurring today in the war on terrorism. The unilateralist policies of President George W. Bush and his insistence on secrecy represent a discontinuity in recent American history. Civil liberties have been limited by the so-called Patriot Act, which followed the September 2001 attacks, giving the government greater powers to develop multiple projects of surveillance, to collect information about persons such as airline passengers, to arrest suspected terrorists, and to hold them in long-term secret detention.

There were similar restrictions of civil rights in the United States, especially during the two world wars. The House Un-American Activities Committee (HUAC) was established in 1938 to investigate people who might engage in "unpatriotic behavior." The Alien Registration Act of 1940 was a special law limiting freedom of opinion: among other things, it required keeping a record of the political beliefs of alien residents. In 1947 the HUAC undertook the infamous investigation of the Hollywood film industry on the suspicion of communist influence. This was followed in the 1950s by the McCarthy era, a particularly poisonous time of demagoguery and intimidation.[3]

Nevertheless, a basic faith in democracy and the Bill of Rights remains strong as a fundamental element of American culture. In all of the above examples, subsequent legislative action restored civil rights. For example, the Nixon years were filled with government secrecy and attempts to hide transgressions. The Watergate burglary and the investigations that followed ultimately caused Nixon's resignation. Yet in the era of George W. Bush as president, secrecy and governmental power have again increased. Nevertheless, the core values of freedom of speech and expression continue to be vigorously defended in the courts and by civil society watchdogs like the American Civil Liberties Union (ACLU).

A certain amount of disorder in American society has always been the result of liberty. However, the United States has an active sector of voluntary organizations, a lively civil society, and a community spirit that exercises some self-regulation. There are many voluntary efforts to deal with community problems. The idea of the open society is generally cherished by Americans, as are freedom of expression, government accountability, and separation of church and state. (Most Americans believe that everybody should have some religious faith, however.) Much information is readily shared in America and civil liberties are defended, albeit with serious restrictions. A comparative survey measuring freedom in various countries gives the United States its highest rating of freedom on both political rights and civil liberties. However, restrictions resulting from antiterrorist measures and the adoption of the Patriot Act in 2001 have given the government greater powers of surveillance and secrecy.[4]

An investigative press and watchdog organizations like the ACLU watch for transgressions, but governments also hide behind secrecy. Political parties and interests groups in turn try to head off the press. Overall, the freedom of the press seems reasonably secure in America, despite pressures that dampen the quality of media reporting. After the terror attacks of September 11, 2001, more than half of Americans believed that some civil liberties needed to be curbed as a defensive move, although the number of those favoring such sacrifices continues to fall as time goes on. Democrats are much more protective of civil liberties and oppose curbing civil rights, whereas fewer Republicans uphold these values and are more willing to see them curtailed for defensive reasons.[5]

We should remember that the United States created its innovative and unprecedented political institutions when the country was young and very small.[6] But it has exerted worldwide influence by encouraging the spread of democracy, advocating the free but regulated market, and endorsing the rule of law.[7] Other important innovations were also born in small peripheral countries: Sweden established a legal definition of press freedom in the eighteenth century and the office of ombudsman in the nineteenth century, while recent innovations in social security originated in Chile. However, the innovations in U.S. political culture extend beyond the Founders. The movements for universal education, for expansion of suffrage, for expanded citizens' rights, women's rights, racial equality, affirmative action, expansion of tertiary education and access to it have led to a reasonably open society. The Freedom of Information Act of 1966–67 mandated free access to a fairly wide spectrum of government information. Admittedly, none of these achievements occurred without a fight. They were usually the result of scandals, massive group pressures, or shifts in the moral and religious value systems of generations. America's roles in the creation of both the League of Nations, which it later deserted, and the United Nations were attempts to create global institutions for world peace. They also enlarged (albeit ambivalently) U.S. openness to the world. Yet at no time did the United States change its nationalist identity and its belief that its form of democracy was of universal validity. Nevertheless, we can refer to these extraordinary innovations in extending freedom of information as contributing to the systemic transparency of American society.

As an imperial power, the United States may begin to pursue realpolitik strategies and may build oligarchic power structures in the government. These are challenges to liberal, democratic values and institutions. Throughout the wars of the past century, and especially during the cold war, strategic considerations became more and more salient in U.S. foreign policy and culture. The McCarthy era was a high point of secrecy and oppressive paranoia. Sen. Joseph McCarthy used intimidation, deceit, and outright lies, often in secret proceedings, to establish that Communists had dangerous access to government agencies and strategic secrets. At the height of his demagoguery he had many followers, but he eventually generated widespread revulsion and ended in disgrace.

Wartime provides excuses for abuses of civil rights and restricting openness. The cold war was a period of special opportunities for hidden projects, strategic intelligence mistakes, and manipulation of developing countries to prevent their alliance with the Soviet Union. The secret intelligence apparatus became huge, and even the number of intelligence failures was enormous. The rules of secrecy are never effective guarantors of accuracy in the production of knowledge. The cold war was largely won through U.S. military dominance and political and economic appeal, but this victory also occurred because the Soviet Union was collapsing under the weight of its own internal contradictions. Stifling secrecy, dictatorial oppression of the citizenry, inefficient bureaucracy, a dysfunctional economy, ethnic conflicts, and the rise of globalization all also contributed to the Soviet empire's collapse.

Recent U.S. administrations have more or less consistently supported secrecy, except for the Clinton administration, which tried to limit it. The rise to power of the Republican party, and especially the influence of its right wing and the "neoconservatives," brought a devotion to government secrecy unparalleled in American history. The emphasis on executive privilege claimed not merely by the president, but for his cabinet and staff, was adopted early in the first George W. Bush administration, whose programmatic objectives can be inferred from its actions better than from its rhetoric. One goal is clearly and deliberately to increase economic inequality among U.S. citizens through enormous tax cuts for the very wealthy. The shrinking of government services and aid to the poor are further examples of such measures. There is also a belief that corporations need to be given new protections and powers, and that major government functions should be privatized. In foreign affairs, the initial posture of the administration was one of simple imperial nationalism, rejecting "nation building" and multilateralism, refusing to enter into international treaties wherever possible. However, it has become involved in global affairs not only by initiating a war on Iraq and declaring a war on terrorism, but also by the need to forge new international alliances. The internal contradictions and the nationalism of the Bush administration's stance have created complex policy dilemmas for the nation and the world.

The policies of the Bush administration have created strongly negative views of the United States in the vast majority of countries, with the exception of Israel. Even before the terror attacks of September 11, 2001, European nations were opposed to American unilateralism. In August 2001 Bush's international policy was disapproved by a plurality in Britain, Italy, Germany, and France. In 2003 the U.S. image abroad had further deteriorated, even though sympathy for the United States ran high for a while after the terror attacks. This was a striking change from 1999, when 83 percent of respondents in Britain, 62 percent in France, 78 percent in Germany, 76 percent in Italy, and 50 percent in Spain held favorable views of the United States. But this had changed by 2003 to 48 percent in Britain, 31 percent in France, 25 percent in Germany, 34 percent in Italy, and 14 percent in Spain.[8]

Actually, these divisions between the United States and Europe mirror the divisiveness in America itself. About half of the voting public roughly favors the national strategies of the government, and about half are critical. Unilateralism in general is not favored by a majority of Americans. Many are uncomfortable with the notion that their country is an imperialist power. A full 53 percent of Americans feel that the United States should participate in the International Criminal Court, as against 22 percent who oppose it, while the government fights fiercely against such participation. The Kyoto Protocol on measures to reduce global warming is favored by 44 percent, as against 22 percent who reject it. There is a battle of values being carried to the political arena.

Given these conditions, the tensions of informational ambivalence have become intense. The insistence on taking government decisions in secret, conducting clandestine investigations, and limiting civil rights is also a result of the cultural values that the ruling elite tries to imprint on the country as a whole: a desire to limit freedom of choice in life styles, to limit political dissent—in other words, to create an "illiberal democracy." As we have pointed out, these programmatic choices by the government parallel the desire of Republican party leaders to increase economic inequality in the United States, already the most economically unequal industrialized country in the world. A study of the effects of President Bush's tax cuts enacted in 2001 reveals that from 2001 to 2010, the top 1 percent of the richest Americans will receive annually $342,000 in tax reductions. This same 1 percent of the richest taxpayers will receive 52 percent of the total tax cuts.[9] Clearly, this policy is deliberately designed to increase the gap between rich and poor. The result could be a domestic shift from openness to governance by a plutocracy and a foreign policy based on radical power rather than on values.

Nationalism can be a tool for leaders with such an agenda. U.S. nationalism has actually increased at a time when much of Europe is moving toward transnational integration and supranational governance. Nationalism has something to do with the scope of accepted solidarities, as noted in chapter 3, where we discussed the discovery by the early sociologists that solidarities can take more than one form. The core EU nations are oriented to both transnational and national solidarities. This affects the mosaic of informa-

121

tion cultures in Europe, as we shall see later. America's special form of nationalism has a powerful impact on the information culture of the nation.

U.S. nationalism is radically different from the forms of nationalism that once prevailed in Europe and exists today in much of Asia. Minxin Pei writes about the "paradoxes of American nationalism" that cause the United States to misunderstand itself and the world. American nationalism cannot be based on ethnic and cultural homogeneity, he argues; after all, this is a country of immigrants and cannot pretend to ethnic superiority. In fact, Americans generally regard the kind of nationalism found in the Old World with disdain. Instead, their nationalism rests on pride in the democratic ideals the country stands for. Pei observes, "First, although the United States is highly nationalistic, it doesn't see itself as such. Second, despite this nationalistic fervor, U.S. policymakers generally fail to appreciate the power of nationalism abroad."[10]

Pei notes that Americans have the highest degree of pride in their nationality among all major Western democracies, while not conceiving of themselves as nationalists. They take it for granted that U.S. ideals are naturally universal and superior. Pei cites the Pew Global Attitudes survey, which reports that 79 percent of those polled agreed that "it is good that American ideas and customs are spreading around the world," and 70 percent said they like American ideas about democracy. Yet, Pei points out, these views are not widely shared, even in Western Europe. U.S. nationalism is part of U.S. social life, says Pei; it is not imposed by the state. Civic voluntarism is a source of pride in the community and in the nation, but it is voluntary. In fact, efforts to impose official nationalistic symbols and gestures by federal legislation have experienced stiff resistance, as seen in the failure, twice in eight years, to pass a constitutional amendment prohibiting burning of the U.S. flag. Americans share a political creed, but they do not recognize it as nationalism. Their nationalism is triumphant, forward-looking, not dwelling on grievances of the past. This leads U.S. policy makers to assume that other cultures should naturally want to build a democratic state following their own ideals. Such attitudes have three consequences for dealing with nationalism abroad: it creates resentment against the United States; insensitive policies abroad tend to backfire; and "finally, given the nationalism that animated U.S. policies, American behavior abroad inevitably appears hypocritical to others. This hypocrisy is especially glaring when the United States undermines global institutions in the name of defending American sovereignty (such as in the cases of the Kyoto Protocol, the International Criminal Court, and the Comprehensive Test Ban Treaty)." The inherent contradictions in U.S. attitudes and behavior are partly the result of the nation's relative isolation and most Americans' lack of interest in international events.

The revolution in information technology has added to the openness of U.S. society. Yet this very openness has become an instrument of surveillance. Although the Internet offered what seemed to be unlimited opportunities for communication and exploration, it is becoming more limited as commercial interests and legislative interventions alter its ground rules and impose more controls.[11] There is controversy about this change—the free spirits of the early era of the Internet are eager to preserve the openness. Limiting Internet access to business-owned sites to subscribers and customers who have to identify themselves and pay a fee is regarded as an encroachment. Yet the domain of noncommercial, free communication has not disappeared.

The Internet plays a special role in the military and in the communication networks of universities and research centers. After all, the United States has the world's largest concentration of scientific and technological enterprises. It is also a major home of social science, being among the countries that have incorporated social sciences methods and concepts into their institutions. This includes the measurements of the economy, polling public opinion, and the sophisticated use of data. Further, there is also an enormous expansion of data collected about people, communities, groups, and institutions. There is little opacity left in American social life. The nation has a very rich information culture characterized by considerable systemic transparency. The establishment of area-focused, domain-specific transparency regimes, like the one created by legislation mandating informed consent in health care, or the information disclosure regulations for financial reporting, auditing, and accounting in business, reach across U.S. society. They take different forms in different sectors, contributing to systemic transparency. However, even such a system of openness can have its failures.

The values underlying the transparency syndrome in the United States are based on a network of support organizations. Civil rights extend beyond the legal structures that embody them, but also depend on watchdog organizations such as the ACLU and the Leadership Conference on Civil Rights (LCCR). Interest groups and political parties take up civil rights issues. Watchdog organizations also oversee access to and disclosure of government information. The National Freedom of Information Coalition and the Society of Professional Journalists are examples. Official agencies charged with carrying out the terms of America's Freedom of Information Act (FOIA), are found in the Department of Justice and other federal departments. Privacy International (PI), a human rights group based in Britain dedicated to advocating privacy, free speech, and freedom of information, created a global assessment of freedom of information and access to government records.[12] The survey results were presented at the Freedom of Information Act Days in 2000, 2001, and 2002. The original FOIA in the United States was passed in 1966 and enlarged in 1996 by the Electronic Freedom of Information Act, which makes it possible to view government records in electronic form. The law provides for exceptions for Congress, the courts, the president's immediate presidential staff in the White House, and the National Security Council. In Banisar's words:

> In 2000, there were 2,235,201 FOIA requests made to federal agencies. The Act's utility, however, has been undermined by a lack of central oversight and in many state agencies, long delays in processing requests. In some instances, information is released only after years or decades. There have been setbacks in access to information since the election of President George W. Bush and the events of September 11, 2001. In October 2001, Attorney General John Ashcroft issued a memo stating that the Justice Department would defend in court any federal agency that withheld information on justifiable grounds. The Bush administration has also engaged in several high-profile attempts to prevent access to information about the secret meetings of the energy policy task force. Many federal Web sites were either closed or some of the information that they had was taken out.

Freedom of speech is avidly defended by newspapers and professional journalists, but other groups also rally to the cause, such as the National Freedom of Information Coalition, the Electronic Frontiers Foundation, and the American Library Association, among a host of others. Again, the ACLU and the Society of Professional Journalists play a role here. Freedom of speech is the dominant value of the American information value syndrome. There are of course infringements through intimidation, attempts to discredit certain views or ideas, and slanted reporting in the media, but the constitutional right to freedom of speech is defended in the courts. This is quite different from certain rules in major European states that prohibit speech advocating Nazi totalitarianism or racial hatred.

Another central value stresses the importance of accountability for governments, businesses, professions, schools, and universities. So-called sunshine laws require governments to hold some meetings in an open way. But accountability not only includes state institutions, but reaches into sectors of private activity in business, foundations, churches, groups such as volunteer firemen associations, wherever there is a legally or ethically determined responsibility for actions taken or not taken. Demands for reform toward greater transparency and accountability in corporate governance and in the accounting profession followed the revelation of extensive corporate fraud and their scandals at the turn of the twenty-first century. Demands for accountability are among the most potent drivers of transparency.

Privacy is a value that has caused heated debates and inspired legislation in the United States, as elsewhere in the world, although U.S. privacy rules are quite porous.[13] There is no reference to privacy in the U.S. Constitution, although the Supreme Court has interpreted some of the provisions of the Bill of Rights to grant constitutional protection for certain specific activities limiting some aspects of government surveillance. Meanwhile, the private sector has established large data bases of personal information against which the public is not protected. There is also no federal office providing oversight on privacy issues, and the Bush administration has decided that self-regulation of privacy is adequate.[14] Many disagree. New legislation was adopted in April 2003 to protect the privacy of medical information, a reform much demanded by the public. The Health Insurance Portability and Accountability Act of 1996 (HIPAA) included a mandate for medical privacy. Final HIPAA privacy rules were released in December 2000 by the secretary of health and human services and became effective in 2003. This is one of the major legal actions for privacy in one sector of American society.

The pervasive practice of using social security numbers as identifiers in many transactions, the ability of corporations to share private information with other firms or to sell these data calls into question the public's right to privacy. There is much political concern with matters of privacy. State governments have formulated their own approaches to the issue, and several legislative initiatives have been launched in Congress. Privacy International reports that since January 2001 well over 100 bills have been introduced in the House and Senate.[15] However, the protection of privacy in the United States remains fragmented and is strongly resisted by the business sector. As we will see, this is a sharp difference with the information cultures in European Union nations.

The concept of information property is based on the idea of ownership of tangible possessions such as goods or land. Ownership of intellectual and cultural artifacts is shielded by laws that protect information owners from the free public use of their property. Patents have been successfully used to encourage innovation and to provide the inventor with a period of time in which to reap rewards from a novel achievement. Copyright law has a simi-

125

lar purpose for intellectual and artistic creations. However, both of these legal protections of property can also be used for unintended purposes. David Brin points out that both patent and copyright law is undergoing great strain in the United States, a strain that is becoming more intense in this era of global transformations.[16]

Patent law can be used to foil innovations instead of promoting them, as in the practice of companies holding secret patents that can be used to deny the granting of a legitimate new patent to a real innovator for the purpose of blocking competition. Obviously, this and similar practices arouse contentious debate, especially since copyright law can be used to restrain access to information. Even broader problems worry David Brin:

> Intellectual Property (IP) law was originally meant to foster public disclosure and dissemination of new ideas, but one new trend pulls in the opposite direction. Trade secrets have been getting increased honor and protection, both under the U.S. Economic Espionage Act of 1996 and through the willingness of courts to grant major damage awards to plaintiffs in trade secret misappropriation cases. . . . But the trade secret strategy denies the public its quid pro quo of public disclosure in exchange for legal protection of the inventor's rights.[17]

On the whole, we can say that the U.S. legal system protects corporate intellectual property to such an extent that one can indeed speak of a phenomenon of "enclosure."

The partial commercialization of the Internet to establish an electronic market, whereby the customer can gain access to information only by paying a fee or to make a purchase, does restrict free access to information. The market strategies of firms engaged in this business rely heavily on a customer data base. Establishing norms to regulate the "enclosure" of information under the claim that it is private property is still an emerging process, capable of distortions. The globalization of these processes brings an even more complex context to the debates about intellectual property in America. In many parts of the world such concepts are not part of the cultural repertory, making piracy of copyrighted materials rampant in many developing countries.

Surveillance, the opposite of privacy, is often conducted in secret, mainly by the government. The enormous private data bases in the private sector are also like surveillance services, but with important differences, as Reg Whitaker explains in *The End of Privacy*. They rarely contain information gathered in secret investigations; they are collected from everyday transactions, such as credit card purchases. Second, whereas secret dossiers are jealously guarded and rarely shared, "Data base operators, on the other hand, tend to regard their data as a commodity that can and should be sold."[18] Third, security intelligence and secret dossiers are controlled by highly centralized structures, whereas private data bases conduct what Whitaker calls "dataveillance," the creation of composite surveillance profiles by digitally tapping into multiple data bases. He concludes that "data bases, despite their dispersed and decentralized structure, form a more or less unified functional system."[19] There are public surveillance processes, especially in the field of public health. Public registers for infectious diseases in the case of epidemics is a form of transparency.

After the terror attacks of September 11, 2001, the United States declared a war on terrorism. Much has changed since then, as has the overall global strategy of the Bush administration. The impact of these changes on the transparency/secrecy syndrome has been significant. The Patriot Act enlarged the powers of the federal government over immigration, requiring the registration of students from abroad, enabling the government to hold "enemy aliens," as well as—under certain circumstances—American citizens on a secret basis, and expanding the governmental effort at surveillance under a Department of Homeland Security. This department links the different intelligence agencies and the FBI, sharing information and supplementing each other's surveillance. Further changes in the oversight of intelligence are recommended.

The war on Iraq intensified the importance of secrecy. The strategy of preemptive military intervention directed at whatever "rogue states" that might attack the United States or support terrorists was a virtual declaration that the United States was the world's only sovereign nation. Paradoxically, while this strategy was the culmination of the president's unilateralist policy of withdrawing from many global treaties, starting with the Kyoto Protocol, the strategy of defenses against terrorism forced the United States to become heavily involved in many global affairs. The administration had earlier announced its criticisms of existing security frameworks, the UN, and "nation building," causing wide distrust of the administration's intentions on a large, global scale. Yet today the United States is committed to an extensive global military presence well beyond Iraq, without advancing the progress of global governance or improving the normative framework that makes global security possible.

The Bush administration envisions an extensive surveillance system to defend against terrorism. The terms of this project seem to disregard the rights of privacy and to limit civil rights in ways not very different from other security measures adopted in wartime as temporary emergency measures. Many Americans support increasing the government's ability to track down terrorist plots. However, technology enables the government to implement surveillance programs of a scope and depth that have never been seen before. The administration's insistence on secret decision making as well as risk assessments will likely raise public concern. Yet the political process on these issues has barely begun in earnest. The enactment of the Patriot Act, soon to be followed by Patriot II has raised alarm about the excessive expansion of government powers and secrecy. Organizations such as the ACLU and political leaders are mobilizing defenses against the apparent plan to create a permanent surveillance society run secretly by the federal government. Privacy and transparency remain important values in America. In March 2003 the *Economist* wrote: "America has jumped too far in one direction. A reassessment is called for, if it wants to avoid rude comparisons with South Africa four decades since."[20]

Information Cultures of the European Union

The steps toward European integration began after World War II to establish permanent peace in Europe. The EU came into being with a treaty signed in Maastricht on February 7, 1992, making it the most successful political innovation of the twentieth century, a community of nations with certain forms of supranational authority. It has made war among the member nations of Western Europe impossible. It has brought nations of very different cultures together in one encompassing and yet limited polity. Therefore, it is best to speak of the European Union's information cultures in the plural, with two levels: the supranational level of the EU itself and the level of the member states. The enlargement of the EU not only creates a bigger polity, but also brings in eastern European nations that had lived through a history quite different from that of the West under the authoritarian oppression of the Soviet empire.

Despite a history of almost incessant warfare over recent centuries, the concept of a united Europe such as existed in the days of Charlemagne and the Holy Roman Empire was always lurking in the background. Heinrich Schneider has studied the guiding images for European politics, beginning with the very early roots of Europe's reflections on itself, as a background for the strategies that led to the creation of the European Union. Schneider's concept, which he terms a *Leitbild,* is difficult to translate. A *Leitbild* is more than a "guiding image," it is both a vision and an image of a strategy to be realized, a combination of interests and ideas, a strategic model.[21]

Visions of European unity appeared in the Enlightenment. Henri de Saint-Simon, a pioneer in sociology who wrote about the industrial era, was convinced that the countries of Europe would eventually discover how useless national interests were. In his account of the reorganization of Europe in 1814, he concluded that the emergence of industrial civilization would transcend narrow national interests, since they would be recognized as costly and irrational. The Enlightenment also produced other efforts to overcome the European nation-state system. In 1867 Garibaldi and Victor Hugo helped to found the International Peace and Freedom League, which advocated the creation of a United States of Europe.[22] These ideas laid the groundwork for imagining possible futures for Europe, but they were not enough to realize them. Saint-Simon articulated the strategic model of industrial economics for European integration, while Garibaldi and Victor Hugo stressed the strategic model of the need to overcome wars in Europe. These became the major strategic models for the European integration that finally occurred.

Movements for uniting Europe became much more substantial after World War I, when serious political efforts were made to achieve some form of European integration. The advantages of European federalism were articulated by scholars in France and Italy. Schneider quotes *Paneuropa* (1923), by Count Richard Nikolaus Coudenhove-Kalergi, a passionate call to action. Its opening sentence reads: "This book is intended to awaken a great movement that slumbers in all the peoples of Europe."[23] His theses resonated. Coudenhove-Kalergi founded the Pan-Europa movement in 1924 and remained its president until his death in 1972. His vision included all of Europe, but excluded Russia and Turkey. The idea was accepted by representatives of industry and finance, who founded the Association for the Union of the European Economy. In 1925 the German Social Democratic party adopted a program that called for European economic unity and the creation of the United States of Europe.[24]

Coudenhove-Kalergi, an Austrian aristocrat, first envisioned a united Europe during the catastrophe of World War I. In the 1930s his movement was denounced by right-wing nationalists as a plot of "plutocratic capitalism."[25] When the Nazi regime came to power, the Pan-Europa movement was outlawed. In 1938 Coudenhove-Kalergi fled to Switzerland, then to the United States. He returned to Austria after World War II and in 1947 became the secretary-general of the European Parliamentarians Union, in which capacity he discussed his Pan-Europa ideas with many leaders, including Winston Churchill. Coudenhove-Kalergi's and Churchill's conceptions of

Europe's future differed from the ideas that became the source of European federalism, and these differences remain in the current EU structure. Both Churchill and Coudenhove-Kalergi had their roots in old, monarchical empires; Churchill remained a champion of the British Empire and saw a special role for Great Britain in the emerging global constellations. He believed in the strategic global importance of three large circles of noncommunist states: the British Empire, the English-speaking world (including the United States), and a united Europe.[26] In Coudenhove-Kalergi's later years, his Pan-Europa Union became an exclusive, conservative-Catholic elite, and his successor was Otto von Habsburg.

The vision of European federalism was embraced by antifascist and anticommunist dissidents during the war, and early discussions of the idea of a federal Europe committed to human rights, liberty, and the rule of democracy and law, occurred in concentration camps. Many European intellectuals, persecuted both by Nazis and by Communists, formulated the idea of Europe as a value-based community. "Never again!" for them was not just a pacifist slogan, but also a call to create a civilized, humane, and just social order. They were convinced that the nation-state had lost its legitimacy through the disasters of nationalism, war, and genocide. Frank Niess writes, "The virtual uniformity with which the European idea arose in the political thought of the resistance groups is striking. It emerged in the countries occupied by Germany like the Netherlands, Poland, Belgium, France or Norway about simultaneously."[27] There was very little communication among these groups, except possibly some contacts to the Swiss organization Europa Union and the secret Resistance newspapers. The same ideas were created almost simultaneously all over Europe.

Another call for a united Europe was the Ventotene Manifesto issued by the Italian antifascists led by Altiero Spinelli. As an advocate of a European constitution, Spinelli later served in the European Parliament. The three Polish parties in the Resistance agreed as early as 1941 that the Polish republic of the future was to be a "member of the Federation of Free European Peoples." The Dutch Resistance paper *Het Parool* spoke of a European directorate or European federation in 1942. Helmuth von Moltke, founder of the German Resistance group Kreisauer Kreise, in 1941 envisioned a future in which peace would bring European sovereignty, "at least in fields like customs borders, currency, foreign affairs, including the armed forces, [and] constitutional legislation. . . . The highest legislative body of the European state will be accountable to the single citizen, not to the self-governing bodies." Finally, the Buchenwald Manifesto of 1945, endorsed by fifty prisoners of democratic socialist (noncommunist) persuasion from several European countries, called for the annihilation of all kinds of nationalism and militarism and the creation of a new community of states, to build European peace: "We don't want any more wars. We will do everything to make another war impossible."[28] The proponents of these ideas created the Union of European Federalists (UEF) and its youthful vanguard, the Young European Federalists, known by their French acronym, JEF.

The democratic, federalist, human rights values of these movements had an important impact on the ideas of European unity. However, the leaders of the major European nations desired a community of nation-states for more pragmatic reasons. Winston Churchill and political figures in France, Germany, Belgium, Luxembourg, the Netherlands, and Italy adopted it vigorously. The British approach was always a statist one. The step-by-step construction of a new community of European states would build the new institutions of what became the European Union. The tension between transparency and secrecy is one aspect of the divergent strategic visions of the federalists and the statists in the construction of a united Europe.

The institutional history of the European Union was at its inception dominated by Robert Schumann and Konrad Adenauer in the 1950s, who established the framework for the emerging community. The first step was to create the European Coal and Steel Authority. The treaty establishing it was signed in 1951 in Paris and it lasted half a century, ending in 2002. It was a strategically decisive step, but a modest one, since it was limited to only two industries. Yet it put the integration of Europe on the path of treaty law. It was a matter of importance that a "high authority" over coal and steel production transcended international rules among countries. Treaties that were incorporated into the laws of member nations helped to create the European communities (the European Economic Community and the European Atomic Energy Community were established in 1957 by the Treaty of Rome) and later the European Union. Many further treaties were concluded that expanded the scope and the policy areas of the European institutions.

The Treaty on European Union was signed at Maastricht in 1992 and took effect in 1993. It added a political dimension to the union among the member states by subsuming the European communities under the European Union and enlarging the domains of cooperation. Among other things, this treaty established the office of ombudsman—a major step toward transparency, since the ombudsman plays an active role in opening up the flow of EU information. The current ombudsman, Nikiforos Diamandouros, observed in 2003,

Since the mid-seventies we have the third wave of democratization; there is an expansion of democratic regimes worldwide. There is much to be done about the quality of democracy. To citizens, "accountability" is the means to better "quality" of democracy. Accountability must take many forms: some are vertical like elections—voters pass judgment on elected officials periodically, but this suffers from periodicity. There are horizontal mechanisms that are capable of checking accountability on a day-to-day basis, such as regulatory agencies such as the U.S. Interstate Commerce Commission, or central banks, auditing systems, electoral commissions; in postauthoritarian regimes there are truth commissions. The office of the ombudsman is part of the new arsenal of accountability and improvement in the quality of democracy.[29]

The European Union made an important step by establishing the position and the powers of its ombudsman, even though his mandate is limited to EU institutions.

A further step beyond Maastricht was the Treaty of Amsterdam, signed in 1997 and entered into force in 1999. This treaty included the concepts of fundamental rights and reaffirmed the establishment of citizenship in the EU (already adopted at Maastricht), and set out frameworks for employment, social policy, environmental policies, public health, consumer protection, and transparency. It is clear that creating the legal structure of the union and its institutions by relying on treaties has been successful this far. It has built a large, differentiated, formidable, and confusing structure. However, while the structure of the Treaty of Amsterdam was both more expansive and ambitious, it was also more complex than the Maastricht agreement. Many worried about the relationships among EU institutions, the member states, and the citizens. The complexity of EU institutions created an infamous "comitology" that made it virtually impossible to determine who was responsible for a particular decision.[30]

The "democracy deficit" in the European Union became an issue of debate. Governance in a supranational dimension required new approaches. The idea of a "democracy deficit" reflected the problem that the institutions of the union did not resemble those of established national democracies. Many Europeans believed that the EU governed without the openness that democratic governance requires. To deal with this issue, the European Commission embarked on efforts to overcome this reproach. It commissioned a White Paper on European Governance that relied heavily on the principles of transparency, subsidiarity (analogous to states' rights), citizen participation in the development of policies, consultations with civil society, and accountability for all levels of governance. The White Paper received much attention, but it was eventually considered inadequate to the serious challenges that had arisen. Nevertheless, it illuminated the struggle between those who wished to maintain secrecy and those who sought transparency. How is one to overcome a "democracy deficit" in a supranational as well as transnational authority that is governed by a Council of Ministers from the member states? How is one to create a democracy that extends beyond the boundaries of democratic nations? The initial answer was: transparency.

The White Paper on European Governance was very much a project of Romano Prodi's commission that followed the famous scandal of the Santer Commission in 1999, when a whistle blower had brought to light serious abuses by members of the commission. Some of the charges were serious, and they caused the collective resignation of the whole commission. The European Court of Auditors and a special Commission of Independent Experts investigated and decided on a policy of transparency in that matter.[31] According to Deirdre Curtin, the first report of the investigating committee in March 1999 "publicly lanced the boils of secrecy and of lack of [collective] responsibility of the Commission as a whole. A secretive administrative culture is the single and predominant reason given by Paul van Buitenen, the whistleblower, . . . to explain why the events in question could happen and how those facts became submerged in what at times amounted to a virtual conspiracy of silence."[32]

The policy of the Prodi Commission became an effort to improve European governance, transparency, and accountability. The work took some time and the White Paper went through several drafts. In the final version, there was less emphasis on specifics. Nevertheless, it said that there was disenchantment with governance in Europe at all levels. This sense of alienation "is not confined to the European institutions. It affects politics and political constitutions around the globe. But for the Union, it reflects particular tensions and uncertainty about what the Union is and what it aspires to become, about its geographical boundaries, its political objectives and the way these powers are shared with the Member States."[33] The White Paper called for comprehensive reform of the way Europe is to be governed at all levels, including the European institutions, the member states, the communities, and not least, civil society. It was initiated by Jerome Vignon and conceived as an important and effective strategy for dramatically improving governance in Europe. According to the commission, there were five principles of good governance: openness, participation, accountability, effectiveness, and coherence. In the early drafts of the White Paper in 2001, the main emphasis was on transparency as such.[34] The final version continued this general idea and specified it in these five principles, seen as equally important for the European institutions and all levels of authority in the member states. These new principles reinforced the principles of proportionality and subsidiarity, weighing whether public action was really necessary for a particular initiative, and whether the European level was really the appropriate one.

The White Paper presented several proposals for change. Almost all of them focused on communication and cooperation, on transparency and accountability, at all levels of governance in the union. For example, one was to expand the functions of the EU's Europa Web site.[35] The White Paper announced a plan to evolve this Web site "into an inter-active platform for information, feedback and debate, linking parallel networks across the Union"[36] Other recommendations were greater involvement of the public in policy shaping, greater flexibility, and overall policy coherence through greater transparency and consultation. Attention was given to the global role of the EU as well, albeit in very general terms. The final chapter, "From Governance to the Future of Europe," anticipates the need for a continuing debate about the functioning of the EU. This debate started very quickly, and in many ways it was not exactly what the creators of the White Paper had hoped for.

In March 2002, Statewatch, an NGO that monitors civil liberties in the EU, published its comments on the commission's *White Paper on Governance*.[37] Statewatch was clearly very unhappy with the document. Many paragraphs open with "It is unfortunate that . . ." For example, "It is unfortunate that the Council has not established a similar reflection upon the accountability, transparency and legitimacy of its work, particularly given the Council's role as a legislative body and its increasing executive powers." The list of criticisms is a long one, particularly that transparency had been reduced, especially in access to documents.

The White Paper was issued in the hope of initiating a major public debate in Europe about the future of the European Union and its policies, and it elicited much criticism. Indeed, the White Paper may have triggered a deeper debate than the commission intended. Christian Jörges writes:

> The White Paper project that the Commission launched with a view to developing prospects of democratically reformed "European Governance" nourished hopes and met with reservations. The skeptics called the practical utility of the whole undertaking into question. They saw their views confirmed when, on 26

February 2001, the Treaty of Nice produced a result that made follow-up conferences not just seem inevitable, but absolutely necessary. . . . Now that the Irish referendum has unleashed its own confusion, the White Paper, finally published on 25 July 2001, may once again reckon on greater attention. . . . Was Romano Prodi, then, well advised to give such a high priority to programmatic renewal of the practices of European governance? Is it even appropriate to bring in historical references and recall Prussia's position in the early nineteenth century, when brilliant, energetic reformers sought, through a "constitution of government," to smooth the path toward an overall constitution?[38]

Jörges ends with a historical analogy: "Those Prussian reformers who, with the help of administrative reforms, wished to meet the demands for a genuine constitution and/or prove it superfluous, were unable to tranquilize their contemporaries, and, instead, paved the way to the revolution of 1848. Prussia's reformers did not have that on their banners, yet it was a good thing for Germany, as we know today."[39] Jörges hinted that maybe a constitutional effort might be the unintended follow-up to the White Paper. Indeed, the episode was followed by the establishment of the convention to prepare a constitution for the European Union.

The member states and their council had concluded that more needed to be done to prepare the Union for the future. The 2001 Treaty of Nice was an early response, also generally considered to be inadequate. It tackled multiple challenges. The negotiations about that treaty in 2001 revealed disagreements and worries among the governments of the member states, especially about the impending enlargement of the EU by adding new states from eastern Europe and the need for new approaches in governing the EU.

The Treaty of Nice, entered into force in February 2003, tried to revise the structure of the EU institutions when the number of members reached twenty-seven. This included notably reviewing rules for the commission on governance and for the European Court of Justice. The commission would no longer have one member from each country, but there would be a rotational system, on the following basis:

1. The Members of the Commission shall be chosen on the grounds of their general competence and their independence shall be beyond doubt. The number of Members of the Commission shall be less than the number of Member States. The Members of the Commission shall be chosen according to a rotation system based on the principle of equality, the implementing arrangements for which shall be adopted by the Council, acting unanimously. The number of Members of the Commission shall be set by the Council, acting unanimously.[40]

Clearly, the principle of unanimity among the member states and the culture of secrecy among them could produce deadlocks and would not be adequate to the challenge of governing the EU with so many members. (In 2004 there were twenty-five member states.) This constellation led to the decision to create a constitutional convention, with great aspirations for success.

The role of the European Union as a constitutional body would be different from its past role, explained Jean-Luc Dehaene, former prime minister of Belgium and member of the constitutional convention presidium. "Political union was always the strongest aspiration of European integration. We must solve this in the convention. . . . The ambition should be at the international level. Europe should speak with one voice." Dehaene stated his "hope that one day the EU will have a seat on the Security Council. We will have to reorganize the Security Council. Europe should be stronger, with one voice and one seat; that is the direction to go." He emphasized that "the convention should organize greater transparency on Europe. Also it needs to make understandable to people what the EU is. Now there is a strongly integrated Europe for internal matters and for the third pillar [of internal security]. We need to have a common position and speak with one voice on external relations, security, policing, and defense." He continued: "We need to have one person, institution, responsible for all, to act as president." He also expressed serious concern about the policies of the United States and sharply disagreed with U.S. unilateralism.[41]

Dehaene's hopes were not quite realized as he expected. In September 2004, when asked about the outlook for the EU constitution, he said, "The intergovernmental council did not change the essence of our draft. This went beyond my expectations. The whole challenge is now: will the constitution be ratified by twenty-five member states? It is difficult to say. We must avoid discussion as to what can be done if some do not ratify. There is no plan B!" Other EU officials emphasize the finality of the draft constitution.

The European Union has to deal with several historic challenges. One is the expansion of the EU through the accession of the new member states. It was viewed as an enormous achievement, but by now a sober mood has taken over. Economic problems and issues of effective governance inevitably will create disappointments as well as successes. The second challenge is the constitution and its approval by the members' parliaments or referenda. As Dehaene said, Brussels is trying to avoid the exploration of alternatives. Yet, the debates are spreading among the European citizenry. In fact, up to now, EU politics were managed by the governments with little citizen participation or interest. This has now changed, and citizen participation, writings by prominent intellectuals and politicians, reveal vigorous debates about the future of the EU, much of it focusing on governance. The third issue is the debate about the accession of Turkey, which EU negotiators appear to assume is necessary. However, this issue also has aroused the interest and concerns of citizens. Finally, a fourth challenge is the spreading sentiment in all of Europe that American unilateralism must be rejected. This is emerging as a unifying theme in Europe, even in countries that had joined the U.S. war in Iraq. These intersecting themes are likely to create a period of debates and political turbulence for at least the next decade. The general direction seems to be toward a greater strength for Europe, but it is not clear what that might mean.

The work of the constitutional convention will inevitably be affected by the world situation. The European Union evolved in an era when momentous events were transforming the world political structure. The end of the cold war, the disintegration of the Soviet Union, the reunification of Germany, and the desire of eastern and southern European nations to join the union produced extraordinary changes. The polarization of the cold war had disappeared, and an entirely new configuration of great fluidity emerged. The European Union had come into being in a peaceful era, under the military protection of the United States. It had engaged itself extensively in foreign aid and in development policies and financing to combat extreme inequalities and poverty in the developing countries. However, the EU was not able to define an international strategic role for itself in global politics.

Many observers saw that the EU had a problematic inward perspective. To be sure, the challenges facing it were enormous, but there was a tendency to take European peace for granted, even in an era of global turbulence. There was no articulated EU policy regarding global transformations. The rise of the George W. Bush administration and its new security strategy of preemptive military strikes was accompanied by the systematic dismantling of the global institutional structure that previous administrations had helped to build. Beginning with the rejection of U.S. participation in the Kyoto Protocol on environmental protection, and ending with the withdrawal from the treaty on the International Criminal Court (and the policy to strong-arm individual nations to enter into bilateral treaties exempting Americans from its jurisdiction), the Bush administration made it obvious that it intended to rely on U.S. military power, not on building transnational institutions. The Europeans were aghast and deeply shocked by these developments. Treaties, after all, had been the instruments for the successful achievement of peace in the European Union. The dismantling of transnational treaties by the

United States was widely perceived as a step backwards into a world of anarchic nationalism and Hobbesian "war of all against all." This was the opposite of what EU citizens had lived in and generally took for granted: a supranational, normative order. The enormous shock of the terrorist attacks of September 11, 2001, reinforced the realpolitik and secrecy strategies of the administration that in turn profoundly alienated the majority of the citizens in the EU.

Reactions by the formerly communist nations of eastern Europe, the aspirants for EU enlargement, were very different. They had experienced the brutal oppression by the Soviet Union during the cold war. Many in these countries still continued to view Russia as a threat to their security. The enlargement of NATO was not much debated in the EU, but it became a symbol of liberation in the East European countries that were accepted in the alliance. On the whole, attitudes in these countries were much more supportive of the U.S. stance than in the western member states of the EU.

This all came to a head during the final months of the EU constitutional convention in debates about the war against Iraq. The arrogance of U.S. policy makers in negotiating with its allies, assuming that in the end they would follow their lead created enormous resentment in Europe and a backlash against the Bush administration. This was also the popular attitude toward European governments that had allied themselves with the United States. Anti-American feelings were especially strong in Britain and Spain. However, Polish sentiments favored the United States because of America's role in the cold war and the collapse of the Soviet Union, their oppressor. By contrast, the governments of France and Germany resisted U.S. pressure, infuriating the U.S. government and many in the American populace. These developments have put a great strain on relations between the EU and the United States and on the relations among the EU member states. France and Germany strengthened their own alliance, but their relationship with Britain became brittle, at the least. These issues influence the value syndromes toward transparency and secrecy in all these countries, and in the EU to some extent.

The final outcome of the negotiations over the European constitution is still unknown. By 2004 it was clear that the most difficult decisions were those concerning governance, especially for Spain and Poland, which demanded equal standing with the much larger nations. There will be more maneuvering, as the commission continues to struggle with a very cumbersome governance structure, albeit with vastly more commissioners. Remember that the U.S. Constitution had to make difficult compromises regarding the relative power of the northern and southern states. Without the "three-fifths clause" and other compromises, the Constitution would not have been approved. The European constitution, of course, is necessarily very different. It is to be a constitution for a union of culturally very different states, with national histories that go back for centuries. The necessary process will take a long time. The tension about President Bush's strategies based on U.S. nationalism continues to rise in Europe. There is also a sense that the EU has become a great power in the world, in both economic and "soft political power." The future, however, is uncertain.

The information cultures of the EU institutions are shaped by the basic value commitments of the organization and by European history. The fundamental values are democracy and the rule of law. The EU is a novel political institution, neither a state in its own right, nor an international organization. Its member states delegate sovereignty to it, establishing in part a supranational form of governance, while in other respects using intergovernmental approaches. As we have pointed out, EU law is entirely based on the ratified treaties among its member states.[42] The EU has always held human rights to be the basis of its values. Its Charter of Fundamental Rights is not part of EU law but is a statement to be respected by its institutions, subject to the principle of subsidiarity. There are exceptions in case of national law provisions. Yet the charter is treated as a fundamental statement of principles and has become part of the draft treaty establishing a constitution agreed by the European Council on June 18, 2004 (with some changes). The original charter states:

> The peoples of Europe, in creating an ever closer union among them, are resolved to share a peaceful future based on common values. Conscious of its spiritual and historical heritage, the Union is founded on the indivisible, universal values of human dignity, freedom, equality and solidarity; it is based on the principles of democracy and the rule of law. It places the individual at the heart of its activities, by establishing the citizenship of the Union, and by creating an area of freedom, security and justice.[43]

The list of freedoms includes the right to liberty and security; respect for private and family life; the protection of personal data; the right to marry and to found a family; freedom of thought, conscience, and religion; freedom of expression and information; freedom of assembly and association; freedom of the arts and sciences; the right to education; freedom to choose an occupation and the right to engage in work; freedom to conduct a business; the right to property; the right to asylum; and finally, protection in the event of expulsion, removal, or extradition.

This is a remarkable statement, quite different from the liberties outlined in the U.S. Constitution, even though an inherent democratic kinship is clear. The charter is certainly a democratic document and yet it has a very distinct profile. It gives privacy a privileged place. It does explicitly deal with freedom of expression and information, and with the securities that were so often lost in European history: the right to property, asylum, and protection from expulsion, removal, and extradition. The document expands the rights of citizens into social rights to work, to conduct a business, to receive an education, and to own property. Nevertheless, making this document into law will require extensive further debate. Specific rights, for example, the rights to work and to run a business, are more generalized hopes than legally binding entitlements.

The information cultures in the major EU institutions are partly shaped by these general values and by the historical legacy of government secrecy. They are further influenced by democratic demands for freedom of information, as well as by economic and broad cultural demands for transparency. Some of these issues were articulated in our discussion of the White Paper on European Governance. The Council of the Member States and the commission carry on the tradition of secrecy probably more vigilantly than any other EU institutions. Tony Bunyan of Statewatch has described the struggle for freedom of information and transparency in the EU over the last ten years. In December 1993, he reports, the EU's major initiative toward freedom of information was its code of access to EU documents. At that time, both the Council of Ministers and the commission wanted to control the documents to be released. "At the heart of the issue was whether citizens could have access to the documents in the policy-making process before the final decision was adopted. Governments and the Commission wanted to keep under wraps all documents until a new policy was in place—except for selective leaks to 'friendly' media outlets."[44] Many civil society groups mobilized and argued that the European Union needed "true openness, that is, full freedom of information."[45] A strong network of support developed over these issues. In 1997 the Treaty of Amsterdam included the right of access to documents in Article 255. Nevertheless, it remained controversial when it came to the specifics of implementing this right. This is not surprising, given the enormous differences in information cultures among the member states. When Sweden joined the EU in 1995, it made a strong commitment to continuing its tradition of freedom of information. The Swedish government attached a declaration to its agreement to join the EU that "access to official documents, and the protection of journalists' sources, 'remain fundamental principles . . . of Sweden's constitutional, political and cultural heritage.' With a taste of problems to come, the existing member states countered this 'unilateral' declaration, with their own, noting that they 'take it for granted that . . . Sweden will fully comply with Community law in this respect."[46] A bitter legal battle ensued. When the Swedish Union of Journalists applied under Swedish legislation for documents relating to the Europol convention, most were released by the Swedish government. However, when the journalists applied to Brussels, most of these documents were refused. The journalists took the issue to the European Court of Justice, to the consternation of the EU. In the council's view, the Swedish release of documents was a breach of community law, since no council decision had authorized such a disclosure. The defense of the council was posted by investigative Swedish journalists on the Internet, further enraging members of the council. This episode illustrates the ambivalence about freedom of information in the EU.

The struggle for freedom of information has made considerable progress in the last decade. Tony Bunyan writes:

> "Democracy" and "democratic standards" are not static, they are ever-changing. Governments and Ministers may or may not be open and transparent and often seek to control what is released and when it is released. Democracy cannot, and should not, rely on them to maintain a democratic culture; rather it is sustained by lively parliaments and an ever vigilant and critical civil society. The fight for freedom of information in the EU and against secrecy is a small, but indispensable, contribution to this process.[47]

Nevertheless, the EU does have considerable systemic transparency, roughly analogous to that of the United States. However, there are areas of resistance to transparency on both sides. In the United States the expansion of secrecy is of relatively recent growth. In the European Union the transparency syndrome is a very recent development, struggling against the gatekeepers of secrecy in European governments, and therefore also in the major EU institutions, especially the Council of Ministers.

Freedom of information in the form of access to government documents is increasing in the EU, but such freedom remains controversial in some EU institutions and certainly in many of the member states, except for Scandinavia. The specialized forms of transparency such as informed consent in the health professions and information disclosures by businesses contribute to the relatively high transparency in the EU. Freedom of speech is a well-established legal norm in all the EU states, but with some differences from the U.S. conception. In Germany, hate speech and advocacy of racism and Nazism are illegal. Similarly, in Britain there are limitations to freedom of speech when the acts in question infringe upon the civil rights of others. Britain and the United States hold two different views of civil liberties. The ACLU is unconditionally committed to the individual right to unfettered free speech. The organization must provide advice even to those who clearly wish to deny the civil rights of others. This policy was applied in 1977–78 when the ACLU was asked for advice by Frank Collin, head of the National Socialist party, about a demonstration he was planning in Skokie, Illinois. His party advocated the forcible deportation of Jews, Latinos, and other minorities from the United States. When Skokie village denied a permit for the demonstration, the ACLU claimed that this was unconstitutional, and the Federal Court of Appeals upheld this position in 1978.

The National Council for Civil Liberties in England and Wales (NCCL) encountered a somewhat similar situation, but after a period of debate reacted in a very different way. In 1984 they provided advice to the National Front (a British neo-Nazi organization). There had been police actions against members of the National Front to which the NCCL would have objected if directed against anyone else. A vigorous debate followed. The annual general meeting of the NCCL changed the policy. It prohibited giving advice to a person or organization whose known objectives were to deny the basic rights of others. There was no doubt that the National Front was such an organization. The NCCL had arrived at a position diametrically opposed to the view adopted by the ACLU. Their argument was the following:

> While acknowledging the civil liberties of all, it would seem inappropriate for this Council to provide aid of any kind to an organization or individual whose publicly stated objectives include the removal of civil liberties from a large section of society and a substantial portion of the membership of this Council. The AGM believes that the provision of such aid could ultimately help bring about the denial of rights to others.[48]

The importance of accountability was a prominent feature of the European Union's White Paper on Governance. It also plays a prominent role in the member states and in many sectors of European society, especially in improving governance and the quality of business or professional services. This value is often cited in relation to financial responsibility, government performance, and education. Accountability, the main tool in many efforts at reform, is of course closely tied to evaluation and to transparency.

In the European Union, privacy is the single most discussed value within the transparency syndrome. Privacy legislation is most prominent in the protection of data. The European Union Directives on Data Protection have evolved since 1995 on the basis of legislation in several states dating from 1970. In 2002 the Council of the European Union adopted the new Electronic Communications Privacy Directive, enabling member states to pass laws mandating the retention of the traffic and location data of all communications by mobile phones and other devices. According to Privacy International, "Such requirements can be implemented for purposes varying from national security to the preventing, investigation and prosecution of criminal offences." At the same time, the directive added new protections to the right of privacy, including protection from precise location tracking and surveillance of mobile phone users.[49] Most important, the directive requires all European Union countries to enforce privacy rights and protection of data. The United States does not have such a system, but relies on voluntary privacy rules adopted by corporations. This has led to difficult negotiations. "The United States lobbied the European Union and its member countries to find the United States system adequate. In 1998, the United States began negotiating a 'Safe Harbor' agreement with the European Union in order to ensure the continued transborder flows of personal data."[50] Of course, the terrorist assault of September 11, 2001, caused further complexities in assessing the balance between privacy and security. The debate across the Atlantic continues.

There is also a European interest in expanded surveillance to prevent acts of terrorism. However, the extent of surveillance is much disputed.[51] It is seen as an infringement of privacy and civil liberties and is regarded with suspicion by civil rights organizations, as is secrecy. However, government secrecy has remained an accepted pattern for a long time. Corporate and professional secrecy have always been part of European information culture, especially in totalitarian states and during the world wars. The felt need by the EU institutions, especially the commission, to enhance their legitimacy through transparency, led to serious debates. Step by step, often with the energetic help from the EU ombudsman and with tireless prodding by civil society organizations like Statewatch, openness and access to information have increased in the EU. However, as in the United States, the demand for secrecy and the struggle for transparency have both intensified in the era of terrorism. The high value given in the EU to privacy, especially regarding personal data, is not shared by the United States, causing strained relations over surveillance and information sharing. Yet in this era the EU and its member states are becoming intensely aware of dangerous conditions in the world at large, so they have adopted compromises with the United States.

The EU nations represent a diversity of information cultures. In dealing with U.S. information culture, we have, for simplicity's sake, presented a unitary picture. Of course, this is a gross simplification. The information cultures of Vermont or Minnesota, on one side, and Texas or Louisiana, on the other, are very different, even though all are parts of a fairly tight federal system. Such generalizations cannot be applied to the European Union. The diversity of national cultures is too great to be ignored. To illustrate this diversity, we will focus on Sweden and Greece. The EU embraces nations of great cultural and regional differences and is about to become even more diverse through its enlargement toward the east and south.

Sweden

We have already identified Sweden as a pioneer in incorporating transparency in its culture as early as the eighteenth century. For other EU countries like Greece, the idea of openness of government information is a radical innovation that came about only in the 1980s and 1990s. The differences are huge, and the harmonization required by EU directives, its charter, and its treaty laws make for difficult changes in some countries that will cause resistance or at least delay. For example, Sweden joined the EU in 1995, but whether it will adopt the euro currency is still undecided. It has a long cultural tradition of openness and democracy. Since becoming a member of the EU, Sweden has lent its cultural influence in favor of more transparent policies and rules in Europe. Its commitment to freedom of information includes the right of free access to government-held information. Its Freedom of the Press Act of 1766 was the first law in the world requiring freedom of information in rather broad terms. This act is now a part of the constitution.

There are, to be sure, limits. Secrecy is also respected. Jan O. Karlsson observed in March 2001 that Sweden draws sharp boundaries between openness and secrecy. "Yes, we have secrets in Sweden," he said, "and the boundaries of secrecy and openness are clearly defined." He pointed out that at the European Court of Auditors, of which he is president, "the boundary between what is secret and what was public is well known."[52] Secrecy in Sweden is recognized as a legitimate value—under certain sharply defined circumstances. Appeals against denials of requested government information can be filed in a judicial system, an ultimate appeals ruling to be made if necessary by the Supreme Administrative Court as the highest authority.[53]

Privacy is also an important factor in the Swedish transparency/secrecy syndrome. The constitution and laws had long protected personal information, but in 1998 Sweden adopted a Personal Data Act to bring its privacy legislation in line with the European Community directive. On the whole, there is a strong cultural endorsement of both freedom of information and privacy. Of course, there are conflicts between the Personal Data Act and the legislation protecting freedom of expression, with priority generally given to the latter. The act specifically states that in the case of a conflict between existing protections under the Freedom of the Press Act of 1949 and the Freedom of Speech Act, the latter will prevail.[54] Similarly, surveillance measures are permitted only under stringent provisions. Secrecy in government, therefore, is limited and carefully guarded. Sweden exhibits the Nordic culture of openness, public participation in governance, and revulsion against corruption. In the Transparency International 2001 Corruption Perception Index, it ranks sixth out of 91 countries assessed, with only Finland, Denmark, New Zealand, Iceland, and Singapore ahead of it.[55] (The inclusion of Singapore at such a high rank underscores the fact that transparency and democracy are not one and the same.) Sweden also has a very high rating in Transparency International's Bribe Payers' Index. Corruption and bribery are distasteful in Swedish culture.

Sweden's information culture and support of transparency are rooted in the history of religion in Sweden. The Reformation brought the establishment of Lutheranism and also expanded public literacy. The Church Law of 1686 that declared was Sweden an evangelical country and that Swedes were expected to uphold the evangelical faith. Freedom of religion was made official in 1952 by the legal separation of church and state, but the new membership regulations of the Church of Sweden, established in 1994, came into force only in 1996. No longer are Swedes born into the Church of Sweden; instead, they must be baptized to join the church. Full legal separation of church and state did not occur in Sweden until the turn of the twenty-first century. While the tradition of Lutheran evangelism continues, Sweden also has undergone significant secularization: whereas 85 percent of the population belongs to the Church of Sweden, only about 10 percent go to church regularly. Nevertheless, 78 percent of all infants are baptized, and 90 percent of all Swedes are buried within the church. Although individualism is important to Swedes, they also respect an overall framework of social institutions. This is the context surrounding the Swedish commitment to the com-

145

plex transparency/secrecy syndrome that emphasizes openness, individual accountability, and also privacy. Sweden has used its influence as a member of the European Union to defend its values and to persuade other countries to follow them. It has often pressed for greater freedom of information in the EU and is an advocate of transparency. Its cultural influence is considerable, considering its relatively small population in relation to that of the European Union as a whole.

Greece

The pattern of information culture in Greece is very different. Over the millennia, dramatically divergent civilizations have clashed in this land. These include the Greece of antiquity, with its spectacular cultural accomplishments that made it a beacon for Europe and Western civilization; it resisted the Persian Empire, the Roman Empire, Byzantine rule, and the Ottoman Empire; then followed the Greek nation-state and the turbulent experience of warfare in the Balkans and during the cold war. In many ways Greece is a special European country, uniquely related both to the East and the West. It is also a country of Orthodox Christianity.

Greece joined the European Union in 1981 at a time when social and cultural change was accelerating in Greece. The momentous events of the end of the cold war and the collapse of the Soviet Union, the wars in the former Yugoslavia, globalization, and cultural changes brought by the EU affected Greece very deeply. Immigration, for a long time virtually unknown in Greece, became a major phenomenon. The idea of equal rights for men and women emboldened feminists and led to major culture changes in family structures, employment, and personal behavior. Social change continues at a breathtaking pace, to the delight of some and to the disenchantment and anger of others. Some prominent Greek intellectuals are very concerned about what they see as a cultural change toward materialism.

Greece has a limited constitutional right providing free access to information. The formulation is a little less than specific: "A request for information shall oblige the competent authority to reply, provided the law thus stipulates."[56] Regulations for freedom of information were established by Article 5 of the Greek Code of Administrative Procedure in 1999, a law that replaces the 1986 law regulating identification cards. The constitution provides also for the rights of privacy and for the secrecy of communications: Article 9 states: "(1) Each man's home is inviolable. A person's personal and family life is inviolable. No house searches shall be made except when and as the law directs, and always in the presence of representatives of the judicial authorities. (2) Offenders against the foregoing provisions shall be punished for forced entry into a private house and abuse of power, and shall be obliged to indemnify in full the injured party as the law provides."[57]

As in other European Union countries, privacy is highly valued in Greece. To enforce privacy protections, the Hellenic Data Protection Authority was established in 1997. It has a broad range of responsibilities, including that for the national identity card, surveillance at work, direct marketing, and other intrusions on privacy. The Greek identity cards once included the religious affiliation of the card holder, but the Data Protection Authority defined this practice as unconstitutional in 2000 and removed it. This led to massive protests by the Greek Orthodox Church, but a year later the decision was upheld by the high administrative court. Other items were removed from the card: fingerprints, name of the card holder's spouse, maiden name, profession, home address, and citizenship. One may wonder what is left on the card.[58]

Virginia Tsouderou, head of Transparency International Greece, described the group's volunteer work and the enormous challenge of fighting corruption. "Little corruption" is a fact of life in Greece. "Big corruption" in politics and business is taken by most people as an inescapable aspect of life. One TI member said: "The problems are so large—where do you start? . . . Corruption is a culture by now. Within the EU there are different approaches regarding corruption, along a dividing line between North and South. We see things differently from the North. The Danes think they are incorruptible, they think they are 'white pigeons.' So do the Swedes. They are very incorruptible within their own society, but not outside of it."[59] In Greece, there is a great need to create an awareness of the cost of corruption: "We explain that corruption is not to the advantage of the simple taxpayer. We are trying to approach the press, TV, through speakers, conferences, interviews, normal things. . . . We published a booklet, giving suggestions on how to succeed in having transparency in various fields of government. We have a special project on local government—there is a great amount of corruption." The TI group discussed the roles of codes of conduct, like the OECD convention against corruption, but emphasized the enormous difference between endorsing a code and implementing it. "Regarding the OECD convention, we were among the first to ratify. It was our first initiative, but implementation is something else." There was a shared sense that Greece is a developing culture. "In the sixties you had to have a political protector. That's not so much any more. There is 'petite transparency.' People now say, 'We don't want to pay'; people feel the moral need not to pay." In 2002

147

Greece was rated 44 on the Transparency International Corruption Perception Index, a low score for a European country, but higher than that of many developing countries.

The Greek government and parliament established the office of the Greek ombudsman in 1997 and appointed to the post Nikiforos Diamandouros, a political scientist with a strong commitment to reform. The Greek ombudsman has two major functions: to resolve individual complaints after an event has occurred, and to make recommendations to the government on how to address root causes. By 2001, Diamandouros's office had resolved about 50 percent of the complaints brought to them. The second objective requires more time, but there is significant movement forward. Innovations concern immigration (a new phenomenon), religious tolerance, gender equality, and other issues linked to government transparency. The ombudsman is clearly a major factor in cultural change and political reform in Greece.

Several scholars we interviewed in Greece expressed ambivalence about the concept and social meaning of transparency. The sociologist Demosthenes Agrafiotis talked about his work on cultural change. He has proposed the concept of a postcultural society, one no longer based on a shared, unique, and homogeneous cultural heritage, but a society of multiculturalism and diversity. In his words,

> Because of transparency and diversity, nothing is mysterious; nothing reaches the level of a saint. A full culture is always something dark and something light. The dark side rests in myths; the bright side is transparency. In a society in which transparency is the main cultural focus, where is the question of evil and darkness? . . . Yes, it is a question of identity. It is quite difficult to think today in terms of identity. Transparency insists on a strict codification so that everybody, or some people, can read the code. The opposite of transparency is secrecy. Identity has something to do with secrecy. . . . In the postcultural situation we have no mystery. Culture is always a mixture of desire and knowledge. Desire is always something dark. When we reduce the darkness, we create an illusion of rationality and reasonableness.[60]

Corruption is part of the reality of life in Greece, Agrafiotis stated. There are very different types of corruption: there is the innocent corruption of local black or gray markets, which is very different from the organized, enforced corruption of the Mafia type. In turn, this type differs from the macrocorruption we have seen in Indonesia and the Philippines, a kleptocracy created by ruthless and self-serving dictators who appropriate large wealth in an obvious, brazen, but powerfully protected way. It is different in its brutality from the often hidden political corruption in democratic societies that involves unethical or illegal election campaign financing, monopolistic control of media outlets, and the informal networks linking political parties, government, and corrupt businesses.

As in Sweden, information norms in Greece are derived from religious tradition. The church claims that 97 percent of all Greeks are baptized members. According to Demetrios Constantelos, "The Greek Orthodox Church of today claims that she is the Church founded by Jesus Christ himself; that the Church was guided by the Apostles, including Saint Paul, who visited many Greek cities; was strengthened by martyrs, saints, and the Church Fathers; and is maintained and propagated by her believers in the modern world."[61] A spokesman for the orthodox heritage, Christos Yannaras, explained that the Western tradition of individualism and its particular definition of human rights are at odds with the communal tradition of Byzantium and of Greece. He said, "The philosophy of individual rights is not an anchor point of the Greek political heritage because politics here means social relations."[62] His communalism and insistence on spirituality, in contrast to individualism and materialism, is in tune with the view of the Greek Orthodox Church.

The church is a major force in Greek cultural life, and its perspectives influence more than information cultures. Thus the Greek transparency/secrecy syndrome of information values is generally tilted toward secrecy, to preserve endogenous identity. The Greek Orthodox Church is quite active also in the debate in the European Union about its constitution. Article 8 of the *Statement of the Orthodox Church of Greece on the Future of Europe* says the following:

> The Orthodox Church, appreciating the contemporary search for a common "European Constitution" as a democratic process whereby the diachronic conscience and spiritual legacy of the Peoples of Europe are to be expressed in specific legal provisions, submits the following proposals on the basic principles which she feels should permeate this Constitution: (a) The Principles of Religious Freedom and basic Human Rights are to be fully and specifically guaranteed and safeguarded, and deceitful proselytism forbidden, as proclaimed by the Treaty of Rome and confirmed by the functions of the institutions of the European Union. (b) Respect for the common conscience of the Peoples of Europe concerning the Christian roots of their diachronic and contemporary spiritual legacy is to be ensured, without thereby violating the principle of Religious Freedom for all Religions or Confessions. (c) Church-State relations, which have an

149

historical diachronic depth for each specific People, are to be left to the internal Law of each Nation, within the framework of religious freedom, as this is specifically foreseen in Statement No. 11 of the Treaty of Amsterdam so as to avoid undesirable and unprofitable tensions on sensitive questions pertaining to religious traditions that have determined or define the national identity of the Peoples of Europe.[63]

This statement indicates the large differences between Swedish and Greek cultures, two very different information value syndromes among the member states of the EU.

Japan

Japan's information culture today reflects the legacy of history, the changing place of Japan in the world, and the maturing of its democracy. It is in a process of change. Democracy in Japan and East Asia is developing in a cultural context very different from that of the West. Its cultural heritage stems from a long and unique history. Traditional culture and the quest for modernization have been the poles of political debates for over a century. The simultaneous desires to establish and defend the continuity of Japanese culture while also pursuing modernization and importing models from the West created the effort at indigenization, assimilating new elements into the continuity of Japan itself. Robert W. Compton summarizes this dynamic: "For contemporary students of Japanese politics, the modern-tradition context encompasses the political and economic system. In many ways, the Japanese economic and political systems resemble the West's modernity, but in many ways remain traditional."[64]

The transition from traditional society began with the Meiji emperor in 1868. In a transformation of breathtaking speed, Japan became the first non-Western country to build an industrial, highly efficient economy and a nation of great power. The process was not supportive of transparency. Secrecy had its roots deeply embedded in the traditions of hierarchy, loyalty, and familistic particularism. The different eras of political change in Japan saw the rise of fascism in the first half of the twentieth century, the nation's role in World War II, its ultimate defeat, and the U.S. occupation. The construction of Japanese democracy in the latter half of the century also meant reconciling a new U.S.-inspired democratic form of government with an indigenous, very Japanese, political and economic culture. What resulted and persisted until the early 1990s was a highly elite-controlled hierarchical system that was in some ways democratic. Japan is now an electoral democracy. The concept of "illiberal democracy" described the Japanese political culture until demands for transparency and reform began to arise. The idea of democracy in other than liberal terms seems contradictory, but it captures an important phenomenon in the global spread of democracy in the diversity of cultures. It is a feature of East Asian democracies, but it is not confined to that area.

The Japanese information culture is characterized by a resistance to change and a simultaneous sense of a need for reform and further change. People we interviewed in Japan described the transparency/secrecy syndrome of a society undergoing dramatic changes and trying to resist them at the same time. These changes are pressing under the influence of internal dynamics, the stalled economy, the demographic shift toward an increasingly aging society, and the forces of global transformations. A managing director of a business research and consulting institute told us that change was coming in the business world, but that there was a Japanese way he cherished and a Western one that he did not. He defined the work of the big international accounting firms as "global," meaning that the work was the same in New York and in Tokyo. He said, "The global standard is flowing into the Japanese business scene; the evaluation criteria will be global. . . . 'Global' in this sense means American. There is a choice. We can improve management in a Japanese way or become global, which is American. . . . We stick to our clients. We analyze their issues, their environments. They vary company by company. We have to be prudent, very careful." Japanese people, he told us, are against the pressure to adopt global accounting schemes. "The global approach wants real-time assessments, Japanese allow book value." In Japan, he said, the invisible rules of the business circle govern the whole system, not transparency. "But the trend exists; it is changing, slowly to more transparency and accountability. Ordinary people talk about this, but nothing essential has changed. We cannot forget about the glorious days of the 1980s." The Japanese government was not active in the international arena to shape the emerging standards of transparency and accountability, he said; indeed, the structure of the foreign service made it virtually impossible for them to do this. "Japanese society is not very well prepared for that sort of social governance structure," he said.[65]

Several professionals at major foundations—in a way, sources of reform in Japan and in Japan's cultural and educational relations with other countries—expressed their views. Ellen Mashiko described the far-ranging academic linkages the Tokyo Foundation had established in the world, clearly with an agenda of global change and an open Japan in mind. She said that reform in Japan was necessary, but it had made few advances. She felt that progress in the Japanese universities, with several notable exceptions, is painfully slow.[66] Hiroshi Matsumoto, director of the International House of Japan, felt a similar frustration, but from a different perspective. He felt that education in Japan actually had lost ground since the rigorous days of earlier decades. In spite of the fact that millions of Japanese travel abroad each year, that experience has little influence on their outlook. "Japan is geographically isolated. Japan is surrounded by the sea. Students can't cross borders by bicycle, as they can in Europe. . . . In Japan, about 4 million people go abroad every year, but keep life in Japan separate from what they see. It is not related to their daily life."[67] He also felt that education in Japan should focus more on Japanese history and on Japanese accomplishments.

The Japanese people we spoke to felt that there was a strong generational difference in perspectives on globalization and cultural change. Change is occurring, says Robert Grondine, of the U.S. Chamber of Commerce in Tokyo, but very slowly. He emphasized the adoption of the Freedom of Information Act in 1999, but noted the serious handicaps in implementing this law. Yet transparency in Japan is increasing, not only because of the freedom of information law. "The relationship between companies and investors is changing gradually. This is what will push transparency." However, one should not expect rapid change; change would occur in the cycle of generations: "Many senior managers are close to retirement, just want to get there. The generational conflict is very stark."[68]

Change in the information culture of Japan began with the creation of the constitution of 1966. Its Article 21 states, "Freedom of assembly and association as well as speech, press and all other forms of expression are guaranteed. No censorship shall be maintained, nor shall the secrecy of any means of communication be violated."[69] In 1988 a law was passed assuring the privacy of computer-processed data in the possession of government agencies. In 1998 a Supervisory Authority for the Protection of Personal Data was established, enhancing the right to privacy in Japan.

Clearly, Japan had established a constitutional and legal framework for the basic elements of democracy. The 1990s saw further changes in the information culture of Japan, and the process seems to accelerate. One major step in the movement for transparency was the creation of the Law Concerning Disclosure of Information Held by Administrative Agencies, passed by the Diet in 1999 and enacted in 2001.[70] The Diet was persuaded to adopt this law only after decades of mobilization. A growing movement of lobbying to "break down the walls of secrecy" started in sporadic initiatives in the

1960s. The Citizen's Movement for an Information Disclosure Law was formed much later. It was created in March 1980, bringing together several civil society organizations, including the Japan Civil Liberties Union, the Japan Consumer Federation, and the Housewives' Federation.

Three factors that helped this movement were a series of major scandals involving serious damage to many people and government secrecy; growing grassroots interest in information freedom in local governments; and the political shift of 1993 that moved Japan beyond the monopolistic hegemony of the Liberal Democratic party. The early efforts of a group assembled to persuade the Diet in 1980 to create a freedom of information act failed, but they prevented the situation from getting worse. They defeated the proposal to create an Official Secrets Act in the 1980s. This initiative was promoted by nationalistic and conservative members of the Diet and could have been a significant setback in the move to transparency. Even today, there are strong defenders of secrecy in Japan. The real political force generating acceptance for freedom of information was a popular, grassroots movement.

The Nishiyama case of 1972 presented a moral problem regarding secrecy that helped to start the movement for freedom of information. A news reporter, Takichi Nishiyama, discovered government cablegrams that seemed to point to a secret deal between Japan and the United States in the agreement on the reversion of Okinawa. Nishiyama reported that Japan had agreed to make secret payments to Okinawan landowners as compensation for damages suffered, even though the agreement publicly stated that the United States was paying this compensation. The secret deal aroused a big public debate. The government sued, and the reporter and "an accomplice" were convicted of revealing state secrets. This caused a serious concern about freedom of information in the public and especially in academic circles.[71]

A series of scandals also caused public outrage. The cases in question included government failures to warn the public in time about harmful drugs like thalidomide and chloroquine. There also were political scandals, including the so-called Lockheed incident of 1977. It involved former Prime Minister Kakuei Tanaka, who was convicted in 1983 for accepting bribes from the Lockheed Corporation to persuade All Nippon Airways to buy its jets. We have noted the positive role of scandals in stimulating moves toward greater transparency; they have helped to uncover malfeasance in Japan as well.[72]

The success in mobilizing for the freedom of information access also had an important, broader effect on Japan's civil society. The Citizen's Movement for an Information Disclosure Law transformed itself into the Information Clearinghouse Japan (IJC). This organization provides an active infrastructure for disclosure and personal privacy by monitoring the government's performance in implementing the new law and by providing information about its use by citizens. Further, the new information clearinghouse is linked to international organizations with similar purposes, like Article 19. A conference held by IJC in 2001 brought activists on information access from South Korea, Thailand, India, and the Philippines together with their Japanese counterparts.[73]

The secrecy/transparency value syndrome of Japan is in a process of change, as Japan moves from its traditional pervasive opacity and secrecy toward growing systemic transparency. However, this cultural shift, while very real, is still in its formative stages. Secrecy still is the rule in many domains of government and corporate activity. Surveillance includes the use of cameras on utility poles and the monitoring of pedestrians by the police. Surveillance is also practiced by corporations, which monitor e-mail and other communications. The basic constitutional values of human rights and civil rights are protected in Japan, as is freedom of speech. The disclosure of information law has worked toward limiting secrecy, but exceptions and defenses against its intent continue to exist. Privacy has received legal protection, following roughly some of the measures adopted in Europe. We will discuss historical transparency in Europe, Japan, and elsewhere in chapter 9, but we note here that Japan was for a long time reluctant to confront the history of warfare and oppression in its past. However, scholars, activists, journalists, and some politicians now raise these issues of the past and their significance for the present and the future.

Information Cultures in Interaction and Change

The very different information cultures in the United States, the European Union, and Japan are undergoing very large changes, with remarkable differences among them. The variations in their architectures of information values are based on different histories and their chosen responses to global challenges. They are even more influenced by their own, often narrow, political interests. The outcomes of these changes are still uncertain, but they all involve shifts that alter the relative scope of the values of transparency and secrecy and their full syndrome of values. In its war on terror, the United States has intensified its surveillance activities, its monitoring of information, and its secrecy in certain security areas. However, defensive measures also include a need for greater transparency in other domains, for example, in banking and business transactions in the fight against money laundering and bribery, in public health, and in government accountability. The emerging changes in information architectures have not yet crystallized, but they show certain continuities. The United States continues to uphold the importance of freedom of speech, even as nationalistic fervor leads to outbursts of intolerance against dissenters and their views. The Justice Department under Attorney General John Ashcroft vigorously campaigned for exemptions from the constitutional protections of civil rights in antiterror pursuits. Yet, there remains in the United States an equally vigorous defense of freedom of speech and civil rights by the courts, the legal profession, and by civil society organizations like the ACLU.

The European Union is in the process of "harmonizing" information structures across different national cultures, at least to the extent that such efforts are required for the single market and other policy domains affecting the entire union. It faces a task of enormous difficulty, given the variety of cultures and traditions in the member states. These diversities are very deep and broad—ranging from the strong commitment to transparency in Scandinavia to the traditional opacity of the Mediterranean South. Like the United States, the EU is also worried about terror risks and illegal immigration, giving surveillance a greater role than before. In general, it has not gone nearly as far as the United States in its expansion of secrecy and limits to civil liberty. Privacy of individuals and protection of individuals from corporate intrusions remain high in the European information value architecture. The debate about security protection is very active in the EU, but it differs from the U.S. debate. There is a conviction among EU members that the death penalty is an unacceptable barbarism. In the United States the death penalty is retained at the federal level and in many states, even though movements toward abolition are gaining ground. The death penalty has recently been challenged over a lack of transparency in the proceedings. A substantial number of executions were legally inappropriate due to court errors, malpractice by prosecutors, or incompetent defenders. California has established an office to assist courts and attorneys in conducting such cases with appropriate care, professional competence, and transparency. Further, the EU states continue to insist on formal, open judicial procedures in prosecuting all kinds of suspects. The general European view of the U.S. approach to the rights given to terrorist suspects is aptly summarized by the *Economist* as "unjust, unwise, un-American."[74] There is a growing emphasis

155

on transparency in corporate conduct, financial affairs, and major aspects of governance in the value profiles of the United States, the EU, and to some extent also Japan.

Relations between the three major industrial powers and the developing regions have also undergone dramatic changes. These changes are only in part shaped by information cultures. Strategic political and economic interests pursued by domestic forces, governments, corporations, and special interest groups are more directly influential. These pressures reflect the role of secrecy/transparency syndromes in the poor countries and their counterparts among the great powers. The relationships are in many cases opaque and distorted by a tradition of "cutting deals," sometimes in utter secrecy. This extends across all the ten dimensions of global transformations identified in chapter 3, most prominently, economic, military, and political dimensions. However, change is on the way. Developing countries are moving toward greater transparency in spite of the regressive tendencies aroused by the reactions to the threats of terrorism.

Political interests, historical ties left from the colonial era or from the cold war have established special—and frequently corrupt—relationships linking the rich and poor countries. In too many cases, these relationships protect special interests in the poor countries as well as in the rich ones. A major example is grossly subsidized agriculture in the United States, the EU, and Japan to protect their farmers' interests. Special laws and regulations influence the conduct of corporations, as do policies for providing development assistance. For example, the antismoking efforts in the rich countries have caused tobacco companies to shift their marketing strategies to developing countries, with very negative consequences for public health. Further, vast criminal networks in many developing countries find markets in the rich regions for drugs as well as for the illegal traffic in human beings. Precisely because of these transnational evils, the demands for transparency have increased. Nevertheless, while in certain strategic as well as criminal sectors secret practices continue and even increase, throughout the world there is greater scrutiny of corporate activities and greater demand for accountability.

Global institutions such as the United Nations, the World Bank, the IMF, and the WTO serve as intermediary links between the rich and the poor. There is in fact a growing awareness that poverty must be overcome and that the rule of law, democracy, and responsible governance is in the interests of rich as well as poor countries. Indeed, an interactive network of organizations and individuals has emerged in the decades of the institutional reality of the United Nations, of major transnational institutions and of long experience with development assistance.

The major global financial institutions are struggling to meet the pressures for transparency. There is a strong and rising demand for information disclosure to their constituents, clients, nongovernmental organizations, and the public at large. Yet they are caught between the tradition of diplomatic secrecy among states and the need to respond accountably to criticism and demands for transparency. Toby J. McIntosh reports that the World Bank is considering expanding the transparency of its bidding requirements and procedures. A new disclosure policy took effect in 2003, a major step toward transparency. When the European Bank of Reconstruction and Development adopted a new information regime that largely protects its tradition of secrecy, it came under serious criticism from the public and notably from the United States. The IMF has adopted a new, cautious transparency policy. Similar efforts at defining new institutional information cultures are now under way in virtually all the development banks, such as the Asian Development Bank, the African Development Bank, and the Inter-American Development Bank. The debate has also reached the WTO. In every case, there is an effort to protect the confidentiality rules among national governments and of the negotiating processes.[75] In every case there is also an intensive monitoring effort by outsiders such as NGOs, but also by governments, corporations, and social movements.

The network of links across the boundaries of wealth and poverty, and across widely different cultures, includes five different types of legitimate actors: (1) governments and their military and diplomatic channels and practices in international relations; (2) the UN and its network of organizations; (3) the World Bank and many other transnational institutions dealing with financial regulation, trade, development policy, and other issues; (4) corporations and their specialized networks; and (5) those representing transnational and global social movements and global civil society. While these actors have made progress in global institution building, they have also generated interlinked "epistemic communities" (knowledge communities that cross cultural boundaries) that have learned from past failures and successes in development strategies and efforts at governance. There are strongly held but conflicting perspectives among these communities. Among them is the dramatic rift between the views of neoconservatives in the United States and the views of most people in the EU and Japan, as well as in the developing regions.

There is an intense clash of perspectives on global change between the

157

United States and most of the European Union, even the entire world. In the United States under the Bush administration, an attitude of "regressive globalization" has taken hold. This is a threat to the advances that have been made in building global institutions as well as to civil society. The *Global Civil Society Yearbook 2003* sees this trend as "a form of displaced, latter-day quasi-imperial nationalist thinking in the context of global capitalism. . . . These are individuals, groups, firms, or even governments that favour globalisation when it is in their particular interest and irrespective of any negative consequences for others. . . . Regressive globalisers see the world as a zero-sum game, in which they seek to maximize the benefit of the few, which they represent, at the expense of the welfare of the many, about which they are indifferent at best."[76] This does indeed characterize the policy perspective of the Bush administration. It in fact resembles the nationalist attitudes of religious and conservative groups that resist constructive global change and reject the open society.

The unilateralist policies of the United States and of Britain in the war on Iraq could well undermine the global institutional framework that has been constructed over the last half century. This global framework has grown especially in the past decade, epitomized by the creation of the International Criminal Court. The general advance in global institutions has created new norms in the economic institutions of trade and finance, as well as in human rights, international law, and institutions of justice. "This global institutional framework made possible the growth of global civil society—and global civil society helped constitute global institutions."[77] Global civil society has recently grown in this space between governments, transnational institutions, business links, and global social movements.

U.S. policies of neoconservatism are designed to disrupt the efforts to build global institutions and to stem secular currents toward the open society and transparency. However, since transparency is demanded and advanced by so many forces, their long-term success is unlikely. At the same time, many developing countries, such as China, India, and Brazil, and to a lesser extent Russia, are gaining in confidence that they can turn the lopsided power system of the world to their own advantage. At the conclusion of the Davos meeting of the World Economic Forum in 2004, these countries expressed confidence that they will become major competitors to the United States, the EU, and Japan. A similar expression of confidence was heard in Cancun at the WTO meeting in 2003, when the major developing countries refused to accept the proposals presented by the rich countries. The effort to change the power system structured around the United States is now under way. China, India, and Brazil are building their political strategies around their potential for growth. Economic globalization on unilateral terms is coming to an end. The era of global companies who invest in manufacturing facilities built in developing countries with low wages continues. But the new phenomenon of outsourcing high-technology jobs to India, for example, has been made possible because of educational progress made in India and other developing countries. It is a new challenge for the West and an advantage to the developing world.

Demands for transparency are being felt in the developing world. While transparency as a cultural value is rooted in the Western Enlightenment, powerful forces now implant transparency into the culture of developing countries. Global trade requires transparency in accounting, investment, and sales. Many countries in Latin America, Africa, and Asia have adopted electoral democracy as their system of government. Several are struggling to overcome the damage and trauma of dictatorial past rulers. They search for historical transparency, but even more urgent is the practical need for credible information flows in business and in governance. China's membership in the WTO has not yet become fully part of China's business culture. An additional concern is the need for public health protection, especially after the SARS epidemic of 2003 and its brief return in early 2004, and this is also a force for transparency. In China, the public health expert who virtually forced the central government to take the route of transparency in the SARS epidemic also spoke out against the official silence about the Tiananmen Square massacre of 1989. He was promptly arrested, but subsequently released. It seems that transparency is on its way also in China.

Hong Kong and Singapore were long under colonial rule, and at the end of World War II both of these city-states were impoverished developing societies. Both made successful efforts to curb corruption and now have a worldwide reputation of being free of corrupt links between business and government. Hong Kong even has a movement for historical transparency; the next round of history textbooks will include references to the demonstrations in Tiananmen Square. In mainland China, this is still regarded as unthinkable.

In India a major movement against corruption and for accountability in governance is the group called Mazdoor Kisan Shakti Sangathan (MKSS), based in Rajasthan, India. It started with local issues, but it has now branched out and has become a national force. Similar groups have arisen in many countries. Some of these efforts have been assisted by Transparency International. The awakening of grassroots movements to articulate citizens' rights, to give women a greater role, to protect the environment, to abolish corruption, and to depose arbitrary rulers have become important parts of the local and national information cultures, and they are finding ways to bring a demand for transparency into the local culture.

In addition to the obvious needs for business transparency in global trade and in the defense of human rights locally and nationally, a new, third force is at work. It protests the fact that in the past the idea of national sovereignty has protected high government officers virtually completely against charges of malfeasance. In the early 1990s the World Bank refused to adopt any programs to reduce corruption on the grounds that such efforts would be infringements of the sovereignty of the countries in question. This does not hold any longer in many ways. Sovereignty of national states is no longer a defense against the implementation of anticorruption laws and regulations. The OECD member countries have adopted rules against corruption, as have the international agencies and donor countries. With these changes brought about by global transformations, transparency is beginning to become part of the information culture in developing countries. There are exceptions, especially in dictatorships or theocratic countries, but these countries remain in misery and not only pose dangers for themselves but also serve as breeding grounds for terrorists.

The international flow of information grows in complexity. Civil society organizations continue to debate the long-term goals to be achieved for a sustainable world. Many innovations have emerged within the development communities serving in the interstices between the poor and the rich countries. The term *community* belies the fact that components of the global networks are often in competition and conflict. Nevertheless, there is considerable interaction among all these agencies and civil society in the form of NGOs and voluntary associations.

Many of these agencies have begun to embrace transparency for their own work—and this is new for them, having been well known and criticized for their secrecy. There is also the startling phenomenon of the globalization of educational patterns and standards, even in developing countries. This development includes a strong emphasis on regularizing educational standards, curricula and degree requirements. To be sure, inequalities in education still remain, but the direction of change is clear. It includes seedlings of openness in the tradition of opacity and secrecy.

Thus, interactions between rich and poor countries continue to expand at a rapid pace, even in the era of "regressive globalism." Many of the rich countries recently have followed the lead of the United States in adopting laws forbidding bribery at home or abroad. This is at least partly the result of the growing influence of global civil society organizations in the rich and some developing countries. Among these, Transparency International has been the most persistent and successful in the fight against bribery and corruption. Peter Eigen, the founder of TI, wrote about "the net of corruption" that connected the rich donor nations with the poor countries receiving aid.[78] TI was able to put corruption on the agenda of the world and advanced transparency in information flows among the rich and poor countries.

There are countervailing forces such as narrow nationalism, corporate fraud, environmental exploitation, and wars. However, accountability is being demanded not only by many governments, but increasingly by their publics. One major change toward transparency has occurred in the international financial institutions, in large measure owing to civil society pressure and the influence of both individuals and nongovernmental organizations. Transparency International has done much to reduce corruption and bribery. This and similar forces have affected the information norms in the developing countries, a trend pointing toward a new form of governance based on transparency and accountability.

The norms of civil society may be the most important links across the chasm of economic inequality in the world. The scope of global civil society has increased; some organizations have learned how to influence governments, international agencies, and corporations in rich countries. Global causes such as the women's movement, the environmental protection movement, the efforts of Amnesty International to abolish torture are gaining ground. Ann Florini's hope expressed in *The Coming Democracy: New Rules for Running a New World* may materialize. It is for a transnational form of democracy based on accessible information, accountability, transparency, and the watchful participation of local, regional, and transnational publics.[79]

6

GLOBAL CIVIL SOCIETY, TRANSPARENCY, AND SOCIAL SYSTEM CHANGE

Transparency is a major force in the rapid rise of global civil society and in social system change in many parts of the world. Transparency changes the flow of information from centers of authority. This alters power relations, with far-reaching changes in local societies as well as in the emerging global society. In the era of multidimensional globalization, civil society is increasingly linked both to local and global themes. Global civil society has recently become a familiar term, but it remains a difficult concept. Like transparency, it is an emerging social fact. Some of the movements emerging from it seem raucous and chaotic, while others appear to be highly ethical, competent, and constructive new organizations.

In the historical struggle for democracy in the European nation-states, and in North America especially, civil society emerged as a democratic achievement. It was a product of the struggle against the hierarchical and authoritarian ecclesiastical polities of medieval Europe. It separated the state from the civil society, which then had overtones of the "society of good burghers." In the nation-state era, civil society came to mean associations of citizens who were members of a state. Thus until recently, the idea of civil society was understood primarily as a space of citizens' movements and groupings within a state. This has now changed. Michael Walzer writes:

> Civil society is usually thought to be contained within the framework of the state: it has the same boundaries as the political community. In fact, both the older and the newer associations reach for connections across those boundaries. The labor movement, the historic churches, contemporary environmentalists and feminists—all these have comrades, friends, and fellow workers in faraway places. There is today an international civil society, the very existence of which raises questions about the usefulness of the state.[1]

162

Walzer's observation about the usefulness of the state today might be put differently: whereas civil society is in transition within states and across states in an era of global change, the functions of states are changing, but the state is not about to disappear because of global transformations.

There is a further difficulty: the idea of civil society draws boundaries around its members and excludes certain associations. In democratic countries the notion of "civility" in civil society means the rejection of criminal organizations, terrorist groups, and others who pose threats to society. In the 1990s the rapid expansion of worldwide communications and expanded opportunities for individuals to become empowered for good or mischief, a negative and threatening phenomenon rose in parallel to global civil society. Thomas L. Friedman writes:

> When you combine the angry men that Americanization-globalization creates with the way in which globalization can super-empower people, you have what I believe is the real, immediate national security threat to the United States today: the Super-Empowered Angry Man. That's right, it's not another superpower that threatens America at the end of the twentieth century. The greatest danger that the United States faces today is from super-empowered individuals who hate America more than ever because of globalization and who can do something about it on their own, more than ever, thanks to globalization.[2]

Moises Naim describes the danger in this way:

> In truth, experts who observed the rising influence of nonstate actors in the 1990s viewed it as a largely benign development. It was the era of civil society. Nongovernmental organizations (NGOs) empowered by democracy, a free press, cheaper travel, and the Internet projected influence and civilizing values worldwide. Banning land mines, fighting environmental degradation, and defending human rights were now missions that could be undertaken by ordinary citizens on a global scale. Less attention was paid to the fact that the changes in politics and technology that empowered NGOs did the same for terrorists.[3]

Terrorism has become a hallmark of security concerns and international policy in the early twenty-first century. States now feel the need to draw boundaries by law and regulation to protect themselves against terrorist threats.

By contrast, the rise of global civil society continues. Global organizations may be granted special benefits by the state, such as tax exemptions. Of course, at times there is a conflict between such associations and the state, and there are usually institutional policies to resolve it. Not-for-profit organizations that produce beneficial services to their communities, such as, for example, the YMCA or the Animal Rescue League, are granted privileges even though they are not exactly charities. Advocacy groups like labor unions, the American Civil Liberties Union, the Nature Conservancy, and Save Our Environment are part of recognized civil society.

Religion played a powerful role in the emergence of civil society, and in many ways it continues to play this role. The relationship between religion and the state takes very diverse forms among the world's nations. In many Islamic countries today, such as Iran and Saudi Arabia, the state and religion are firmly linked. In the West the struggle between religion and the state has found different solutions. In the United States, a sharp line has been drawn between state and church to assure religious tolerance. Religious fervor does boil up from time to time in the United States, and the boundary between state and church can become a contentious issue. Nevertheless, the rule of religious tolerance usually holds. In several European countries the official church was an important unifying frame of the nation. Different relations between church and state emerged in Europe, where the church in many cases may still have a close, even official relation with the state. It is not unusual (if controversial) for European countries to collect taxes for a state church. Nevertheless, religious tolerance has taken hold in most of Europe. All European Union member states insist on religious freedom and tolerance. They have created a peaceful framework and cherish it, aware of a memory of devastating religious wars. Still, churches, sects, and religious movements play a major role in democratic politics in Europe.

To summarize, the boundaries of civil society may vary, owing to great diversity in history, culture, and religion. However, there are normative boundaries around civil society. Cults engaging in dangerous and illegal practices are excluded. Criminals, terrorists, hate mongers, and members of secret societies seeking to overthrow the government are clearly outside civil society. Obviously, disputes arise about these boundaries: political and religious extremists may challenge these boundaries and may be outraged at being excluded. Or there may be conflicts between entrenched interests whose behavior threatens the environment and those who protest against their practices. Protesters may be denounced as harming the economy, or even labeled as terrorists. Just as members of civil society addressed centers of power in the era of the nation-state, they do so now in the international era, whether power resides in government, business, or the professions. Today's eastern European countries have an even more value-charged conception of civil society, having emerged only recently from Soviet oppression and totalitarian rule. As they initiated movements to reform the state and thus to create democratic forms of governance, dissidents against this rule crystallized the concept and reality of civil society. Here activists from civil society were able to transform the state.

In the creation of the modern state, associations multiplied, often with the blessing of political authorities, but sometimes in conflict with them. Labor unions, social movements, sport clubs, professional associations, learned societies, beneficent societies, religious groups—a great variety of voluntary associations grew in Europe and the United States. Such associations came to have at least some relation to the national state, although it was a sometimes strained or even antagonistic one. In a time of unquestioned national sovereignty and intense nationalism, the state was the main context for a nation's civil society, even after civil societies became transnational. Organizations such as the YMCA, Rotary Clubs, international labor unions, the Red Cross, and many others flourished within and among nation-states.

Now, civil society is again undergoing dramatic and rapid transformations in a global context. Civil society is now transnational. It also has boundaries of legitimacy, although often contested and fluid. The distinction between legitimate global civil society and its illegitimate outcasts is even more controversial and heated today than what defined civil society in a national state. Global transformations are changing civil society, as they also change the nature of states. This is one of the ten dimensions of global transformations we introduced in chapter 3. It is closely linked to the transparency phenomenon. Being concerned with global risks and deficiencies in governance, global civil society is oriented to global solutions.

The spectacular and unruly protests against economic globalization in recent years dramatized the rise of global civil society. Many of the protesters meant to trash the policies of the rich countries, most of all the United States, in pursuing free markets and free trade worldwide, and especially the policies pursued by the WTO, the IMF, and the World Bank. The rejection of these policies became a creed among several social activist groups, ranging from radical anticapitalists who hoped to abolish markets altogether, to proponents of world peace as well as nationalist movements for protectionist causes. Participants included protesters against American hegemony and the exploitative policies of the advanced capitalist nations, including some who simply wished to "stop globalization." However, even policy critics from within the development community sensed that global change needed to be redirected. Frustration with failures in the world financial system

165

and with development policies that did not work affected many professionals in the development community and in universities and research organizations. Something strange—and important—had occurred in the debates about global change in the late 1990s.

The most noted event in the public perception of global civil society at the end of the twentieth century was the huge and disruptive demonstration against the World Trade Organization (WTO) during its 1999 ministerial meeting in Seattle. In late November, about 700 organizations and 40,000 demonstrators converged on Seattle and effectively disrupted the meeting. The passionate demonstration was a motley gathering of many groups with widely disparate views and issues in mind. There had been previous protests against meetings of the WTO. Because it deals with some of the most sensitive issues in world trade and global interdependence, it has become a symbol of the "Washington consensus" favoring free markets everywhere and open global trade. The protests in Seattle, which attracted worldwide media attention, were organized by Internet communications. It was a surprise to the authorities, who clearly had not anticipated anything like the fury of the protestors and their enormous numbers.

Demonstrators in Seattle included students, members of labor unions, environmentalists, those favoring protectionist trade policies, religious groups, nongovernmental organizations committed to various global issues, and consumer organizations—congeries of people who certainly did not agree on many issues. But they shared their anger at the WTO and its policies.[4] The Seattle meeting was a shock to the institutions and corporations that had for so many years committed themselves to economic globalization under the banner of free markets and the "Washington consensus." This attack was initially misdirected and misstated as an attempt to stop global change.

The event had several consequences for the debate over the direction of global change. It crystallized the multiple, unconnected groups into something like a worldwide movement. However, although it is not an organized movement, with clearly defined goals and leaders. It is a network with loose ties capable of mobilization into collective action. The Seattle protests did shock the international institutions into serious reflection—some of their own members shared the criticisms expressed in the demonstrations. It also encouraged scholarly critics and dissidents from the established policy centers to come forth with alternative ideas. Prominent among them was Joseph E. Stiglitz, winner of the 2001 Nobel Prize in economics, once an official of the World Bank, and chairman of Clinton's Council of Economic Advisers. He writes:

> International bureaucrats—the faceless symbols of the world economic order—are under attack everywhere. Formerly uneventful meetings of obscure technocrats discussing mundane subjects such as concessional loans and trade quotas have now become the scene of raging street battles and huge demonstrations. The protests at the Seattle meeting of the World Trade Organization in 1999 were a shock. Since then the movement has grown stronger and the fury has spread. Virtually every major meeting of the International Monetary Fund, the World Bank, and the World Trade Organization is now the scene of conflict and turmoil. The death of a protester in Genoa in 2001 was just the beginning of what may be many more casualties in the war against globalization.[5]

Until recently, such protest had occurred almost exclusively in the developing countries. Now it is occurring in the rich countries as well. In Stiglitz's account: "It is clear to almost everyone that something has gone horribly wrong. Almost overnight, globalization has become the most pressing issue of our time, something debated from boardrooms to op-ed pages and in schools all over the world."[6]

On September 11, 2001, almost two years after the protests in Seattle, terrorists attacked the World Trade Center in New York City. That event changed the strategic posture of the United States, which unleashed a "war on terrorism" and the wars in Afghanistan and Iraq. Globalization became even more a focus of concern. In late September 2001 the conservative British journal the *Economist* published a special overview of the globalization debate. It was a spirited defense of capitalism, and an equally spirited attack on the muddled demonstrators in Seattle and their expanding movement. Nevertheless, the article admitted, "Anti-globalists see the 'Washington Consensus' as a conspiracy to enrich bankers. They are not entirely wrong."[7] Similarly, it recognized that there were other points in the protesters' agenda that needed to be taken seriously, such as criticism of the rule of secrecy followed by the WTO and its lack of a transparency policy. Conduct by all important international authorities should be transparent, they argued. The protesters had made some valid points.

The protests in Seattle and subsequent events gave the global civil society movement a new direction. One vehicle for strengthening the coherence of some parts of global civil society was to organize "alternative forums" as rebuttals to the official meetings of major international agencies and conferences.[8] Such vehicles for civil society debates and mobilizations appeared at the G-8 meeting held in Genoa in 2001, where demonstrations turned violent; the meeting in Bonn, Germany, in 2001 about the follow-up to the Kyoto Framework Convention on Climate Change, which Greenpeace declared to be a great victory; and the World Conference against Racism in Durban, South Africa, which aroused extreme controversy and nasty conflict. These events attracted enormous, worldwide media coverage and discussion. Such occasions were not only novel forms of demonstration, they were transnational and brought many groups together. They were also learning processes for activists. Actually, there are now training programs for global activists.

There have been failures but also successes in using the approach of "alternative" assemblies. Some movements of global civil society are in fact converging and in part uniting. This includes the by now annual assemblies of the World Social Forum of 2001, 2002, and 2003 held in Porto Alegre, Brazil. A fourth forum met in India in 2004. These events were intended to be alternatives to the World Economic Forum held in Davos, Switzerland. They have grown in attendance and in attracting the interest of several governments and corporations.

The World Social Forum is a large, multifaceted, and chaotic assembly. Patrick Mulvany, senior policy adviser to the Intermediate Technology Development Group (ITDG), described the conclusions of the 2003 Porto Alegre meeting:

> Amid the chaos caused by crashed computers and thus no published venues and timings for around 1,700 workshops, 100,000 people from every corner of the world crowded the streets of Porto Alegre for the opening march of the World Social Forum. In a riot of colours and sounds, the voice of the people was raised in cacophonous harmony in a spirit of renovation asserting that "Another (peaceful) World is Possible." This is the third Porto Alegre World Social Forum that expresses the diverse demands of Civil Society for peace, justice and equality, held in opposition to the government-dominated Davos World Economic Forum that fixes the economic rules that impoverish the majority.[9]

Mulvany saw reason for optimism:

> As the echoes of 40,000 marchers' demands rumble North towards Cancun, participants in this third World Social Forum in Porto Alegre are celebrating the coming of age of a global social movement that is challenging the economic orthodoxies of the powerful. Noam Chomsky said on Monday that the more optimism rises here in Porto Alegre, the more despondent they become in

Davos. To the leaders of the crumbling neo-liberal model gathered at the World Economic Forum in Davos, he said "Party time is over! . . .Wherever the optimism comes from: the figures with 100,000 activists present at the forum including 20,763 delegates, representing 5,717 organisations from 156 countries and more than 25,000 young people who camped by the river; or from the quality of the 1,286 official workshops and numerous parallel rallies, conferences, assemblies, panels and testimonies that drew together the world's foremost thinkers and analysts and cemented opposition to inequality, injustice and war; or from the unity of realising that the political vision of a more just and equitable world, locally responsive and with democratically accountable institutions can now be achieved; or that Brazil has eventually elected a leader of a national social movement as its president who energised a mammoth rally with his commitment to end inequitable polices and violence against the poor and replace them with equality, justice and dignity; the World Social Forum is established as a new global force. But to strengthen this position will require more openness and transparency from the organisers, less focus on the Gurus and more on the grassroots, more resolution of differences on policy issues.

This movement is concerned with inequality, poverty, hunger, and human rights, but it remains diffuse and loose. It is capable of organizing the World Social Forum, but it is far from being tightly organized. It is also primarily *against* the ruling powers and their policies. Bridget Anderson reported on the experience: "Nothing could have prepared me for the chaos of the World Social Forum, not even the email that told me to bring a sleeping bag because, all else failing, I could sleep in the public park. I was invited to dinner with Chomsky, I was to speak on a WSF panel with an audience of 'a few thousand possibly' and I was to be sleeping in a park! Well, this seemed grimly egalitarian, so I couldn't complain." The assembly was also anarchic and "out of control," she reports, "willingly or not, increasingly out of the hands of those who originally began it." Her final note was: "And migration is certainly rising on the agenda of those who believe Another World is Possible."[10]

There are many branches and twigs in the tree of the emerging global civil society, with its passionate and woolly "movement events," temporary occasions of great mobilization of people connected to many diverse networks. Continuity can grow out of a series of such events, but continuity cannot be assured. Certainly, the global antiwar movement produced another historical event of far larger scope: the worldwide outcry of demonstrators against America's determination to go to war in Iraq. On February 15, 2003, about 11 million people demonstrated in approximately 800 cities all over the world—a demonstration without precedent in its global scope, size, and coordination. The *New York Times* called this a sign that global civil society had become the second superpower. But it did not stop the war. And the 11 million people have not created an organized, continuous social movement. Nevertheless, they are part of global civil society.

What Is Global Civil Society?

Global civil society today seeks to find solutions to major worldwide problems. How has this concept been defined in the past? In ancient Rome, *societas civilis* meant a well-governed, political society under the rule of law, in contrast to barbarian tribes who lived violent and brutish lives outside such a society. From its very beginning, the concept had a value-charged meaning. Whereas serious social scientists today seek to avoid facile value judgments, this is not easy; the concept of civil society has inherently an evaluative charge. No one would define it simply as "the entirety of associations within a state" (or, to put it more broadly "polity"), since this would include criminal organizations, secret societies, hate groups, and other scoundrels. But, on the other hand, in the words of Helmut Anheier et al.,

> The problem with a purely normative definition of civil society is, however, that defending civil society as a "good thing" threatens to become tautological: civil society is a good thing because it espouses the values we hold. Anyone who fails to hold these values is not part of civil society. And whose values are these? The desirability of absolute non-violence, for instance, is not something everyone agrees about. And are nationalist and fundamentalist movements parts of civil society? Where and how do we draw boundaries?[11]

Civil society became a concept of the Enlightenment as an element in the construction of the enlightened, law-based, national state. This certainly was the conception of Adam Ferguson and of Georg Wilhelm Friedrich Hegel in his effort to systematize everything into reason and the dialectic. Hegel lived in a period of great change, when the French Revolution cast a shadow of horror yet held out promises of freedom. Napoleon's imperialism aroused the spirit of nationalism in all of Europe. The search was on for progress without revolution and the building of a secure state. Hegel's mature time was that of post-Napoleonic reconstruction and reactionary restoration. The period saw the creation of the University of Berlin, where Hegel taught, the establishment of the Prussian military state, and the growth of civil associations. Hegel conceived of civil society as *bürgerliche Gesellschaft* (citizens' society) in a dialectic, but reasoned, tension with the state. Karl Marx ridiculed this idea: by contrast, he defined *Bürgertum* (solid citizens) as the exploitative capitalist bourgeoisie. Hegel saw his *bürgerliche Gesellschaft* as a force of reason, but Marx was convinced that the revolution would come from the proletariat. Thus the concept of civil society had a very political and ethical coloring in the nineteenth century and through much of the twentieth. It remains controversial today, as global society continues to emerge.

This controversy poses a challenge for the analysis of global civil society. The literature offers three kinds of definition: first, the empirical-operationalized version; second, a definition that links civil society conceptually to other parts of social life; and third an "ideal type" in the style of Max Weber's methodological construction. We will then offer our own classification of the components, boundaries, and dynamics of civil society, with a reference to transparency.

Even describing the empirical-operationalized definition requires a special approach to understand the difficulties. Particular aspects of global and transnational civil society have been studied, but very few systematic data collection programs are of the same quality as the records about associations in advanced national states. The Union of International Associations, founded in 1907, was for a long time the only organization registering international associations.[12] Certainly, the United Nations has a formidable capacity for data collections, but it, too, is limited by "methodological nationalism," since most social statistics are based on data collected and organized by nations. The problem is summarized in this way: "Simply put: existing statistical systems are based on the notion of the nation-state—a unit that seems ill-suited for the kinds of data and information needed for mapping and measuring global civil society."[13] Measuring global civil society requires international data, not just aggregates of national data.

The emergence of the *Global Civil Society* yearbook is an intriguing innovation in social science. The yearbook provides carefully documented and analyzed information; at the same time, the international group of scholars and researchers who put it together are part of the phenomenon they study, part of global civil society itself. Their project required them to develop the very concept they were exploring, where to begin, how and where to collect their data. The editors explain:

> We have learned, at least to some extent, where we need to look to find out more about global civil society and with whom we need to engage to develop the conceptual underpinning of the project. So we are not informing our readers as we

imagined, although we hope there is a lot to be gleaned from this first Yearbook; rather we are, in effect, asking our readers to participate in the journey of discovery. As we see it, the Yearbook itself is a part of global civil society: a terrain for developing ideas, investigating issues, and gathering information that does not readily fit existing categories and cannot be found in conventional sources.[14]

The editors of the yearbook acknowledge the existence of multiple definitions of and perspectives on global civil society. Their working definition is this:

> Global civil society is the sphere of ideas, values, institutions, organizations, networks, and individuals located *between* the family, the state, and the market and operating *beyond* the confines of national societies, polities, and economies. While we recognize that global civil society is ultimately a normative concept, we believe that the normative content is too contested to be able to form the basis for an operationalisation of the concept.[15]

The collection of data, tables, and chronologies of events in their yearbook represents a growing number of such "records of global society" and contains an invitation to correspondents to add further facts. It is an impressive effort to create transparency about global civil society, a phenomenon that is still somewhat opaque. In fact, the yearbook's definition seems very loose and in itself emphasizes the diffuseness of the phenomenon.

Others define the concept of global civil society by mapping the conceptual location and links of civil society structures. Philip Nord focuses on its "publicness," or as we would say, its allegiance to transparency. He sees it as the "spawning ground of social movements" and the source of democratization of the state and the market alike. For Nord,

> Publicness is its lifeblood, which sets it apart from family and property, domains of intimacy and private right. Yet, it has not the overt partisan coloration of political society or the policing pretensions of the state. It ends where government and public administration begin. The borders defining these various realms are neither fixed nor impermeable. But fluid as they are, they demarcate the terrain that is civil society's—an irregular topography dotted by institutions, associations, and movements that are never altogether freestanding but do together sculpt a space for self-activity.[16]

This definition speaks to the potential significance of the role of civil society as an influence in emerging global governance, and the need to pay attention to the gaps in such governance.

Sudipta Kaviraj and Sunil Khilnani discuss the cultural variations of civil societies and their limitations.[17] Khilnani believes that all uses of the term *civil society* see it as limiting the state. Some identify civil society with the free economy (the private sector), some with society, and others with culture. None of these formulations, especially those that limit civil society to the private sector, is very helpful, in our view. Antony Black writes about the European origin of the phenomenon. He places the beginning of civil society roughly in the twelfth century, which we also have identified as a crucial cultural turning point toward greater social openness. The rising role of guilds, cities, universities, and the law created special conditions for the rise of manifold associations, including many religious groups. Values began to emerge that made the growth of civil society possible. Black explains:

> These civil values and practices belonged to a society which arose in a highly specific cultural milieu, combining Germanic, Greco-Roman, and Judeo-Christian influences. This mixture goes far towards explaining why the outcome of European history was different from that of other histories. What we have uncovered is a unique set of values in a unique society. It is, therefore, unlikely that civil society (in the modern sense) can be used as an analytical tool for understanding other pre-modern societies or their pasts. . . . [However,] there is no reason why, under certain conditions, other societies may not now acquire as many features of civil society as modern Europe. But the evidence of this chapter clearly indicates that this would need, as one of its preconditions and perhaps the most difficult, the adoption of favorable cultural norms.[18]

In Black's view, a functioning civil society requires certain broad cultural conditions of civility, toleration of differences in interests and outlook, and the ability to make compromises. It also requires structural conditions such as a division of labor and a functioning state. Otherwise, the outlook is bleak. While civil society has become a force for democracy and hope in parts of the world,

> those regions that have emerged from authoritarian rule or from close political regulation of the economy—that is, in regions which seemed to have created what were assumed to be preconditions for the emergence of civil society—the picture has been much darker. The common pattern has been the appearance of a multiplicity of non-negotiable identities and colliding self-righteous beliefs, not a plural representation of malleable interests. Civil society remains as distant and precarious an ambition as ever.[19]

However, Black does not specifically deal with the emerging global role of civil society that we have to keep in mind.

Civil society was established in some colonies under European rule—for example, in India. This may have been primarily for the benefit of the colonial administration to limit the scope of its responsibilities. However, it may have contributed to the origin of endogenous civil society groupings and movements after the colonial period. In other regions, especially in Latin America, civil society has often been connected with Marxist or at least left-leaning traditions. It tends to take an antagonistic attitude toward the state. Recent developments in Latin America accompanying the growth of democracy show an expansion of civil society activities and the establishment of many connections to transnational and global organizations, a remarkable shift.

There are broad variations in perspectives on civil society in different contemporary cultures. Wherever the idea of civil society came from, it is growing worldwide. Today's emerging civil society at the global level is in the process of defining itself around the challenge of global problems. John Keane has created an "ideal-type" of global civil society. This is not a normative ideal, but a simplified conception of a complex phenomenon that makes analysis possible. For Keane, the term global civil society

> refers to a dynamic non-governmental system of interconnected socio-economic institutions. . . . [It] is neither a static object nor a *fait accompli*. It is an unfinished project that consists of sometimes thick, sometimes thinly stretched networks, pyramids and hub-and-spoke clusters of socio-economic institutions and actors who organize themselves across borders, with the deliberate aim of drawing the world together in new ways. These non-governmental institutions and actors tend to pluralise power and to problematise violence; consequently, their peaceful or "civil" effects are felt everywhere.[20]

The ideal type of global civil society for us deals with the search for global solutions to global problems.

An important domain of global civil society is the search for solutions to the threats of war, poverty, overpopulation, and environmental destruction. Bill McKibben writes:

> The bottom-line argument goes like this: The next fifty years are a special time. They will decide how strong and healthy the planet will be for centuries to come. Between now and 2050 we'll see the zenith, or very nearly, of human population. With luck we'll never see any greater production of carbon dioxide or soil erosion. . . . So it's the task of those of us alive right now to deal with this special phase, to squeeze us through the next fifty years. That's not fair—any more than it was fair that earlier generations had to deal with the Second World War

or the Civil War or the Revolution or the Depression or slavery. It's just reality. We need in these fifty years to be working simultaneously on all parts of the equation—on our ways of life, on our technologies, and on our population.[21]

Bill McKibben calls for action on the impending global risks. Environmental degradation did not begin yesterday, and it will not stop tomorrow. Slavery is still a reality in parts of the world. Wars still break out and cause innumerable deaths and great devastation. There is a still diffuse but emerging consensus that global action is required. This growing consensus is, of course, heatedly attacked by those who do not have a global perspective. Yet the charter of the United Nations contains a list of human rights and duties that are pursued vigorously by social movements. Even powers hostile to them find them difficult to ignore, and they are at least in principle acknowledged by governments, international agencies, and global civil society movements. The rights include civil liberties, freedom of expression, freedom of speech, and freedom of association; women's rights, children's rights, patients' rights; freedom from coercion and torture; and access to pure natural resources. The duties include accountability by both citizens and authorities; respect for law and the rights of others; transparency by authorities; and ethical norms of business conduct.

In the face of global threats and risks, these rights and duties oblige governments, international and supranational agencies and institutions, and global civil society to acknowledge a new set of global ethics and norms. We are not concerned with all networks or organizations of global reach, but with social movements that advocate solutions to global problems. Some of these have large numbers of supporters. Global civil society is necessarily related to centers of authority such as governments, international agencies, corporations, and the professions. Some of these connections are firm, others still emerging. Since the framework of global governance is still very fluid, with many gaps, global civil society is also in flux. However, growth is under way.

How Global NGOs Compete

The growing awareness of global interdependence has created an enormous, competitive "quasi-market" for effective solutions and new norms that respond to new global challenges. Competing in this market are those with the capacity to create influence and to find solutions to emerging problems. Demand for and the supply of such solutions are linked, but such transactions occur outside a monetary marketplace and without commercial compensation. The quasi-market creates rank orders of credibility for actors in the field of influence. This in turn can build or dissolve coalitions among competitors. The quasi-market concept strengthens the argument that influence as a medium of exchange is itself a powerful element in effecting global change.

We have already referred to Talcott Parsons's four symbolic media of exchange: money, power, influence, and value commitments. In the processes of global change all these play a role, but influence is a special medium in the formation of global civil society. In the competition for influence, competitors adopt strategies that are akin to, but also unlike economic strategies. Influence is based on credibility, known competence, knowledge, and even the prestige of "eminent persons." We will describe how these quasi-markets work among global civil society organizations. National governments are not always successful in this market because they are often limited by concerns for their sovereignty and national interests. No national government feels a primary responsibility to improve the state of the world, even though it may have entered into numerous treaties and regimes that serve global purposes.

International and transnational institutions are held responsible for some aspects of global governance, but they, too, are limited by the national interests of their members and sponsors. Many NGOs in this quasi-market have achieved a high level of credibility and acclaim. The Nobel Peace Prize is increasingly awarded to global institutions; the United Nations and Kofi Annan were recipients of the award in 2001, and several UN agencies have been earlier recipients. The following organizations have won the prize: Amnesty International in 1977; International Physicians for the Prevention of Nuclear War in 1985; Joseph Rotblat and the Pugwash Conferences on Science and World Affairs in 1995; the International Campaign to Ban Landmines (ICBL) and Judy Williams in 1997; Doctors Without Borders (Médecins Sans Frontières) in 1999. In addition, some global civil society organizations have been recognized by governments, corporations, international agencies, and universities who have sought their cooperation, with attendant acclaim and global publicity.

Of course, some might bemoan the "cooptation" of such organizations by world powers—much as Karl Marx belittled Hegel's fondness for civilized citizenship as bourgeois. Nonetheless, voluntary, nongovernmental organizations make up a significant component of global civil society and have entered vigorously into the quasi-market for ethical solutions to meet the new human condition and a new, global normative order.

A quasi-market for identifying risks and finding solutions exists not only among NGOs. It is also linked—often in conflict, sometimes in alliances—to global business itself and to politics, both global and local. NGOs have risen in power and influence, and their numbers have increased, because of the widely felt need for global ethical norms. There are demands for ethical codes of conduct among corporations and the professions—demands that have intensified after the recent waves of business scandals. Corporate enterprises have learned that malfeasance can be costly. Yes, there are countercurrents among Machiavellian "realists" and unscrupulous, even outright criminal organizations do exist, but efforts to contain them increase.

The definition of ethical conduct is a matter of some dispute, but there is also a large area in which it is quite clear what the ethical path is, even if it is not always followed. To be sure, NGOs often become aware of established practices by governments, corporations, and even communities that are harmful. Their main strategic tool is transparency: shining the light of the "publicness" of global civil society on the evils of corruption, suppression of free speech, child labor, sweatshops, environmental damage, land mines, unscrupulous sales of dangerous products, enslavement of women for the sex trade, crimes against human rights, torture, and genocide. Of course, those who profit from these evils do not like this. Furthermore, some accusations by NGOs may not be valid. So the complaint has been raised: where is the transparency in the NGOs? Who authorized them to set new standards for ethical conduct and governance?

One example of such contest is the effort of the American Enterprise Institute for Public Policy Research and the Federalist Society for Law and Public Policy Studies to make available information about NGOs.[22] Both institutions pursue a conservative agenda and are both ideologically close to the views of the Republican party. Their objective might be called "regressive globalization." However, they are demanding transparency from NGOs by publishing information about them, including financial data that (in the United States) must be filed with the Internal Revenue Service.

The organizers have a clear rationale for this project, which is to curtail the growing power and influence of NGOs. Sudipta Kaviraj and Sunil Khilnani write:

> While it is true that many NGOs remain true to grassroots authenticity conjured up in images of protest and sacrifice, it is also true that non-governmental organizations are now serious business. NGO officials and their activities are widely cited in the media and relied upon in congressional testimony, corporations regularly consult with NGOs prior to major investments. Many groups

have strayed beyond their original mandates and have assumed quasi-governmental roles.[23]

Whereas NGOs are unregulated in much of the world, they are regulated in the United States. These conservative institutes have set up a Web site with "interactive" pages that invite comments or observations about an individual or organization in question. There will be links to articles and authors, most of which reflect the most strident nationalism. These institutes have in their own way entered the struggle in the quasi-market for new ethics.

Today there are almost 60,000 international, not-for-profit organizations registered by the Union of International Organizations.[24] There has been an enormous increase since the early 1900s, when there were only a handful of organizations. Rapid growth accelerated in the 1970s. Active international NGOs were estimated at about 25,000 in 2001, a rise from about 10,000 in 1981.[25] The diversity of the purposes of such organizations has grown as well. As Kofi Annan, UN secretary-general, states: "If the UN's global agenda is to be properly addressed, a partnership with civil society is not an option; it is a necessity." The UN has established an "information platform" because many civil society organizations are important sources of knowledge about specific global issues and are advocates of informed (if at times controversial) views.[26] The UN's information platform encourages INGOs to cooperate and form networks and alliances.

Major international and transnational authorities have established official patterns of cooperation with INGOs and thus with global civil society. This is also the case with many national governments, since several types of civil society organizations may have a high level of expertise in their field of activity. Specialized UN agencies have established similar databases for INGOs such as the United Nations Development Program (UNDP) and the United Nations Environment Program (UNEP). The latter has further established a global reporting initiative to foster accountability and to provide a common framework for the civil society organizations with which it works.[27] Clearly, many very diverse organizations of global civil society form a tight network with UN agencies, international development institutions, national development agencies, and foundations. The activities and concerns addressed by international nongovernmental organizations listed by the United Nations include the following: humanitarian issues; the rights of children, youth, women, indigenous peoples, minorities, and refugees; education and training; economic development, labor, trade, transportation, and energy; science, technology, and telecommunications; environmental protection and biodiversity; health, food, and nutrition; population problems; intellectual property; international law and international relations; and disarmament and conflict resolution, among many others. It illustrates a quasi-market that offers ideas and services for addressing global problems.

Types of Global Civil Society Organizations

Many global civil society organizations are based in popular movements for peace, against capitalism, even against globalization itself. Movements involving political confrontation call for political solutions to problems such as environmental degradation or the lack of affordable drugs. Another type of global organization is comprised of a special corps of engaged experts. In some cases, activists also include networks of knowledgeable experts who form "epistemic communities," or interactive, bounded associations of informed professionals.[28] Some of these may be found in the United Nations' NGO information database. Epistemic communities share criteria and standards for the specialized knowledge they produce and use. For example, there are groups of scientists who study global warming, or the effects of fiscal policies, or water quality in the Mediterranean, or new vaccines. They also include professionals with expertise in accounting, health care management, or fish farming—among myriad other activities. These epistemic communities are bound by the standards by which they assess truth claims —that is, how they judge the quality of knowledge developed in their field. Membership in these communities is based on certified competence. Some epistemic communities may be ambivalent about transparency, wishing to protect some secrets from the general public. Communities of research scientists have specialized structures and communication patterns that differ from those of engineers or physicians, but central to their value system is knowledge.

Today communities of professionals responsible for knowledge production often cross national and cultural boundaries. They may develop collective learning capacities and change the body of knowledge with which they deal. Within a broadly shared frame of reference, there may be hot contests about the validity of knowledge claims. As we have pointed out, such debates have been under way in the global development community since the 1990s.[29]

While members of epistemic communities can be passionately committed to social change, they rarely themselves demonstrate in the streets. However, members of many other social movements are also part of global civil society and some do actively seek confrontations, even warfare. From the conflict-oriented pole to its opposite, global social movements and formally designated INGOs intersect in many ways. Some movements are devoted to a single cause, such as taking action against AIDS, or regulating child labor, or eliminating land mines. Such diversity of views is reflected in the variety of strategies civil society organizations pursue. Direct confrontation can be very effective, as in the case of Julia "Butterfly" Hill. As an activist of Earth First, she settled more than 150 feet high into a California redwood to stop Pacific Lumber from "harvesting" these giant trees. She was supported by civil society organizations and by various celebrities, and the media dramatized her actions. Pacific Lumber helped her case by harassing and threatening her, arousing public sympathy. After she had spent two years in the tree, Pacific Lumber agreed to preserve the tree and the forest around it.[30] Another dramatic example was the conflict between the environmental protection organization Greenpeace and the French government about nuclear tests in the southern Pacific. Another activist, but definitely democratic, international movement is Attac, founded in 1998 and now represented throughout Europe and in some Latin American countries. It seeks more democratic control of financial markets, the abolition of public debt of poor countries, and the defense of nations whose sovereignty is now threatened by international finance.[31]

At the other end of this spectrum are the NGOs that rely primarily on persuasion and strategic cooperation. This includes, for example, Transparency International (TI), dedicated to reducing corruption and bribery worldwide, and Conservation International (CI), dedicated to the preservation of biodiversity. TI's overall strategy is to publicize information about the costs of corruption and how to reduce it. CI's strategy is to find ways to integrate environmental sustainability with economic needs. Between the poles of confrontation and persuasion, there are multiple strategies open to NGOs, including court action, lobbying governments, mobilizing shareholders in stock companies, and forming cooperative partnerships to develop codes of conduct. In all of these strategies, the credibility of the NGO's information is of crucial importance: transparency and truthfulness are potent instruments for change.

A second way to classify global civil society organizations is by their organizational structure and rules. Those that act globally must deal with local cultures and problems as well as with national laws and global pressures. Global NGOs take a wide variety of organizational forms and include many innovations. The most basic difference is that between large-membership organizations like Amnesty International and nonmembership organizations that rely on supporters or donors, like Greenpeace. Membership organizations are more likely to respect democratic voting rights, whereas this is not necessarily the case in nonmembership, sponsored organizations. Examples include Article 19, the highly professional group devoted to encouraging free expression worldwide by developing freedom of the press laws. Nonmembership organizations have greater difficulty in demonstrating the legitimacy of their decision making. A group's organizational form is influenced by its leadership dynamics, its mission, its funding sources, and the customs and laws about the governance of associations in different countries. Among these, an emerging form is that of the global federation—an organizational type that relies on a central office or secretariat and affiliated organizations that may be local or national chapters or branches. This type can accommodate diversity in the forms of its affiliates; but it has problems with maintaining central leadership dynamism and a focus on the mission. Networks have surpassed the hierarchical form of traditional bureaucracy; new communications enable the creation of new organizational forms. The search for the most effective, democratic, creative, and transparent organizational form of INGOs is in full progress, but by no means will it be ended soon.[32]

Among the funding sources of INGOs are individual donors, individual volunteers, governments, corporations, development assistance programs of various kinds, and foundations. Global civil society, of course, is not limited to the development community, even though it is a major part of it. According to the OECD, the total resources from donor countries and multilateral agencies to recipient countries in 2000 amounted to $212.9 billion. Of that, direct official aid was $52.3 billion.[33] However, even these sums are not sufficient. Nevertheless, the development community is deeply engaged in global change, employing many professionals from both donor and recipient countries, and working with many INGOs. In 2000 an estimated $7 billion from bilateral government funds and multilateral agencies went specifically to NGOs, only a fraction of the total.

Many major donors are involved in aid, including the OECD states, the international agencies, the European Union, which takes a special interest in civil society organizations, foundations, religious organizations, corporations, labor unions, and individuals. U.S. foundations that contribute to the growth of global civil society include the Bill and Melinda Gates, MacArthur, Ford, Rockefeller, and Soros foundations. Foundations worldwide are the second most important funding source for INGOs, giving

$2 billion in 2000, with the largest single share of this coming from U.S. foundations.[34] Japanese foundations play an international role as well.

Where are the homes of global civil society organizations? According to the *Global Civil Society 2002* yearbook, their headquarters are predominantly in Europe.[35] Brussels is home to 1,392, London to 807, Paris to 729, Geneva to 272, Rome to 228, Vienna to 190, Amsterdam to 162, Madrid to 140, Stockholm to 133, Copenhagen to 108, and Berlin to 101. The United States also is home to a substantial number, with 487 in Washington, D.C., and 390 in New York City. Within the EU, the greatest concentration is in northern Europe. There are also NGO offices in certain developing countries, with some concentrations in Kenya, Senegal, India, and several Latin American countries, but none in China. The presence of INGOs around the world is about to change, as is their function. More and more grassroots local and regional NGOs are arising in Latin America and in many parts of Asia, as well as in some regions of Africa. Everywhere they will have to embrace transparency, including about themselves.

Brokers and Evaluators in the Quasi-Markets of Influence

The process of learning in global civil society extends beyond the needs of poor countries. It is part of the epistemic community presence. Such collective learning, and the changes pursued as a result, are belittled by reactionaries and opponents everywhere, especially those who realize that their own social system is changing as a result of global pressures. INGOs focus much of their attention on the social problems of poor countries, inequality, and global governance. However, the idea that changes in social norms can lead to more sustainable and equitable societies, embraced by rich industrial countries for their own purposes, has begun to spread. Other nations have recognized that social system change is inevitable and must be guided in constructive ways, on the basis of valuable information. The quasi-market for innovations has its brokers, such as the Rockefeller Foundation, the Ford Foundation, the Kurt A. Körber Foundation, and the Bertelsmann Foundation. The Carl Bertelsmann prize illustrates the role of knowledge brokers in global-local innovations, as well as the transparency phenomenon itself.

The Bertelsmann Foundation originated as a modest German publishing house that had created loyal readers through its book clubs. In 1977 its director, Reinhard Mohn, established the Bertelsmann Foundation, transferring most of his shares to a management company. Today it is one of the most active European foundations concerned with solving local and global problems. Its central mission is defined by two questions: "How can we efficiently manage continuous change in our society? How can we keep moving forward, maintain competitiveness and yet shape our transitions in a humane and socially responsible way?"[36] Working from a global perspective, its focus is on improving German national governance. Thus it is politically independent but does not shy away from political issues.[37]

The Bertelsmann Foundation awards its annual prize to stimulate social and political awareness by drawing attention to international approaches to social problems. To accomplish this, it selects successful models of reform that have led to beneficial social change. In 2001 it awarded its prize to Poland and Bolivia in recognition of their peaceful transition from authoritarianism to democracy and a market economy. The 2002 prize was concerned with creating sustainable alliances of business, government, and civil society. The winner was Transparency International, with three runners-up: the Coalition for Environmentally Responsible Economies; Conservation International; and the World Business Council for Sustainable Development.[38] By studying a large number of global NGOs, the foundation hoped to discover the best practices worldwide for social reform and improvement *in Germany*. This award had a more limited objective than the enormously prestigious Nobel award: to help Germany learn from the innovative practices of these organizations. Examples from global civil society were seen as models for better practices at home. At the same time, the Bertelsmann Foundation also acted as a broker in the quasi-market of global civil society by examining a number of organizations in the search for a winner.

Bertelsmann's survey results concentrate mainly on four INGOs. This presents an intriguing opportunity to understand the specific dynamics of a certain type of INGO: the high-expertise, epistemic community–based, and issue-driven INGO working in alliances and global "federations" seeking to establish lasting reforms and effective new norms and standards for their mission. In reviewing these organizations, we concentrate on the winner, Transparency International. Not only did TI win this prize, it is an INGO of very wide reach and demonstrated success, and it is strongly engaged in social system change.

All of the INGOs on the short list were founded by a remarkable person with enormous energy. All participate in what we have called the quasi-market of global solutions. A remarkable example of this group is Joan Bavaria, cofounder of the Coalition for Environmentally Responsible Economies (CERES). Bavaria was the founding president and CEO of the Boston-based firm Trillium Asset Management, incorporated in 1982. Before that, she cofounded the Social Investment Forum, an organization providing advice to loan fund organizations engaged in socially responsible investing.[39] At the time of the grounding of the Exxon tanker *Valdez* in March 1989, causing a catastrophic oil spill in Prince William Sound, Bavaria was able to bring both investment companies and environmentalist organizations together and to motivate businesses to measure the environmental costs of their activities. Such a reliance on measurement and business data underlies the CERES principles, rules for sustainable business practice. CERES promotes the idea that businesses may benefit by incorporating environmental practices into their core business strategy.

This emphasis on standards and measurement, indeed transparency, also led to the establishment of the Global Reporting Initiative, a vehicle for reporting on the social and environmental impact of companies. Kofi Annan called this organization "an admirable response to one of the primary challenges of our times: making global markets more stable and inclusive."[40] Obviously, Joan Bavaria worked with many other leaders in her network linking environmentalism and business. Her persistence created an organization of limited, but wide-ranging influence when the *Valdez* disaster mobilized the initial cadres of CERES "to do something."

The World Business Council on Sustainable Development (WBCSD) came about in response to the United Nations' need to organize a program for linking environmental and development problems on a global scale. It was necessary to reduce the distrust between environmentalists and industrialists, at least to get them to attend the same conference. Maurice Strong, organizer of the 1992 UN Conference on Environment and Development in Rio de Janeiro, turned to Stephan Schmidheiny to tackle the assignment of mobilizing a substantial participation of corporate leaders for this program. Schmidheiny, a Swiss industrialist with an established record in both environmental awareness and business, believed that businesses could actually benefit from incorporating environmental responsibility into their core functions.[41] In 1991 he founded the Business Council for Sustainable Development (BCSD) and financed its work in preparing the Rio conference. Instead of disbanding after the conference, several participants found the discussions so significant that they established a permanent organization. By this time, many corporations had begun to feel public pressure for environmental protection. The BCSD now defined its long-term mission, which was to create a forum "for businesses to promote sustainable development and corporate social responsibility" by building networks to provide expertise for industrial practice.[42] This required a large membership. In 1995 the BCSD merged with the World Industry Council for the Environment, based in Paris, and increased its membership to 120 leading corporations; the merger created the World Business Council for Sustainable Development (WBCSD), with about 160 global corporations as members in 2002.

As a knowledge "platform," the WBCSD set up a large network of connections, including partnerships with international agencies like the UNDP, the World Bank, universities, and INGOs like the World Resource Institute and CERES. WBCSD developed the concept of "eco-efficiency," with the goal of using less raw material and energy to make superior products at lower cost. Thus WBCSD became the catalyst for a variety of cooperative projects. One of the most ambitious is the Sustainable Mobility Project, with thirteen member companies, to develop new automotive technologies. In May 2003, Dow Chemical and General Motors came to an initial understanding regarding a huge project utilizing hydrogen in giant fuel cells to be built by GM.[43] This technology is claimed to be able to generate enough energy to power 25,000 homes. The WBCSD was not a response to an appalling environmental disaster, but to an invitation by the United Nations to help bring business leaders and environmentalists to cooperate and to implant environmental ideas in the culture of many major corporations.[44] Again, one remarkable individual was a crucial factor in creating this catalytic organization.

The founder of Conservation International (CI), Peter Seligmann, had been a professional in a major environmental organization. During field visits in Latin America, he saw hopeless poverty in countries of incredibly rich biological diversity. He concluded that conservation could not possibly succeed if it ran counter to the economic needs of the population. Economic factors had to be incorporated in sustainable environmental protection. Seligmann's employer did not share his views, and they parted ways. Thirty colleagues went with Seligmann, agreeing with the premise that "only solutions that integrate both economic and ecological factors can succeed in the long term."[45]

Founded in 1987, Conservation International was a major undertaking, with thirty-five staff members and a new board of directors. Funding was to come not from memberships but from generous individuals. CI's annual budget expanded to $70.3 million in 2001, by far the largest among the INGOs described here. CI's strategy was to balance the interests of all parties in solving conservation problems. Those who benefited from exploiting the environment had to be shown workable alternatives to solving their needs. This meant taking their cultures and traditions seriously, assuring the livelihood of those living in the environment while attempting to preserve it.

Finding such solutions required a high level of scientific and social expertise. The appointment of Russell A. Mittermeier, a zoologist, as president of CI assured its commitment to research as well as to action.

CI convinced a number of rich donors to invest in its innovative strategy of offering economic incentives for ecological improvements. The "debt-for-nature swaps" provide funding for part of a country's debt on condition that its government protect specific areas as nature preserves. The complexity of conservation issues requires solid research conducted on site. Thus CI created a Rapid Assessment Program, whereby a team of scientists gathers the necessary data as quickly as possible to assess the problem and how to solve it. The program was expanded to marine research, focusing on the coral reef regions in the Pacific. CI focuses on the most endangered areas with the greatest biodiversity. This is a clearly delimited niche in the quasi-market for global solutions.

In 1998 Gordon Moore, a wealthy Intel executive, donated $35 million to CI, enabling it to establish its Center for Applied Biodiversity Science.[46] Reliance on wealthy donors enables CI to pursue its strategies independently from government funding sources. CI's rigorous research standards and scientific expertise give it great credibility. This has enabled it to work with local politicians in arriving at politically and economically viable solutions for conservation as well as protecting the economy. CI organized its own platform for knowledge exchange with business corporations by establishing the Center for Environmental Leadership in Business in 2001.

Transparency International

By the beginning of the twenty-first century, Transparency International had become the most influential INGO among the global efforts to fight corruption. Peter Eigen, its founder, was never a revolutionary activist, but his life was changed by the experience of hitch-hiking in South America in 1963: "On this trip I first got a sense about the injustices of the world, a feeling that was to change me forever. Whoever picked me up on this trip or let me stay with them, I got to know the rulers as well as the workers and students." He met dictators and their friends, leftist students, Communist artists and workers as he traveled. In Argentina he saw Jewish refugees, old Nazis, members of the military junta. He observed the arrogance of the ruling classes and "how chauvinistically they lived at the expense of the vast majority of citizens."[47] He decided that he would come back there "and do something useful." In 1968, Eigen joined the World Bank as an attorney dealing with international trade and procurement. In 1971 the Ford Foundation sent him to Botswana to help establish a legal system and international economic transactions. His wife, Jutta, a physician, played an important role in his life. She moved to Botswana with him, where she worked in a hospital.

On his return to the World Bank in 1975, Eigen was responsible for the seven central African countries Cameroon, Central African Republic, Chad, People's Republic of Congo, Equatorial Guinea, Gabon, and São Tome/ Principe. It was a turbulent time in Africa and in Eigen's work. From 1983 until 1988 Eigen was responsible for the World Bank's work in Argentina, Chile, Ecuador, Paraguay, Peru, and Uruguay. In 1988 he moved with his family to Kenya, where he became intensely aware of the enormous harm done by corruption.

At this time, what we should call macro-corruption by dictatorial rulers had become a matter of public concern in many parts of the world. In 1986 there was the fall of Ferdinand Marcos and the democratic revolution in the Philippines, with the revelation of huge riches amassed by the corrupt government. Massive corruption was discovered in many other places, especially with the end of the cold war and the collapse of the Soviet empire. The cold war was waged not only by the direct confrontation of the two superpowers, but also by indirect diplomacy and bribery by countries in the developing world. It was a period of secrecy and opacity. Stealth operations by both sides were carried on in all continents; development and military aid were tools of the contenders. Bribery and government corruption were taken as matters of course, especially in the Third World. The emerging new states in the former sphere of Soviet power were trying to adapt to a new era of democracy and open markets. Opportunities for enormous corruption arose with the privatization of formerly state-owned enterprises and by the widely promoted doctrine of deregulation.

Toleration of corruption was endemic virtually worldwide, but especially in Africa. In 1990 representatives of the World Bank working in Africa met to examine how to improve governance in the countries under their responsibility.[48] Peter Eigen and his colleagues were extremely frustrated by the devastating effects of corruption. Many of the projects they were expected to oversee were unnecessary, overpriced, and handled by corrupt businesses in the rich countries.

There was also frustration on the part of donors. At that time, Hansjörg Ellshorst was the manager of the German Society for Technical Cooperation, a state-owned organization of about 122,000 employees and one of the world's largest development agencies. Ellshorst's refusal to practice bribery led to the loss of a lucrative project in Indonesia, a $100 million undertaking. Some of his employees protested—jobs in the agency were at stake. Instead of tolerating bribery, Ellshorst resolved to abolish corruption.[49] This was exactly the spirit of Peter Eigen and his colleagues. The World Bank representatives assembled around Eigen agreed that it was now important to launch an anticorruption effort by the World Bank. Fredrik Galtung reports:

> At the Bank's Washington headquarters, however, doubts quickly emerged. The Bank's legal department was implacably opposed, repeatedly citing the Bank's articles of confederation prohibiting it from being involved in a member government's political affairs and claiming that corruption was therefore beyond the Bank's legal mandate. This view dominated senior and middle management circles. In spite of encouragement from the field generated by staff members' experiences, from certain individuals within World Bank headquarters, and from some (though by no means all) political leaders in the African region, *many of the Bank's managers felt that tackling corruption would interfere with the Bank charter's "requirement" to abstain from "political" considerations in lending decisions and was therefore not an option.*[50]

This attitude was shared by many governments. The World Bank under President Conable was stubbornly against any policy to curb corruption. Conable personally forbade Eigen to work against corruption. "It would shed a bad light on the World Bank." Eigen then left the bank to devote all his time to the creation of Transparency International. Since 1990, such views are perceived to be astoundingly wrongheaded. The moral framework has shifted. Peter Eigen's book describing a "net of corruption" contains a remarkable postscript by Conable's successor at the World Bank. It recognizes the enormous accomplishment of Eigen and Transparency International in putting corruption on the agenda, even praising him for undertaking his work outside the institution.[51] This was an unusual statement by the leader of the World Bank and proof of the dramatic change TI has effected in that institution and elsewhere. When Eigen left the bank to devote himself entirely to the cause of fighting corruption, he mobilized credible and visible elites, including Oscar Arias, Nobel laureate and former president of Costa Rica, and former presidents of Germany, the United States, and Botswana.[52]

Transparency International was set up in an unusually decentralized way. The office in Berlin, and to some extent the one in London, are "central" only in that they provide expertise and resources as well as connections to influential people who can help to realize TI's objectives. National chapters support their own work financially. Each was founded by local citizens and each sets its own agenda. They share a common concern for the effects of corruption, but their priorities may be quite different. In one chapter the highest priority might be the health sector, in another it might be municipal government procurements. They all abide by the ground rules of the TI approach: there must be no confrontational attack on "evildoers"; instead, there must be a shared approach to build "integrity systems." All chapters must abide by TI's integrity norms. They all see themselves as an international network devoted to transparency. They have annual meetings and communicate frequently with each other. By 2003, TI chapters were found in nearly 100 countries.

The relationship between the Berlin secretariat and local chapters is complex and often intense. Each chapter is part of the local culture (something we observed by visiting chapters in various countries). The Greek TI chapter's president, Virginia Tsoudero, told us that she had met John Brademus in New York and learned from him about the importance of Transparency International. She explained: "He was amongst those who were a founding member of Transparency. I said, 'Well, we need it also in Greece.' And we formed a committee. We formed a committee here completely accidentally." She also explained to us the different types of corruption in different part of the European Union. As we pointed out before, the Scandinavian countries are proud of their clean approaches in politics and business, but the presumption of bribery in developing countries did continue (even though now strong efforts are made to eliminate it).

The culture of corruption is not easily changed. It requires strong efforts in the public media, and in educational undertakings. People need to understand that corruption is actually very harmful to them. This will not be obvious to many of them, until the recognition of using public resources for private uses is actually recognized as a crime and a distraction of public policy decisions. Virginia Tsoudero continued: "We are not in favor of having many members. We are in contrast, for example, to TI Argentina. Our membership is by individuals—could be organizations, but we don't do that yet. We have distinguished members of the business world as members, for example the ex-president of the industrialists and the present chairman of the industrialists."[53] The Greek example illustrates very well several facts about the national chapters. They set their own agendas, very much aware of cultural differences and different patterns of corruption in their countries. They do not generally recruit large numbers of members, but influential experts. Indeed, TI networks deliberately work through the symbolic medium of exchange of influence.

TI at first focused on reducing corruption in the southern developing countries and in the "transitional" countries in the former Soviet realm. It would remain a single-issue organization, not spreading its efforts thinly in too many directions. It was a natural choice to describe itself as a "coalition against corruption in international business transactions."[54] However, another matter of strategy had to be resolved: should TI follow the model of Amnesty International in exposing human rights abusers? Should TI confront corrupt officials?

A senior leader of Amnesty International recommended against adopting the role of muckraker. This would make it more difficult for TI to reach its goal. The best strategy was to fight corruption by using transparency and forming influential coalitions for reform. This meant creating public awareness of the horrendous costs of corruption and establishing cooperative networks that would insist on integrity in government and in business. Of course, TI welcomed the publications of investigative journalists to expose corruption cases but did not see this as its own task. TI sought to make the problem of corruption highly visible worldwide, to combat the assumption that corruption is a fact of life that one must live with. To achieve this daunting task, in 1995 TI created the Corruption Perceptions Index (CPI) through cooperative arrangements with universities and research centers. To create the index, TI worked with Johann Graf Lambsdorff, of the University of Passau, where he established the Internet Center for Corruption Research. The index measures the perception of corruption as recorded by knowledgeable experts in specific countries, merging several parallel surveys into one worldwide index. Since its inception, the CPI has become the most visible measure of global corruption.

For the 2002 Corruption Perception Index, fifteen different surveys were used, conducted by nine independent organizations. Countries were included in the CPI only if at least three such surveys had been conducted there. Scores (10 points means no corruption; 0 means extreme corruption) are based on the composite of the surveys.[55] Lambsdorff reported in the Corruption Research Center Web site how some countries of low standing reacted to it in its early days:

> The index, being a politically sensitive and provocative instrument, resulted in some strong international reactions. Indonesia was rated worst in 1995 and clearly rejected this assessment—just to experience a bitter economic crisis shortly afterwards. Argentina's president Carlos Menem called TI a criminal organisation in 1996. Had he taken the warnings more seriously and contained corruption among his administration, he may have spared the country from an

awful economic crisis. Criticism of the index was not always well-founded and sometimes came from those with a bad conscience—in some cases comparable to authoritarian regimes rejecting a negative human rights report as being culturally biased.[56]

By now, the CPI is of high political relevance the world over. Countries are painfully, or proudly, aware of their rank in the index.

More recently, TI created the TI Bribe Payers' Index, an effort that measures the proclivity of international businesses to pay bribes.[57] It, too, was the result of cooperation between TI and expert organizations; it is built on special surveys conducted in fifteen "emerging market" economies by the Gallup International Association. It was an important step for the TI strategy: while the initial focus was on corruption in developing countries, now the frame had widened. Corruption was affected not only by the proclivity to accept bribes, but also by the proclivity to offer them. The purview of TI now included some of the problems of the industrial countries.

The index was constructed on the basis of interviews conducted by the Gallup International Association with 835 senior executives of domestic and foreign companies, executives of accounting firms, binational chambers of commerce, national and foreign commercial banks, and commercial law firms in emerging market countries. They included Argentina, Brazil, Colombia, Hungary, India, Indonesia, Mexico, Morocco, Nigeria, the Philippines, Poland, Russia, South Africa, South Korea, and Thailand. Questions probed the propensity of companies from twenty-one rich exporting countries to bribe senior public officials in emerging market countries. The rating also included the countries that had ratified the OECD convention against bribery. According to the Bribe Payers' Index, Australia and Sweden are the countries least inclined to bribery, the United States is placed about midlevel, at rank 13 (in spite of the laws prohibiting bribing), and Russia is the most bribery-prone country, at rank 21.

There was a widespread belief in the international business community in the late 1980s and early 1990s that one could not do business in poor countries without paying bribes. In fact, some Western governments allowed tax deductions for bribes paid abroad, since bribing was considered a necessary business practice and expense. The United States' Foreign Corrupt Practices Act (FCPA) of 1977 was an early effort to change this. It was passed because it had become known that over 400 American companies admitted to bribing officials in foreign countries. This was seen as a scandal. The purpose of the law was to "bring a halt to the bribery of foreign officials and to restore public confidence in the integrity of the American business system. The antibribery provisions of the FCPA made it unlawful for a U.S. person to make a corrupt payment to a foreign official for the purpose of obtaining or retaining business for or with, or directing business to, any person."[58] The law was amended in 1988 and provided specifics for its enforcement; it was even then a pioneering legislation, not adopted elsewhere. TI built upon this U.S. initiative by enlisting a network of supporters in southern countries and in other Western countries to ban corruption and bribery. It was a long process, but TI succeeded in persuading several governments to follow the U.S. lead. In 1997 the OECD countries formed a treaty to ban all bribery abroad. This was a breakthrough for TI and a cultural milestone in the advance of transparency.

A further element of the evolving TI strategy was the creation of a guidebook, entitled *National Integrity Systems: the TI Source Book,* for effective action to advance integrity in social systems.[59] This work may be as important as TI's major indices that have made corruption and bribery a highly visible public issue. Translated into twenty languages, the *Source Book* is designed to generate effective and workable norms for integrity. It is a tool enabling local activists to use practical strategies for transparency and accountability in their countries.

Locally initiated projects for reform have had deep effects in several countries. Changes are occurring in the transparency/secrecy syndrome, the moral climate, and thereby in the institutional structures of several communities. The *Source Book* is a work in progress that builds on the experience and insights of many actors in various countries. It is in touch with the activists in TI chapters around the world. The key concept in this strategy is that of the "integrity system," designed to make corruption a risky undertaking that offers low rewards. Jeremy Pope puts it this way:

> The first version of this Source Book . . . advocates the need to adopt an holistic approach to any anti-corruption reform programme. It also recognizes that every society, in whatever stage of development, has evolved a series of institutions and practices that collectively serve as its national integrity system. Few have been consciously developed as such—and most will be in need of repair. Country "Integrity System Audits" are now being developed by Transparency International to this end.[60]

An integrity system must be free of needless restrictions and obstructions to government effectiveness. While Pope takes a positive outlook, he is a realist who is well aware of the ocean of corruption in the world; he believes that the

European Union suffers from enormous corruption and nepotism. He saw TI's effort as an audacious "uphill battle."[61] Both the practical and ethical thrusts in the guidebook are articulated in the foreword by Oscar Arias, former president of Costa Rica and Nobel peace laureate, who notes the difficulty of eradicating corruption in totalitarian regimes. "In Latin America, many dictators justified their governments for years by pointing the finger at corrupt regimes of the past. These same dictatorships were often fronts for thieves and embezzlers. . . . Corruption can only be examined and eradicated in an environment of pluralism, tolerance, freedom of expression, and individual security—an environment that only democracy can guarantee."[62]

The *Source Book* defines corruption as "the misuse of entrusted power for private benefit." It is "trans-systemic." It has existed in to some extent in all known social systems, feudal, capitalist, socialist, and liberal.[63] The damage done by corruption is not only that large resources are diverted from the public good to private exploitation, but also that important decisions are determined by ulterior motives without regard to the public interest. The costs of corruption can be extraordinarily high, although they are difficult to ascertain, since corruption is done by stealth and secrecy. The World Bank estimates that corrupt African leaders have placed several billion dollars in European banks. The cost of corruption in Mexico is said to be greater than the entire budget for educational system of the country. Corruption also occurs in the private sector. Its control requires a comprehensive integrity system and a functioning state based on the rule of law. This reminds us that global transformations are not necessarily destroying nation-states. A reliable state is the major condition for protecting the common good in the era of global change. Accountability, both vertical and horizontal, requires effective institutional structures.

Vertical accountability is demanded by voters to whom the elected government is responsible. However, in the words of the *Source Book,* it is insufficient:

> Politics has become a profession, and as such has acquired its own rules and standards, to which the political class subscribes—those who govern and those contesting for power alike. Transparency vis-à-vis the people is seldom seen as being an advantage to the rulers, who have a vested interest controlling what the governed know and precisely how what is going on is presented to them (hence the emergence of "spin doctors").[64]

Instead, there must also be the checks and balances made possible by horizontal accountability—that is, interlocking different agencies in governance, including independent reviewers that create a sense that fraud is likely to be detected.

> Monitoring corruption cannot be left only to public prosecutors and to the forces of law and order. Action cannot depend solely on detection and criminal prosecution. Rather, action must include a combination of interlocking arrangements. In part, this approach includes improving the transparency of relationships, and to the extent possible, preventing the development of relationships which can lead to corruption. It includes transparency in the financial affairs of key players and the prospect of reviews being conducted by independent institutions which are likely to be outside any particular corruption network.[65]

The National Integrity System, the core of the *Source Book,* takes a holistic view of the institutional structures that are necessary for the integrity of a state. This system is essential to the successful functioning of markets and the private sector as well as of civil society. The approach is a very detailed framework of checks and balances by assigning multiple government functions to separate agencies, a division of powers. The *Source Book* specifies the requirements of sustainable development, the rule of law, and the quality of life. All this depends on public awareness and solid social values.

Civil society can play an important role in advancing an integrity system. As part of civil society, TI can be effective only by forming influential coalitions. It relies on national chapters, independent "owners" of the transparency movement, but under two conditions: they must not investigate and denounce specific individual cases of corruption, and they must avoid partisan politics. This would compromise their credibility and that of TI. National chapters set their own agendas as local circumstances require. They must establish credibility and win the confidence of both politicians and the public. Finally, the TI strategy requires a step-by-step approach. "Rather than arguing for dramatic, sweeping programmes that attempt to cleanse the stables in a single onslaught, TI argues for achievable and highly specific plans of action."[66] The *Source Book* contains specific guidance for action and describes both successful and failed efforts to contain corruption. TI offers an even more substantial account of these learning episodes and the state of corruption worldwide in the *Global Corruption Report 2003.*[67]

The evolution of Transparency International illustrates the role that civil society can play in social system change. This organization grew and its knowledge base matured in a remarkably short time. Its emergence coincided with the growth of global civil society at large in recent decades. Michael Wiehen divides this period into three phases: "In the first phase, we started with narrow expectations, and now we are blooming, blossoming, expanding. We have also seen some hurdles. TI itself is now at a stage where it begins a new strategy discussion. At the beginning, even if we just look at the slogans we used then, the focus was on corruption in international business transactions."[68]

Phase two turned to a network of national chapters in developing countries. However, TI confronted the problem of widespread political corruption, which undermined its efforts. In Wiehen's view:

> If governance is corrupt, we cannot start. So, the early message with its narrow focus could not last. We accepted that and turned to the issues in political corruption. We talked with administrators, politicians, and very quickly developed tools to get into debates with these people. . . . In the second phase TI became much more systematic. We wrote down our experiences with issues in certain countries. The *Source Book* became a tool. We became more prescriptive. Just as we structured our themes of the TI mission and strategy, we structured our national chapters, even in countries that had not come to us. When we looked at the map five years ago, Russia, Japan, China, Indonesia, and many others were not on our map. We were never successful in Japan. In China there is no civil society, so we work with the government. We had a hard time in Russia; now we have a chapter. We had a difficult time in Indonesia. They had a rich tapestry of NGOs before we came on the scene. Some had dealt with corruption; we were not the first there. We still do not have a strong chapter there, but a small one that cooperates with other organizations.

In this second phase, TI formed coalitions against corruption with government, business, and civil society, working mostly with the first two, and gradually with civil society organizations. Wiehen described his negotiations with OECD and Hermes, the German export-credit institution:

> I said to various export-credit institutions that they had an important role to play so that corruption is not continued. I went to the German institution Hermes, owned by Allianz, but connected to the government because whatever losses they make is covered by the government. They support exports by national industries. I asked them: "What do you do to make sure you don't support deals that are clearly corrupt?" They said: "Why should we care?" I said: "You have public money. You should not support deals that are clearly corrupt." I have been there six times, brought in the federal government, and after two

years they said: "All right. We will adopt a few of your suggestions. Hermes coverage is not available for deals that engage or result in corruption." Since that date, Hermes requires each applicant to sign "This deal is not obtained by corruption." That is a major step forward.

Now TI is entering phase three, where several new tasks need to be solved. When Wiehen joined TI, he recalled,

> We were dealing exclusively with problems in developing countries. Everyone then was from development assistance work. I did notice that, but accepted it in the first year. Then I said: "We must broaden out"—we can't say that we don't have corruption here in Germany. I accepted the post of leading Transparency International–Germany on a condition: there needed to be a shift in the German chapter from working only on corruption and bribery in the developing countries to focusing on corruption and bribery in Germany. We slowly found our area of activity.

In phase three, Wiehen returned to Hermes; he wanted more. He told them, "Talk to your colleagues in OECD. You certainly want to make sure that all your competitors play by the same rules." At the OECD in November 2000, he discussed with the German representative twelve items TI wanted export credit institutions to adopt. "The representative told the group, 'We do this and it has not messed us up.' They adopted 60–70 percent of the first action paper." When Wiehen checked with the OECD export credit group two years later, they reported mixed results. He sent a questionnaire to all members, and they addressed the issue again. Wiehen said, "Most of you have done quite nicely in terms of papers, but there are no cases. You allow the commissions that companies pay to be included in the total. But you do not identify the amount of the commissions. If you discover that it is 15 percent, that is quite different from 2 percent. I gave them a list of fifteen points, which they are still struggling with. . . . This has been a dialogue among equals. They accept us as professionals, not ideologically driven, who want something they want."

In its third phase of evolution, TI confronts the challenges of a widening mission and its own growing complexity. It is forming coalitions with other global nongovernmental organizations. Wiehen has met with Greenpeace and the World Wildlife Fund (in Germany), who proposed joining forces. In joint meetings with Hermes, Wiehen made it clear that there was a point beyond which he would not go. An approach had to be nonconfrontational. He described the meeting with Hermes:

It started professionally and realistically. Then, within weeks we got a draft letter from environmental NGOs that said, "We have prepared a catalogue of demands for the ministry—on every deal there must be an environmental impact study." I looked at it and said, "This is not our approach and we won't sign." That has happened several times in the past few years. Each time we get a phone call from the ministry involved saying, "It has been noticed that you did not sign." Our coalition building with other NGOs is always very cautious. We work with them to the extent that we could benefit from it. Right now, we have a different problem.

That different problem turned out to be a complex set of further issues. TI has matured into a widely recognized, respected, and influential INGO. It now faces also the complexity that comes with success and intergenerational transitions. One of the issues of growth, says Wiehen, is TI's position in relation to other groups:

We must define our position especially with other actors in civil society. Right now we have an issue relating to the WTO—we want to have a special concern with transparency in government procurements. Developed countries want to expand markets and we, and I personally, have jumped on this wagon. Every society will benefit from this. Now, suddenly, Oxfam, Greenpeace, and others are fighting our issue on the grounds that developing countries are so overtaxed, they can't handle more issues. . . . Developing countries have a problem with that, and rightly so. This is now a case where we may well decide not to push our narrower technical issue because . . . this will be seen as a breach in the NGO community. For us this is a telling moment in the third phase, since as a member of civil society we have a broader responsibility. Let me just say, just two weeks ago, Eigen invited the heads of about ten major NGOs and talked about issues like these. We took the initiative. We acknowledge that we are a power. We must be much more strategic for example in relation to the World Bank. It is now very active. In economic analysis the bank is way ahead of us. It forces us to rethink our own position.

Another issue concerns the evolving structures in TI, including the gradual transition in leadership, the very large number of national chapters, and the expansion of TI's projects. Wiehen said that TI will continue to rely on unpaid professional volunteers. "There is no NGO that could pay me. Peter Eigen's special talent is to convince people to work eighteen hours a day, and be happy doing it. His successor must have that gift. . . . TI in its present strengths will continue if the head can mobilize these people." It can be done.

197

Beyond Transparency?

Since its early efforts, Transparency International has branched out in many directions.[69] One extraordinary achievement in 1998 was bringing eleven banks together to adopt the Wolfsberg Principles, a code of conduct for their international network and with their major competitors to fight money laundering. The banks involved were UBS AG, ABN AMRO Bank, Barclays Bank, Banco Santander Central Hispano, S.A., Chase Manhattan Private Bank, Citibank, N.A., Credit Suisse Group, Deutsche Bank, AG, HSBC, J. P. Morgan, Inc., and Société Générale. Representatives from the banks met with Peter Eigen, Frank Vogl, and Fritz Heimann (the latter two from TI USA) to agree on the code. This agreement has become even more important in the fight against money laundering by terrorist organizations.

A second achievement was the Partnership for Transparency Fund created to provide small sums of money to fight corruption. For example, experts in TI chapters in such countries as Kenya, Argentina, or Ecuador can provide help to anticorruption efforts in other countries. Such people were often invited by World Bank teams as consultants. Because TI worried that they might lose credibility by being integrated into these teams, the Partnership for Transparency Fund provides enough money for them to do their work without losing their independence. These grants are enlarging the mobility of the anticorruption network. Support comes from development agencies such as the German Ministry for Economic Cooperation, UNDP, and private foundations.

The third project is the Forestry Integrity Network (FIN). Peter Eigen pointed out to a professor of environmental studies, Theodore Panayoto, that corruption leads to the destruction of the environment. This is certainly occurring in large forests in developing countries: through bribes, illegal licenses are awarded, leading to wholesale deforestation in some areas. FIN was established to fight this form of corruption; it included the World Bank, academic institutions, environmental INGOs, and activists from the countries most affected by this abuse: Cameroon, Nigeria, Indonesia, Brazil, and Colombia.

In spite of its many successes, TI was only a small global civil society organization in its first decade. As it is today, it was a network of valiant, competent activists. Its agenda has become broader, more complex, more involved with outside forces. It is now entering a new, much more ambitious era.

The Next Decade: The Transparency International Strategic Framework

By 2003–04, TI had completed a comprehensive assessment of how it should be organized for the next decade and how to define its strategies. It had seen a number of spectacular successes over its first decade. The need for coalitions and a coherent worldwide network called for a comprehensive self-examination. TI began the new era by involving its national chapters and the Berlin secretariat in the comprehensive self-assessment that resulted in the Transparency International Strategic Framework of 2004. The framework begins with these statements:

> In 2003 TI celebrated its 10th anniversary. The organisation has accomplished much during its first decade and is recognised as the leading NGO focusing on fighting corruption at the international and national level. However, corruption still distorts political, economic and social life and as TI grows and continues its fight against corruption new challenges open up. To identify the strategic directions for the organisation for the next three to five years, TI has undertaken a process of strategic planning. This document is the result of that process. Consultations with the Movement and with external stakeholders have helped define the following vision and mission for TI:
>
> • TI's vision is a world in which government, politics, business, civil society and the daily lives of people are free of corruption.
>
> • TI's mission is to work to *create change* towards a world free of corruption.[70]

There is a sense of pride in past accomplishments, but also an awareness that much more can be achieved. The programs to be undertaken will focus on changes to be made to effect "a world free of corruption" and on a limited list of "Global Priorities which have been identified on the basis of consultation within the TI Movement." The scope of these global priorities is limited and focused on TI's mission and capacities, but it is far wider than its initial, much narrower objectives. TI recognizes six global trends: Concerns about terrorism may lead some governments to play down the issue of corruption; greater attention must be given to corruption at the international level, to creating legislation and anticorruption policies; codes of conduct, conventions, and standards on corruption must be established with resources for implementation and enforcement; there are rising concerns about the social and environmental costs of globalization efforts pursued by governments and multinational corporations; there should be more "public and media attention to the governance of businesses and the relationship between business and party politics"; similarly, there should be more public and media concern with the transparency and accountability of NGOs; finally, technological developments are needed, particularly in telecommunications (Internet, wireless), facilitating access to information.[71]

TI has the ability to pursue these priorities. The capacities of the national chapters have increased and so have those of the secretariat. As a result, there are many sources of expertise available. The knowledge resources needed for this work have grown; more coalitions have been formed. Also very important is the fact that TI can mobilize highly qualified experts as volunteers. The strategic framework outlines how to strengthen these resources and bring them to bear on needed programs. Bold global priorities have been carefully identified: to reduce corruption in politics; to curb corruption in public contracting; to encourage anticorruption standards in the private sector; and to advance international conventions against corruption.

The problem of corruption in politics is staggering in many countries, including the United States. To combat it requires movements by citizens, members of congress/parliament, parties, and business. The United States saw extensive and raucous debates about this issue, only to have new legislation imaginatively circumvented by election campaign managers in 2004. Much more needs to be done. Cleaning up contracting procedures can begin by drawing on established TI tools, such as the "integrity pacts." There is a plausible idea for providing "an independent global perspective on the theme of corruption in public contracting and therefore facilitate national, regional and international awareness, improvement, exchange of experience and benchmarking."[72]

Enforcing anticorruption standards in the private sector involves the establishment of business principles. TI plans to focus specifically on the abolition of corporate bribery. This will require a legal framework to enforce these rules. National chapters of TI are specifically called upon to help in monitoring these arrangements. There are seven more major programs that focus on (1) securing access to information, (2) combating money laundering and recovering stolen property, (3) fostering education for ethics and anticorruption norms, (4) advancing accountability of civil society organizations and preventing corruption by development cooperation, (5) promoting judicial reform and enforcement of anticorruption laws, (6) working against corruption in—for example—environmental industries, and (7) measuring corruption even better than TI has done in the past.

The realization of these goals requires cooperation in a well-organized way. The strategic framework provides ideas for cooperation between the national chapters and the secretariat, and for creating regional programs around the world. This vast network needs access to knowledge and practical tools. Each regional network and each programmatic theme has a specific person responsible in the secretariat. Policy and research play strategic roles with responsibilities for measuring corruption, the anticorruption handbook, the TI *Source Book*. The Knowledge Centre provides access to existing knowledge. One of its features is Corruption in the Education Sector, available through CORIS (Corruption Online Research and Information System). In addition, the TI Web site includes country reports, corruption news, the *Source Book,* and other useful information. The use of the Internet has become very intense. A further instrument of the global efforts of TI is the series of International Anti-Corruption Conferences (IACC), which have been biennial events since 1983. The programs of these conferences are administered by a special council and the secretariat of TI.

TI has now decided to apply its transparency principles to itself. Just as codes of conduct have become instruments for transparency in many governments and organizations, TI now has a code of ethics and an ethics committee, a special TI secretariat code of conduct, and the TI conflict of interest policy. Several national chapters have adopted such codes. It is clear that TI has a thought-out framework for its next decade.

It is very important that TI has attended to the realities of its governance structure, because interaction between the chapters and the secretariat is intense. The strategic framework has been a collective creation. Peter Eigen continues as chairman of the board of directors, a globally recruited body. The new chief executive is David Nussbaum, chosen from about 600 candidates by unanimous vote. He is of a younger generation and yet has had much experience in global civil society organizations, having been finance director and a deputy chief executive of Oxfam GB, the British-based development and humanitarian charity. A new, much larger, much more diverse and ambitious organization has emerged.

Global Civil Society, Transparency, and Social System Change

Movements in global civil society have risen in the last few decades with remarkable speed. We have seen the enormous scope of their missions, ranging from the diffuse and varied protests in the streets to the focused, single-cause INGOs. These movements have attracted people of vitality and unreserved dedication to their causes. There is competition in a quasi-market for solutions to global issues that need to be addressed. Brokering institutions in this competitive quasi-market include the Nobel Peace Prize award and, at a lesser level of distinction, the Bertelsmann Foundation, in its effort to evaluate the choices for their award. A learning process is taking place within and among the INGOs and the social movements that spawned them, and also a learning process among the major international agencies and at least some of the world's governments. It is not an easy process, but the case of Transparency International shows that a complex evolution is taking place in global civil society.

To a limited extent, these movements and these engaged people are moving toward better global governance. The demand for transparency is clearly increasing, but so are the conflicts about this trend and the determined resistance by the enemies of the open society. Corruption may actually be spreading in the industrial countries. When we asked Jeremy Pope in 2002 whether corruption was increasing, he answered: "Definitely. There is actual growth. TI is a tiny little NGO." He continued by urging that the fight against corruption be carried out in Europe as well as in other parts of the world. "Yes, opportunities for corruption have grown. And the culture has changed. Now it is that you go into public life to make money. The World Bank should pay market rate, less 20 percent. Then it will get the best people, because you want people who want to make a difference. But last night I was talking with a businessman and I said, 'Don't you wish you were younger? You could make $50 million a year.' And he said, 'What would I do with it?' That ethic has been gone for a decade in Europe."[73]

Pope talked about greed in the film and sports industries. "Opera stars have killed opera. Football stars have killed football. FIFA, the head of the governing board for soccer, has taken bribes. There's a move to get the Olympic movement to check these out, bring accountability. Some good came out of Enron, like ongressional votes for campaign finance. The people enriched by Enron felt pressured. . . . None of the money reaches the kids at the bottom." He concluded that in order to make progress, "TI would have to go on forever."

In 2004 Peter Eigen observed, on the basis of the results of that year's Corruption Perceptions Index: "Corruption robs countries of their potential. As the CPI of 2004 shows, oil-rich Angola, Azerbaijan, Chad, Ecuador, Indonesia, Iran, Iraq, Kazakhstan, Libya, Nigeria, Russia, Sudan, Venezuela, and Yemen all have extremely low scores. In these countries, public contracting in the oil sector is plagued by revenues vanishing into the pockets of Western oil executives, middlemen, and local officials."[74] On the other hand, in the TI quarterly newsletter Eigen wrote that several new presidents in Kenya,

Brazil, and Georgia have made commitments to cleaning house and fighting corruption. Mexico's Vicente Fox and Nigeria's Obasanjo reiterated their engagement in the struggle against corruption. He is hopeful that these leaders may keep their word. Elsewhere, the fight is still under way. "The success of any government cleanup can be assessed only in the long run. But if these campaigns are to have an effect on reducing corruption, political will and sustainable institutional reforms are needed. Civil society must be vigilant in lobbying for such reforms and in ensuring they are implemented. This task will define the years ahead for many TI chapters around the world."[75]

Yes, global civil society is in a period of turbulent change, with many hoping to advance the open society and transparency. But others hope to avoid transparency. They hide in the cloak of stealth and secrecy, yet their malfeasance and crimes, once discovered, may actually advance the cause of transparency and accountability.

7

CORPORATE GOVERNANCE AND TRANSPARENCY

From Exuberance to Scandals to Reform

Recent decades have seen turbulent changes in corporate America, providing a drama of struggles for and against openness, for and against transparency. This chapter presents the dynamics of the transparency syndrome and the confluence of local and global forces pressing for greater transparency and more enforceable rules in business corporations. The business scene in America at the turn of the twenty-first century was a time of huge successes as well as crimes and calamitous collapses. Corporate governance was changing, with an impact on the information values and the conduct of business, certainly in the United States, but in different ways also worldwide. The result has been an intensified rise in pressures for transparency in the corporate world. The social dynamics of the scandals first saw a phase of denial, then a demand for reform and resistance to it, then gains in transparency and improvement in its infrastructure. The forces of transparency can press its dynamic forward, can divert it, and ultimately prevail—creating new challenges.

The business world has seen such turbulence before. One may think of the events following October 1929 after the stock market collapsed. The idea of transparency was almost unknown in the boisterous expansion of the "bubble" years of the early 1920s. Opacity was just fine in the years of wild speculation. After the calamitous crash, the market fell further. In the early 1930s the Great Depression devastated the global economy. High unemployment in all industrial countries led to major reforms in firmly democratic nations and to the catastrophic rise of totalitarianism in countries without such rugged democratic foundations. The 1929 stock market crisis in America led to new legislation providing regulations for the stock market and establishing the Securities and Exchange Commission. Major steps were taken to limit opportunities for fraud, beginning the movement toward financial transparency. Thereafter, management of economic turbulence became more sophisticated and the regulatory institutions more effective. By the late twentieth century, one had every reason to believe that the disasters of the 1930s would not, could not, be repeated.

There is no parallel today to the upheaval of 1929. However, since that time opportunities for malfeasance have reappeared and the scope of economic crime has grown, in spite of the safeguards built by modern states and their institutions. Human ingenuity inspired not only honest people, but also scoundrels who invented new forms of fraud. And like the reaction to America's early efforts at reform of the market, the crisis led to further steps toward transparency. This time the story began in the 1980s, but the full drama did not unfold until the 1990s, an era of the rapid expansion of global civil society. This was a period of growing concerns with global issues and global threats, but especially in America it was a time of exuberant confidence. The wave of new democracies after the end of the cold war and the decline of dictatorships increased the chances for the open society and for open markets. Even more was going on in America's business performance and expansion. Information technology and new business strategies created enormous economic successes. Productivity grew. The stock market rose to unlikely heights. The "Washington consensus" on open, free markets and general acceptance of faith in the efficiency of the market, presumably worldwide, seemed to have won the day. Economic globalization was to follow the American model—which most Americans accepted as a matter of course and fervently believed to be good for the whole world.

This was a remarkable turn after the 1970s and much of the 1980s, when many U.S. industrialists saw Japan as outdistancing the United States. In the 1980s, America's steel industry collapsed. In a way, it was the perception of a loss of competitiveness that motivated the American government and industry to do everything possible to overtake Japan and to adopt a strategy of exports and open markets. Japan had been viewed as a model, albeit a threatening one. This turn to opening foreign markets had much to do with the United States' emergence as the leader of economic globalization.

But in the 1990s there was a conviction, vigorously advocated and spread by the creators of the new technology and IT businesses and their admirers, that the world had entered a "new economy" era. Traditional economic rules had forever yielded to the new rules, they were convinced. The new technology would open the path into the future, would create enormous productivity, wealth, and an expansive, inevitably successful world. Stock options as rewards for business leaders would encourage them to take risks for corporate growth, driven by these incentives and other perks for vast increases in their personal wealth.[1] There developed large, growing companies that existed for long time without any earnings, but with the confidence that their future success would be assured in the new economy. All this added to an exuberant sense of confidence in America.

The Rise of the Celebrity CEO

The major economic and political changes of the late twentieth century produced a cascade of novel phenomena in economies and in the structure of corporate governance. Several of these involved dramatic changes in property. One trend was the spread of state policies of privatization in many countries in the world. It was a movement toward greater liberalization of the economy and a restructuring of state functions.

Paul Starr identifies three general programs for privatization: the institution-building program, the balance-building program, and the boundary-blurring program. The institution-building program means the creation of "an enabling framework for civil society and private markets in parts of the Eastern bloc and some developing countries." The balance-shifting program is "the divestiture of state-owned enterprises and other efforts to redraw the public-private balance in capitalist societies with relatively large public sectors." The boundary-blurring program means using "private providers for public services" and creating "public-private partnerships in carrying out public policies."[2]

During these processes of privatization, major opportunities arose for shifting property not through sales by the state in an open market but in opaque and indirect ways. This occurred through legally sanctioned, private appropriation, and sometimes by outright corruption. It took one turn in the brazen appropriation of public goods for private gain in the countries of the former Soviet empire after its collapse. That process was also called privatization and turned huge state-owned industries into privately owned enterprises. In some cases, former managers of state property became private owners. It created tycoon-oligarchs in Russia and to a lesser extent in other countries like Ukraine. This is one kind of appropriation. There is a rainbow of meanings for the verb *to appropriate*. It means to set apart, to authorize (a sum of money, for example) or to legislate; to take to or for oneself; to take without consent, to seize; and finally: to steal. This is akin to Max Weber's concept of appropriation as economic action.[3] It means *taking* of property, of privilege, of economic advantage, of monopoly, limiting open competition and finding a way to *legitimize the taking*. In Weber's sense it also means closing access to opportunities in economic relations to some while opening and maintaining opportunities to the appropriators and, if at all possible, legitimating their arrangement. Weber's illustration of the concept is the case of "ambulatory" cultivation of land by a household unit: when one's land has been exhausted, new land is taken. According to feudal seigneurial rights over land and persons, "the land itself and the workers are appropriated by the lord, the *use* of the land and rights to work by the peasants." Another example is the plantation where "the land is freely appropriated and worked by purchased slaves." Weber gives many other examples, ranging from simple economies to monopolies of capitalist entrepreneurs.[4]

Appropriation requires some form of closing of economic relationships. In competitive relations, interest groups have incentives to look for lasting advantages. "In spite of their continued competition against one another, the jointly acting competitors now form an interest group toward outsiders" that strives for monopolistic interests and political influence, that is, appropriation.[5] Appropriation in this sense is a form of closed or closing economic relationships, where special economic (and political) advantages are taken by privileged groups. Obviously, appropriation is well known in any economic system, even in advanced and regulated capitalism.

In contrast to the process of privatization in the former Soviet Union, appropriation of property took a different and for a long time much more silent form in America, with some spillover into Europe. This was the emergence of the celebrity CEO. The role of the chief executive officer had evolved because of efforts to improve the efficiency and ingenuity of corporate governance. The dilemma was that publicly traded corporations are typically managed by salaried staff, not by the owners—the shareholders. In privately held companies, the incentives for vigorous dedication to succeed is in the hands of the private entrepreneur, who is also the owner. The change was to search for a combination by providing the chief executive officer and other leading employees of publicly held corporations with incentives similar to those of the owner-entrepreneur. A variety of such incentives, such as stock options and awards of special perquisites (such as bonuses for performance and retention grants), were increasingly used. In fact, the productivity of U.S. companies thrived initially under this system. However, it also led to distortions of intent. The system has enabled boards and CEOs to pursue their own private appropriation of wealth.

Pathways to Appropriation

There were major political battles in America to legalize the process of appropriation. One was the battle to keep the costs of stock options, given to CEOs as incentives to better corporate performance, off the company reports (except as footnotes). The charge was led by Sen. Joseph Lieberman in the belief that showing the expense of stock options would ruin the successful growth of high-technology firms. It was a bitter battle.

Arthur Levitt was chairman of the Securities and Exchange Commission (SEC) from 1993 to 2001. The Financial Accounting Standards Board (FASB) had initiated a new rule to "expense" stock options, that is, to mention them in full financial statements of a company as an expense and not only as a footnote. Levitt said about this event:

> When I came to the SEC, this new FASB rule to expense stock options had galvanized the American business community and brought literally hundreds of CEOs to my office in Washington to urge me to prevent the FASB from going ahead with this proposal. . . . But what happened during the course of this fierce debate and dialogue was that the Congress changed, and Newt Gingrich brought to power a group of congresspeople who were determined to keep FASB from enacting this rule proposal. My concern was that if Congress put through a law that muzzled FASB that would kill independent standard setting. So I went to FASB at that time, and I urged them not to go ahead with the rule proposal. . . . It was probably the single biggest mistake I made in my years at the SEC. . . . Investors should care deeply about expensing stock options, because those options represent a distortion of the earnings of the company. Right now, options are treated as a footnote, but that's not good enough.[6]

Lynn Turner, SEC chief accountant from 1998 to 2001 and director of the Center for Quality Financial Reporting at Colorado State University, was asked about stock options. He saw them as a good tool for appropriate incentives, but open to abuse. On the issue of transparency, he was uncompromising:

> There is no question what these things [stock options] have value. If they didn't have value, heck, we wouldn't be giving out so many of them to everyone. And to turn around and say, "Let's not show that number to investors," is no different—absolutely no different—than turning around and saying, "Let's not show investors the debt. Let's keep it off the balance sheet." So when a congressman turns around and tells me, "Let's put all the debt on the balance sheet, but leave

the stock option expense out," in the back of my mind, I can only assume that there's someone else out there with money that's influencing their decisions.[7]

In a number of cases, stock options improperly used created incentives to mislead investors and regulators, leading in several cases to fraud on a grand scale.

Another factor was the 1995 Tort Reform Act, which limited the scope of lawsuits against corporations to be held responsible for an alleged harm. Its purpose was to reduce the number of frivolous lawsuits against firms. Many business leaders—and also much of the general public—felt that such a limitation was needed. The Tort Reform Act did that, but it also had the effect, according to Lynn Turner, of reducing the risk to corporations and to their auditors of being held accountable.

> The auditing firms now view this, to some degree, as risk management. Not an issue of, "Do I get the audit done right?" but, "I do trade-offs between how much audit work I'm going to do, versus how much risk do I have," or, "Exposure to litigation, given that the passage of that 1995 act, actually reduced the chances that someone's going to successfully sue me." That trade-off is not a healthy situation in the profession right now.

A third factor was the change in the accounting industry to combine auditing with consulting services. Accounting firms became more and more focused on "financial engineering," providing services that allied them increasingly with management rather than with investors. The financial incentives for the accounting firms were great, shifting their very sense of mission. Efforts by the SEC to limit the ensuing conflicts of interests were vigorously fought by the accounting profession. Lynn Turner was asked why it was so important to separate accounting and consulting. He replied:

> In the cases we had seen and what was going on with them, like Waste Management, it had become clear to us that the auditors were not as independent as they should be. And it was becoming a growing trend. At the same time, we'd seen a growing trend in the number of financial restatements, 85 percent of which came out of actions other than the SEC. We'd never seen them before they'd showed up in the paper. So we were very concerned about the trend. Given that, we decided that we couldn't wait any longer, that we needed to go try to do that fix. We'd actually talked to the accounting firms for quite a period of time even before we proposed the rule, trying to get the firms in agreement on a plan that might address the issues. When we couldn't get them to agree to any-

thing—and, in fact, there was a violent split amongst the profession about what the fix could be—then we decided we had to act on our own.

In response to a question about the fight, Turner replied,

It was easily described as a fifteen-round, knock-down, drag-out-to-the-final-bell type of fight. It was the accounting firms using the power of their money, using the power of their Washington, D.C., lobbies, heavy lobbying in Congress—and using that to get Congress at every turn to oppose what we were trying to accomplish. And that was very difficult. . . . It basically took everything we had, every resource within the commission, to avoid having Congress actually cut off our appropriations so we could do no more reform. And that forced us into watering down quite a bit the final reforms that were eventually passed.

A fourth factor was a weakness in the transparency infrastructure of financial reporting: "the number." Alex Berenson asserts that quarterly earning reports by corporations could be—and often actually were—manipulated. Companies have to publish their earnings per share on a regular, quarterly basis. That is "the number," as it is called on Wall Street. It is important since it powerfully influences the price of stock shares and is a barometer of a company's health. How this number is measured by a large corporation is necessarily complex and requires difficult accounting decisions.

Because they're not simply measuring cash inflows and outflows, companies need to make hundreds of assumptions to calculate their earnings each quarter. They must estimate everything from how much money they will earn on their pension funds to how quickly their assets will lose value. With so many assumptions to make, even honest companies sometimes make mistakes. Those who want to cheat have an almost infinite number of ways to do so. They can book sales to customers who won't ever be able to pay them. They can hide ongoing, day-to-day expenses as investments in long lived assets. They can shift research and development expenses to supposedly independent partners. They can make sham deals with other companies, swapping overvalued assets in a way that allows both sides to book a profit on the trade.[8]

This creates a weakness in the information infrastructure for keeping investors and the public informed. There were strong incentives for corporate leaders to keep "the number" as high as possible. The rewards for keeping stock prices high were great. The professionals, for the most part, took "the numbers" at face value. For Berenson, "a reasonable estimate is that fraud and gimmickry added several hundred billion of dollars to the reported profits of the S&P 500 from 1997 to 2002."[9] The weakness in the information infrastructure aided the process of appropriation.

Appropriation by insiders was not the only factor that created a change in corporate conduct. However, it was a central factor. The rise of the celebrity CEO in the 1980s and 1990s was a significant phenomenon. The procedures that made CEOs extraordinarily rich were quite legal and even sanctioned by professional business experts. They were also admired by business schools and the American public, since several of the celebrated CEOs succeeded in creating extraordinary wealth, and not only for themselves. But quite a few of them stepped beyond the border of ethical corporate governance. There was a historical shift. Events affecting business not only created a new pattern in the role of chief executive officers but also changed the culture surrounding them, which extended to networks of politicians. Opportunities for appropriation were pursued by relatively closed networks that also included legal advisers, accountants, and other consultants. Although officially expected to promote the cause of business growth, they sometimes produced the opposite, the looting of the business by insiders. These are classic examples of appropriation efforts: closing opportunities to others while opening them to insiders and their networks. For long-term results, appropriation must be legitimate. After the public scandals of corporate appropriations, the search for business legitimacy expanded. This time the pursuit of gain emerged within high, sophisticated capitalism mostly in the United States, and in a more brazen form in the new "transition countries" of the former Soviet empire. In these countries a peculiar form of modern patrimonial authority arose out of the chaos of the collapse of totalitarianism. These countries tried to build both democracy and a modern free market, but privatization created vast wealth for only a few.

However, there were other forces of change at work as well, pointing in different directions. These currents were visible to careful observers of the "bubble" well before the 1990s. For example, Pittsburgh saw the collapse of its steel industry in the 1980s and later the splintering and demise of the venerable Westinghouse Electric Corporation; there were mergers of companies that changed the business landscape but did not necessarily improve it. Many saw an economic bubble developing in the 1990s. Yes, the "roaring nineties" created "the new economy." Yet there was also apprehension. Such turning points in the structure of major institutions tell us to expect turmoil, uncertainty, and conflict, not just expansion and progress. Advances in the highly specialized rationalization of firms and confidence in growth bred not only wealth, but also losses, scandals, conflicts, and demands for reform. At the beginning of the twenty-first century, capitalism is at such a turning point.

The challenges faced by business leaders are summarized by Jeffrey F. Garten, who interviewed forty CEOs, including several heads of the world's largest companies, to learn how they thought. He wanted to understand their perspectives on their roles and responsibilities. His interviews reveal the pressures created by the Internet, the enormous speed of change, the risks of corporate mergers and their culture conflicts, the ferocious competition in global markets, the foreign policies of the United States and other countries that can derail their business plans, security threats, and the rising need for transparency. Some CEOs even try to influence and redirect these forces, very often with unintended consequences. Garten summed up with his personal conclusions:

> If I had to guess . . . I would say that today's CEOs will be seen as captains of ships in a turbulent sea—unable to chart a steady course and to maintain control of their own fate, at least to the extent most people imagine they can. Their considerable skills and determination notwithstanding, the pressures of this era will have proved much greater than anything these individuals could handle well. The challenges that will have arisen—of the Internet, of globalization, of creating trust in the face of rapid change, of putting forward a bold vision and executing it exquisitely, of balancing shareholders and stakeholders, and of understanding the need for broader vision and leadership in society—these challenges will be assessed by historians as having been too difficult for most CEOs to successfully handle all at once.[10]

Garten noted that in the period between his interviews and writing his book several major business leaders had encountered serious setbacks and three were toppled. The vulnerabilities of CEOs began to become apparent, and they continue to increase. In many ways, Garten's critique seems much gentler than it might have been only a few years later.

The change in the CEO's role reflected the growing economic inequality in the United States. From 1980 on, the gap between rich and poor Americans widened, in sharp contrast to the much more egalitarian developments in the European Union and Japan. And one of the main signals of this development was the rapid financial rise of the CEOs (as well as sports celebrities and film stars). The AFL-CIO Web site cites the following facts:

> Since 1980 the average pay of regular working people has increased just 66%, while CEO pay grew a whopping 1,996%. According to *Business Week*, the average CEO of a major corporation made 42 times the average worker's pay in 1980, 85

times in 1990 and a staggering 531 times in 2000. If runaway CEO growth continues at the current exponential rate over the next 50 years, the average CEO would be paid more [than the compensation received by] 250,000 workers.[11]

We should notice that this staggering phenomenon of growth in CEO compensation is especially American, even though some of these excesses have also occurred, but quite rarely, in Europe. It definitely has not evolved in Japan. While the annual total compensation of major CEOs in the United States is in the range of multiple millions (up to several hundred million), total compensation for Japanese CEOs is in the range of several hundred thousand dollars. Takao Kato reports annual CEO compensation for all Japanese firms in his sample (using data from 1985) at 41,577,000 yen, 40,198,000 for Keiretsu firms, and 45,788,000 yen for independent firms.[12] Darrel Taft and Gangaram Singh also affirm the large differences in salary between American and Japanese CEOs.[13] Takao Kato and Katsuyuki Kubo report similar results from a more recent study.[14]

Another factor explaining the enormous gap between rich and poor are the tax cuts introduced by President George W. Bush that dramatically reduced the taxes of the wealthiest American citizens. This legislation implemented a policy that deliberately aimed to increase social inequality in the United States. Something very important had occurred in the culture of American society even before Bush's tax cuts: the deliberate choice of inequality over social cohesion and social equality, a choice that many see as driving achievements in the society as a whole. This value choice was one of the factors that made the celebrity CEO possible.

The role of the chief executive officer had already begun to change in many corporations in the 1980s and 1990s. Some of them became charismatic leaders; others were feared for their ruthlessness but admired for their efficiency. The escalation of CEO financial compensation was only one change in the CEO's role. The priorities and the strategies of business leadership changed as well. They included the creation of entirely new and large corporate entities through mergers, an uncompromising effort to heighten the efficiency of the market and to reduce costs. Jack Welch, chairman and CEO of General Electric Corporation, provides an illustration. Welch was a popular speaker. After all, he was one of the most celebrated business leaders in the world. He had taken General Electric from a market value of $12 billion to over $500 billion while he led the company. When he lectured at the Yale business school, a student asked what he would advise to anyone in charge of a large business conglomerate. Garten reports his response:

Welch took off his coat and threw it on the chair behind him. He walked in front of the podium, rolling up his shirtsleeves at the same time: "You have to think about that company as a big house," he said. "The house has several floors. Think of each floor as a layer of management. Then there are the interior walls. Think of them as separating different divisions of the company." His eyes were glistening and he moved closer to the audience. "Then you get a hand grenade," he said, his arm curling upward and his fist tightening around an imaginary object. "Then you pull the pin." He paused. It seemed as if all the students were leaning forward. "And then"—now he dropped his shoulder, stooped and slowly swung his arm in a long arc as if he were bowling—"you roll the sucker right through the front door of the house and blow up every floor and every wall." He straightened up, smoothed one hand against the other. "And now you are ready to do something with that company."[15]

Like many other CEOs, Welch believed that the successful company would be one without internal boundaries. It would be a company in which information flowed freely across divisions and branches of organizations. Hierarchies must be flattened for this strategy to succeed (but note: this "non-hierarchic structure" was seen as entirely compatible with enormous financial hierarchies). The expectation that employees would thus be empowered entrepreneurs was widely shared. It was an exciting, challenging, and promising time for leaders of business. They did accomplish a great deal in increasing productivity and profits. However, some of the entrepreneurially spirited business leaders degenerated into a cultural isolation from society at large and from their own employees. There were powerful CEOs who in their exalted, lavishly financed, bullish confidence in unlimited possibilities lost contact with common sense. Even GE's Jack Welch had to make concessions when his retirement package became publicly known in the course of a contested divorce. His enormous retirement perquisites raised a storm of criticism. After the public fury, he asked GE to eliminate all perks except the traditional ones of an office and administrative support that all previous GE chairmen and vice-chairmen had received.[16] Another example is L. Dennis Kozlowski, chairman and CEO of Tyco International, famous for his lavish spending and resulting corporate and legal troubles. Kozlowski's "annual compensation went from $950,000 in 1992 to $26 million in 1997, $70 million in 1998, and $137 million in 2000."[17] It is difficult to imagine how common sense can survive in a cultural environment of people who believe that these levels of payments are appropriate and even necessary.

A special, inverted culture had developed around the celebrity CEO: interconnected boards of directors, accountants, and lawyers who sometimes crossed into the realm of evasion of laws and rules. A culture emerged in some of U.S. corporations that encouraged ignoring, distorting, and breaking the rules of integrity. Of course, not all CEOs became celebrities—in many companies the tradition of integrity and solid work continued. However, celebrity business leaders moved to the very top of the social pyramid, cultivating their networks of intimates, politicians as well as subservient professionals, and fostered their dependence on them. Something was lost in a number of corporations: accountability and ethical integrity.

By 2002 the business scandals and startling cases of malfeasance broke into public awareness. The climate of public opinion on CEO compensation had begun to change. In an article for the *New York Times Magazine,* Roger Lowenstein covered the compensation history of Edward E. Whitacre, CEO of SBC Communications, described as a "sprawling Baby Bell with headquarters in San Antonio," a rather ordinary large enterprise. Lowenstein picked this company for his study because of its "unspectacular" qualities. In his words, "It is profitable and professionally managed, and its CEO is well regarded in the industry. Like many CEO's, he pursued a bold growth strategy for much of the 90s, had some good early years and recently gave back much of his gains. In the last three years, his stock has fallen 27 percent."[18] It serves as an illustration of how the compensation the CEO in such companies changed.

Whitacre took charge SBC Communications in 1990. In 2001, Lowenstein reports, he "received the largest pay package of his career—one with a present value of $82 million." This level of compensation is now not unique in America. It is noteworthy that the level of payment reaped by the CEO did not parallel the performance of his company. In the twelve years of his tenure the stockholders of the company increased their return from appreciation and dividends by 11.5 percent annually. This was roughly like the return of similar companies. However, the CEO's compensation grew at an extraordinary rate: his compensation was about 3.1 million in 1992 and two years later it was $4.4 million. "But as SBC grew, Whitacre was rewarded with options that gave him the chance to earn a small fortune over many years. For instance, in 1994 Whitacre received options entitling him to buy 161,739 shares, at the price prevailing in 1994, over the next decade." In the following year Whitacre received an even bigger grant. In 1995 the shares rose, but in 1996 they fell. In 1997 he received the biggest option grant, 345,000 shares. Lowenstein continues:

> The other way his pay changed was that his board began to grant significant compensation aside from options. In 1995, Whitacre got $4.9 million. In 1996,

an off year for SBC, he got $6.6 million. In 1997, the total rocketed to $15.7 million. Including options, the total for that year was $21 million. The sums were distributed over seven different categories: salary, bonus, "other," restricted stock, options, long-term incentive plan and "all other." This seven-pocket approach served two purposes. First, the dollars that Whitacre received in any one category were only a fraction of the total, minimizing the appearance. Secondly, the board determined the total for each category by different yardsticks, as if each were independent of the other. He would get millions out of one pocket for overall leadership, millions out of another for directing some special events like a merger and still more to "retain" his future services.

Lowenstein went on to ask how the SBC's board members justified a compensation package of $82 million in 2001. He checked the pay level in a peer corporation. Verizon had not only one, but "two CEOs, each of whom received $14 million last year in addition to at least $14 million apiece in options value. Whether SBC or Verizon got more for the C.E.O. buck becomes a senseless debate; indeed, at such levels, all attempts to rationalize pay become meaningless." When Lowenstein finished this article, he called the general counsel of SBC, who took strong objection to the idea that his CEO was overpaid. He found several reasons why it was reasonable and fair. In fact, many people in the culture around the celebrity CEO were convinced that their heroic, giant leadership figures had ushered in a new era of growth and success. A business school professor stated that it is healthy for people to make lots of money, that without the CEO's incentives for growth there would not be as much wealth as there is today. After all, he said, these leaders had improved the efficiency of the market, and the market would correct any aberrations.

The Business Scandals

Sunbeam, an appliance manufacturer, had fallen on hard times in the late 1990s, and "Chainsaw" Al Dunlap was brought in as CEO to improve its fortunes. Dunlap was known as a harsh business leader, and the hope was that he would lead the company back to prosperity. In 1997 he claimed success in turning the company, but this claim was not correct. In March 1998 Sunbeam had to announce that its sales report had been inflated. Later in that year, Sunbeam fired Dunlap after only two years as CEO. The company had to reduce its profit reports for those two years. It fired its auditor, Arthur Andersen, after an SEC investigation found that unacceptable accounting methods had inflated Sunbeam's earnings. Nevertheless, Dunlap left the company several million dollars richer. Sunbeam filed for bankruptcy in

2001 and its stock was reduced to 4 cents.[19] Also in that year, Waste Management had to restate its earnings after inflating its report by $1.7 billion, a staggering sum. In both cases Arthur Andersen, the accounting firm, was involved.

There were business scandals in Europe as well. In Germany the Flow-Tex scandal may well have been the largest case. The firm Flow-Tex had manipulated nonexistent drilling equipment into a fictitious, hugely valued corporation. "Criminal damage" of this fraud was estimated at more than 2 billion euros.[20] Further, questionable bookkeeping in the construction firm Holzmann brought criticism to the accounting firm of KPMG. Problems surfaced elsewhere in Europe as well, including the case of the Dutch trading firm Ahold. The EU Commission reacted with concern and called for reforms somewhat similar to those debated and implemented in the United States.

In the 1990s Enron, a Houston-based company that started as a natural gas pipeline business, grew into the world's largest energy trading company dealing in gas and electricity. Enron's leaders claimed in January 2001 at a conference with analysts that the total value of their company was more than $100 billion. This would have been $126 a share. Enron gloated that it was on the way to being the world's "greatest" company, and its claims seemed convincing to Wall Street and to the larger public. Enron's trading strategies seemed to be the ideal of the effective market. Fund managers made major investments in Enron stock.[21] An early warning that there might be something wrong came in March 2001, when *Fortune* printed an article entitled "Is Enron Overpriced?" The article noted that Enron's financial reporting was extremely hard to interpret and "impenetrable to outsiders . . . because Enron keeps many of the specifics confidential for what it terms 'competitive reasons.' And the numbers that Enron does present are often extremely complicated."[22] In August 2001, Jeffrey K. Skilling, the CEO of Enron, left the firm. He said it was for family reasons. While Wall Street analysts continued to encourage buying Enron stock, investigative journalists and the SEC began to wonder. In the fall, Enron stock slid lower. In November Enron hoped to find a major investor and partner. Dynegy, also an energy firm located in Houston, offered to buy Enron for a low share price and an infusion of cash. When Enron confessed that it had overstated its profits for the last three years and could not account for its cash, Dynegy left. On December 2, 2001, Enron filed for bankruptcy and fired thousands of employees.

Of course, given U.S. oversight and regulatory institutions, this catastrophe should not have been possible. However, it did occur because Enron was able to conceal its manipulations for a long time. The company had made losing investments, and its leaders wanted to hide these losses. According to Berenson,

> Enron's bankruptcy finally brought to the public how bad corporate accounting had become. Investors may not fully understand the details of the Fastow partnerships or the vagaries of market-to-market accounting. But they saw that Enron's financial statements were filled with sawdust and that a few dozen executives at the top of the company had reaped enormous profits from what looked like a Ponzi scheme. In the three years before Enron collapsed, twenty-nine executives had sold more than $1 billion in stock. Skilling took home $67 million; Fastow sold $30 million. The biggest winner was Lou Pai, the head of Enron Energy Services, which used an especially egregious version of market-to-market accounting. Pai sold $354 million in stock.[23]

The Enron catastrophe was an immense disaster for the employees, for their pension plans, for the businesses linked to Enron, and for the credibility of American business. It also had serious consequences for lawyers and accountants. Enron's auditor and consultant, again the firm of Arthur Andersen, was convicted on November 15, 2002, of obstruction of justice in the government investigation of the energy company. The collapse of Enron and the conviction of Arthur Andersen were turning points: Congress became seriously concerned; the public reacted with shock and worries. Huge investments of pension funds were lost. It was the beginning of the public's awareness that something was seriously wrong.[24] A seemingly endless string of "restatements," of investigations of fraud and malpractice, of lawsuits and bitter accusations, followed, and continue as we write.

Denial

Commenting on these scandals in July 2002, former SEC official Lynn Turner saw an entire pattern of denial:

> The facts are in. In 2001, 270 public companies restated the numbers in their financial statements. That was a record high, the peak of a trend. Between 1997 and 2001, there were 1,089 such restatements, according to a recent study by the Huron Consulting Group, from companies including many whose names are now notorious (Enron, MicroStrategy, Cendant and Rite Aid). They have cost investors hundreds of billions of dollars. . . . Those numbers prove that there are more than the "few bad apples" in the orchard that President Bush would have us believe following his Wall Street speech on Tuesday. The accounting profession's refrain that 99.9 percent of audits are solid is no longer credible. The

financial statements of Enron, Waste Management, WorldCom, Adelphia Communications and Xerox were, after all, part of that 99.9 percent.[25]

When Turner made these observations, most Americans believed that the U.S. corporate system was healthy and that only a few companies had done bad things. Denial was evident in President Bush's "few bad apples" speech. The troubles of Arthur Andersen, the public hoped, were also unique. Turner did not believe that at all. During his years at the SEC he found that the restatements of financial reports between 1997 and 1999 "were spread fairly equally among the major accounting firms: KPMG was the auditor for such companies as Xerox and Rite Aid; Ernst & Young for Cendant and Informix; Deloitte and Touche for Livent and Adelphia; and PricewaterhouseCoopers for MicroStrategy WR Grace." And Turner was right: in August a survey of chief financial officers found that "17% of all respondents report being pressured to misrepresent their results by their companies' CEOs during the past five years." They also found that some companies have started to disclose more information to investors—almost 60 percent of all companies surveyed. However, 40 percent felt that such action was not necessary.[26]

In September 2002 Frank Vogl, a cofounder of Transparency International, argued that the corruption of the business system could no longer be denied.[27] He had consulted a large number of knowledgeable people within the Transparency International network worldwide. He learned that the scandals had caused not only an American business system crisis, but that it had huge worldwide repercussions and a loss of trust in U.S. business, oversight institutions, and corporations at large. The U.S. scandals had been publicized across the world, inevitably leading to the belief that U.S. firms worked at lower ethical levels than they professed to the public. Trust had been lost, at home and abroad.

Vogl noted that the domestic debate had not yet included the global aspects of corporate integrity reform. There was a problem here: U.S. perceptions of foreign cultures are generally not very sophisticated, and most Americans assumed that basically all was well at home, that corruption and malfeasance occurred elsewhere. However, with the enormous spread of corporate malfeasance in the United States, this attitude is now changing. Vogl commented:

> Research . . . suggests that experts agree that there are no cultural differences when it comes to understanding the term business integrity. This may shock those in U.S. business who have long felt that this country alone possesses the golden key to corporate ethics. It may also shock U.S. business leaders to learn

that corruption in many developing countries is seen by their citizens as a disease that has been brought to their nation by Western multinational corporations and is not a home-grown product.

The practice of bribing officials in developing countries, often used by multinational corporations, is believed to be involved in the growth of corruption in these countries.

Actually, denial of the significance of the flood of business scandals persisted in the United States, even though the dreary march of investigations, and even some indictments, continued month by month. Enormous sums of money have been lost to fraud; losses at WorldCom appear to have amounted to $4 billion, according to its own admission of overstated profits. In the case of Tyco, the loss of investors' value from the fall of the share price amounted to roughly $100 billion.[28] Serious accusations of malfeasance by managers of some mutual funds surfaced in 2003. Nevertheless, according to the Transparency International Global Corruption Barometer, in 2002 only 7.4 percent of American respondents believed that corruption affected the business environment in the country "very significantly," 53.8 percent said business corruption was "insignificant," and 38.8 percent thought it was "somewhat significant."[29] Yet in one of the world's least corrupt countries, Sweden, 32.6 percent of respondents worried about a "very significant" impact on business by corruption. A question asked in the same study was: "If you had a magic wand and you could eliminate corruption from one of the following institutions, what would your first choice be?" A full 39.1 percent of American respondents chose political parties as needing for the "magic wand" to deal with their corruption. (Actually, people in most surveyed countries chose political parties as needing to be cleansed of corruption.) The *Atlantic Monthly* commented, "Survey the American people and they'll tell you that despite the recent wave of corporate scandals, U.S. businesses remain paragons of virtue."[30] It is possible that this assessment of the public mood may be incorrect, however. Many Americans think of corruption as bribery of government officials only and categorize the business scandals as fraud, obviously a serious crime.

Denial continued for a long time in U.S. public opinion, but awareness of American business malfeasance fueled spreading anti-American sentiment abroad. The impact of the waves of bad news, however, brought a new perspective to the public debate among investigative journalists, politicians, business leaders, prosecutors, regulators, and other professionals in accounting and law. The themes of urgent reform of corporate governance, of the role and responsibilities of CEOs and corporate social responsibility, are prominent in the press and in professional circles, and especially in the Congress and in prosecutors' offices.

Fallen Idols

Many were shocked by the revelations of scandal and malfeasance among business executives. The *Economist* used harsh words about the CEOs, some of whom they had admired.

> Business leaders are being knocked off their pedestals faster than Communist heroes after the fall of the Berlin Wall. Bernie Ebbers, a deal maker from Mississippi whose creation, WorldCom, was the epitome of telecoms excitement, was forced out this week. Diana "DeDe" Brooks, a forceful former chief executive of Sotheby's, was sentenced to house arrest and narrowly missed jail—the fate handed out to her former chairman, Alfred Taubman. Even Jack Welch, the former boss of General Electric who was perhaps the best known celebrity chief executive of all, has seen his reputation dive. The vehemence of today's reaction against business leaders is partly a reflection of how far their companies' shares have fallen, and also of the extent of their personal greed. But it is also a reaction to the worship heaped on them in the 1990s. Revolutions devour their children, and the impact of new technology and the bull market on business was little short of a revolution. Now for the devouring.[31]

The change in the perception of former celebrity CEOs has even turned to the possibility that their compensation should be scrutinized and reduced. This was triggered by the case of Richard A. Grasso, the toppled chairman of the New York Stock Exchange. Outrage over Grasso's deferred compensation of $187.5 million forced him to resign. The *New York Times* wrote:

> There is no more evocative monument to the vibrancy of American capitalism, and to New York City's claim to be the world's financial capital, than the graceful, colonnaded building that houses the New York Stock Exchange on Wall Street. The imposing structure exudes a sense of reassuring permanence, befitting the market place that has served through boom and bust, for 211 years. . . . So much for the aspirational architecture. Inside, utter disarray reigns. The controversy that led to Richard Grasso's resigning last week, when it became clear that he would never outlast the furor created by the disclosure of his absurd $187.5 million deferred compensation plans, has given the investing public a peek into the Big Board's clubby boardroom. It's been a frightening sight. . . . As part of [regulators'] effort to restore investor confidence, the S.E.C. and Congress will have to make fixing the Big Board a top priority. It will do no good to reform

companies' behavior if people remain leery about the integrity of the market-place.[32]

Even the *Economist,* usually enthusiastic about business, capitalism, and the wisdom of the market, concluded, "Something has gone wrong with the bosses' pay. The solution has to lie with shareholders." They even venture to suggest a move that until recently was almost unthinkable in America's corporate boardrooms: "Some corporate boards ought to at least consider a return to what was once the norm in both America and Europe (and still is in Japan) and largely ditch pay-for-performance and instead pay largely through a straight salary (most lower-level employees are paid this way)."[33]

The Agenda for Reform

There are many demands for reform in American business governance, regulation, legislation, and voluntary codes of conduct, all increasing the pressures for transparency. The domestic and worldwide reverberations are enormous and have occurred in a tense international cultural climate. The first major step to reform was the Sarbanes-Oxley Act of 2002, which established the new Public Company Accounting Oversight Board.[34] Accounting firms must register with this board. It has important powers of investigation and of disciplinary action, it can impose significant financial penalties on accounting firms or their personnel, and it can bar such firms from auditing companies. The board is funded by fees of all public companies and is under the oversight of the SEC. The board has the authority to set rules determining quality standards for audits. The establishment of this board (like the SEC) was marred by conflicts over how to appoint its leadership. These conflicts were really about how far the new tools of oversight and disciplinary action would actually be used. By 2003 William J. McDonough was chairman of the board, determined to be vigorous and aggressive. Regarding a Senate inquiry of suspect tax shelters, he was quoted as saying that the major accounting firms had "suffered a complete ethical collapse." He "found the willingness to sell faulty tax shelters and hide them from Internal Revenue Service auditors 'immensely and immorally repugnant' and warned that his board has told the firms they must change or face dire consequences. 'If they do not save themselves, we will save them and it will not be pleasant.'"[35] The struggle, no doubt, will continue.

The Sarbanes-Oxley Act covers a broad range: (1) it establishes the Public Company Accounting Oversight Board, just mentioned; (2) it sets up rules to limit conflicts of interest and assure rotation of auditors; (3) it holds audit committees, corporate officers, and lawyers responsible for financial reports, with penalties for infractions; (4) it requires enhanced financial disclosure; (5) it prohibits conflicts of interest; (6) it regulates commission resources and authority; (7) it oversees studies and reports dealing with studies of such issues as the consolidation of public accounting firms, credit rating agencies, violators, enforcement actions, and investment banks; (8) it demands accountability for corporate and criminal fraud and defines criminal penalties for various infractions and protection for whistle blowers; (9) it introduces criminal penalties for attempts to commit fraud and sets up sentencing guidelines and mandates corporate responsibility for financial reports; (10) it regulates corporate tax returns by CEOs; and finally (11) it increases penalties, for example, under the Securities Exchange Act of 1934, giving the commission the authority to prohibit certain persons from serving as officers or directors. Certain other provisions of the law impose a new regulatory regime on the accounting profession and on brokerage firms, analysts, and lawyers.[36] Major changes are required in how public companies deal with their financial system and with their disclosures to the public. The legislative intent of Congress is to compel chief executive officers and chief financial officers to certify, personally, periodic financial reports as required by the Securities Exchange Act. The legislation provides serious criminal penalties for violations of this certification—a fine of up to $1 million and imprisonment of up to ten years for knowingly false certification and twenty years for willfully certifying untrue statements.

The law directs the SEC to create new rules, to create a "continuous disclosure" regime. This means that companies are no longer allowed to remain silent about financial events (good or bad) occurring between the periodic disclosure reports. They must provide information on material changes in their financial condition and operations. "This will make disclosure decisions an everyday part of public company management."[37] In fact, this may force a dramatic increase in corporate transparency. There is a call for establishing codes of ethics and for new regulations of audits. The SEC rules on corporate codes of conduct require that a company disclose whether it has adopted a code, and if not, what the reasons are. This is, of course, a further step toward establishing an infrastructure for corporate transparency. New rules are also established for the compensation of executives and their trading in stocks. In the case of restatements of profits because of substantial noncompliance with SEC rules, "CEOs and CFOs must disgorge bonuses and other incentive-based compensation and profits on stock sales received during the 12 month period following the initial release of the financials that were later restated, if the non-compliance results from 'misconduct.'"[38] There are to be no loans to executives from the company, and there are trading restrictions for them. There are protections for whistle blowers. In other words, the Sarbanes-Oxley Act tries to remove incentives for manipulating information, and it trims the role of the celebrity CEO. It also envisions further reforms. Yet there remains some skepticism about the lasting effectiveness of this legislation. Early comments by politicians, business leaders, and regulators about the debate following the Sarbanes-Oxley Act were ambivalent, cautioning against too much regulation.[39] However, as the scandals continued into 2003, the sentiment for further inquiry and regulation became more intense. There was a dramatic demand for comprehensive reforms.

Accounting and Further Reforms

Paul Volcker, former chairman of the Federal Reserve and head of the International Accounting Standards Committee Foundation, stated in 2002: "The profession of auditing and accounting is in crisis. It is hard to make meaningful change when there is a sense that things are going reasonably well. There is a silver lining in Enron. We do now have a sense of crisis." To this statement, the *Economist* added: "Fingers crossed."[40]

The sense of crisis in accounting is not only caused by the catastrophic impact of the business scandals on the accounting profession. Business scandals almost invariably become accounting scandals. The conviction of Arthur Andersen executives was an extreme warning sign for the profession. But these are not the only problems to be resolved. The need for innovation is also a result of the global expansion of economic transactions and the multiple problems that arise as a result. The accounting profession requires solutions to its new challenges. It must reconsider its mission, its rules, and what new ethical standards are needed. Accounting is an indispensable "transparency infrastructure" without which a modern economy cannot function. It must be accurate, reliable, and clearly accountable. It must also be of global scope. Here major obstacles still exist. There has to be a worldwide movement toward harmonizing accounting standards across different cultures. The movement is already more than three decades old, moving very quickly, and it contributes to the worldwide transparency phenomenon in a compelling way. According to a current textbook:

> Accounting is a branch of applied economics that provides information about business and financial transactions for users of that information. International

accounting is distinct because the information concerns a multinational enterprise (MNE) with foreign operations and transactions, or the users of the information are in a different domicile than the reporting entity.

And it warns its readers of the complexity of the task:

Those who want to manage a business, or obtain or supply financing across national borders, need to understand the international dimensions of accounting. Accounting amounts may vary significantly according to the principles that govern them. Differences in culture, business practices, political and regulatory structures, legal systems, currency values, foreign exchange rates, local inflation rates, business risks, and tax codes all affect how the MNE conducts its operations and financial reporting around the world. Financial statements and other disclosures are impossible to understand without an awareness of the underlying accounting principles and business culture.[41]

That is a statement of extreme complexity. Indeed, "accounting amounts" can vary greatly. For example, the net income of a Swedish firm calculated in accord with Swedish accounting principles could yield a substantially different value than if net income were calculated according to U.S. Generally Accepted Accounting Principles (GAAP) rules.[42] Another example is the difference between valuing the equity of the German company BASF (a chemical firm) by using U.S. GAAP and German rules: One approach would be to change the German accounting by choosing legitimate alternatives within German rules that are more like GAAP rules. By contrast, using GAAP rules that are not compatible with German rules makes a huge difference. The equity value according to the German rules was DM 23 billion, but when calculated by GAAP rules it was DM 25.2 billion. For a third of the companies studied, there is no material difference between the U.S. and German accounting systems. However, some differences are massive. "The notorious Daimler case—a gain of DM 602 million under German accounting rules was reconciled to a DM 1.8 billion loss under U.S. GAAP—also had such a technical explanation that it was fully understood only by some analysts."[43]

Like the larger business environment, accounting is shaped in part by a country's cultural environment, legal structure, and history. However, as national economies enter the global economy, there are moves toward convergence. Similarly, the challenge of harmonization confronted the creators of the European Union. The differences in national accounting practices pose problems for firms engaged in international transactions. Multinational companies are seriously concerned with the diversity in accounting standards.

They face competition every day and sense that accounting diversity affects competitiveness. If a European corporation can bid for a U.S. acquisition target company and immediately write off all premium payouts to owner's equity (bypassing the income statement), it might outbid an equally interested U.S. corporation that must amortize the same premium payouts as goodwill through subsequent income statements. MNCs like "level playing fields" for their global operations. Distorting factors cause barriers and retaliation.[44]

Goodwill is a complex and slippery concept that illustrates very powerfully the problem of diversity in international accounting. The value of a company that another company buys may be estimated to be greater than the fair market value; there may be an especially promising constellation in the combination of the two firms; there may be patents that can generate a greater potential through a merger, or still other factors producing a greater value. When the purchase price is higher than the fair market value, accountants speak of goodwill. If the firm being bought is in trouble, the goodwill can be negative. This value is accounted for differently among different countries. "The goodwill accounting diversity is aggravated by a taxation effect. For instance, goodwill amortization is not tax deductible in the United Kingdom or the Netherlands, but it is deductible in Canada, Japan, Germany (post-1986), and the United States (post-1993)."[45] It is easy to see the potential inequities in this state of affairs.

Transnational companies may wish to list their stock shares in foreign stock markets as a way of raising capital in countries where they have activities. Investors are even more interested in reducing the expense and frustration of international accounting diversity.

> Investors experience frustration when they do not understand whether financial statements merely look similar or are in fact similarly prepared. Underwriters consistently report that worldwide accounting diversity causes some underwriting (i.e., pricing of new securities issues) difficulties. If investors, analysts, and underwriters indeed experience difficulties with GAAP diversity, financial markets are not as efficient as they could be and therefore returns to investors are less than they ought to be. This is a powerful indictment of GAAP diversity.[46]

Many powerful forces urge the harmonization of accounting practices worldwide. They strongly support transparency rules and professional reforms for the accounting profession. At the center of these professional movements is the International Accounting Standards Board, a private effort at developing global regulations for accounting. It also encourages the establishment of sturdy professional frameworks that provide transparency and resist fraud and corruption. The mission statement of IASB is short and direct:

> The International Accounting Standards Board is an independent, privately-funded accounting standard setter based in London, UK. Board Members come from nine countries and have a variety of professional backgrounds. The Board is committed to developing, in the public interest, a single set of high quality, understandable and enforceable global accounting standards that require transparent and comparable information in general purpose financial statements. In addition, the Board cooperates with the national accounting standard setters in all participating countries to achieve convergence in accounting standards around the world.[47]

The IASB grew out of the International Accounting Standards Committee (IASC), founded in 1973 by accounting organizations from Australia, Canada, France, Germany, Japan, Mexico, the Netherlands, the United Kingdom, Ireland, and the United States. Professional organizations of accountants were organized under the International Federation of Accountants (IFAC) in 1977. However, the process yielded several different proposals for the eventual organization of global accounting rules.

Günther Gebhardt suggested that not only the accounting professions should be represented on the IASC board because the situation in 1998 was not satisfactory. He argued:

> The IASC board in its current structure has thirteen part-time country members and three co-opted institutional members. The broader country representation is deliberately biased toward the developed countries (nine members). Founded by the national accountancy bodies cooperating in the International Federation of Accountants, membership of the IASC is still dominated by the accountancy profession, even though many country delegations (normally two representatives and one technical adviser) include representatives of preparers, users, or national standard setters. With about seventy persons . . . sitting at the table, IASC board meetings are not an efficient forum for detailed technical discussions.[48]

Gebhardt wanted something akin to a global accounting standard parliament comprised of national standard setters, representatives from parliaments and users, as well as accountants.

Actually, the direction of development turned toward creating an independent, highly respected professional board. It was an epistemic community rather than a parliament, with legitimacy resting on knowledge, expertise, and known integrity. Sir David Tweedie, chairman of the IASB, characterized this history:

> What happened sometime in the 1970s was that the United States, Canada and the United Kingdom came together and founded an Accountants' International Study Group. They looked at the different practices of each country, recommended what they decided were best practices, but nothing happened. In 1973 the World Congress of Accountants passed a motion to set up a board. . . . There were at least four ways to tackle anything—you could follow any. By the late 1980s people despised this approach; they didn't really create standards. A committee of sixteen delegations . . . did not produce any clout. What was needed was to have real standards that could be accepted in any stock exchange. IOSCO, the International Organization of Securities Commissions, and the SEC, the U.S. Securities and Exchange Commission, were big players. There were discussions about an international standards committee—but some believed this, and others believed that. . . . But the idea was there.
>
> At the time I was chairing the British board. We wanted to persuade others that we were best. It all became more competitive. Convening a meeting three times a year wasn't going to accomplish anything, so we set up a restructuring committee. Some at the European Commission wanted a representative board with a full-time chair, but the SEC rejected that. The SEC prevailed: there were to be nineteen trustees, six European, six North American, and seven from the rest of the world. They were highly competent people, like Paul Volcker. They were told to go out and find fourteen people of high caliber, including auditors, users, academics, et cetera. They were meeting four times a year, producing think pieces. The board sucked them in. The emphasis was on independence and expertise.
>
> The International Accounting Standards Board was established in 2001. There were seven central members from the U.S., Canada, Great Britain, Australia, France, Germany, and Japan. There is pressure in the European Union: by 2005 all listed companies have to use the IASB standards. We have a staff of eighteen. IASB is financed worldwide with $1 million each from the four major accounting firms, $1 million from central banks, and $3 million from industry. We have established the IASB Trust Foundation headed by Paul Volcker.

It is clear that the legitimacy of IASB, a private organization, rests on its independence and ethical clarity. (The United States has its own accounting standards board, the FASB, and has not yet adopted the IASB standards). The structure that has been built protects their work from political or other self-interested pressures. Tweedie underlined these points: "There is an advantage we've got; we're not subject to the same political pressure as the American board. Congress can't extradite me. The board can fire us; a lot of us would like to see the ship sink rather than go back to safe harbor. Enron helps. It is a blow to the solar plexus—deceit, fraud, abuse. People want to know what we're up to."[49]

Kevin Stevenson, director of technical activities of the IASB, emphasized the special structure of the IASB, deliberately designed to make it both credible and independent:

> The structure of the IASB is quite unusual. It goes back to Sydney in the 1960s. Until the end of the International Accounting Standards Committee in 2001, it was sponsored by the professional world associations in management accounting and in public sector accounting. There were about 160 bodies as members. They did not influence what the IASC did. I was secretary to a review done in the late eighties, early nineties to see if these bodies and IASC should merge. There was a resounding response: IASC should remain independent. IASC was really born out of the need to get technical matters taken care of. Board members wanted to keep this work independent. There was and is a desire to professionalize the profession completely. Standard setting is an important, independent ethical enterprise.[50]

The core of the professional activity is, indeed, a fusion of an ethical and a technical mission for IASB. Stevenson told us more about how the structure of IASB functioned.

> IASB has twelve full-time board members, two half-time board members, twenty-one technical staff, and twenty administrative staff. The only equivalent in the world is the American Accounting Standards Board. The other national groups are only slightly professionalized. . . . It was impressive how IASB got structured: the professional organizations agreed to give up membership in it. Several "eminent persons" were appointed to select a board of trustees, and then went out of existence. The board of trustees is chaired by Paul Volcker, who is not an accountant. They hired a technical board, made sure that the infrastructure was in place; they have to find funding through donations, and they have oversight. They have no involvement with our work. They provide the money side. We have no connection to the professional accounting bodies. They are not involved with us.

Stevenson explained that the United States first set accounting standards because of its early industrial prowess, starting in the late 1930s. The U.S. FASB is "heaven on earth for standard setters. A year ago, it was the biggest challenge to our organization to gain equivalent recognition to FASB. One year later on, Enron hammered the FASB. It is under pressure to change. The new chairman of FASB is one of our board members, Bob Hertz."

The IASB is so far an experiment, established in 2001 as an independent board with full-time members serving three to five years. Stevenson called it the most impressive effort he had ever seen. The thinking has changed, he said:

> Most standard setters follow a conceptual framework, very widely drawn. The purpose is to provide information for common user needs. The information is for all stakeholders, not just shareholders. Our standards . . . are principle-based. The American standards are specific rules: if you tell an accountant that rules forbid him to do A, B, C, and D, he will look for E and do that. Standards that are defined as principles are different in that accountants are reluctant to breach the required principle. I think America will be changing to principles-based standards.

In a second interview, Tweedie took this view of the ethical mission of IASB:

> That is the way I was taught. I was brought up in Glasgow. I was an indentured apprentice, and that's the type of ethics practiced. Their professional ethics were very strong. If something was wrong, it was wrong. There was no question of bending to a client. You were to work for the investor, not the client. You would turn clients away if you had to. That stays with you. And it comes through in standards setting. It makes you careful. Some people might say it's very Presbyterian, very narrow-minded, but it's just the way I was raised.

We asked whether this ethic had eroded in America. He replied that it had been lost in Europe, too.

> In 1990, I was chairman of the British standards-setting board. Companies were collapsing. Suddenly accounting was very poor. Investment banks came up with schemes. Sell something to someone in order to show lots of money. When the board came on, they banned a lot of these schemes, and they were not grandfathered. Lots of firms said, "Thank goodness." People don't like to do things that are unethical. They'll say that competitors do it, so they have to go along with the flow; but people came round pretty quickly. The press is a great ally: "Name and shame!"[51]

In 2003 the European Commission ordered that the International Accounting Standards of the IASB should be compulsory for all member states by 2005. Frits Bolkestein, the EU's internal market commissioner, commented:

> Adoption by the Commission of this Regulation, endorsing most of the existing International Accounting Standards and publishing them in the EU's official languages, will help the 7000 or so listed EU companies affected to get ready for 2005, when their consolidated accounts will have to be in line with IAS. That will put an end to the current Tower of Babel in financial reporting, improve competition and transparency and make the free movement of capital much easier.[52]

A major step toward accounting harmonization has been taken.

Legal frameworks, like that set by the Sarbanes-Oxley Act, as well as voluntary global reform based on expertise such as the efforts of the IASB, are essential steps. Of course, they are often criticized as either too demanding or too lenient and ineffective. They do, nevertheless, set landmarks in the growth of transparency. Another movement is the evolution of corporate codes of conduct. Much of this effort is voluntary, but even reluctant or recalcitrant corporations are compelled to adopt such codes. What the codes are about, what activities they cover, what responsibilities they entail, how they are to be enforced—all is still in flux. However, the crisis of accounting, the fall of the celebrity CEO, the need to rebuild trust, all provide powerful incentives for corporations to adopt a new stance.

Can Corporate Codes of Conduct Be Global?

Codes of conduct are not new. Many associations and groupings have relied on them throughout history—in religious communities, craft guilds, schools, codes of conduct have shaped communal existence. Codes of behavior have been part of the civilizing process studied by Norbert Elias, even though he did not use the term. He rather spoke of *sociogenesis* in the social construction of *civilization* and *Kultur* as transformations of human behavior into civilized, cultivated conduct. He saw how France's *civilization* and Germany's *Kultur* differed in the social construction of those nations and their codes of behavior.[53]

The word *code* itself has several meanings. Among them are: "any systematic collection of the existing laws of a country, or of those relating to a particular subject"; or "any system or collection of rules and regulations." In the broadest sense a code prescribes what is desirable and permissible; it also presents an image of appropriateness and is a vehicle for self-presentation.

An early code of corporate conduct was the Credo of Johnson and Johnson, the medical products company, written by General Robert Wood Johnson, in 1943. It listed the company's responsibilities first to the doctors, nurses, and consumers, second to the employees, third to the wider community, and fourth to their stockholders. "Shareholder value" here comes last in the company's self-presentation. The Credo was important in 1982 and 1986 when its product Tylenol was adulterated with cyanide and used as a murder weapon. "With Johnson and Johnson's good name and reputation at stake, company managers and employees made countless decisions that were inspired by the philosophy embodied in the Credo. The company's reputation was preserved and the Tylenol acetaminophen was regained."[54] Other corporations have also created codes, credos, ethical standards, or "visions." The necessity for codes of conduct dawned only slowly. They became a topic of interest in the business community only in the 1970s. It was a controversial idea at first, since many corporate leaders did not see the need for such codes.

An important and controversial event in the evolution of codes was a part of the fight against apartheid in South Africa. This was the international boycott spearheaded by the Rev. Leon Sullivan, pastor of Zion Baptist Church in Philadelphia who also served on the General Motors board of directors for twenty years. He was a pioneer in fighting for human rights and liberty. In 1977 he formulated the Sullivan Principles, "a code of conduct for human rights and equal opportunities for companies operating in South Africa."[55] These principles rallied an international movement to end apartheid in South Africa, an enormous factor in transforming South Africa into a democratic state. Reverend Sullivan was praised and celebrated for his leadership and awarded fifty honorary doctorates. In 1997 he formulated the Global Sullivan Principles of Social Responsibility, which was endorsed by many corporations.

Another illustration of codes for corporate behavior was the legalization of the social market economy concept in the early days of the German Federal Republic. In 1948 the currency reform and the social regulation of the capitalist market economy became law in the three Western-occupied zones of defeated Germany. Its creator was Minister for the Economy Ludwig Erhard. His policies included the equitable distribution of the economic losses caused by the war among German citizens, Germany's return to an open world economy, and the inclusion of employees in corporate governance. Joint decision making in corporate affairs by management and employee representatives became the special hallmark of German business, in sharp contrast to practices in the United States and Britain. It was a legally determined code of corporate conduct. The model of a social market economy also influenced the economic cultures of other West European countries. Its enormous success helped to produce Germany's "economic miracle" after the war.

Business codes are established for a variety of reasons. Although many are called voluntary, that is not always true. Johnson and Johnson did adopt a code for its own reasons—a truly voluntary action. The Sullivan Principles were created by an engaged leader determined to fight the human rights violations in South Africa. The adoption of these principles by corporations was voluntary in some cases, but ultimately adoption was due to pressure from boycotts and the fear of loss of reputation. This was not exactly pure voluntarism at work. The corporate governance norms for German firms in the late 1940s were imposed by law. Voluntarism was not an option.

Codes that guide the behavior of employees as well as corporate leaders were also designed to reduce risk. Honest trading practices, labor relations, safety and work rules, concerns about child labor, environmental damage, violations of human rights, and differences in business law in different countries became increasingly complex questions as international operations expanded. Firms increasingly needed guidance in defining norms and good practices. Again, scandals helped this development, especially the adverse impact of disastrous events such as the deadly explosion at the Union Carbide plant in Bhopal, India; the grounding of the Exxon oil tanker *Valdez* on Alaska's shore; the boycott of Nestlé products to protest its promotion of artificial feeding of babies in developing countries; the "essential action" boycott of Shell Oil because of alleged human rights violations in Nigeria.

To help corporations avoid loss of reputation and to provide needed services, special professional associations and consulting firms began to address business ethics. Two will serve as illustrations. The U.S. Ethics Officer Association has about 600 corporations as members, each of which has a professional ethics officer.[56] (The median total compensation for ethics officers is $225,000.) Another organization is the Ethical Trading Initiative of the UK, an alliance of companies, nongovernmental organizations, and trade unions set up "to identify and promote good practice in the implementation of codes of labour practice. [Its] ultimate goal is to ensure that the working conditions of workers producing for the UK market meet or exceed international standards."[57]

The industry of organizations helping firms with codes of conduct, providing monitoring and auditing to assure compliance, has become a large business. A Salvadoran labor union professional discussed with the German Informationsstelle Lateinamerika the role of codes of conduct in improving the maquiladoras in El Salvador. He said that there were some improvements for workers, but they were limited to correcting worst excesses. Moreover, there are problems with the auditing system; audits are conducted by businesses that want to make a high profit and please their clients but are not interested in the major problems of low wages and long hours.[58] This is not the only voice that finds fault with the implementation of codes of conduct.

The demand for corporate codes of conduct grew rapidly at the end of the twentieth century in cooperation with international organizations, corporations, labor unions, and many governments. The avalanche of business and accounting scandals created a crisis for the reputation of many companies. Civil rights organizations and investigative journalists began to scrutinize the conduct of corporations for their role in causing environmental damage and for abuses such as employing child labor. State regulators and inquisitive politicians have also conducted hearings into alleged improprieties, calling for better enforcement of regulations and greater transparency, since just following the letter of a law may be inadequate. Formal compliance is often not enough; there needs to be a principled ethical framework. In many countries there is the risk of being sued in a court of law.

Mellon Financial Corporation has had a code of conduct since 1977, says Michael Bleier, chief legal counsel for the firm. Bleier explains:

> Jim Higgins, who was then chairman of Mellon Bank, was also a member of the Board of Gulf Oil. Gulf had problems. . . . There were slush funds, money spent incorrectly overseas. Then there was the Foreign Corrupt Practices Act of 1977. . . . Anyway, Jim came back and said: "We want a code of conduct." It was approved in 1977 and there have been about five updates since then. These were triggered by a variety of things. A change of laws, events, IRS situation . . . we put together a video: "Raise your hand if there's a problem." There is an Office of Ethics, web-based training for everyone, on the right things to do. We use third parties; we use their videos and modify them for our own purposes.[59]

There are solid internal reasons for having a corporate code of conduct. The CEO of a firm producing medical apparatus proudly reported on the establishment of his organization's code, although he had not seen the need for it at first. Then he learned that the U.S. Department of Commerce had declined to give his company distinguished recognition because it did not have a code. After this not too gentle prodding, the firm's general counsel, with broad employee participation, set to work. Employees welcomed the code because it established clear channels of communication and helped with decision making in difficult situations. It also helped in relations with suppliers who might suggest a questionable action: "Well, you see, we have our code and we just can't do this!" The same can be true of relations with customers. The CEO appreciated the observable benefits of the new code to the organization.[60]

Given the enormous increase in global businesses searching for risk protection (and innovation) through codes, there are thousands of participating organizations. In addition to national governments, the EU, and the UN, others involved include the International Chamber of Commerce (ICC), Organization for Economic Cooperation and Development (OECD), World Bank, World Trade Organization (WTO), International Labor Organization (ILO) of the UN, and many global civil society entities, prominent among them Transparency International and Amnesty International. The Business and Human Rights Resource Centre, an independent organization in partnership with Amnesty International Business Groups and leading academic institutions, offers a vast collection of sources regarding codes of conduct and the work of international bodies concerned with enforcing them.[61]

The OECD, with thirty members, has played a particularly active role. In 1997 it set up a convention on combating bribery of foreign public officials in international business transactions. It was revised in 2001.[62] Transparency International is an important partner with OECD in promoting this worldwide prohibition against bribery. Michael Wiehen, a prominent member of Transparency International, is especially involved with OECD. The OECD takes a sustained interest in corporate governance and conduct. In 2003 it published guidelines for multinational enterprises that are part of a larger effort to clarify rights and duties in international investment and in the conduct of multinational corporations. These guidelines are not obligatory, but each country is expected to have a national contact point—in many cases, a government office. OECD reports that the guidelines "are becoming an important international benchmark for corporate responsibility."[63]

The OECD studied 246 voluntary codes of corporate conduct from around the world. The firms included enterprises in high technology, mass retailing, heavy and light manufacturing, primary production, and financial services. The codes address a range of topics, focusing prominently on environmental and labor issues. They also frequently address consumer protection, measures against bribery and corruption, and issues relating to shareholder value. Some codes emphasize limiting risks of liability and abiding by the law. Others emphasize successful competition in the market and protection of the firm's reputation. What is striking is their diversity: "Codes addressing labour and environmental issues differ considerably in how they approach these two issues. While some codes mention labour and environment only in passing, many of them are devoted exclusively to one of these two issues. Especially in these 'single issue' codes, the overall level of commitment is often quite high, although the specifics of the commitment vary."[64] Environmental codes often deal with community concerns, training employees, and encouraging dialogue about environmental issues. In the labor area there is variation, too, but the main topics are the work environment, discrimination and harassment, child labor, and compensation. Different industries vary in their codes and in the sources of the codes. This is especially true of the apparel industry, which focuses on labor issues, especially child labor; and the extractive industries emphasize environmental and labor questions. The codes are derived from a variety of sources, including industry associations, the companies themselves, industry and trade associations, NGOs, unions, and a few intergovernmental agencies.

The most visible efforts to provide guidance to corporations comes from the UN institutions, the World Bank, and the Global Reporting Initiative. There are now efforts under way to harmonize these undertakings. The United Nations Global Compact was initiated by Secretary-General Kofi Annan in 1999. He saw this enterprise as an invitation to companies to adopt voluntary and transparent principles to achieve a more humane and sustainable global economy. The nine principles at the ethical core of this compact are based on three basic documents: the Universal Declaration of Human Rights, the ILO's Declaration on Fundamental Principles and Rights at Work, and the Rio Declaration on Environment and Development. The principles inform multinational corporations that they should "support and respect the protection of internationally proclaimed human rights within their sphere of influence . . . and make sure that they are not complicit in human rights abuses." On labor issues, they should "uphold the freedom of association and the effective recognition of the right to collective bargaining; the elimination of all forms of forced and compulsory labor; the effective abolition of child labor; and eliminate discrimination in respect of employment and occupation." With regard to the environment, they should "support a precautionary approach to environmental challenges; undertake initiatives to promote greater environmental responsibility; and encourage the development and diffusion of environmentally friendly technologies."[65] This is a list of very broad admonitions, not a specific code. More than a thousand companies have signed up for this program. It is an effort at a very abstract level, lacking in detail regarding practical application.

A more recent call from the UN is the statement of human rights norms for transnational businesses. It is far more specific than the Global Compact and lays out a daunting array of international laws and charters that give legal weight to the norms. The norms give the states "primary responsibility to promote, secure the fulfillment of, respect, ensure respect of and protect human rights recognized in international as well as national law, including that transnational corporations and other business enterprises respect human rights."[66] (It is very clear that the whole document has been written and rewritten by lawyers!) The rights to equal opportunity, security of persons, and protection of workers are spelled out. There are norms respecting national sovereignty and human rights, consumer protection, and environmental protection. There are even directives as to how they should be implemented. Enterprises are to report on the measures they have taken and will be subject to periodic monitoring by the UN and other agencies. This is a language of command, not suggestion.

The debate about corporate responsibility and codes of conduct has evolved beyond voluntarism. The continuing business scandals that elicited the Sarbanes-Oxley Act in the United States and the UN action on norms has moved ethical codes more toward formal regulation. An important player is Transparency International, which provides guidance for establishing and enforcing corporate codes of conduct in a handbook based on a survey of about 100 U.S. companies. The handbook examines the laws affecting these codes and requiring compliance. Its purpose is stated at the beginning:

> Recent court decisions have indicated that a director could be held liable for a company's failure to exercise good-faith judgment in developing an information system that is likely to detect misconduct in a timely manner. It should be noted that exposure to civil and criminal liability is not limited to the top executives of the organization. Liability may also arise from the conduct of an organization's lower level employees. Therefore, it is essential for companies to implement initiatives that prevent and manage employee misconduct. To accomplish this objective, *an effective Code of Conduct/Compliance Program must become a part of everyday corporate governance.*[67]

The survey found that many of the companies included the elements of the compliance program that TI-USA considered to be essential. Of the companies queried, 78 percent said that their compliance program had been very effective. However, there remained weaknesses that need to be remedied. TI-USA made six points:

- Many organizations do not have a compulsory training program on their code and many do not have job-specific compliance training.

- Only 56 percent of the surveyed organizations have multilingual codes.

- 80 percent had implemented auditing and monitoring procedures, but only 52 percent had an outside, independent party involved.

- 74 percent had not established a dedicated resource to take responsibility for the compliance function.

- Due diligence before a merger or acquisition was a practice in most companies, but 23 percent did not consider corporate compliance to be part of this process.

- 24 percent did not include compliance as part of performance assessments.

The detailed approach of TI-USA differs dramatically from the general guidelines approach of the UN Global Compact and other similar approaches. Obviously, these efforts by international organizations have been valuable, but they inevitably fall short of emphasizing compliance. TI-USA, of course, wrote its study with a new, legal framework in mind. Their work will bring greater rigor to many organizations.

However, the road to well-functioning, legitimate codes of conduct with a workable compliance function at the global level will still be long and difficult. Just as we found the harmonization of international accounting standards to be difficult, requiring great sensitivity to both principles of universal validity and flexibility in special cultural settings, establishing codes for all settings remains a challenging task. There are universally binding principles concerning human rights, transparency, and the abolition of all bribery and corruption. But there are also special circumstances that differ by country, by the nature of the enterprise, and by myriad other factors.

One difficulty is the relationship between corporations and the national governments with which they must work. To be sure, a private multinational company must abide by human rights standards, but it is the government that must establish and protect a corresponding legal and enforcement system. In a "Memorandum to U.N. Secretary-General Kofi Annan," Daniel Litvin argues that both the Global Compact and the UN human rights norms for businesses fall short: "The failure of these initiatives to set reasonable and well-defined limits on the human rights responsibilities of companies helps explain the current hostility of business lobbies to any effort to create an enforceable code of conduct. A more realistic and fair approach can resolve this problem and win the support of both businesses and non-governmental organizations (NGOs)."[68] Litvin asks whether a company like General Motors working in China would be obliged to break Chinese laws in order to implement the norms. Falun Gong in China is an illegal organization—would General Motors have to permit Falun Gong meetings at their plants? His main point is that the boundaries between the rights and duties of states and of corporations must be clearly defined. This is a very difficult area: these different values cannot easily be harmonized. A balanced set of norms must be established over a limited period—maybe five years. A panel of experts from business, NGOs, the labor movement, and the UN, and from both the North and South, should be entrusted with drafting the new norms and rules for their enforcement. If this is done, Litvin is convinced, businesses will follow. It is probably good advice for the UN to take a step similar to the much more specific task of the IASB—which is on its way to success.

In *The Naked Corporation,* Don Tapscott and David Ticoll argue that transparency in business can be a powerful incentive for integrity as well as for success.[69] It is no longer a matter of choice, but of necessity. The open corporation reveals information readily to all its stakeholders; it generates trust among employees and customers alike. They found in their research that transparency encourages success; resistance and denial can bring public relations catastrophe. Their advice to business leaders is very direct: transparency brings business achievement and will be the mandate of the new business era.

Conclusions

The struggles for the social construction of the celebrity CEO and the appropriation of huge amounts of money to these leaders (and their networks) created incentives that led to a wave of business scandals of enormous scope. They destroyed many companies, jobs, investments, and pensions. They occurred mostly in the United States, but Europe had its troubles as well. The incentives that encouraged some business leaders to stoop to fraud were based on flawed parts of the transparency infrastructure for financial accounting and governance. They were tempted to manipulate "the number," the quarterly earnings report. These reports, of course, were designed to be part of the transparency infrastructure, but this design turned out to be not entirely secure. These flaws inspired multiple efforts to limit fraud and malfeasance in business corporations and to rebuild investor and stakeholder trust. Another, converging current of events was the growing movement to create new global norms for corporate social responsibility. These two forceful movements intersected in a way that energized the pressure for far-reaching reform of corporate governance, creating new global business norms and a demand for transparency and accountability. The crossing of two initially separate initiatives created serious complications.

The effort to reestablish trust in corporate accounts yielded changes in the profession of accounting, in its networks, and in the legal structures defining the duties of corporate governance, and it certainly changed America's mode of running corporations. Simultaneously, the movement for global social responsibility accelerated. The constellation of concerned governments (especially in the United States but elsewhere, too), the effectiveness of certain global civil society organizations and movements, and their partnership with international organizations created dramatic new challenges for the new transparency syndromes for business that are now being worked on in every corporate board room.

We find again, as in the functioning of civil society described in chapter 6, that combining social movements and their ethical commitments with powerful, effective expertise can produce a change in norms. To be sure, we have observed only one sliver of the dramatic historical process that is bringing pressures for transparency. There will be more struggles for and against efforts to appropriate wealth by people who see opportunities of stealth and fraud. The transparency syndrome is building codes of conduct, mechanisms for compliance, regulations with the force of law, and a new stream of information flowing to the public. The process is, of course, expensive. The infrastructure will grow in size. It will—inescapably—be successful in many ways, but it will also generate its own powerful networks. Some of its members will seek and find new opportunities for appropriation in the future. However, the framework of norms, disclosure, surveillance, compliance, and enforcement will create a new set of criteria by which the workday in corporate governance will be shaped.

8

THE CHANGING ARCHITECTURE OF INFORMATION VALUES IN HEALTH SYSTEMS

Changes in social morality have propelled changes in health systems, and changes in medical knowledge, technology, and practice have caused further social change. The information values of the health system have changed dramatically in the space of a few decades. Because health systems deal with matters of life and death and human well-being, these systems are critical, with political implications. As demands for transparency and privacy have increased in this domain, other values have been displaced or altered.

Health Institutions in Flux

Pressures for transparency are growing in global civil society and in the corporate world. These pressures work in several dimensions of health care: informed consent, patient privacy, and transparency and monitoring in public health. Concerns with health systems and public health have become urgent political concerns worldwide because they depend on the policies of states, the economies, and the moral frameworks of the cultures of which they are a part. The rich countries of Europe and North America have seen policy reforms in their health systems and policies, particularly in the twentieth century, when they grew in size and complexity. The transition from the profession of independent medical practitioners of a century ago to the enormous, multidisciplinary systems of today was a comprehensive professional, economic, and political transformation. Biomedical research establishments and the industries producing pharmaceuticals and medical apparatus are huge. The public's expectations of health care in 1900 were modest, as was the stock of medical knowledge. By 2000, medical knowledge had become sophisticated, complex, and opaque because of its complexity. At the same time, the public's expectations and demands are high.

Today, health systems face simultaneous challenges: the needs of aging populations, rising costs of treatment, enormous increases in the price of medical equipment and drugs, a rapid flow of technological innovations, the fiscal problems of hospitals, changing management systems, new formations in the structure and roles of the health professions, as well as turbulence in their political and moral frameworks. These challenges dramatically affect health information rights and duties. Health has become a hot topic for reform through legislation and regulation by governments and market forces.

The medical sciences and technologies have transformed the practice of health care in ways not even imaginable a few decades ago, even though biomedical research was making rapid progress even then. Biomedical advances also have entailed new expenses. These changes are occurring in the developed countries in a tense and contested political context, where health policy has become one of the most controversial issues in national politics. Heated disputes have arisen about the value changes and moral choices brought by growing scientific knowledge, medical skill, and new conceptions of morality.

The growing body of medical knowledge has brought new curative possibilities because of changes in the information norms that relate to illness. When medicine could act only as a palliative, serious illness inevitably meant death. With more effective and more available treatment, cancer is no longer a terminal illness. This circumstance has had two effects: on one hand, more effective medical knowledge increased the political demand for further advances and greater budgets for research and new treatments. On the other, it also enhanced the demand for patient privacy as well as more access to knowledge about one's condition. Because some employers may have a negative view of a patient's future as a worker and take actions against the employee, concealment of illness was common among those with terminal illnesses. Today, these taboos are shrinking. However, the need for privacy remains, and now it is the goal of social movements and some politicians to protect private information from abuse.

A society's moral framework and the values embedded in its institutions affect the political forces shaping its health systems. Increasingly, the global transformations of the nation-states add a new dimension to health institutions, both private and public. Further, global transformations affect health systems: the risks of new infectious diseases and of environmental health threats crossing national borders have become very real. For example, a wide variety of social movements have arisen to address health care issues such as

Britain, with publicly financed health services, and of France, Germany, Brazil, and Korea, with multiple payers. All the European countries and Canada have comprehensive national health systems, and all continue to work on further reforms, even though these systems were established more than half a century ago.

By contrast, the United States has seen many efforts to establish a national, comprehensive, and inclusive system, but, according to the *AJPH* editorial, they were always thwarted by:

> powerful interest groups blocking constructive reform efforts; the tendency of reformers to work only from the inside; and the focus of grassroots groups on single issue reforms, such as hospital desegregation, abortion rights, and access to AIDS drugs. What seems different today is that every sector of U.S. society feels an increased level of health insecurity. Working people are concerned about shouldering ever larger premium costs. Students fear that new jobs won't provide health insurance. The elderly are worried about the privatization of Medicare and the affordability of medications. The poor are distressed that Medicaid has become unreliable and subject to state budget crises. More and more the public feel anxious about their health care coverage and are dissatisfied with security threats. This incendiary moment may be just the time for rekindling reform.[3]

The health systems of Sweden and Canada illustrate the wide difference between those countries and the United States. Sweden, undoubtedly a leader in universal health care legislation and practice, makes access to medical care a right and necessity for all citizens. Services are provided more or less without charge. The dominant value is equality.[4] By contrast, the U.S. system is entrepreneurial and values freedom over equality. Clearly, Canada is closer to Sweden rather than to the United States:

> Although Canadian health care seems to be perennially in crisis, access, quality, and satisfaction in Canada are relatively high, and spending is relatively well controlled. The Canadian model is built on a recognition of the limits of markets in distributing medically necessary care. . . . Lessons for the United States include the importance of universal coverage, the advantages of a single payer, and the fact that systems can be organized on a subnational basis.[5]

A national health system depends on a country's political structure and its values. In the United States, at this time, universal coverage is not under serious political consideration, even though 43 million citizens do not have health insurance. Beatrix Hoffman argues that in the twentieth century in the United States all national health campaigns were initiated, organized, and led by elites. None tried to create a popular grass-roots movement for a universal health care system. Many special movements have raised particular concerns, such as the fights over the release of AIDS drugs and treatment, over abortion, over gender bias in medicine, and more. "These types of activism have ostensibly focused on a single issue . . . or on demanding benefits for a particular group."[6] However, some groups are now beginning to see the need for universal health care in the United States.

Corruption in Health Systems

There is corruption in health care, both in wealthy and poor nations. The details may differ, but corruption is a major problem everywhere. In the rich countries health care has become a big industry, a substantial part of the economy, involving large flows of money. In poor countries, health care is often a rare commodity, and underpaid health workers can be tempted to extort bribes from their patients. Corruption in health care systems can distort health care policies, services, and budgets, and it can contribute to system failures. When Peter Eigen became the new World Bank official responsible for Central Africa in 1975, he and his wife, Jutta, a physician, decided to study firsthand the medical care available to the population of Cameroon. Eigen writes:

> We visited on this trip many clinics in villages, in the settlements of forestry enterprises, in the development projects financed by various donor organizations, at missionary stations, but also in the larger cities. Wherever the state had the responsibility the results were simply devastating. The hospitals had almost no medicines or bandages, the shelves were empty; the patients had to find medicines and drugs themselves and bring them to the hospital. The only places in which sick people could hope to find appropriate medical care were the missionary stations and the worker settlements of the forestry corporations.[7]

Peter and Jutta Eigen found that underpaid personnel in the clinics and hospitals depended for their own livelihood on extorting bribes from their patients. Because suppliers paid lavish bribes, health authorities often bought inappropriate or outdated medicines for their clinics. Indeed, health care corruption appears to be everywhere in the world. Dr. Virginia Tsouderou, chair of Greece's chapter of Transparency International, discussed the problem of corruption in Greek health care. She noted the two-tiered system of expensive private care and the low-cost semi-public system. There are seri-

245

ous differentials in the speed of admission to hospitals that are simply a function of cost.[8]

In advanced countries like Germany or the United States, corruption in the health care system is affecting the quality of care in some institutions. Peter Eigen referred to alleged cases of fraud by German dentists and to the practice of pharmaceutical firms of providing "incentives" to physicians to prescribe their products to patients. He also noted that some care providers charged for services that were not actually carried out and other types of fraud. The German chapter of Transparency International is conducting a major project to introduce transparency norms into the health care system. Dr. Michael Wiehen stated that patients in Germany cannot possibly understand the bills paid by their insurance companies.[9] There is management malfeasance in some U.S. institutions quite similar to that in Germany, even though the basic institutional frameworks of the systems are different. Where great sums of money are involved, the probability of corruption cannot be disregarded.

Corruption connected with health care ranges from the needs of underpaid workers to systematic, institutional fraud in some large corporate health organizations, where very large sums are at stake. In the legal marketplace, the allocation of financial resources can also be distorted and may approximate corruption, even if not in an openly illegal form. Marcia Angell in *The Truth about the Drug Companies: How They Deceive Us and What to Do about It,* raises very critical points about the commercial practices of the pharmaceutical industry.[10] She observes that in 2002 the major drug companies spent more than twice as much on marketing and administration as on research. In fact, they do not contribute as much to research as they claim to do. These firms are enormously profitable but do not serve the public well, driving pharmaceutical costs to enormous heights. Many are European firms, but increasingly they take advantage of the U.S. market because of the pricing opportunities. The drug companies maintain a huge lobby in Washington and have formed links with politicians that will be difficult to break. This is an instance of official, legal advantages given to an industry because a lack of regulation benefits the corporations, not the public.

These facts about modern health systems provide a background for our discussion of the information values in health care and the role of transparency in public health. The political and ideological contexts of the health professions have changed. The most drastic ideological distortion of ethical values occurred in Nazi Germany. Those abuses were followed by denial and eventually a new emphasis on historical transparency and the values of human rights in the provision of health care.

Transparency in Informed Consent and Privacy

In current practice, the necessity of informed consent turns on the moral and legal duty of health professionals or researchers to inform patients, or research subjects, of the benefits and risks of a medical procedure, or research study, so they can make reasoned choices. Transparency is necessary for informed consent because it requires full disclosure of information to the patient or subject. An important precondition of informed consent is that the patient must be educated about the medical situation, the alternatives to choose from, and the risks to be taken. It is a very complex matter of morality, law, and practice. Ruth R. Faden and Tom L. Beauchamp see three intersecting moral principles in informed consent: the principle to respect autonomy, the principle of beneficence, and the principle of justice.[11] The moral ground for requiring informed consent involves duties and rights that are based on respect for a person's autonomy and self-determination. The principle of personal autonomy is a part of the idea of human rights and the dignity of the person. The Universal Declaration of Human Rights adopted by the United Nations Assembly in 1948 sees human rights as a matter of the "conscience of mankind." The declaration refers to the barbarous war crimes of World War II and other events that have outraged the world as undergirding this significance given to conscience. This is the most general statement of the moral and legal framework for the principle of autonomy. However, this idea is relatively new in medicine.

Medicine has always been guided by a principle of beneficence. While the care giver has a duty to act for the patient's benefit, the principle also created a paternalistic frame for the medical profession. Dieter Giesen writes:

> Medical ethics, from the Hippocratic Oath on, has taken a thoroughly paternalistic position, emphasizing the patient's somatic well-being above his dignitarian interest in determining whether and to what extent he shall undergo *any* recommended medical procedure. A doctor's primary ethical duties within *this* framework are owed to his fellow medical professionals, his obligation to his patient (merely) being to apply his training and skills with competence and diligence to ensure attainment of the unshakeable goal of full health. Such professional norms and paternalistic attitudes, transmitted from generation to generation of doctors, were of little significance in former centuries when medical knowledge was scant and the usage of health care services was infrequent. But in

our contemporary, medicalized society, health care is a large and ever-expanding sector of the economy and doctors have become a select and powerful elite, truly standing as the gatekeepers of life and death. The potential for medical paternalism is increased by the growing informational imbalance that exists between doctor and patient, extending the power of the former and the dependency and vulnerability of the latter.[12]

Strong currents of paternalism remain in medical practice, and therefore the legal definition of self-determination for a patient will decisively change the traditional practices of the profession. Giesen cites court rulings by the German federal supreme court and by the French supreme court on this issue, in which "self-determination is as much to be respected as good health."[13] However, Faden and Beauchamp observe that "informed consent as a practice of *respecting autonomy* has *never* had a sure foothold in medical practice."[14] The beneficence model of medical ethics has always prevailed in the past. "The autonomy model is, in the light of history, still a novel, provocative, and even radical idea. Yet we shall see that it *is* the idea that underlies the movement to informed consent."[15]

Nevertheless, the principle of beneficence remains a basic ethical value of the medical profession. It is compatible with the principle of patient autonomy, even if these two value principles need to be balanced against each other. Informed consent would give the greater weight to autonomy or self-determination. A third principle is that of justice, which entails broader guiding ideas about social norms granting equal access to essential services, integrity, personal rights and fairness to all people. It is a matter of importance at a time of rising costs and limited access to care.

The moral bases of informed consent and the national and international laws protecting it are not identical. Faden and Beauchamp comment: "The history of informed consent is rooted in multiple disciplines and social contexts, including those of the health professions, law, the social and behavioral sciences, and moral philosophy; the most influential fields have been law and moral philosophy; the central problems of informed consent have been framed in their vocabularies. Yet these disciplines, each with distinct methods and objectives, serve strikingly different social and intellectual functions."[16] The principles and practices of informed consent are matters of law in many countries.

Medical Atrocities under the Nazis

The movement for informed consent is part of the moral framework of human rights and personal dignity. Laws guaranteeing patients' rights reflect the revulsion toward the experiments or other misuses of medical knowledge that have been carried out on unsuspecting or helpless victims. The outstanding examples in recent history occurred during the Nazi-inflicted Holocaust. Changes in attitude also came with the creation of the United Nations and the declaration of universal human rights and subsequent movements.

Nazi ideology placed German medicine in a starkly destructive framework. The genocidal Holocaust and the cruel medical practices of German physicians and researchers, once revealed, aroused revulsion. The Nuremberg war crimes tribunal (1945–46) uncovered an appalling record of horrors. Since then, the moral framework of human rights has been often violated in civil wars, in failing states, by brutal dictators who have suppressed free speech and enslaved their citizens. Wars, terrorism, human subjugation, and genocide demand intervention by the international community. New institutions have been created to deal with extreme violence and destruction carried out in many parts of the world. The United Nations established the International Criminal Court in 1998 to deal with the worst of war crimes. The United States government has unfortunately chosen to boycott this institution. Nevertheless, the struggle for human rights remains vigorous and is the basis of a new emerging and compelling moral framework of global scope.

The 1933 Nazi revolution in Germany drastically affected the general moral framework of public discourse in Germany. The German medical profession contributed to this shift in attitudes away from human rights. The Nazi crimes in medical research and practice (which began well before World War II) had their roots in history. The doctrine of "racial hygiene" that rose in the nineteenth century and became fashionable not only in Germany, but also in the United States and elsewhere, was believed to be based in science. The idea that some human lives were superior to others was a preferred doctrine of conservatives who adopted the theories of social Darwinism in a crude misconstruction of Darwin's ideas about evolution. This doctrine appealed to those who saw life as a competition for success, a struggle in which only the fittest would survive. Successful people were therefore superior to the poor, who had demonstrated their lack of fitness by their economic failure. Racism applied this idea to entire populations by devising a hierarchy of human races that introduced truly appalling ideas about the value of human life in "racially inferior" groups. This conception played a major and destructive role in German medicine and medical research.

In *The Nazi Doctors*, Robert Jay Lifton presents interviews he conducted in the late 1970s and early 1980s with Nazi physicians who were among the perpetrators of the Holocaust. These oral histories of those who persecuted Jews and others deemed to be "unworthy of life" understandably contain many forms of self-defense. Yet they show to what extent the Nazi conception of the ideological role of the medical profession was shaped in an earlier time.[17]

The idea of eugenics, the "scientific" approach to improving of a race by controlling or eliminating the reproduction of genetically "inferior" people, was popular in many countries in the nineteenth century and even later, including in the United States. The practice of coerced sterilization by vasectomy, for example, was applied to the criminally insane. By the 1920s twenty-five states in the United States had adopted laws for compulsory sterilization. But in Germany a different pattern of thought (not universally accepted) advanced a much more extreme conception of eugenics. In 1933 Fritz Lenz, a German physician advocating sterilization of the "unfit," criticized the German government and the Weimar Constitution for being so backward in this field, by contrast to the United States.[18] Lenz became one of the most ardent advocates of racial hygiene and an enthusiastic supporter of the Nazi policy of racial purity. He was also ardently anti-Semitic. Lenz's views were not those of the mainstream medical tradition in Germany before the Weimar era, but they became that in the Nazi era. He claimed to be a neutral scientist, but in spite of his claim to objectivity he strongly endorsed the Nazi ideology. His arguments turned into advocacy of medical killing rather than mere sterilization.[19]

Ironically, in 1900 the Prussian minister of medical affairs had stated that the use of medical procedures for anything other than beneficial purposes would be absolutely forbidden if the patient had not agreed to the procedure. Only two years before Adolf Hitler came to power, even more stringent guidelines were issued to protect patients. Pre-Nazi Germany had certain pioneer ethical rules for medicine, but it also had the opposed thematic. Nazi rule ruthlessly destroyed the ethical practice of medicine. The regime's value system could not tolerate the idea of personal autonomy of individuals. In fact, the notion of eugenics enabled some in the medical profession to shift to the concept of euthanasia, direct medical killing, or "mercy killing." Advocates extended the concept to include killing those whose lives were "unfit to live." Discussion of these ideas created the concept of the *Deutsche Volksgemeinschaft,* or "the community of the German people," which was conceived to be an organism superior in its essence to any individual person. People who were seriously ill, handicapped, or a "burden on society" were candidates for killing in order to "enhance the quality of the *Volksgemein-schaft.*"[20] In 1920 Karl Binding, a judge, and Alfred Hoche, a professor of psychiatry, published a work entitled *The Permission to Destroy Life Unworthy of Life.* Lifton writes:

> Carefully argued in the numbered-paragraph form of the traditional philosophical treatise, the book included as "unworthy of life" not only the incurably ill but large segments of the mentally ill, the feebleminded, and retarded and deformed children. More than that, the authors professionalized and medicalized the entire concept. And they stressed the *therapeutic* goal of that concept: destroying life unworthy of life is "purely a healing treatment" and a "healing work."[21]

Social problems were to be solved by biological means. This euthanasia movement aimed to achieve the therapeutic goal of "health" for the collective body of the national community, the *Volksgemeinschaft.* This was the intellectual basis on which the Nazi movement built its policy for health care, but also the policy for mass killings by medical means. The theory of racial hygiene was ferociously put into practice.

Medical professionals in Germany joined the Nazi party even before it came to power in 1933, but even more joined after 1933. Robert Proctor estimates that 45 percent of all German doctors ultimately joined the Nazi party. Proctor gives several explanations: "Professional opportunism certainly played a role: driving out the Jews, jobs could be created for non-Jewish physicians—an important motive, given the overcrowding and financial stress suffered by the profession in the years before the rise of the Nazis."[22] The infamous anti-Semitic events of 1938 included many special restrictions against Jewish physicians. In 1933, 60 percent of Berlin's doctors were Jewish. By 1937 they were 23 percent. In July 1938 all Jewish doctors were barred from practicing medicine as of September 30, and on November 9 the pogrom of Kristallnacht took place.[23]

Other motives for joining the Nazi party included the very conservative and nationalistic views of most in the medical profession. Doctors had suffered from the economic hardships in Germany. "Impoverishment after the war and economic collapse during the final years of the Weimar Republic polarized the profession politically. At the same time, physicians warned of a 'crisis in medicine,' a crisis variously construed as the bureaucratization, specialization, or scientization of medicine—problems blamed on the socialists, the Jews, or the numerous quacks that eternally plague the profession."[24] Many imagined that National Socialism might solve their problems.

251

The severe distortion of the ethics of the profession included racial hatred, especially anti-Semitism. The ultimate crime was the Holocaust, the systematic killing of millions of Jews and other victims, including political enemies, members of other minority groups, handicapped children, tuberculosis patients, retarded people, the institutional elderly, homosexuals, and alcoholics. Their extermination was seen as a matter of expediency, a way to free hospital beds and to have fewer useless people to feed.[25] Those events became a horrible reality in part because of the ethical disaster that overtook much of the German medical profession. The Holocaust was not only based on anti-Semitic hatred and the arbitrariness of the violent totalitarian regime, but also on the acceptance by the medical profession of the concept of racial hygiene and permission to kill in the service of cleansing the German people and the Nordic race. To be sure, some doctors were greatly disturbed by the political turn to dictatorship, and socialist and communist groups were the most active in resisting the Nazis. In January 1933 the Association of Socialist Physicians raised an appeal for the working class to rise against the power grab of fascism. However, by then the Nazi movement had engulfed the country. Many German dissident physicians had to emigrate, many were killed, and criticism of Nazi policy was silenced in Germany.

From Denial to Acknowledging Historical Fact

Christian Pross, a physician, has taken an active role in creating a new spirit in German medicine. He has worked to overcome the attitude of denial that prevailed earlier in the postwar period. In 1992 he established the Treatment Center for Victims of Torture in Berlin, which has been a leader among an emerging global network of similar institutions. Pross gives an account of the evolution of the medical profession in Germany after the revelations of the Nuremberg war crimes tribunal. The denial phase continued long after the trials, Pross writes:

> It was not only the tiny number of 350 black sheep among the German medical profession who were involved in medical crimes, but that many more were involved directly or indirectly, among the cream of German medicine—university professors and outstanding scientists and researchers. As Alexander Mitscherlich and Fred Mielke noted in 1947, "Only the secret consent of the professions of science and politics can explain why the names of high-ranking scientists are constantly dropped during this trial, of men who perhaps did not right off commit any crime but took advantage of defenseless individuals."[26]

Pross reports that Mitscherlich presented to the West German Chamber of Physicians the documentation of the Nuremberg doctors' trial, but the book remained unknown to the public, was not reviewed, inspired no letters to the editor. "It was as if the book had never been written," Mitscherlich recalled. Pross concludes:

> One must assume that 10,000 copies had disappeared in the basement of the West German Association of Physicians without a single German doctor ever having read the book. The World Medical Association received a copy, however, and took it as proof that the German medical profession had distanced itself from the medical crimes committed under the Nazis and thus was qualified for renewed membership. In return Mitscherlich, who had helped save the international reputation of the German medical profession, faced a campaign of slander by his colleagues, who labeled him a traitor to his country and were successful in damaging his career.[27]

Actually, Alexander Mitscherlich had a distinguished career in Germany that transcended the attempt to slander him. He had been opposed to the Nazi regime even before the war and was arrested by the Nazi secret police and held in Nuremberg for eight months in 1937. After a period of exile in Switzerland, he returned to Germany following the war, established a psychiatric clinic at the University of Heidelberg, and coauthored with Fred Mielke *Doctors of Infamy,* a revealing book about Nazi medical crimes.[28]

Over the next three decades there was a growing awareness of the Nazi crimes in Germany, with a number of trials and revelations about medical crimes in the 1950s and 1960s. However, there were also attempts at resistance. For example, Pross writes:

> In 1968 the director of the National Cancer Institute in Heidelberg, Karl Heinrich Bauer, faced a sit-in by medical students confronting him with his involvement in compulsory sterilization during the Third Reich. Documentation of this fact was published but did not become known beyond the Heidelberg academic community. The whole medical faculty backed Bauer, and the document's author was expelled from Heidelberg University.[29]

Pross also takes the historians of medicine to task, noting that they "produced the literature on the profession's past that its leaders were asking for."[30] In many cases the 1933–45 period was simply skipped over, and documents about prominent professors and physicians with Nazi backgrounds were difficult to find until the end of the 1970s. It was fortunate that a Canadian historian, Michael H. Kater, discovered files about the revocation of the licenses of Jewish doctors after 1933, copied most of the material, and moved it to the York University archives, because by the time researchers asked for these files, they had mysteriously disappeared. After repeated requests for information, in 1986 Kater received an official letter from the Federal Association of Health Insurers in Cologne informing him that "unfortunately" the papers had been destroyed.[31]

Debates about the facts of Nazi medicine had begun in earnest in the 1960s, but by the early 1980s the political climate in Germany had changed dramatically. The television series *Holocaust* had made an impact. Archives were now opened. Holocaust memorials had been erected throughout the country, and history textbooks recounted the horrors of the Third Reich. Pross writes, "Grass-roots historians feverishly sought out reminiscences, their activities reaching a crescendo in the commemoration of the fiftieth anniversary of the *Machtergreifung*, the Nazi seizure of power, in 1983, and the fiftieth anniversary of the Kristallnacht pogrom, in 1988."[32] There was a general shift in the German public's definition of the nation's past. A new generation began to see the Nazi crimes as a reality that could not be met by denial and silence, but that required transparency and intense reflection. This movement to historical transparency also applied to Nazi medicine. In the 1930s and 1940s doctors were members of a high-status, traditionally secretive and paternalistic elite able to ward off calls for transparency about their misdeeds. A conference of physicians and health professionals held in 1980 entitled "Medicine under National Socialism: Repressed Past or Unbroken Tradition" included five Jewish refugee physicians from abroad and started a new wave of studies of Nazi medical practices and crimes.

In 1989 the Chamber of Physicians of Berlin hosted the 1989 Deutscher Ärztetag and forced the topic of medicine under the Nazis on the agenda. This led to a vigorous and angry debate within the profession. The matter of historical transparency took a decisive turn in 1993 when a former member of the Nazi SS, Hans Joachim Sewering, was elected president of the World Medical Association, then had to resign after U.S., Canadian, Israeli, and German physicians protested.[33] It was a turning point. Pross concludes:

> The system of silence, lies, half-truths, excuses, and angry denials of the last four and one-half decades is on the retreat, however. The open debate about the Nazi past has raised the consciousness of many German doctors and parts of the German public about contemporary medical abuses. It has shaken the German doctor's self-image of infallibility, of belonging to a profession that stands neutrally

above political and social forces and that presumably has always had a clean record and acted out of noble, altruistic motives.[34]

It had proceeded gradually over a long time, but the change was complete.

From the Nuremberg Code to Informed Consent

The evolution of informed consent as a legal reality and moral code for the medical profession reveals the forces that moved the process. The general adoption of informed consent took a long time and required fundamental changes in moral frames. It began early in the twentieth century in the form of ethical and legal arguments and a growing body of case law in the United States and elsewhere, including Germany. By the end of the century, it was an institutionalized system of legal requirements, formal codes of ethics, a large research literature, and specialized institutions.

The courts played a major role in introducing patient consent in treatment in both the United States and in Europe. In 1914 Judge Cardozo ruled in the famous case of *Schloendorff* v. *Society of New York Hospitals*: "Every human being of adult years and sound mind has a right to determine what shall be done with his own body; when a surgeon performs an operation without his patient's consent, he commits an assault for which he is liable in damages."[35] Other early cases that dealt with medical malpractice emphasized the importance of self-determination. Several cases in which a medical malpractice was treated as "battery" and "negligence" indicated the growing tendency of courts to require doctors to provide vital information to their patients. The courts were busy in the 1960s and 1970s creating case law dealing with informed consent.[36] U.S. courts had begun to move toward *informed* consent by the late 1950s. In the much earlier *Schloendorff* case, the decisive concept was "assault" or "battery." Gradually courts moved toward the idea that the practice of clinical medicine imposed the duty of informing the patient of available courses of action and their risks. A critical court proceeding was the *Salgo* case. In 1957 Martin Salgo sued Stanford University for the permanent paralysis caused by an operation. The court ruled that physicians had failed to warn him of the possibility of paralysis as a risk posed by the procedure. According to Faden et al., "The *Salgo* court suggested "that the new duty to disclose the risks and alternatives of treatment was a logical extension of the already established duty to disclose the treatment's nature and consequences, rather than a duty different in kind." This was a case of malpractice. However, the court's decision established the concept of *informed* consent. "*All* pertinent topics of consent—the nature, consequences, harms, benefits, risks, and alternatives of a proffered treatment— were therefore conceived as information needed by patients in order that they know what they are choosing."[37] In the long run the most powerful force behind the demand for informed consent was worldwide revulsion against the Nazi medical experiments on prisoners and the revelations of the Nuremberg war crimes trial. The Nuremberg Code of 1948 became a historical landmark for informed consent in human subject research.

The Nuremberg Code contained ten principles, with an emphasis on consent: "The voluntary consent of the human subject is absolutely essential." A forceful commentary is added:

> This means that the person involved should have legal capacity to give consent; should be so situated as to be able to exercise free power of choice without the intervention of any element of force, fraud, deceit, duress, over-reaching, or other ulterior form of constraint or coercion; and should have sufficient knowledge and comprehension of the elements of the subject matter involved as to enable him to make an understanding and enlightened decision. This latter element requires that before the acceptance of an affirmative decision by the experimental subject there should be made known to him the nature, duration, and purpose of the experiment; the method and means by which it is to be conducted; all inconveniences and hazards reasonably to be expected; and the effects on his health or person which may possibly come from his participation in the experiment. The duty and responsibility for ascertaining the quality of the consent rests upon each individual who initiates, directs or engages in the experiment. It is a personal duty and responsibility which may not be delegated to another with impunity.[38]

The code outlines principles justifying the purposes of the experiment: it must yield fruitful results for the benefit of society; it must be so designed that the anticipated results are worthwhile; it must avoid all unnecessary suffering and injury; no risk of disabling injury must exist, "except, perhaps, in those experiments where the experimental physicians also serve as subjects"; the risk to be taken should never exceed the "humanitarian importance of the problem to be solved"; preparations have to be made to protect the experimental subject from even remote harm; the experimenters have to be scientifically qualified persons; the human subject "should be at liberty to bring the experiment to an end" if he concludes that it is physically or mentally not possible; the experimenter must terminate the experiment if it may result in injury, disability, or death of the subject.[39]

The World Medical Association (WMA) recognized that unregulated biomedical research would be a threat to the legitimacy of the entire medical research profession. In the early 1960s the WMA began to draft rules governing research on human subjects. The Declaration of Helsinki of 1964 made informed consent a central requirement for such research. (It was revised in 1975, 1983, and 1989.) The declaration differentiates between therapeutic research, that is, medical research combined with professional care, and nonclinical biomedical research. In the former, "the physician must be free to use a new diagnostic and therapeutic measure, if in his or her judgment it offers hope of saving life, reestablishing health or alleviating suffering." With regard to the latter, it states that "in research on man, the interest of science and society should never take precedence over considerations related to the well-being of the subject." The emphasis was on safety of the experiment, its value to society, and respect for the patient and on informed consent. The governing principle throughout focuses more on beneficence than on autonomy of the person.[40] Nevertheless, the Helsinki Declaration was a milestone in the emergence of informed consent.

Despite the general endorsement of the Nuremberg Code and the Helsinki Declaration, practical implementation under the law occurred only much later. More than twenty years elapsed between Nuremberg in 1948 and the beginning of a major movement toward informed consent in the United States, and it took another twenty years to the 1990s to see it become a fully institutionalized system in all advanced countries. There were several reasons for this. Most U.S. professionals saw the scandals of Nazi experiments as events that "could not happen here." They believed their behavior to be far in advance of the rest of the world. There was little perceived need to create an elaborate code, let alone the large-scale apparatus that has in fact since emerged. But a number of scholars, including Henry K. Beecher, who published *Experimentation in Man* in 1959, were seeking to establish a new discipline of research ethics and informed consent.[41]

The strong moral concern about experimentation with human beings had led to the creation of a new epistemic community. In 1966 Beecher described twenty-two cases of unethical research in the *New England Journal of Medicine*. According to H. Y. Vanderpool, "The impact of Beecher's article was all the more confounding because it probed the actions of recognized cultural benefactors, those who in a few years' time had discovered 'an array of antibiotics . . . a cure for tuberculosis; a variety of drugs for treating cardiac abnormalities; a new understanding of hepatitis.'"[42] Many of these advances relied on research that disregarded basic principles of the Declaration of Helsinki.

Several cases of widely publicized unethical or at least questionable medical research in the United States created public outrage in the 1960s. The Jewish Chronic Disease Hospital case in Brooklyn in the early 1960s involved the injection of live cancer cells into twenty-two patients without cancer to discover whether the rate of rejection of the cancer cells was affected by debilitation. Because they believed the experiment posed no risk, they did not inform the patients of this action so as not to agitate them unnecessarily; they were convinced that the cancer cells would be rejected. (Actually, the cells were rejected. The ethical problem was that patients had not been informed of the procedure.) The investigation led to serious criticism of the experimenters, and they were placed on a year's probation. This case alerted the Public Health Service to the looseness of the regulations in medical research.[43]

Another troubling case from the 1950s involved the Willowbrook State School for "mentally defective" children. According to Faden et al., sanitary conditions at the school were so poor that they "facilitated the rapid spread of fecally borne infectious hepatitis of a relatively mild strain. By 1954, virtually all susceptible children contracted the disease within six to twelve months of residence in the institution."[44] Saul Krugman and his associates tried to develop a preventative. They used an isolated strain of the hepatitis virus and deliberately infected newly arrived children in the hope that this would immunize them against the particular hepatitis virus. They presented information about the experiment to the children's parents, but critics charged that the information was not adequate and the consent given may have been faulty. A major debate followed in professional medical circles and in public discourse. Krugman's research unit was closed, but the debate about the ethics of the studies was never resolved.

The Tuskegee syphilis study became a turning point in setting U.S. norms for experimentation on human beings. It was an experiment to study the natural consequences of advanced syphilis in African American men that started in 1932 and ended in 1972. Conducted by the U.S. Public Health Service, it became, over forty years, the longest experiment on human beings without any therapy in the history of medicine. This project aroused criticism in the 1970s and casts a shadow over race relations even today.

In the early twentieth century America suffered an epidemic of syphilis. The U.S. surgeon general in the 1930s, Thomas Parran, outlined the need for an urgent, comprehensive national campaign to control the disease. He described its threat: "There is reason to believe that if all conditions due to syphilis were reported as such it would be found a leading cause of death in the United States."[45] By 1937, the Tuskegee syphilis study had been under way for five years.[46] When the Public Health Service examined 2,000 black workers at the Delta Pine and Land Company in Mississippi, they found that 25 percent had syphilis. The Public Health Service then approached the Julius Rosenwald Fund of Chicago for help, and together they established syphilis control programs. Test programs conducted from 1929 to 1931 revealed that in Macon County, Alabama (where Tuskegee is located), 35–40 percent of those tested were infected with syphilis. Charles Johnson was commissioned to study exacerbating conditions, such as extreme poverty, and the presence of other ailments, such as tuberculosis, in Macon County.[47]

The Depression brought an end to the Rosenwald Fund's contribution to the testing program. At the same time, a major controversy arose concerning the relation between race and the incidence of syphilis. The dominant American medical view was that the disease had different outcomes for whites and blacks. Blacks, it was believed, suffered more cardiovascular damage, and whites suffered more neurological harm. However, in Norway in 1929, Dr. E. Bruusgaard published a study of syphilis cases between 1891 and 1910 recorded but not treated at the Oslo Clinic. He found that cardiovascular damage was common and neurological damage rare. This, of course, suggested that the U.S. hypothesis regarding racial differences might be wrong.[48]

A new study designed by Taliaferro Clark, M.D., of the Public Health Service recommended working with living patients, in contrast to past research. He stated, "The result of these studies of case records suggest the desirability of making a further study of the effect on untreated syphilis on the human economy among people now living and engaged in daily pursuits." He also said that Macon County, Alabama, presented a "ready-made situation" for studying untreated syphilis in Negroes.[49] There was no concern with the ethics of the plan to study the natural course of syphilis in African Americans without treatment.

There can be no doubt that these decisions were grounded in racism and authoritarian paternalism, pursuing science in the service of the U.S. national interest. Scientists were convinced of the physiological differences of the races and expected that Negroes would trust the white authorities. They also assumed that the advance of medical science was exclusively the prerogative of medical doctors. They did, however, show considerable political skill in making alliances with the local authorities in Tuskegee and its churches, as well as with plantation owners. The subjects of the project were never informed of its purpose, especially not that treatment would be withheld. Yet the project was not kept secret. It became the subject of conferences, reports, and papers in medical journals.

Aware of the national interest in studying and combating the syphilis epidemic, arguments for budget allocations stressed the threat of syphilis to individuals and the public. Withholding treatment was required for the success of the experiment. In 1942–43, when the local draft board ordered treatment for some of the subjects, they met strenuous opposition. The medical staff was proud to report: "So far, we are keeping the known positive patients from getting treatment."[50]

Withholding treatment became more obviously problematic after penicillin was shown to be an effective medication for syphilis. A Public Health Service official, however, saw it as a further argument for continuing the experiment. James H. Jones reports Dr. Parran's reaction in 1943:

> The study had become "more significant now that a succession of rapid methods and schedules of therapy for syphilis had been introduced, and the finding of syphilis has become practically a routine periodic testing of the citizenry." These developments increased the experiment's value, [Parran] explained, because it now could be used as a "necessary control against which to project not only the results obtained with the rapid schedules of therapy for syphilis but also the costs involved in finding and placing under treatment the infected individuals."[51]

By 1951 there was no longer any doubt about that penicillin could treat syphilis. By that time the Nazi medical crimes and the Nuremberg principles about human research were generally known. Nevertheless, Jones writes, the PHS professionals saw no relevance to their work.

> There is no evidence that the Tuskegee Study was ever discussed in the light of the Nuremberg code, the ten basic conclusions or principles on human experimentation that emerged from the trials. . . . And yet there was a similarity between the Nazi experiments and the Tuskegee Study, one which went beyond their racist and medical natures. Like the chain of command within the military hierarchy of Nazi Germany, the Tuskegee Study's firm entrenchment in the PHS bureaucracy reduced the sense of personal responsibility and ethical concern. For the most part doctors and civil servants simply did their jobs. Some merely "followed orders"; others worked for "the glory of science."[52]

Yet there were questions in 1951 about whether the study should continue. Procedural improvements were discussed. A major examination of the

AIDS and tuberculosis. The health threats that can cross national borders make it imperative to compare health systems for their vulnerability. The outbreak of severe acute respiratory syndrome (SARS) is an example.

In the developing countries also, health care issues are fueled by moral demands. Efforts to improve and expand health systems are under way, often encountering frustration and strife. Inadequate budgets, a scarcity of qualified medical professionals, and lack of physical resources in clinics and hospitals make these systems especially vulnerable. Measures to combat epidemics strain resources and become even more troublesome for the political system. The difficult experience with AIDS in South Africa under President Mbeki is an example. His initial, politically motivated denial and rejection of the scientific knowledge about the causes of AIDS slowed the fight against the epidemic. As a consequence, the disease spread without effective countermeasures. Gradually, international pressures helped to change the stance of Mbeki's government. In the case of AIDS and other major epidemics, the struggle for public health security has become increasingly global. It is one of the many urgent problems being tackled by global civil society, international agencies, and national governments. Public health has become a major concern for the World Health Organization (WHO) and many global civil society groups.

Comparisons of Health Systems

Many countries have at least nominally embraced the right to health, an idea expressed in legislation and even national constitutions. The Charter of Fundamental Rights of the European Union contains a general, albeit qualified, endorsement of the universal right to health care. It reads: "Everyone has the right of access to preventive health care and the right to benefit from medical treatment under the conditions established by national laws and practices. A high level of human health protection shall be ensured in the definition and implementation of all Union policies and activities."[1] Also, current health systems all have a general commitment to the values of patient rights and the importance of informed consent. They also need to consider the value of justice. It is remarkable that these values are at least nominally adopted, since they were not universal at all in the first half of the twentieth century, and even today there are important differences in the political frames of health care systems.

In 2003 the *American Journal of Public Health* examined health system reform in many countries so as to enlighten the U.S. debate about national health system reform.[2] The journal presented case studies of Canada and subjects was carried out, but the study continued. In June 1965 Dr. Irwin J. Schatz raised the first serious criticism of the project. He wrote:

> I am utterly astounded by the fact that physicians allow patients with a poten-tially fatal disease to remain untreated when effective therapy is available. I assume you feel that the information which is extracted from the observations of this untreated group is worth their sacrifice. If this is the case, then I suggest that the United States Public Health Service and those physicians associated with it need to reevaluate their moral judgments in this regard.[53]

The letter was not answered. Another critic, Peter Buxtun, who worked for the PHS in San Francisco, had learned about the Tuskegee study in conversa-tions with colleagues and concluded that this was not what the Public Health Service should be doing. In 1966 he wrote to the head of the Division of Venereal Diseases, but received no reply. When he was later contacted for discussion, his ideas were furiously rejected.

In 1967 Buxtun resigned from the PHS and enrolled in law school. He wrote a second letter in 1968, but this time the political scene had dramati-cally changed. Buxtun had become even more alarmed about the Tuskegee study in view of the civil rights movement and the outbreak of race riots in several cities. The Public Health Service responded by convening a blue-rib-bon panel to discuss the study in 1969, but it recommended against treat-ment.[54] Finally, in July 1972 Buxtun went to an Associated Press reporter with his knowledge about the study. Jean Heller broke the story on July 25, 1972, in the *Washington Star*. This was the definitive end of this project.

The consequences of this disastrous experiment were great. Informed consent now became a requirement for experiments with human subjects. Jones writes, "In December 1974 the U.S. government agreed to pay a $10 million out-of-court settlement to subjects-plaintiffs and their survivors. In addition, the U.S. Department of Health and Human Services (DHHS) has been making yearly payments to cover the medical, nursing care, and other expenses of the research subjects, their spouses, and their progeny—pay-ments that exceeded 1.8 million in 1994."[55] In 1997 President Clinton apol-ogized for this government study, and in 2001 the government of Alabama apologized. On January 16, 2004, the last survivor of the Tuskegee study died at age ninety-six.

One legacy of this experiment was lasting distrust in America's black community of public health projects. The cultural and political damage cre-ated by the Tuskegee study has affected the AIDS epidemic among African-

Americans, among whom infection is spreading more rapidly than among other groups. The problem of distrust has led to beliefs among some groups (including the Nation of Islam) that "AIDS is a form of genocide, an attempt by White society to eliminate the Negro race."[56] Even now, beliefs of this kind are in circulation. There is a great need for AIDS education and community support to improve this condition.

The Tuskegee study was not a unique event. There were many other instances of medical treatment of patients without proper precautions, let alone informed consent. Many became public knowledge. Several were carried out by the U.S. military. Some experiments tested exposure to nuclear radiation, the hazards of which were not well known in the 1950s and even in the 1960s. As late as October 2002, new revelations appeared of U.S. military experiments on human subjects. Some of these dealt with exposure to biological and chemical weapon materials in the 1960s and 1970s in various locations in the United States, at sea, and elsewhere. In Vieques, Puerto Rico, the military sprayed trioctyl phosphate on troops at a firing range in May 1969.[57] This substance is said to cause skin and other irritations and even cancer. The revelation caused outraged protests, even thirty-three years later.

Many more cases of the victimization of subjects in experiments by medical and behavioral researchers, as well as violations of patients' rights by hospitals and other institutions, have come to light. Military secrecy about such activities contributed to the irritation of the public. The result was the mobilization of political forces to create a system of laws, government regulations, and oversight for patient care, control of experimentation with human subjects, and regulation of exposure to dangerous substances. These efforts have now grown into a veritable industry, with a focus on informed consent.

In the United States, federal policies have emerged to protect human subjects in experiments and patients from medical practices that involve risks. The beginning of federal concern with informed consent occurred in the early 1960s, at about the same time as the adoption of the Helsinki Declaration by the World Medical Association. In the 1960s various initiatives were taken by the National Institutes of Health and the U.S. Food and Drug Administration to advance the rules for human subject research and practice. In 1966 the government mandated the creation of institutional review boards (IRBs) for bioethics research on human subjects. This established the group review of the ethical aspects of each government-sponsored project. While this was an important step, these early initiatives remained very limited. Two federal commissions played a major role at the federal level: the

National Commission for the Protection of Human Subjects of Biomedical and Behavioral Research worked from 1974 to 1978, and the President's Commission for the Study of Ethical Problems in Medicine and Biomedical and Behavioral Research worked from 1980 to 1983. The first produced the landmark Belmont Report, while the second recommended preparing a guidebook for institutional review boards.

The Belmont Report (1979) outlines principles for research on human subjects, calling attention to the boundaries between practice and research. Practice is "designed solely to enhance the well-being of an individual patient or client and to have a reasonable expectation of success. . . . By contrast, the term 'research' designates an activity designed to test a hypothesis, permit conclusions to be drawn, and thereby to develop or contribute to generalizable knowledge (expressed, for example, in theories, principles, and statements of relationships)."[58]

The report discusses principles in some detail: "Individuals should be treated as *autonomous* agents, and second, . . . persons with diminished autonomy are entitled to *protection*." Beneficence includes efforts to respect "their decisions and protecting them from harm, but also to secure their well-being." Beneficence is considered an obligation. "Two general rules have been formulated as complementary expressions of beneficence actions in this sense: (1) do no harm and (2) maximize possible benefits and minimize possible harm." Justice involves the question, "Who ought to receive the benefits of research and bear its burden? This is a question of justice, in the sense of 'fairness in distribution' or 'what is deserved.'" Justice is a prominent value for public health, where universal health care for all is an urgent goal.

These principles are very complex, especially in the intersection between justice and respect for persons. Justice can mean access to benefits, which also involves political will and economic resources. It connects the ethical principles to the politics and economics of national health care systems referred to earlier. The Belmont Report discusses applications through informed consent, voluntariness, assessment of risks and benefits, their nature, scope, and systematic assessment, and the selection of subjects. It is basically focused on the protection of the individual.

The *Guidebook for Institutional Review Boards* is very different in its purpose. Growing out of the 1983 commission report, the IRB guidebook has since been revised and remains a helpful and practical guide for the institutional review boards. Since that time, their functions have been expanded and they have become a prominent element in the infrastructure of informed consent. In 1991 the Common Federal Policy on research with human subjects was established. As a result, there is now a huge infrastructure for informed consent and its contexts in the United States. It consists of the IRBs, federal granting and oversight agencies like the National Institutes of Health, assurance of compliance contracts, federal and state regulations, approved ethical principles, and continuing updates for new developments.[59]

Researchers enroll in training programs to learn how to deal with their IRBs. The administrative apparatus for informed consent has meant the rise of an elaborate structure in hospitals and clinics, dental clinics, and independent medical practices. Because there are legal sanctions against infringements of federal and state regulations, lawyers and other consultants are employed in addition to the health professionals. However, the least developed of the ethical principles is justice. As we have seen, in the United States access to health care is very uneven and many citizens have no health insurance. However, the progress on informed consent at all levels is impressive. It has also become part of daily routines for health care professionals, despite grumbling about the additional legal formalities.

The Rise of Medical Ethics as a Discipline

Declarations of ethics and of codes of conduct have become ubiquitous in associations, corporations, and institutions around the world. An Internet search yields an almost endless list of associations of funeral directors, professionals in massage, automobile sales, realty brokerage, specialists in the study of dreams, the hotel managers of Tobago and Trinidad, and many others—and all have an ethics code of conduct, most recently adopted. Some of these codes make fairly preposterous demands on their members and all claim the highest possible standard of ethics. Most are serious attempts to clarify the norms for their vocation. The apparent duty to create guidelines and adopt new norms responds to the uncertainties of rapid and often global change, and the need to be trusted.

The rise of medical ethics as an organized disciplinary effort worldwide is an especially important phenomenon. It is a respected academic discipline, with powerful organizations to create standards, exchange ideas, and develop educational programs. Leaders of the profession have asked all medical schools to teach medical ethics. In 1982 the Standing Committee of the Doctors of the European Economic Community declared that medical ethics should be taught in all medical schools, a declaration repeated in

1991. Similar proposals have been raised in the United States and in other countries.

The World Medical Association (WMA), founded in 1947, established its Committee on Medical Ethics in 1952 and an Ethics Unit in 2003, with an even more ambitious mandate. The WMA has always considered it its main duty "to establish and promote the highest possible standards of ethical behaviour and care by physicians."[60] Its Web site includes information exchanges such as a Syllabus Exchange Catalog for teaching medical ethics internationally.[61] For example, the Task Force on Graduate Medical Education on Bioethics and Humanities serves as a resource for ethics educators to meet the requirements of the Accreditation Council for Graduate Medical Education (ACGME), and the American Society of Bioethics and Humanities has established a model curriculum that meets these requirements.

In short, the ethics movement in health care has grown into a formidable infrastructure for informed consent and the linked norms of medical ethics. Professionals draw on a great diversity of views representing many religions, secular attitudes, and the legal systems of different countries. Again we encounter the daunting challenge of harmonizing diverse ethical norms while avoiding the dangers of ethical relativism. The struggle between particularism and universalism is not over, and the drive is on for mandatory medical ethics rules worldwide.

Privacy for Patients

As noted in chapter 5, privacy is not one of the higher information values in the United States. There is no comprehensive privacy law or a specific constitutional right to privacy, but there are specific sectoral laws, such as the relatively new privacy law regarding health care. Here the United States is in sharp contrast to the European Union, where a comprehensive privacy directive is in force with sturdy enforcement provisions. This is Directive 95/46/EC of the European Parliament and of the European Union Council of Ministers, adopted in 1995, which has the effect of law. It protects the processing of personal data and the free movement of such data. In 2003 the EU Commission found that the law was "achieving its main aims," although several member states were tardy in implementing it. The commission then addressed the European Court of Justice, forcing Germany, the Netherlands, Belgium, and Luxembourg to implement the directive. France still has not quite adopted the directive over its own law of 1978. An additional Directive 2002/58/EC, dealing with privacy in electronic communications, was adopted by the European Parliament and the Council of Ministers on July 12, 2002. It preserves the spirit of the older privacy directive but adapts it to the specifics of information technology. In 2003 the EU Commission found that businesses initially hostile to the directive had found it acceptable, but they suggested specific alterations to lessen some of the burdens of specific practices. The health aspect of privacy protections was addressed by IMS Health, a firm that collects data from hospitals, medical practices, and pharmacies, which proposed detailed modifications. Overall, Europeans think that their health privacy law is working.[62]

In the United States the legislative context for health privacy issues is the Health Insurance Portability and Accountability Act of 1996 (HIPAA). Several amendments to the HIPAA were added: the Women's Health and Cancer Rights Act, the Mental Health Parity Act, and the Newborns' and Mothers' Health Protection Act. Congress had determined that the privacy part of the HIPAA legislation would become the responsibility of the HHS as a rule maker if Congress had not taken action by 1999. It did not take that action. Thus the HHS created the HIPAA privacy rule, effective April 14, 2003, with a later compliance date for small health plans of April 14, 2004. It is still in progress, even though the rule has become official policy.[63]

The legislative process to create the law permitting workers to carry health insurance from one employer to another took much time and involved multiple changes. The health care community took a strong interest and had a generally positive attitude toward the legislation. However, there were serious challenges from the start. The HIPAA's very complexity reflected the fragmented structure of the U.S. health care system, as well as the sequential approach to health care concerns addressed by Congress, as indicated by the number of amendments to the act.

Many different types of health care institutions and actors had to be fitted into a comprehensive framework of standards. This was also an enormous technological task. It involved a mandate from Congress to the HHS setting requirements for technological initiatives on electronic transactions by all the covered entities, the various institutions and their affiliates in the U.S. health care system. They are to modernize their management and record keeping and to implement privacy rules and security systems in line with HHS requirements. This will improve performance and save costs.

There was a compelling need for the HIPAA.[64] A shared business language for medical records, diagnoses, procedures, and services would replace the varied formats for bills, payments, and records throughout the enormous system. Individual insurers had previously designed their own forms and codes that health care providers had to use. The HIPAA law was generally welcomed as a necessary reform, although implementation would be complex. Moving the entire system to information technology instead of paper files was daunting. With unintended irony, the HHS developed new rules to help the covered entities adapt to the new procedures and technology called "administrative simplification" provisions.

Lawmakers were convinced that the HIPAA would be beneficial to health system management, especially in setting standards for electronic transmissions. However, the health industry had less experience with information technology than other domains of the economy. According to Goldsmith and Richel, in 2001 "less than 10% of U.S. hospitals had adopted computerized patient records. And less than 5% had adopted computerized physician order entry. The bulk of the $20 billion or so investment in health care information technology (IT) went to the financial infrastructure (billing)."[65] A strenuous process of learning and implementing the "simplification rules" is under way.

The HIPAA privacy rule of 1996 established for the first time "a set of national standards for the protection of certain health information."[66] We focus on the main features of the introduction of privacy rules into the U.S. health system. The HIPAA was primarily intended to assure the portability of health insurance from one job to another and to upgrade the infrastructure of health care. Privacy was one motive, but lawmakers could not specify the privacy requirements themselves. Three years later, the task went to the HHS, which issued a draft in March 2002 and asked for comments. It received more than 11,000. Nevertheless, the rule enforced by the HHS Office of Civil Rights is causing difficulties. The problems are in the details.

In 2003, *USA Today* published an article about the confusion created by the law. It reported a critical episode that occurred in Colorado, where 911 emergency dispatchers in the Denver area had stopped giving ambulance personnel the names of persons to be rescued, believing that the HIPAA privacy rule forbade it. In the rural town of Craig, 200 miles west of Denver, where there were no street addresses, emergency crews were unable to reach a heart attack victim because they had not been given his name. As a result, neighbors could not direct them to his home. This incident "was a dramatic example of the widespread confusion created by part of the Health Insurance, Portability and Accountability Act (HIPAA), which set a national standard for medical privacy by making the unauthorized release of medical information a crime."[67]

Many other examples of mistaken interpretations of the law have occurred. It covers 500 pages and is difficult to read even for lawyers. However, it does not prevent 911 dispatchers from using residents' names in radio calls. But there are other problems: "One of the main sources of medical errors is poor communication," says Deeb Salem, a Boston cardiologist. "HIPAA is another barrier to communication. The principles, the ideals are fine. The costs of chaos, money and possible patient injury have not been taken into account."

The *USA Today* article cited Richard Campanelli of the U.S. Department of Health and Human Services, who said the law requires that "reasonable safeguard" be taken to protect patient information. "The two goals were to protect privacy of patient information and to do so in a way that does not impede access to quality care." This, of course, is a classic case of balancing different information values in what we call the "architecture" of values. It requires detailed adjustments. Campanelli stated:

> The privacy provision is applied to hospitals, doctors, pharmacists and health insurers, and was designated initially to protect computerized medical records and billing. But it has been interpreted much more broadly and at times incorrectly. Thousands of doctors, for example, have stopped sending out appointment-reminder postcards, figuring the cards could be read by someone other than the patient. Some doctors have stopped leaving messages on patients' telephone answering machines, fearing that other family members might listen to them. Wives have been told that they no longer could verify dental appointments for their husbands.

These communications are allowed under the law, said Campanelli, but confusion does arise. In addition, "in the medical community, there is rising concern about the cost of complying with the privacy rules. Many doctors say the government has issued a mandate without providing funds to pay for it. Blue Cross estimates the cost of complying with the privacy law at about $43 billion over five years to cover new staffing, computer software and paperwork." In 2003 a lawsuit was brought against the secretary of health and human services by consumer, physician, and health advocacy groups seeking an injunction against the HIPAA privacy rule. They feel that the regulations were written so broadly that the medical records of patients could be shared with market research firms and that patients did not have enough protection.[68]

Other problems are surfacing. The biomedical research community is concerned about the impact of the privacy rules and their detailed requirements on their capacity to conduct research with human subjects. Mostly their objections are not about the values of privacy, security, and informed consent, but about the burdensome ways in which the actual procedures are prescribed by the government and implemented by the IRBs. The University of Pittsburgh *Times* reported in 2003, "Besides inducing writer's cramp in patients suddenly required to sign reams of release forms, the federal Health Insurance Portability and Accountability Act (HIPAA) is having an enormous impact on institutions.... Protected health information under HIPAA includes a patient's name, address, phone number, diagnosis, and test results, among other things."[69] There had been a vigorous discussion about the way in which the Institutional Review Boards interpreted the HIPAA rules—allegedly in far too narrow ways. Similar discussions have taken place in other American universities. There will be undoubtedly much discussion between the research community and the government as well as Congress. The HIPAA privacy rule remains a work in progress.

Overall, the legislative process of the HIPAA showed the fragmented approach of Congress regarding health care policy. Health privacy rules had to be specific to this sector, rather than being part of general, comprehensive privacy legislation. Laws dealing with special domains such as women's health, cancer, mental health, newborn children, and mothers were added later. The legislative edifice makes improvements to the U.S. health care system, but only in pieces and at the cost of the value of justice for all.

This brief overview reveals that creating and changing information infrastructures is a very complex and contested process. Privacy has always had a relatively low place among the values of the U.S. health care system. Surely, there was very little thought given to patient privacy in the past: social security numbers were used as obvious identifiers, medical records were treated rather carelessly, physical arrangements in hospitals made privacy extremely difficult as physicians' conversations with patients can easily be overheard. Data banks built by commercial corporations on their clients or customers also included health care data. Today privacy in American society is given more attention. Since the privacy rules in health care intersect with many other domains of society, difficulties are inevitable. The HIPAA privacy rule is a major revolution for virtually all U.S. health care institutions.

The dissemination of valid information about the meaning of the rule has turned out to be a slow and difficult process. Misinterpretations have caused real problems and frustration almost everywhere. Training programs are needed to teach staff how to handle the new requirements; a whole industry of lawyers, consultants, trainers, advisers about the HIPAA is emerging. Adherence to rules will gradually become routine, but there is an obvious need for flexibility. An additional difficulty is that all this is occurring when health care budgets in the United States are overburdened with enormous deficits. State governments are grappling with very large shortfalls in their budgets. The entities covered by the HIPAA also have budgetary difficulties, as does the federal government. Full implementation of the HIPAA rule will take resources. Maybe these problems will become an impetus for more comprehensive privacy legislation, despite opposition by powerful special interests.

Public Health in the Era of Globalization

A core feature of modernization in all nation-states is a concern for public health. It has an especially strong record in the United States. The nation's harbor cities have had to deal with immigration, intensive overseas trade, diverse ethnicities, and poverty. Immigrants often brought with them infectious diseases and helped to spread epidemics. The major public health innovations were seemingly simple: clean drinking water, safe food, sanitary dwellings, well-built sewer systems, and wide access to health care in hospitals were the elements that have significantly prolonged life expectancy in industrial countries. These advances are now under threat because of globalization.

Laurie Garrett, in *The Coming Plague: Newly Emerging Diseases and a World out of Balance* and *Betrayal of Trust: The Collapse of Global Public Health,* warns of the serious dangers posed by deficiencies in public health worldwide.[70] Indeed, she notes, public health infrastructures weakened in the late twentieth century and have altogether collapsed in many parts of the world—in Russia, central Asia, parts of eastern Europe, and the very poor countries. For Garrett,

> Public health is not an ideology, religion, or political perspective—indeed, history demonstrates that whenever such forces interfere with or influence public health activities a general worsening of the populace's well-being usually followed. As envisioned by its American pioneers, public health was a practical system, or infrastructure, rooted in two fundamental scientific tenets: the germ theory of disease and the understanding that preventing disease in the weakest elements of society ensured protection for the strongest (and richest) in the larger community.[71]

The perspective of public health practitioners is necessarily different from that of clinical physicians, even though their commitment to health is shared. Public health deals with the well-being of entire populations and with the safety of communities, not primarily with curing an individual's disease. Medical professionals everywhere work in legal frameworks set by the state. However, public health has a very special role to play in relation to the state: it must provide information about threats to a population's health, which means monitoring health conditions on a large scale. And it must recommend measures to overcome these threats through appropriate actions by the state, such as quarantine, allocating resources, and mobilizing assistance in health emergencies. Public health can insist that the state take unpopular measures to isolate an epidemic outbreak, or allocate resources to deal with the health threats resulting from disasters, natural or man-made.

Public health has a lot to do with safety, and that includes the threat of terrorism. Relations between public health workers and the state can be very complex. To build credibility and legitimacy, public health professionals need to practice transparency and demand transparency from the state. Surveillance, monitoring, data collection, and analytical systems are among the necessary tools of public health—and all of these interact in sometimes painful ways with the information values of individual privacy, secrecy, accountability, and transparency. Governments do not necessarily give public health a high priority in their actions. There are other goals to be pursued with limited means. Public health policies often conflict with special interests—even violent forces protecting drug cartels, organized crime, or beneficiaries of environmental exploitation.

The public health profession lost influence in the second half of the twentieth century. Infectious diseases became somewhat less spectacular than earlier epidemics of plague, tuberculosis, typhoid, and others. Smallpox was actually eliminated. Public health professionals tried to combat other health threats, such as tobacco use and environmental pollution as sources of cancer, fatty foods as a source of heart disease, and radiation as a cause of deformation in babies. Nevertheless, these campaigns did not easily convince the public that these risks had the immediacy of a microbial pandemic. "Public health in the wealthy world, therefore, struggled to maintain respect, funding, and self-definition in the late twentieth century."[72] Garrett points out that the public health profession in the United States had lost its focus. The successful rise of biotechnology seemed to be so promising:

No two deans of the West's major schools of public health agree on a definition of its goals and missions. While one school—the University of California, Berkeley—selected a biotechnology executive in 1998 as its dean, another—Harvard—opted that year for a leader whose battle was against the most ancient—even traditional—scourge, tuberculosis. A schism appeared and widened in academia, pitting technologists and health managers against the more traditional advocates of disease prevention and epidemiology.[73]

The public health infrastructure has been shrinking in the United States, and the demand for affordability puts the focus on economic aspects of health care, with an emphasis on managed care.

In fact, there are discussions among public health leaders about expanding the scope of public health. Some are advocating broadening the profession's mandate to include social issues that imperil health, such as war, poverty, and ethnic discrimination. Others warn that this leads to diffuseness and call for a narrower approach that focuses on individuals affected by these conditions. There is peril in judging social problems merely by their health consequences. Ilan H. Meyer and Sharon Schwarz speak of the "healthification" of homelessness as an example of inappropriate broadening of public health:

> Public healthification implies that homelessness is problematic because it is a health-related problem. But would homelessness divorced from its health impact be any less troubling? In a wealthy country, the sight of people living in subways and in shelters is evidence of a wrong that needs no further justification for action. Similarly, should an argument against inequality be dependent on research findings that document the negative outcomes of inequality? Is discrimination any less unjust if it does not lead to adverse health outcomes? We think this is a perilous stance.[74]

Public health must rely on reliable information about direct health risks and threats—it is the requirement of transparency for the profession. However, there has to be a focus, a boundary for the responsibilities of the profession.

The search for a focus and a comprehensive mission may now be under way; but there is more than one view. Two public health leaders, Alfred Sommer and Mohammad N. Akhter, raise the call: "It's Time We Became a Profession!" They point out that public health measures can be credited with 80 percent of the increase in longevity and better health in the United States, but this historical fact is not known. "Investments in public health have declined from a minuscule 3% of U.S. health spending to a microscopic 0.9%; local health budgets and staff are being slashed and their responsibilities transferred elsewhere, often to managed care and other clinical/treatment enterprises; and the public health workforce is traditionally undervalued and underpaid."[75] They are concerned that public health as a profession lacks "definition, appreciation, and visibility." What needs to be done is to create a visible, organized culture of professionalism in public health. This would raise the visibility of the public health work force and improve the quality of public health services. They also agree that the core of public health knowledge, with its focus on the health of populations and prevention of disease rather than the treatment of individuals, is a core of shared ethical values. Sommer and Akhter conclude their call for professionalization with this statement:

> This is a strategic moment. The organization and financing of health-related activities are in profound flux, not only in the United States but across the world. As other professions stake out their claims and positions, public health is uniquely focused on those issues that most profoundly affect health. As a recognized profession, we will be more visible, influential, and effective in improving the health status of all people, not only in the United States but around the globe.[76]

Christopher Keane, John Marx, and Edmund Ricci in 2003 published the results of a survey of the directors of local health departments in the United States, focusing on management, privatization of public health services, and professionalization of the field. Concerned about the future of public health in America, they worry that privatization of what had been public services may blur the boundaries of the profession. Some public health directors who are inclined to adopt a broad view of their responsibilities are also inclined toward privatizing services. The managerial tactics of many directors—often influenced by budgetary constraints that lead them to use private, cheaper labor, to evade regulations—may not support high-quality professionalization. Indeed, the focus on "core public health functions" of "assessment, assurance, and policy making" reflects a managerial rather than a professional point of view. This is dangerous, "especially if managerial criteria displace professional expert knowledge in decision-making. Here we have shown how such beliefs are associated with the decision to privatize."[77]

The growing public recognition that the well-being of populations depends on the prevention of health risks of all kinds has raised worries about health protection in a global context. The threats to health produced by global inequalities are reflected in the discussions of public health codes of ethics and professional strategies. The social and economic impact of diseases—some of them new like AIDS and some of them old like tuberculosis or malaria—has become a threat in both developing and rich countries.

Global and domestic inequalities in living conditions and diet, for example, are gradually being perceived as a worldwide hazard. The World Bank and the World Health Organization have launched important initiatives, as have private donors like the Bill and Melinda Gates Foundation, which has started a major initiative on improving health in developing countries in collaboration with the NIH. The foundation contributed $200 million to this program. In addition, there is the fear of bioterror attacks. This threat clearly requires technological defenses, but also monitoring of health conditions.

The domain of public health is probably most dependent on the information value of transparency, even if it means cutting through oceans of opacity in the world. Monitoring the incidence of disease, the path of epidemics, assessing the state of health in many nations and across the world is a major task of this profession. Public health also has always worked directly with governments as well as with civil society.

The global context as well as the various domestic contexts that are affected by global change place public health at the center of the politics of global transformation. The World Federation of Public Health Associations (WFPHA) has built wide-ranging networks and programs, often in cooperation with the World Health Organization (WHO), the specialized UN agency for health and various global NGOs. The WHO was created in 1948, soon after the establishment of the UN itself. Under the leadership of Gro Harlem Brundtland from 1998 to 2003, the WHO became an active central institution for global health efforts. Brundtland is followed by Lee Jong-wook, a Korean physician who headed the campaign against tuberculosis. There are many global initiatives under way, such as the "3 by 5 initiative" to provide HIV/AIDS treatments to 3 million people by 2005. The WHO's readiness to deal with disease outbreaks requiring immediate intervention has been indispensable in emergencies.

The World Health Organization and the World Association of Public Health Organizations (WAPHO) are rallying points for new initiatives in public health and new conceptions of what the profession is or ought to be. One important episode was the role of the WHO in relation to the Chinese government after the outbreak of SARS (severe acute respiratory syndrome) in 2003.[78] The disease was first reported to the WHO in Vietnam, when a Chinese American businessman was admitted to a small hospital in Hanoi on February 26, 2003. His symptoms seemed to indicate influenza because he had come from South China and Hong Kong, where several apparent influenza cases had been detected. Since his case seemed to be difficult, it was also reported to the WHO. The patient who triggered the concern in

Hanoi was sent to Hong Kong, where he soon died. In Vietnam, several other cases among the care givers of the first case fell ill. The Vietnamese government reacted with great speed on the advice of the WHO. Dr. Carlo Urbani, a WHO professional, saw the first and subsequent cases of SARS. He died on March 11, 2003.

The reactions in different states to this dangerous infectious disease varied. Vietnam responded quickly, but others experienced problems. Taiwan suffered from two sources of the disease converging there: business travelers who came from mainland China and inexperienced health care workers. The WHO sent a delegation to Taipei, then issued a warning against traveling to Taiwan on May 8. The disease spread as far as Canada and elsewhere and was recognized by the WHO as a serious global threat.

The turn of events in the People's Republic of China was at first unfortunate, with the exception of Hong Kong. While Hong Kong's medical and public health establishment acted quickly and successfully, with a high level of transparency, provincial governments and for a time the national government of China did not. The WHO issued a statement of praise: "Hong Kong has introduced a rigorous contact tracing procedure. All close contacts of known SARS cases are quarantined at home. In addition, their Hong Kong identity card numbers are passed to the Immigration Department to ensure that these individuals cannot leave the territory."[79]

SARS was another story in Guangdong Province and in Beijing. Officials in Guangdong suppressed news of the disease. Lynn T. White writes about this situation:

> Rulers in China have an odd belief: that natural disasters, such as earthquakes or new diseases, reflect on their legitimacy. Guangdong cadres repressed news of early cases of SARS out of fear that knowledge of this mysterious illness would disturb the populace and sow "disorder" (luan). Their delay caused real disorder. Nosy, impolite news reporters might have published data, from the unwashed masses, that would have helped doctors contain the disease early. Elite superstitions about chaos throttled them. More trust of lowlier citizens could have avoided gigantic costs.[80]

The political consequences of the denial phase of the SARS episode in China laid bare the internal structure of the country and its inefficiencies. The lies and mistakes actually increased the severity of the outbreak. White quotes Xu Zhiyuan, an economic reporter, who claimed, "SARS has been our country's 9/11. It has forced us to pay attention to the real meaning of globalization. . . . China's future seemed so dazzling [that it] lulled people into thinking that our country was immune from the shocks of history."[81] Actually, the outbreak started in January and the government restricted reporting of cases only to superior authorities, not to the public. Finally, in April 2003, the government admitted its mistakes and its lies. The mayor of Beijing and the minister of health were fired. The new order issued was "transparency." Soon after that decision, it became clear that twenty-six of thirty-one Chinese provinces had SARS cases. A new reporting system of epidemics was put in place. A small opening for transparency has occurred in the Chinese political system, now that party leaders are aware of the huge damage that occurred. Truthfulness would have been the more promising course of action.

New Directions for Public Health

The public health profession in the United States is undergoing introspection and some change. Highly dependent on technology and surveillance, it has focused on prevention of disease and reduction of morbidity and mortality; however, more recently it has contemplated a wider mandate as it fashions a new ethics code. But the U.S. system continues to stand in contrast to the public health systems of Canada and the European Community.

Indeed, world public health enterprises espouse new perspectives. Recent undertakings by the World Federation of Public Health Associations (WFPHA) include a number of initiatives. The question was raised at the 2001 annual meeting of WFPHA: what is the role of the public health profession in globalization? The answer listed many efforts: the International AIDS conference in Durban, South Africa, the malaria summit in Abuja, the meeting of health and finance ministers to discuss TB in Amsterdam, and the climate summit in the Netherlands. In the words of the WFPHA report,

> Heads of State from developing and developed countries alike have called for stronger responses to the diseases most closely linked to poverty alongside international efforts to promote sustainable development, Within and around the World Health Organization, a number of international partnerships have been supported: Healthy Cities, and Health 21, Roll Back Malaria, Stop TB, the Tobacco Free Initiative, the Global Alliance for Vaccines and Immunization, the Campaign to Eradicate Polio, and the International Partnership against AIDS in Africa, to name a few.[82]

The WFPHA has already assumed the role of world leadership among NGOs in public health and now needs to work more actively with UN agencies, especially the WHO, "to clarify areas of emerging public health risk associated with globalisation, ranging from infectious and occupational diseases to diseases which are a product of the growing world-scale for anti-health forces."[83] It proposes an activist program to identify national inequalities in health due to economic change, to draw attention to the need for international intervention for health, to pursue sustainable development, and to create stronger cross-national responses to public health challenges.

Major initiatives by the WFPHA show that it sees itself as a movement, not just a professional association. They include: international debt relief, an effort to reduce global poverty,[84] global tobacco control, a call for action on the "devastating global epidemic." The WFPHA reports that tobacco is "a known or probable cause of some 25 diseases, is responsible for one death every ten seconds worldwide, killing nearly 3.5 million people each year."[85] It has called for including health considerations in international trade agreements, and prepared a brief on the negative health effects of the General Agreement on Trade and Services (GATS).[86]

In May 2003 the WFPHA approved a "Declaration on Public Health, Peace, and Human Rights" offered by members from southeastern Europe, that broadened the concept of public health to include "a constructive spirit of collaboration and peace building." The promotion of peace, the prevention of violence to assure the well-being of Mother Earth, the eradication of poverty, all are included in the declaration. Its final paragraph presents a comprehensive definition of the role of public health:

> We are convinced that public health has important social roles for the advancement of practical techniques for disease and injury prevention, as an early warning system for sudden or gradual changes in vulnerability; for the protection of women, children and other vulnerable groups; in fighting the scourges of bioterrorism, substance abuse and drug trafficking; in addressing the problems of refugees, any kind of torture, prisoners of war and starvation; in combating hate organizations and their ideologies, as well as all forms of humiliation, abuse, and the trafficking in human beings. We therefore state our resolve to integrate the issues of war and peace and human rights into the practice and scholarship of public health, and we call upon all national Public Health Associations and teaching institutions of public health worldwide to take the appropriate steps accordingly.[87]

This declaration, "an expression of the social conscience of public health," covers the entire range of the UN's public health goals.

An equally innovative and impassioned vision for public health arose from cooperation among Canadian and European public health associations and the WHO. It is a strong alternative to the American public health model. The initiative started in Canada in the mid-1980s, adding to the U.S. conception of public health as "reduction of disease" a "social model of health." It was based on a WHO-sponsored conference held in 1986 where the Ottawa Charter was created. According to a reporter for the *AJPH*, the charter

> initiated a redefinition and repositioning of institutions, epistemic communities, and actors at the "health" end of the disease-health continuum, a perspective that had been labeled the "salutogenic approach." . . . In overcoming an individualistic understanding of lifestyles and in highlighting social environments and policy, the orientation of health promotion began to shift from focusing on the modification of individual risk factors or risk behaviors to addressing the "context and meaning" of health actions and the determinants that keep people healthy.[88]

Sir George Alleyne, director of the Pan American Health Organization, said that "it is perhaps not accidental that the impetus for the focus on health promotion for the many should have risen in Canada, which is often credited with maintaining a more egalitarian approach in all health matters."[89] There is talk about a "third public health revolution" that would shift the emphasis from disease prevention to "capacity building for health."

The European Health for All program deliberately did not follow the U.S. public health model. Europe has a long tradition of seeing a strong relationship between public health and social reform, just as there is also a strong link between the state and health care in Europe. By now, twenty-seven European countries have adopted this public health strategy. According to the *AJPH*,

> In 1998, WHO's Regional Office for Europe published a detailed report exploring the intersection between population health and the Health for All strategy. It underlined that the common ground between population health, Health for All, and health promotion resides in the recognition that the majority of health determinants reside outside the health sector and drew attention to the strategic competence and experience that health promotion is able to bring to the table. The more recent target documents of WHO have reinforced the commitment to address health determinants and to seek strategic entry points outside of the health sector.[90]

Three European developments in public health are indeed the "third public health revolution." The first was the effort to deal with improving sanitary conditions and fighting infectious diseases. The second focused on helping individuals to avoid harmful behaviors (like smoking) that produce non-communicable diseases and lead to premature death.

> The third public health revolution recognizes health as a key dimension of quality of life. Health polities in the 21st century will need to be constructed from the key question posed by both the health promotion and population movements: "What makes people healthy?" Health polities will need to address both the collective lifestyles of modern societies and the social environments of modern life as they affect the health and quality of life of populations.[91]

In the United States, the public health code of ethics was first discussed by a "town hall meeting" of leading public health professionals in 2000. The code of ethics is a latecomer among the codes in medicine and differs from the codes for human subject research and for clinical practice. It is described as inherently a moral document, carrying "an obligation to care for the well being of others and it implies the possession of an element of power in order to carry out the mandate. The need to exercise power to ensure health and at the same time to avoid the potential abuses of power are the crux of the public health ethics."[92] The code is not intended to define all conceivable ethical dilemmas a public health professional may encounter. Instead, it states broad principles and ideals of the profession that can serve as a guide to understand the nature of public health and that allows elements for clarifying disputes that can arise.

The ethics code emphasizes the need of the profession to attend to "the fundamental causes of disease and requirements to health, aiming to prevent adverse health outcomes." To do this there must be concern for the rights of individuals; community members should be consulted, including empowering "disenfranchised community members." Public health information must be ethically managed, must be accurate and valid, should be relevant to decision making, and should be timely. Attention should given to the diversity of cultures and their sensitivities, and public health policies should enhance the physical and social environment. Privacy of individuals should be protected, and necessary exceptions must be carefully justified. Moreover, "public health institutions should ensure the professional competence of their employees" and they should "engage in collaborations and affiliations in ways that build the public's trust and the institution's effectiveness."[93]

It is interesting to what extent information principles stand out in this code of ethics. Responsibility in conveying significant health information—

and especially about immediate threats and long-term health risks—is an ethical hallmark for this profession. For Nancy E. Kass, criteria for an ethics framework of public health are grounded in the history of the profession as well as its commitment to science and the scientific method. It is also a recommendation to transparency.[94] Public health is devoted to improving the health of populations, therefore not primarily with individuals. It also has a special relationship to the state. Kass says that, given this focus on population health, public health faces ethical conundrums in balancing individual liberties with the interests of the collectivity. The basic criterion is that programs must reduce morbidity or mortality. Solid data must validate these claims. Equally important are social justice, fairness, and acceptability by the community.

Advances have been made in bioethics for medical care and research on human subjects. Nevertheless, given the different responsibilities of public health, these precedents do not always apply to public health. Kass writes:

> Today, public health practitioners use tools in addition to epidemiology to accomplish their work, still focusing primarily on communitywide, typically prospective, approaches to improve health. Some public health functions—surveillance, vital statistics, disease and injury reporting, and disease registries—relate to epidemiology and the collection of data. In addition, practitioners investigate outbreaks, conduct contact tracing, provide health education and other preventive interventions and conduct research related to public health. Last, public health professionals sometimes create or enforce health-related regulations and legislation, for example mandating screening, treatment, immunizations, or—rarely—quarantine.[95]

One element of public health is its police power, which must be exercised in an ethical way. While bioethics insists on the right of patients for noninterference, this is problematic for public health because of a larger goal, the security of the collectivity. A code of ethics for public health must be a code of restraint, "a code to preserve . . . the negative rights of citizens to noninterference." Citizens have positive rights to improved health of the collectivity and the reduction of social inequities impinging on health.[96] A methodology is needed for an ethics analysis to clarify the specific ethical issues at stake, as well as to provide a procedural legitimation such as that outlined by Jürgen Habermas (discussed in chapter 4).

The need for a code of ethics for public health, and the extension of health risks to global dimensions, and the obligation to reduce inequalities and injustices in health systems have motivated U.S. public health leaders to call again for universal health coverage. We return to the debates in the American Public Health Association and its formal resolution passed on New Year's Day, 2000, to launch a new campaign for universal health care. "Rekindling Reform" may well be the beginning of change in the U.S. health system.[97]

Conclusions

Changes in the information values of health systems have been slow, but they are now accelerating. Major damage occurred under totalitarian regimes in the last century, and the medical and health professions have labored ever since to create a higher standard of transparency and to establish ethical codes. The public health profession is currently working on a commitment to transparency and to a code of ethics and procedures for resolving disputes. New challenges are created by the increasingly global nature of risks to public health.

These historical changes have occurred at an astonishingly slow rate. Informed consent is now institutionalized in America, but as late as the 1970s it was not. Today, informed consent is part of the medical ethic worldwide. The German medical profession did not reach the point of accepting historical transparency until the 1990s. It took roughly a half century to come to this conclusion. Medical ethics has become a prestigious academic discipline, with a focus on the values of autonomy and informed consent. In addition, privacy is being forced into the architecture of information values for health. It had a rough start in the HIPAA's privacy rule in the United States. It fares somewhat better in the European Union, but it remains somewhat undefined. Special interests can still block further movement toward patient privacy. Finally, public health is gathering momentum after a period of decline because of global threats and a new awareness of the essential role of national and international political entities in controlling threats to health. Public health professionals are ready to endorse universal health systems with the capacity of care for all. Could that help to develop a more effective health system in the United States? Further, the new direction of public health as a profession could contribute to the growth of global governance. The transparency phenomenon pervades this sector of society, like the others we have examined. It is a factor in the moral and practical growth of the profession.

9

HISTORICAL TRANSPARENCY

The theme of transparency in global change is new, requiring new concepts and new frameworks. Nowhere is this more true than in the effort to understand how countries have dealt with dictators and evils of their past. Making the transition from a criminal and oppressive regime to the rule of law and human rights is not easy. It requires transparency, made possible by a moral culture shift that breaks the taboos and the "silences" about the past. Public recognition of the evidence can only then become possible. Global change has expanded the reach of historical transparency far beyond national histories and into a wave of support for "universal jurisdiction," the movement to limit sovereign immunity for governments' crimes against humanity.

Facts, once revealed, can take on different meanings in different contexts. They may be about a financial investment, or a new policy, or the recall of a commercial product presumed to be safe, or any other information made public. In the quest for transparency about historical events, further factors enter—a society's emergence from a great trauma, acceptance of knowledge about injustice, and the search to regain moral credibility and respectability. Inevitably in these situations there are demands for revenge, for justice, and there is also resistance, denial, and fear by the guilty. There is somehow the hope for reconciliation and the creation of a viable, changed society. In seeking historical transparency, the information culture of a society has come to the point of demanding public disclosure of past secrets. The disclosure of disturbing facts long kept hidden creates demands for justice and restitution, but also for the dialectical politics of punishment and reconciliation. Historical transparency is a very complex phenomenon.

Many choices must be made about what to do with the facts that historical transparency has bared. Facts may be denied or accepted, and the conflicting goals of justice and punishment must be balanced. Yet, there must be hope. Creating a future that overcomes the conditions of the past may take many different paths. Historical transparency requires convincing proof of the deeds of perpetrators; it also must allow the building of a new society committed to human rights and the rule of law.

In a very broad sense, the demand for historical truth no longer applies to one nation or culture by itself, nor is it limited to defeated nations. Different nations do criticize each other's version of history, just as they may criticize another nation's policies that might hurt their own interests. Interdependence and the demand for transparency have not come just to business or politics or health care. They have also come to national histories and to a nation's versions of world history. Transparency presents truth claims, but they have to withstand examination, criticism, counterclaims based on new evidence, new perspectives, and new challenges. National history books are scrutinized by historians (and politicians) in other countries and may be debated across the world.

Like so many other elements in global transformations, writing and evaluating history have become more demanding. National myths may be revealed as fairy tales, especially those that prop up fervent, wishful patriotism. And while patriotism no doubt will endure, it will have to take into account international debates about its worth. Leopold von Ranke, the nineteenth-century German historian, had a simple definition of what history can do: "You have reckoned that history ought to judge the past and to instruct the contemporary world as to the future. The present attempt does not yield that high office. It will merely tell how it really was."[1] Well, understanding the past in the light of historical transparency is more complex than just telling "how it really was." Legitimate perspectives may change and historians may discover different aspects and new values. Historians must meet new global demands for evidence to document previously accepted historical claims.

The turning point for this new way of assessing history and seriously attempting to uncover war crimes and genocide came at the end of the Second World War. The Allies struggled to overcome the tyrannical and aggressive regimes of Germany and Japan and to thwart their and their Axis partners' plans for world domination. Allied leaders took major initiatives to build a lasting peace, as well as to pursue justice in punishing the war criminals. The establishment of the United Nations in 1945 at the initiative of the United States was soon followed by the war crimes tribunals of Nuremberg and Tokyo. The UN passed the Genocide Convention and the Universal Declaration of Human Rights in 1948. The general framework for articulating basic international values was beginning to be shaped. The investigations of genocide and war crimes proved the horrendous scope of Nazi activities— above all, the genocide of Jews in the Holocaust. Beyond that there was forced labor, the persecution of dissidents and of minorities like the Roma, the murders of many in the Nazi-occupied countries, and the medical "experiments" (discussed in chapter 8)—all documenting the Nazis' brutality against civilians. The Tokyo court also revealed serious war crimes on the part of some Japanese leaders. The moral shock at these facts resounded worldwide.

Uncovering the truth about the past happened very differently in the East and West. Germany's path to historical transparency included two complex historical transitions, unlike the Japanese case. Further, Germany went through a long period of truth-seeking, with extended tribunals, while in Japan, the entire process was truncated for what seemed to be prudent political reasons, leaving a residue of misunderstanding.

The tribunals in Nuremberg and Tokyo became historic events of immense significance as demonstrable efforts to uncover the past in pursuit of what we call historical transparency. From these efforts grew multiple institutions and movements around the globe that, half a century later, still seek "transnational justice," thus to expand the quest for historical truth well beyond collective memory and the "politics of memory" to place the facts within nascent institutions of global governance. Many countries other than Germany and Japan have experienced this transition from a painful past to a hopeful future. South Africa, Argentina, Chile, Rwanda, Spain, Portugal, the former Soviet-dominated countries, and many others have found it hard to make the transition from oppression to a just society working for a better future. It is important to understand what happened between the first meetings of the German war crimes tribunal and the new global era of governance.

The crucial issue of clearing the historical record has now acquired an international dimension. The European Union has become a force behind the demand for historical transparency—for example, in the efforts of member states to scrutinize and debate the contents of each other's history textbooks. National governments, the UN, and global civil society groups have generated a veritable industry in support of transitional justice in overcoming criminal regimes and building a future based on human rights. Networks among shared cultures and regions stimulate debates and critiques and suggest innovations for expanding historical honesty. Much has been written about the Holocaust and German postwar history, but much less about

Japan. Still other studies cover the struggles in the Republic of South Africa, and the genocide and civil wars in Cambodia, Rwanda, the former Yugoslavia, Sudan, and elsewhere.

The literature about Germany and the Holocaust introduced the concept of collective guilt. Karl Jaspers made the distinction between personal responsibility for perpetrators of crimes and the political responsibility for past evils that includes all citizens of a nation. The focus on collective memory has made it possible for researchers to focus on what citizens of a country believe to be true about their own history. In many ways this measures the knowledge of myths as well as facts, of acceptance and resistance. A sophisticated concept going beyond collective memory is the notion of *Gedächtnispolitik,* or memory politics, whereby the contents of memory are socially constructed by political moves in a contentious arena. Those who appeal to memory politics may be spreading propaganda and may desire the public to believe things that are not true; on the other hand, it may be valid public education. Several concepts are specific: the Holocaust and the Jewish version of the Shoah have acquired the status of memory politics because of their uniqueness in history. Other concepts are *Vergangenheitsbewältigung,* that is, dealing with and overcoming the past, and *Wiedergutmachung,* or compensation and restoration of victims. And finally, there is the scholarly topic of construction of national identity. Examples of different paths that memory politics can take may be seen in the very different developments in East and West Germany *after* the tribunal at Nuremberg and the even more different paths taken in Japan *after* the Tokyo tribunal.

The necessity to break with history and establish a new, viable future existed long before World War II. Although the United States has begun to deal with the issue of slavery and its impact on the nation's history, less has been said about the experience of Native Americans and the crimes committed against them. Coming to terms with the past is a challenge in many other countries as well. Many Latin American military dictatorships have given way to fledgling democracies but still must wrestle with past crimes. Many of the authoritarian and dogmatic regimes of eastern Europe that were long under Soviet domination are now members of the European Union and accept its values and democratic rules. These nations must confront the historical facts and devise their own strategies for transitional justice. This goes far beyond the revision of collective memory. Seeking the truth about a nation's history and the institutionalization of transitional justice will occur in the context of an emerging system of global governance in which cross-national debates, critiques, and mutual corrections will play a major role.

The quest for historical transparency will be a part of local, regional, and global change.

Forward-looking leaders also seek to "transcend history." This undoubtedly seems a strange idea, but it means escaping the rigid molds rooted in the past and looking for new solutions. The totalitarians, whether fascist or communist, did try to create a "new man"—with disastrous consequences. Similarly, revolutionaries in the American colonies also broke with the patterns of the past, not to establish "a new man" but new and durable institutions. Several successful examples of "transcending history" after World War II include Konrad Adenauer's carefully orchestrated strategy for West Germany to become the core of a Western nation, the great achievement of the European Union in securing peace among its nations, and today's movements toward transnational justice.

Many countries have long national histories and a past enshrined in stereotypes and myths that limit innovation and progress. The political construction of "national identity" may be based less on valid realities than on cherished nationalism and loyalty. The historical rigidity imposed on political thinking can lead to the continuation of disastrous errors. This was clearly true in Europe with its militaristic imperialism before World War I and the extreme nationalism (led by Germany and Italy) that brought on World War II. Transcending history means an effort to "think outside the box" of established, inherited structures and enmities, and creating new solutions, solidarities, and reconciliation. Of course, efforts to transcend history often fail, but in several cases they have succeeded.

War Crimes and Germany

In October 1945 the United States, Great Britain, France, and the Soviet Union issued indictments against leading Nazis and their organizations for the systematic murder of millions of people and for planning and launching a war of aggression in Europe. Germany was in ruins. Its defeat was total. As of May 1945 there were about 7 million members of the Nazi party. The Allies had complex tasks to tackle: to get essential everyday functions working again, to lay the groundwork for a future democracy, and to embark on a course of de-Nazification. The Nuremberg trials of 1945–46 were providing compelling evidence that enormous crimes had been committed under the Nazi regime. News reports of the proceedings were carried worldwide and broadcast throughout Germany.

In *Divided Memory: The Nazi Past in the Two Germanys,* Jeffrey Herf focuses on the continuities and breaks in German political culture before and after

World War II. He describes the events of the tribunal: "Before the Allies would permit the Germans to govern themselves, they had to make sure that a record of the crimes of the Nazi era was presented to the Germans and to world opinion. The International Military Tribunal that met in Nuremberg from November 20, 1945, to October 1, 1946, and the successor trials from 1946 to 1949, was at the center of this endeavor."[2] The trials were widely reported, in the press and on radio. They made it abundantly clear that Hitler and the Nazi government apparatus had planned and implemented policies of racism and violence, leading to the systematic murder of massive number of European Jews in concentration camps. Several further categories of victims were included in these murderous crimes: the attempted destruction of the Roma and Sinti, the destruction of "unworthy lives" such as homosexuals, mentally handicapped people, critics of the regime such as Communists or dissenting Christians, and what the Nazis called "inferior races." The entire enterprise was aided and abetted by multitudes of officials in the government, the military, and the Nazi party of the Third Reich. After the major defendants were tried in October 1946, "surveys indicated that 55 percent of the German population found the guilty verdicts to be just, 21 percent thought them too mild, and only 9 percent found them too harsh. Overall, 78 percent regarded the proceedings as fair."[3]

Trials continued into 1947. These successor trials included as defendants a considerable number of professionals, including physicians, judges, industrialists, and others who had contributed to the Nazi crimes. They included also the personnel of the concentration camps. In addition, the American, French, and British occupation forces held their own military courts. In all, according to Herf, "5,025 persons were convicted of war crimes or crimes against humanity by the occupying powers; 806 were condemned to death, and 486 of the death sentences were carried out."[4] Overall, the number of Germans indicted for war crimes and crimes against humanity in the four occupation zones is estimated at about 90,000 persons in 1945–46.[5] Further, German trials against Nazi war criminals continued for decades after the establishment of the Federal Republic of Germany in 1949. "De-Nazification" went on.

The breakdown of the Nazi party was complete, not only because of these judicial punishments and the campaign to eradicate Nazism, but also because the Nazis had failed totally. Immediately after 1945 most Germans dealt with just the necessities of daily life as best they could. The war was lost and Germany's cities were destroyed. About 12 million Germans were driven out of their homes in lands settled for many centuries by German populations in East Prussia, Silesia, and other areas like the Sudetenland—which represented an enormous effort at "ethnic cleansing." The large population forced to migrate into the remaining German territory became more or less integrated over time, but the immediate postwar years were difficult in the extreme. World opinion understandably did not object to these events, harsh though they were. After all, the Nazis' attack on the countries of eastern Europe had been designed to take over their lands. The idea of *Volk ohne Raum* (a people without space) was one of the slogans of the Nazi party. The implication was that Germany could simply take land from others.

Konrad Adenauer: Building a New Germany in Europe and the West

The paths of events in West Germany and in the Soviet zone soon diverged.[6] The war alliance between the West and the Soviets was falling apart and the cold war became a harsh reality. The interpretations of Nazi crimes and "collective memory" in the West and East became very different. In the West the priority was to build a functioning democracy and economy. The single most prominent figure in this effort was Konrad Adenauer.[7] He became active in the rebuilding of the Christian Democratic party in 1946. In 1948 he served as the chairman of the Parlamentarischer Rat, the assembly that created the basic law of the new Federal Republic. He was the first chancellor of the Federal Republic from 1949 until 1963.

Adenauer set out to transcend German history by giving it a dramatically different direction. Indeed, he had thought much about the past. He was convinced that the German admiration of the authoritarian state was grounded in Prussian traditions and in the intellectuals of the idealist philosophy creating the German conception of the state as an overwhelming, godlike entity more important than the individual citizen. Adenauer decided to change this dramatically. First, to avoid backsliding into nationalism or even Nazism, a rapid economic recovery and building a democratic state were essential. He was committed to making Germany a Western, European, democratic nation, and he saw Germany as part of an integrated and peaceful Europe that could resist any resurgence of Nazism and could protect itself from Communism.

Adenauer's political convictions were linked to Germany's democratic traditions that predated the Nazi regime. He had been a *beigeordneter* (councilor) of the city of Cologne in 1906 and mayor of Cologne from 1917 to 1933. When Hitler was to visit Cologne in March 1933, Mayor Adenauer ordered the removal of the swastika flags from the Deutz-Bridge over the Rhine and refused to receive Hitler. As a result, he was promptly removed from office by the Nazis and until the end of the war lived in "inner emigration" near Cologne, although harassed and detained by the Nazi police on several occasions. He was sixty-nine years old at the war's end and became chancellor of the Federal Republic of Germany in 1949, at age seventy-three, serving until 1963. He died in 1967.

Adenauer's views on German history were rooted in conservatism, Catholicism, and dedication to Western democracy. His Western orientation was clear. In 1950 he said:

> In the area of foreign policy our line is fixed. In the first instance it is aimed at a close relationship with our neighbouring states in the Western World and, especially, with the United States. We will devote all our energy to ensuring that Germany is accepted as quickly as possible as a member of the European federation with equal rights and equal obligations. In carrying out these intentions we will cooperate particularly closely with the other Christian Democratic forces that are growing in strength among the West European peoples.[8]

Adenauer was committed to the idea of a federal Europe. His hope was for a German democracy based on peaceful values that would have shed all remnants of Prussian militarism. He wanted to integrate Germany into Europe. Adenauer's early projects of creating a European defense community failed, as did the hope for a political community in Europe. However, the Schuman plan for uniting coal and steel production in France and Germany became the beginning of an active policy of European integration. Hans-Peter Schwarz writes about the events of May 1950:

> There now began the week which was quickly recognized by the public as a turning-point in the history of post-war Europe. On the morning of 8 May 1950, exactly five years after the unconditional surrender of the Wehrmacht, Adenauer approved, with some amendments, a draft memorandum on West German entry into to the Council of Europe. It was published immediately. At noon on the same day, in the most confidential manner, a letter from Robert Schuman was delivered to Adenauer. It was the beginning of the planning for the European Coal and Steel Community in 1951, the first integrative policy linking France and Germany. Jean Monnet, the creator of the Schuman plan, revealed the ambitious long term purpose of the plan: "World peace cannot be guaranteed without creative efforts proportional to the dangers that threaten it. The contribution which an organized and living Europe can make to civilization is indispensable for the maintenance of peaceful relations."[9]

The French government proposed that all Franco-German coal and steel production should be placed under a joint high authority "within the framework of an organization which the other European countries can join." To Adenauer it was a move toward a federal Europe. He joined in the endeavor with enthusiasm.

Adenauer recognized the political and moral imperative of providing restitution to Israel and to individual survivors of Nazi persecution, and in 1953 he persuaded the Bundestag to agree. The Federal Republic of Germany joined NATO in 1955—partly as a reaction to the rising tensions of the cold war, partly to join in peace the countries that had fought against Germany and Italy in World War II. The Treaty of Rome, signed in 1957, created the European Community with France, Italy, the Netherlands, Belgium, Luxembourg, and the Federal Republic of Germany as founding members. Adenauer had anchored the Federal Republic of Germany in Western Europe and in the Atlantic Alliance.[10]

While Adenauer worked hard to assure that Nazism was not revived and that the most heinous war criminals were punished, this era was not marked by a strong pursuit of historical transparency: "With considerable circumspection, Adenauer was successful in neutralizing, up to the end of the 1950s, the negative effects of the recent past. He was successful because he spoke only of the new realities to the outside world and to his own people at home."[11] He dedicated his energies to building the future for Germany and Europe. However, the demand to recognize the past grew after the 1960s. Many who worked for Adenauer had played awkward roles in the Nazi era. "Theodor Heuss and Ernst Lemmer had been prepared, in a weak moment, to vote for the Enabling Act [which empowered Hitler], as a measure to fight alleged terrorists. In fact, in 1953 Hans Globke, a trusted aide of the chancellor, was criticized in the press for his Nazi past—he had played a role in the Nuremberg race laws. Nevertheless, Adenauer made him the chief of his chancellor's office."[12] It may have been a deliberate choice to have Globke, since he knew which figures from the past civil service might be useful to the new government. It also may have been a move of opportunistic realpolitik to staff a functioning state rapidly.

Other high officials in Adenauer's staff had been part of the Nazi government, Schwarz reports:

> The Chancellor was, then, more than well aware that he governed a nation of "turncoats," as it was put later. Everyone knew, including Adenauer, that it was best to keep quiet about the twelve-year period of Nazi rule. The attitude was controversial and not without its problems. But Adenauer succeeded with it. In the decades after 1945, the question of the Nazi past had a similar subordinate

political status as during the 1950s. In 1960, however, the stench of the Nazi past could again be smelled at home and abroad and Adenauer had to do something about it in the last years of his chancellorship.[13]

The silence about the Nazi era was a matter of great concern to those who feared a return to anti-Semitism in Germany, or worse. There was little attention given to the Holocaust at that time, even though the Nuremberg trials had documented its catastrophic scope and evil. Jeffrey Herf has a rather chilling explanation for the rule of silence in the 1950s. Although the Western Allies placed more emphasis on the Holocaust than the Communists did, it was not the central issue even for the Allies. Continuing anti-Semitism was surely a factor. Yet, Herf notes, "the Nazis had killed many millions of non-Jews in Europe. Those Germans who wanted to remember what Germans in Nazi Germany had done to others, as opposed to what Nazi Germany had done to the Germans, were a minority. The fact was that four million German soldiers and civilians had died in World War II." If one counts all who died as a result of the Nazi war and their crimes, one arrives at the colossal number of 36 million people. "The six million Jews of Europe—killed as members of the only group whose very existence the Nazis were determined to destroy with a 'final solution'—constituted about one-sixth of all those Europeans who can legitimately be called the victims of Nazi Germany."[14]

Thus, Herf concludes:

> The postwar historian of German memory does not face much difficulty in explaining the problem of why so little was said publicly about the Holocaust in postwar West or East Germany. The presence of mass death, with its multiple claims to memory, and the fact that, aside from a tardy, failed effort to overthrow the regime in July 1944, the Germans fought in support of the Nazi regime up to its bitter end provides sufficient reason.[15]

But as these postwar years passed and new states were built in the West and in the East, other factors played a role: building governments and society. The highest priority in the West was the creation of a functioning democratic state and a social market economy. In the East it was the creation of a Soviet socialist system.

Democratic Continuities

The silence about the Holocaust did not mean that the memory of the Nazi regime had disappeared. Quite early in the 1950s German schools included some curricula of current history. Programs and institutes in *Zeitgeschichte* (recent history) covered the Nazi period.[16] Several strands of political tradition connected the democratic traditions of pre-Nazi Germany to the new task of building a new political moral framework. Adenauer, as we have seen, was grounded in the conservative tradition of German democratic thought. The social democrat Kurt Schumacher was an outspoken enemy of the Nazis and as a member of the Reichstag in 1932 had attacked the Nazi party. After the Nazis' ascent to power, he was arrested and spent a decade in several concentration camps. Though ill after his release, he rebuilt the Social Democratic party (Sozialistische Partei Deutschland, SPD), beginning even before Germany's surrender, and helped to initiate the program of restitution to the Jewish victims of Nazism. This became a major effort in compensating victims, which amounted to about $50 billion by the end of the century, and also an effort in diplomacy.[17] Schumacher was prominent among those who led the effort to break the silence about the Nazi past.

Debates during the Adenauer era covered many basic political issues. The demarcation of democratic values and institutions involved, inevitably, not only the Nazi dictatorship, but also the Communist dictatorship of the Soviet Union. Anti-Communism was an important theme in political discussions. There arose also an awareness of the German resistance against the Nazis. The anniversary of the failed attempt to assassinate Hitler in July 1944 became a memorial day. The link to the memory of a "better Germany" was an important symbol that the new democracy had its own roots in German history.[18]

Other leaders took a role in building a new German political culture. Most prominent were the presidents of the Federal Republic, especially Theodor Heuss and Richard von Weizsäcker. Heuss was also a politician in the pre-Nazi time, of the liberal tradition. Although in 1933 he supported the Enabling Act that gave the Nazis extraordinary powers, he became the first leader of the Free Democratic party in 1948 and pursued a vigorous policy of frank and open debate about the Nazi crimes, emphasizing the Holocaust. Richard von Weizsäcker, president from 1984 to 1994, emphatically carried on the debate about the political responsibilities of Germany and Nazi history. Subsequent presidents continued this function.

The reawakening of German democratic traditions by figures like Schumacher, Heuss, and von Weizsäcker brought to Germany the moral and political convictions that led to the breakthrough to historical transparency. This acknowledgment of German history and the Holocaust meant the creation of many memorials to victims of Nazi crimes, most visibly in the large and centrally placed Holocaust memorial in Berlin. West Germany's public account of the history of the Nazi period gradually became more focused, not only on war crimes but also on broader German crimes against humanity—especially the Holocaust. Over the years there were four debates in the parliament about extending the statute of limitations in murder cases. These debates attracted great public attention. The first occurred in 1960 at the initiative of the Social Democratic party, which insisted that many perpetrators of Nazi crimes still had not been identified and brought to trial. The conservatives demurred. The proposal failed, but it did bring the issue into public debate. In 1965, the SPD was joined by other Bundestag members, and a majority voted to extend the statute by four years. The third debate was again initiated by the SPD, as the statute of limitations was running out in 1969. The outcome was an extension by thirty years. The last of these debates took place in 1979. The Bundestag voted—over the opposition of most conservative members—to eliminate the statute of limitations altogether. These debates helped to change the political climate: there was now a public understanding that crimes against humanity could not be ignored, even if the perpetrators were found only after years.[19]

The Emergence of a New Generation and a New Sense of Morality

By the end of the 1950s, and into the later decades, the public search began for facts about the Nazi regime. There were outbreaks of anti-Semitism that required action. A long series of trials of Nazi crimes in Germany took place, such as the Auschwitz court case and the Eichmann trial in Israel, that received great public attention. University students especially raised the question of the Nazi past. The 1968 student uprisings worldwide articulated deep distrust of authorities in many countries, and certainly in Germany. The Vietnam War, with U.S. military operations from 1964 to 1975, became an issue of outspoken resentment and gave rise to a powerful peace movement virtually worldwide. The policy of silence in Germany had become untenable. Pressure for historical transparency started to become a cultural force in Germany and reached high-priority status in the late twentieth century.

The late 1960s saw a shift in the moral framework of the younger generation. By 1968 Americans had become clearly aroused by the Vietnam War, which finally ended in 1975 with the fall of Saigon and American defeat. Protests against the war in the United States coincided with the civil rights movement. Astonishingly, it spread virtually worldwide. To many, it appeared to be a conflict between generations. In Europe demonstrations against the Vietnam War became a movement for liberty and rejection of all forms of authoritarianism—in the state, in schools and universities, and in the family. Students of that time were very politically active in France, Italy, and Germany, and a small minority adopted a strategy of terrorism that took years to be contained.

With the rise of a generation of activists in Germany, a new moral framework became part of the public reality, to the consternation of the older generation. In an interview, Karsten D. Voigt, of the German Foreign Office, emphasized the importance of the intergenerational shift. He himself was not "a member of the generation shaped by CARE packages," he said, but by the Vietnam War. He continued:

> In the 1950s the young left of Germany was culturally very much pro-American. Anti-Americanism was moderated by anti-Sovietism. Now, there has been a shift. Conservative youth as well as the left youth have more a bipartisan view of America. And the leaders like [Foreign Minister] Fischer and [Chancellor] Schroeder now had their formative experiences in the era of the late 1960s. I have known them since 1969, and they are very different from the last generation of politicians.[20]

Voigt made his point about historical continuity with the example of the German Foreign Office building. In the nineteenth century it housed the central bank of the German Reich; it was frequently used by Hitler as a place for conferences and became the center of financing the German war effort from 1939 to 1945; it then became the headquarters of Central Committee of the Socialist Unity party during the German Democratic Republic. An impressive book about the building has been published because, Voight says, "We want all our people to be aware of all the complex strands of German history. It is necessary that our history become transparent."

The German Democratic Republic and Soviet Dominance

In East Germany the Communist leaders' strategy was very different from that of the West. These leaders had, for the most part, spent the war in the Soviet Union. People like Walter Ulbricht and Wilhelm Pieck, central figures in establishing the German Democratic Republic, admired the bravery of the Soviet soldiers. They had fruitlessly called on the German people to resist the Nazis and urged the German armies to lay down their weapons. As the war continued, Ulbricht and Pieck became increasingly frustrated, even enraged, with the German people. According to Herf's account:

> For these returning exiles, the memory of the Nazi past, its crimes, and the absence of an anti-Nazi German revolt reinforced their already-powerful Com-

munist-bred suspicions of liberal democracy. As one can see from their "Appeal to the German People" in June 1945, their memory of the past included, too, the memory of their past rejection by the German people. Despite public declarations of support for a democratic anti-fascist government in the early postwar months and years, their texts contain abundant evidence of fear and distrust of their fellow Germans. The more they remembered their own past persecutions by the Nazi regime, its popular support in German society, as well as its attack on the homeland of revolution, the more they were inclined to impose another dictatorship on this dangerous people.[21]

The German Democratic Republic (GDR) became a dictatorship with an unsurpassed machinery of surveillance by the state security apparatus. It also turned into a regime that adopted Stalin's "anticosmopolitan" campaign as part of the cold war strategy. A curtain of myth was laid over history. The Soviet interpretation was that the Nazis' crimes were the doing of its capitalist class. In Prague in 1952 a show trial was held of Rudolf Slansky, the second-ranking official in the Czech Communist party, and other party members, most of them Jewish, accusing them of plotting to destroy Communism in eastern Europe. The East Berlin leadership used this trial as providing "lessons" for their party.

In East Berlin a debate about the role of Jewish victims during the war and the Holocaust had been initiated by the Communists Merker and Zuckermann, who had been in exile in Mexico during the war. They saw the Holocaust as a crucial historical event in World War II and wanted the GDR to respond to the victimization of Jews as a central theme of policy. The reaction of GDR leaders was drastically anti-Semitic. They ended the debate by accusing its advocates of being part of the "Slansky conspiracy." In *Lessons from the Trial Against the Slansky Conspiracy Center,* Herman Matern created the tale of a vast espionage conspiracy that involved "American imperialists, Zionists, Jewish capitalists, and some members of the Communist party, such as Slansky."[22] It was the old story, this time in a Communist discourse. According to Herf,

> In Matern's statement, the Jews ceased to be "victims of fascism." Instead, they emerge as the active and powerful perpetrators of an international, anti-German conspiracy. Once again, a German government attacked the Jews as cosmopolitans, rather than as true members of the nation. Once again, German nationalists, this time of a Communist variant, defined themselves in opposition to a Western, capitalist, international, liberal, Jewish conspiracy. Remarkably, at a moment of extreme Jewish weakness, Germany's anti-fascist regime denounced the Jews for their supposed power.[23]

The GDR was thus deliberately constructed by Ulbricht and his party as a state that would transform its people into docile socialists. It was also to be an economic and political asset to the Soviet Union, whose Communist ideology held the "dictatorship of the proletariat" as a fundamental element of their program. Furthermore, the GDR was occupied by the Soviet army. As a matter of fact, this army was a force for suppression in the entire East European realm. The Communist politicians in the GDR could rely on the imperial power of the Soviet Union. The construction of the wall between East and West Berlin and the terrifying boundary dividing the two parts of Germany were not only symbols of blocking ideas from abroad, but also a violent reality: many who tried to leave the East were killed in the attempt. It was generally believed in the West that the GDR was the economically most productive region in the Soviet empire. That turned out to be an error. It remained a poor country, albeit one with a secure standard of simple living—always under the shadow of surveillance by the state security police, the feared Stasi. The collapse of the regime was a special, German component of the collapse of the entire Soviet empire after 1989. The GDR had become hollow inside, partly because of the rising moral critiques by churches, people's desire for personal independence, and irritation with the extremely dysfunctional structure of the planned economy and the rigidity of the government. It was a history full of misunderstandings about what was actually happening in the GDR, and within the GDR what was happening in the West. Much of what led the West to believe in the manufacturing power of the GDR in fact represented Potemkin images.

The Unification of Germany

A reunited Germany was a historical inevitability by 1990. There was no politically viable alternative, even though certain politicians, especially Margaret Thatcher, prime minister of Britain, tried to stop the process. The Communist GDR government had collapsed, and the absolute need to integrate the two Germanys into one became apparent to all, even to Thatcher. In the Federal Republic of Germany, it was believed that the integration of the East into the Western success as a prosperous democracy would be easy. A senior official of the Treuhand, the trust organization empowered to rebuild the East German economy, stated in 1991 that it would take about five years to accomplish this task of effective integration. The same official had changed his mind by 1999—with sadness, he said that "it might take another twenty-five years."

There was another reason for rapid unification: the integration of all of Germany into the European Union. Heinrich Schneider provided the following information:

> It is generally assumed that [Chancellor] Helmut Kohl wanted to achieve unification as fast as possible, since it was not clear that the supportive attitude in Moscow would persist. [It was conceivable that Gorbachev might be toppled by neo-Stalinists.] Holding elections for a constitutional National Assembly, the creation of a new constitution, the public campaign to gain support for all this were very time consuming and risky. But, there are still other considerations. About four weeks before the signing of the Treaties of Rome [the European Economic Community, EURATOM], on February 28, 1957, the leader of the German delegation, Carl Friedrich Ophüls, declared in the framework of the treaty negotiations that "the Federal Government assumes that in case of the re-unification of Germany a new assessment *[Überprüfung]* of the treaties of the European Economic Community and EURATOM will take place." It was very clear and not contested that in the case of reunification, the federal government would have the right to adopt the treaties—or not. . . . At the time, the Federal Government of Germany took the position that a reunited Germany should have complete freedom of decision. . . . The leading actors in this matter were aware of the need for prompt action for unification under the European roof. After the fall of the Berlin wall, it was necessary to avoid placing the question to the Germans whether there was a choice of *either* German unity *or* European integration.

The solution was to refer to an earlier article that allowed the integration of the Saarland after World War II as a model for creating the treaty joining the two Germanys.[24]

In 1989 the socialist control had collapsed and the people of East Germany wanted to see the system of the GDR abolished.[25] Unification was understood in the West as the East German state's integration into the Federal Republic. Not all East Germans welcomed this arrangement. They had a different understanding of the past and different values from those in the West. Mike Dennis and Eva Kolinsky summarize this unexpected rift:

> Conditioned more substantially by GDR policies and practices than anyone had thought possible, east Germans have responded differently to the system and its mixture of gains and losses. Far from bringing the east in line with the west, unification encouraged the east to articulate its sense of difference, and added a new diversity to the meaning of Germany. Rooted in a sense of past and present injustice perpetrated in the east and imposed on its allegedly luckless residents,

eastern distinctiveness has tended to doubt the ubiquitous supremacy of the democratic model and looked to the GDR as a corrective. Unification relocated east/west division from the state level of borders, governments and national symbols to the societal level of living conditions and expectations. After the first flush of system change, eastern needs and misgivings about the validity of the western model proliferate.[26]

The unification of Germany relied predominantly on West German laws and economic practices. A huge effort at privatization of industry was undertaken, strongly encouraged by the Treuhand. Original assumptions about East German industrial capacity were simply wrong, and an enormous allocation of West German resources rapidly became necessary. There were many points of friction. How should party functionaries of the SED (the Communist Socialist Unity party) be treated? Some complained that too many continued in their positions, while others complained that their treatment was too harsh. Some argued for drawing a "judicial line" between the past and the present, the equivalent of an amnesty. In fact, even access to GDR government documents became a controversial issue, but on the whole the principle of access prevailed. There were trials for manslaughter in which serious cases of charges of indirect responsibility were entered. Nevertheless, complaints arose that there was too much action as well as too little. Some East Germans felt that only they could truly understand the realities of the GDR. Further, they were taken aback by the changes in their life style that their new leaders expected them to adopt. A sense of frustration and dissatisfaction arose.

Fundamentally, the political strategies of the postwar leaders in the West and East were diametrically opposed. Adenauer succeeded in creating a Western democracy, and his successors continued the effort. West Germany became West European, and, of course, Western Europe changed through the European Union. This was a massive cultural change for Germans. The predominant sentiment in prewar Germany had been critical or at least ambivalent about the West. East Germany under Ulbricht had taken the opposite direction, an eastern course, connecting with old anti-Western sentiments. The GDR government denied any responsibility for the Holocaust—it was simply a crime of the fascist imperialists. There was no major public debate about German responsibility for the war; this was the guilt of the fascists and their masters, the capitalists. Furthermore, a socialist economy defined very different relations between individuals and the state from those in the Federal Republic. Mike Dennis writes:

A dismantling of the wall in people's heads remains a distant goal, given the differences in inherited mentalities and patterns of socialization, the socio-economic gap between eastern and western Germany and the prevalence of mutual grievances and resentments. However, the new historical discourses and the conceptual variety may at least serve as a warning against treating the inner unity as a monolith and assuming that easterners must somehow "catch up" with the norms and values of their western counterparts.[27]

Historical Transparency in Germany

The search for historical transparency in the united Germany has two major public foci, the Holocaust being by far the most salient. As an issue, it has a strong force field in Europe and in global debates. The other is the second effort at "dealing with the past" in the East, discussed earlier. In the united Germany, Holocaust education has taken high priority for governments and for citizens, although there have been attacks on Holocaust memorials, desecration of Jewish cemeteries, and exhibition of Nazi symbols by "skinheads." Such gestures have occurred in both West and East Germany, but millions of Germans have taken to street demonstrations against these crimes. School curricula in West Germany started to include the history of the Holocaust in the 1950s and 1960s, but this was not the case in East Germany. After unification, education about the Holocaust became institutionalized in all of Germany. Here we see how historical transparency unfolded along different pathways in the two Germanys, leading to very different institutionalized patterns. Significantly, the Holocaust became a central issue first in the West, then for all of Germany.

In Germany there is a sense of urgency about educating the younger generation to understand the full scope of the Nazi regime and its ideology that culminated in the Holocaust. The new democratic institutions created since World War II are recognized as safeguards against repeating the horrors of the Nazi era. The history of the Holocaust is taught at all educational levels and in many different contexts. According to a government publication:

> The treatment of the Nazi period in all its aspects—Hitler's rise to power; his establishment of a dictatorship in Germany; the abolition of the rule of law; the persecution of all kinds of political opponents; the racially motivated persecution of the Jews, culminating in the Holocaust; the reticence and opposition of German citizens; and Germany's instigation of World War II—is compulsory teaching matter at all types of schools in Germany and at all levels of education. The Holocaust is treated as the most important aspect of the period of Nazi rule.[28]

Germany has struggled with its national past, like all countries that make the transition from dictatorship to democracy and then attempt to clear the historical record. Herf concludes:

> Some of the most perceptive German participants and observers who lived through the war and Holocaust, the Nuremberg interregnum, and the postwar decades understood that whether and how they remembered or forgot the Nazi era and the persecution of the Jews would be of great importance for the nature and prospects of dictatorship and democracy in Germany after Auschwitz. This history of memory, democracy and dictatorship in the occupation era, the era of two Germanys, and the era of a unified Germany has confirmed their judgment. Those political leaders who urged their fellow citizens to look the truth of German history straight in the eye raised issues of general significance for any country emerging from a period of dictatorship, crime, and catastrophe. They left behind an often unpopular, discomforting, demanding, yet precious legacy.[29]

War Crimes and Japanese and Asian Views of History

Japan came out of World War II very differently from Germany, and the trajectory of change in postwar Japan pointed in a different direction. The Tokyo war trial lasted from May 1946 to November 1948. Participating countries were the United States, the Soviet Union, China, the Philippines, and India. The supreme commander of the allied powers in the Far East, General Douglas MacArthur, had the decisive role. The tribunal not only dealt with the culpability of the indicted war criminals, but also took into account the political and social consequences in Japan and in the Far East. The trial posed several political risks; many feared that social instability in Japan would require a very large U.S. occupation force, and further instability could result from tensions in China and problems with the Soviet Union.

General MacArthur's decisions were influenced by his conservative beliefs. He was a strong-willed military man who hated President Roosevelt and his policies, all liberals, and Jews. He wanted to pursue realpolitik. His single most important decision was to protect Emperor Hirohito from indictment as a war criminal and even from embarrassment. Hirohito would continue as Japan's monarch, in order to help the occupation forces keep Japanese society stable. Keeping the monarchy intact would require a great deal of careful planning. In fact, Hirohito had an extremely central and powerful role in the war. Under MacArthur's plan, it was necessary to portray him as a powerless figurehead, a constitutional monarch who had no responsibility for Japanese war crimes and atrocities. Herbert Bix writes:

300

MacArthur's truly extraordinary measures to save Hirohito from trial as a war criminal had a lasting and profoundly distorting impact in Japanese understanding of the lost war. Months before the Tokyo tribunal commenced, MacArthur's highest subordinates were working to attribute ultimate responsibility for Pearl Harbor to Gen. Tojo Hideki. So too were Tojo's own army colleagues. Back in September, Tojo, on receiving word that his arrest was imminent, had attempted suicide. While he was recovering, his former subordinates had again gotten word to him that he had to live in order to protect the emperor. Tojo understood, and wanted to own up to his disgrace by shouldering all responsibility for the defeat. Since his testimony would be vital, either absolving or implicating Hirohito, it could not be left to chance.[30]

The choice of war criminals in the spring of 1946 was determined by directives coming from Douglas MacArthur and in cooperation with the Japanese cabinet. Further, in mid-1947 MacArthur urged the Allied governments not to hold any more trials.

In response to MacArthur's request, the United Kingdom took the lead to stop further trials. On April 1948, the Overseas Reconstruction Committee of the British Cabinet decided that "no further trials of war criminals should be started after 31 August, 1948." Three months later, the British Commonwealth Relations Office sent a secret telegram to Australia, Canada, Ceylon, India, New Zealand, Pakistan and South Africa suggesting that no new trials should be started after 31 August 1948. "In our view, punishment of war criminals is more a matter of discouraging future generations than of meting out retribution to every guilty individual. Moreover, in view of future political developments in Germany envisaged by recent tripartite talks, we are convinced that it is now necessary to dispose of the past as soon as possible."[31]

The last sentence of the secret telegram of 1948 refers to the consultation of the three Western Allies occupying West Germany: the United States, Britain, and France. The "future political developments" were, of course, the development of the cold war with the Soviet Union.

The result of these policies was that Japanese people had no realistic understanding of their defeat and of the moral shame the war crimes had brought to their country. As a consequence, many Japanese considered the war a tragedy but did not see it as immoral. Seven cases led to the death penalty by hanging. Bix writes, "Their bodies were then cremated and most of their ashes scattered at sea in the mistaken belief that this would prevent them from someday being enshrined as martyrs."[32] The executed war criminals were symbolically placed in the Yasukuni Shrine. Two Japanese prime ministers visited the shrine to honor Japanese war dead, Nakasone Yasuhiro in 1985 and Koizumi Junichiro in 2002. Japanese public sentiment is widespread, but not universal, that the war criminals were actually victims of the war, even martyrs of their country, not criminals. The International Military Tribunal of the Far East aroused controversy and criticism from almost all directions. However, Tim Maga describes the conduct of the trials by judges and defense attorneys, particularly the American jurists, as highly professional and concludes that the trials were well carried out. From the circle of these jurists, after the trials in Tokyo, came a call to establish a permanent International Criminal Court.[33]

Both in Japan and in Germany, President Truman softened the effort to oust officials who had shared responsibility for the war, limiting de-Nazification in Germany and adopting similar leniency in Japan.[34] However, there were sharp differences between the postwar experience of the two countries. In Germany, the Nazi regime was demolished and discredited. There was no possibility of governmental continuity. Further, as Herf points out, the new Germany could pick up several historical strands of democratic traditions.

> Allied victory made possible multiple restorations of political tradition of the "other Germanys" which Nazism had suppressed from 1933 to 1945. Even where the victor's control over the vanquished in both East and West was total, this power was manifested less in the imposition of previously foreign interpretations than in the repression of Nazism and the encouragement of other previously *local* German political traditions. As representatives of those traditions German political leaders played a central role in bringing the memory of the crimes of the Nazi era, including the Holocaust, to the attention of their fellow Germans.[35]

In the case of Japan, however, there were no such "restorations" because Japanese history did not include substantial, vigorous traditions of democracy. Bix summarizes:

> As the twentieth century ended, although developments in Japan hinted that constitutional change might take place, it seemed unlikely that Akihito would ever be brought forward to lead the nation as dramatically as Meiji or as disastrously as Showa.[36] His personality, abilities, education, and interests all seemed to rule out such a role. So too did the many problems still unresolved from World War II—problems inherent in the institution of the Japanese monarchy itself rather than in the particular occupant of the throne. Nonetheless, like Ito and the *genro* with Meiji; and Kido, the militarists, and MacArthur with Showa, some future national leadership may rise and find effective ways to make use of

the new monarch or his successors. Whether they will move the institution as their predecessors did—to prevent the deepening of democracy and growth in the sense of political empowerment—is a critical issue for Japan in the new millennium.[37]

The problem for postwar Japan reveals the lack of transparency by centers of Japanese power. Only recently have researchers been able to learn much about the past. It took roughly half a century to get the historical record to this point, and it is as yet incomplete. While Japan was in the grip of economic stagnation at the turn of the twenty-first century, we interviewed several well-informed professionals, all of whom were concerned in various ways about the condition of their country. Here are the anonymous comments of a business consultant and planner:

> The pattern of global change affects Japan in a different way. I talk to students and they say to me that Japan has had so many prime ministers. All of them have used the word "reform" and so we know we need "reform." It is needed in administrative structure, in economic structure, and in education and social security. There is also the information technology revolution and there are huge fiscal problems. Each one of the prime ministers has had his own slogan as a "platform." . . . All the prime ministers missed the important point: it is the spiritual problem we have to face. We have to have an ideology that is pragmatic, but it has to come from our own history. Can Japan again become a model, not an example, but a model? The twentieth century was also a century of Japan. Japan broke the orthodoxy of the Occident. Through wars we were defeated as a nation, but we set a model. It led to decolonization in the Pacific. It was a model of high growth and good management. It encouraged Asian countries (and Western ones) to emulate us. We have now so many defects, after the bubble burst.

He felt that Japan had the capacity for effective reform but was pessimistic about the likelihood that business leaders and politicians would act. Drastic measures are needed but can be taken only if there is a revival of the Japanese spirit.

Another very elderly academic told us that a new reform of education was necessary. He felt that the Meiji educational reform had prepared Japan's elites in the prewar era, but that the American reforms had diluted the traditional rigor in secondary school curricula. In his words:

> The students under the Meiji educational plan had to study many classics from Europe, America, and Japan. They had a global outlook. They read Kant in the original language. They were Japanese, but they also learned a great deal about

the Western way of thinking. . . . After the war, many new schools and universities were set up. I do not criticize the American occupation, but so many students now have become rather easygoing. . . . Their point of view is to get credits from their mother campus, but they do not have a global outlook.

This informant also felt that Japan had lost the war, but that it had contributed to positive developments—the end of colonialism. This was a major achievement in Japan's history.

A business leader, head of a major consulting firm involved in international investments, discussed the difference between the Japanese way of doing business and the American perspective. "We have changed drastically since 1988. Information services industries have changed rapidly, leading to amalgamation of contract, consulting and system development and maintenance functions." He emphasized that his consulting division worked essentially in Japan and followed the Japanese way. His competitors were U.S. firms, Anderson Consulting and IBM, but he felt that they had nothing like the scope of the business his division had.

Globality, international culture, that is a basic capability we appreciate. But it is not essential. My division is not global, we work in Japan. . . . We started as a domestic company; now try to be a little global. We started a tiny business in Hong Kong. In Singapore we have a small pilot company. . . . Our consulting work is very domestic. What Anderson Consulting is saying is global. We don't agree. Lots of companies are doing business here, but so far not on our scale. There is global pressure to open up. The global standard is flowing into the Japanese business scene. The evaluation criteria will be global. The substance of Japanese business is so far detached from this trend. "Global" business methods in a sense are simply American. . . . There is a choice. We can improve management in the Japanese way or become "global," which means becoming American. We are not for that. We must adapt to global accounting schemes. Japanese are against that. Global wants "real-time" assessments. Japanese allow "book value." Over time, there is a difference between the two assessments. Then what should Japanese companies do? Simply accepting those changes and try to enhance productivity? The current wave of accounting actually comes from European sources. The trend exists. It is toward transparency, accountability. The Japanese practice is entirely opposite to these. We have invisible rules of business circles that govern the whole system. It seems that it is changing to more transparency and accountability. We stick to our clients. We analyze their issues, their environments. Those environments vary company by company. We have to be prudent, very careful. There is no single global model, there has to be variety across countries.

He concluded the conversation with the remark, "Transparency is coming to Japan, but I will be retired by then."

Young professionals in the major Japanese foundations have other views and are committed to building links with other countries, especially in Asia. One said,

> Japan—I feel like Japan is on the wrong channel, just missing the boat. For example, I'm not a scholar but people use a vocabulary without defining words, then they shift gears in the course of a discussion. For example, shifting between self-assessment and evaluation. . . . The press, especially, refers to the shift from director control to autonomy. They refer to this as "privatization" but it's not; . . . it's just sloppy. . . . For another example, there is the phrase, "compulsory voluntary service."

Another problem is that the Japanese are committed to "process" in arriving at a consensus, which slows down necessary reforms. The pace of change in Japanese universities is especially frustrating. Drastic reform is needed, our informant stated: "During the past calendar year, I've been to Turkey, the U.S., Indonesia, then Romania and Bulgaria, Leipzig, Sweden, Latvia, back in the U.S., Mongolia, and Korea. What I'm finding, in Bulgaria, Mongolia, even Seoul, is the emergence of issues revolving around the fact of life, of globalization." This individual was also concerned that Japanese students are not oriented to the "fact of life" of globalization.

Another foundation officer, also energetic and reform-minded, found that throughout Asia among young people there is a disenchantment with globalization; many simply equate it with Westernization, and that means to them Americanization. "We must find our own way and not just adopt Western ideas" was his emphasis. He felt that students in Japan are becoming very conservative and local. He is, however, aware that Japanese people support development assistance from abroad, especially in Asia. This feeling is in part based on the world war; Japan has a moral obligation to support the development of other Asian countries.

The Japanese understanding of the history of the war is very different from the views of most people in Asia, especially China and Korea. In various interviews in Hong Kong we found a sense of outrage at the denial of responsibility about Japan's role in the war in Japanese history textbooks and in statements by politicians. John Nathan writes about the volatility of Japanese society and the role of Japan's past and future in public attitudes. He speaks of Japan's "bewildered children," with accounts of resigned teachers and schools almost in anarchy: "There is also an alarming communication problem: Turmoil at home and pressure at school, which includes rampant bullying, have created reclusive children who are unable to build friendships with peers that will enable them to talk about their lives. The addiction to computer games and cell phones that Japanese sociologists are calling 'thumb culture' has further eroded direct communication skills and deepened isolation."[38] There is a search for a new sense of collective harmony. One aspect of this search is Japan's new nationalism. Nathan describes the rise of neonationalism, giving a vivid description of the extreme "arrogance comics"—picture books created by a famous author of "arrogant-ism" that glorify Japan's role in the war. This spirit has had its effect on Japan's history textbooks. The Society for the Creation of a New History was founded in 1996 for the purpose of ending the "masochistic version of history" and creating a "balanced" treatment of Japan's past. The texts produced as a result were strongly endorsed by the conservatives (including the Liberal party), but they were criticized by many others. The Ministry of Education approved of the *New History* text in 2002. However, there was heated debate by school boards. According to Makoto Watanabe, a small number had initially accepted the text, but in the end, "all but 3 of the country's 543 textbook boards had rejected the *New History*. In total, about 10 of Japan's 10,000 middle schools would be using it beginning in April 2002."[39] This seemed to be a victory over the nationalists. However, the *New History* was—a rare exception—marketed by its publisher to the general public. It became a huge best seller. As a result, other textbooks speak much more delicately—even defensively—about Japanese malfeasance in the war. In a more general way, beyond textbooks, the nationalist distortions of history are presented as facts in popular books of cartoons. One author of such books, Yoshinori Kobayashi, presents images of heroic Japanese soldiers in World War II, glorifying their fight against Western colonialism. This kind of publicity gained hold in the 1990s.[40]

Public opinion seems to sway in the direction of nationalism in Japan. However, newer efforts by some Japanese historians are making progress toward historical transparency. A Web site devoted to the history textbook controversy examines Japanese and other Asian history textbooks. There is a serious effort to monitor what the textbooks in Japan, China, and Korea have to say about each other. Watanabe concludes by confessing that his report on Japan's transition from denial to acknowledging responsibility for the Nanjing massacre does not cover the whole issue of Japanese history education and textbooks. He is certain, however, that the Ministry of Education strongly influences textbook descriptions of the past, even though the specific choices are made by school boards:

> It looks like the influence is less than that of China and Korea, where the first and central issue of textbooks is the screening by government. If changes are needed, as I believe, we have to think about a new system of checking the "quality" of textbooks, rather than hiding the facts and the truth. The serious attitude toward the reformation of the textbook selection process will contribute to a better feeling between our neighboring countries, specifically Korea and China.[41]

Clearly, the issue of historical transparency in Japan is in flux.

Germany and Japan Compared

Historical transparency has come to Germany and Japan in very different ways. First, their histories are dissimilar. Germans, after the Third Reich, had cultural and institutional memories of a time before fascism; there were precedents for democracy, for rational and just government structures. Japan had no such precedent. The best that could be hoped for was a strong vision of a new future, one radically different in its political culture from the past. A second difference pertains to the quality of leadership during the transition period. In Germany, politicians were committed to restoring and improving the democratic traditions of their early careers, in a transparent atmosphere and with a purpose to build a new, open democratic Germany imbued with Western values. In Japan, however, under General MacArthur and his government partners, there was an entirely different style at work. Transparency was not a priority. Personal status and its benefits were very salient. Perhaps as a misreading of what was possible, perhaps more deliberately, MacArthur shielded the emperor, and many who planned and executed the war, from serious retribution. It was a style of realpolitik.

Third, the cultural and geographic contexts of Japan and Germany are very different. Japan is a nation of islands, geographically close to Asian nations that in 1946–48 were much less developed and also close to the tumultuous and soon-to-be-Communist China. Japan saw itself as technologically superior to these other countries, even given its defeat in World War II, and having no need to seek their approval or cooperation. On the other hand, Germany sits in the heart of Europe and its recovery meant reconciliation, striving for equality with other large European nations. Continued isolation within Europe and a failure to seek and recognize cultural affinities with other Europeans would be catastrophic. Hence, Germany sought integration into the European Union and NATO.

Moral recovery has proceeded along different paths in Germany and Japan. The concept of moral recovery was introduced by Akiko Hashimoto, a sociologist who sees both countries as having gone through a period of silence and denial, but after half a century having very different views of their war history. Hasimoto writes:

> Despite similarities in their basic patterns of response, it is fair to say that there is now a clear international consensus that the Germans have accomplished more by far than the Japanese in facing up to their war legacy. The Germans are more willing to confront the memory upfront; they are more willing to assume responsibility for what happened; they have also long established textbook committees with the neighbor countries they victimized, to write history in ways that are agreeable to both sides. They have also thoroughly incorporated the Holocaust in the school curriculum and in their educational program as a whole. By contrast, Japanese responses give the impression of just barely fumbling through, awkwardly, and apparently without clear direction. Many observers have noted their awkwardness in speaking about the war, and their strong victim consciousness.[42]

Hashimoto points to the many inappropriate remarks made by prominent Japanese politicians about their denial of the Nanjing Massacre or the notion of Japan having "liberated" Asia from Western domination. "In many ways, Japan is today still in a messy place when it comes to war memories."[43]

Hashimoto's approach is to define the different strategies used by Germany and Japan in order to focus on the notion of recovery. Economic recovery did succeed in both countries. However, moral recovery is another, more complex matter. Germany could draw on cultural resources to restore democratic traditions. Hashimoto argues that the Japanese opted for a future-oriented strategy, "to recover their dignity and moral standing, not by examining the past, but by promising something for the future. The promise was *peace,* the promise to become a reliable, peaceful nation."[44]

A "peace emphasis" also exists in Germany, but not quite in the same way in which it was installed in the Japanese constitution. In a dangerous world, both countries now deal with a further challenge: how to redefine the value structure of moral recovery when the issue of security has to be resolved as well. John Nathan describes Japan as a "volatile nation" much affected by the battle about historical transparency. In Germany the issues are different. They concern Germany's future in the European Union—indeed, the future of the EU in the world—with economic reforms and the strategic conception of Germany's playing a global role through the EU based on "soft power."

The Global Demand for Justice and Transparency

Since the war crimes tribunals in Nuremberg and Tokyo, more than a half century has passed. The world has changed in that time, and the pressure for transparency about the past has grown stronger. Obviously, valid tribunals must be legitimated by proving and publicizing the facts and by sound judgments. A truthful account of past events is therefore an important element in such tribunals, which have had the dramatic effect of establishing rules of justice that transcend national sovereignty. Many countries have made the transition from criminal dictatorships or autocracies to some form of (maybe illiberal) democracy. All of these transitions are difficult and their outcomes are often unclear. Yet, increasingly, the actors responsible for transition movements for truth, justice, and reconciliation can turn to a growing body of knowledge about the skills and rules needed to carry them out ethically and effectively. And there is a growing network of "epistemic communities," experts linked to each other to extend the body of knowledge and to work for the realization of global governance under international law.

The number of countries undergoing major transformations today is substantial. In Europe the newer members of the EU—such as Portugal, Spain, and Greece—must undertake substantial changes in policy, economy, and especially how to deal more openly with their complex pasts. In fact, it has taken some time even to make a beginning. For example, in Spain, twenty-five years after the death of Francisco Franco, Spaniards are beginning to acquaint themselves with the problems of almost four decades of fascist domination.[45] And the newest EU members, namely, the ten countries that joined the EU in May 2004—Cyprus, Czech Republic, Estonia, Hungary, Latvia, Lithuania, Malta, Poland, Slovakia, and Slovenia—have daunting challenges ahead.

Not all of these countries had been dictatorships, but most were. In the Balkans and especially in the new countries that suffered from civil war after the collapse of Yugoslavia, volatile and tense situations have required interventions by NATO, with active leadership by the United States. The collapse of the Soviet Union broke it into the Russian Federation and an array of newly independent states. Some forms of transition are under way in those new nations with as yet unknown consequences.

Latin America has seen the emergence of democracies from former military dictatorships. Some of these democracies have to be classified as illiberal, or even as weak democracies, but they struggle to build a new future. In particular, Argentina and Chile have had to overcome their dictatorial pasts. And in Asia there are debates about "Asian values" and "electoral democracy" in many countries. India has been a democracy for many decades, but has historical problems with Pakistan and Bangladesh. In many countries like the Philippines, Indonesia, Malaysia, as well as in Taiwan and Hong Kong issues of governance are hotly debated but carefully shelved. In some of them and certainly in the People's Republic of China, historical transparency is not high on the official agenda at this time. (For a blatant example, look at Myanmar, the former Burma.) However, it became a hot international issue in Cambodia after the genocide carried out by the Khmer Rouge.

Africa provides a shining example in the innovative strategies led by Nelson Mandela in the Republic of South Africa. The continent has other democracies like Ghana, but also too many examples of failed states, civil wars, and dictatorships. The countries of the Middle and Near East are for the most part in disarray, in spite of the oil wealth in some of them. There is the conflict between Israel and the Palestinians, the cultural crisis of Islam confronting modernity, the war in Iraq, the arrest of Saddam Hussein, the scandal of torture used by U.S. soldiers in Iraq, the appointment of a new Iraqi government under the direction of the United States and its allies, and the violent insurgency in that country. An Iraqi tribunal is to establish the facts of the crimes of the Baathist regime and administer justice. Saudi Arabia and several other traditional countries suffering from extreme corruption are under serious threat from terrorist movements. Large countries like Egypt are trying to build nascent democratic institutions—an enormous task requiring strong, honest leadership and the creation of a new political culture. The cultural, religious, and political barriers to historical transparency at this time are enormous. Nasty secrets are coming out, and the quest for historical truth cannot be ignored.

This cursory overview of change in the world makes the complexity of expansion and transformation in the European Union look almost orderly. In much of this disorderly world the hopes for peace, justice, and wealth are hard to satisfy. We focus here on the growing role of historical transparency, using selected illustrations to identify evils.

The tribunals of Nuremberg and Tokyo had a deep personal effect on the judges, prosecutors, journalists, scholars, and others associated with the trials. Some dedicated their lives to acting on their experience with evil and to work for world justice. One was Telford Taylor, chief prosecutor at the Nuremberg trial, who learned so much about the war, the Nazi crimes, and the need for stronger international laws that he devoted the rest of his career to strengthening the moral standards of the United States. He was an outspoken critic of Joseph McCarthy and demanded that President Nixon and Congress create an investigative commission on the origins and conduct of the Vietnam War. His Nuremberg experience inspired him to become a force for moral reform and advancing international law.[46]

Among those whose lives were changed by the trials was Benjamin B. Ferencz, the prosecutor at Nuremberg who charged the SS extermination squads with responsibility for the murder of more than a million Jews. He became a peace activist and a distinguished international lawyer who campaigned for the establishment of the International Criminal Court in the UN framework. The experience of Nuremberg never left him.[47] Another prosecutor, Henry T. King Jr., who became chairman of the American Bar Association's Section on International Law and Practice, is now part of its special task force on war crimes in the former Yugoslavia.[48]

Sir William Webb of Australia, chief justice at the International Military Tribunal for the Far East in Tokyo, recommended as a long-term legacy of the tribunal "a permanent legal apparatus . . . that would always be poised to try and convict war criminals."[49] This recommendation was made in 1948, but it was not well received by the allied governments, especially not by the United States. It was taken up by Australia during the 1990s to support the idea of the International Criminal Court. Maga writes: "This new, long-incoming tribunal constituted one of the only obvious legacies of the Tokyo War Crimes Trial era."[50] These judges were convinced of the concept of global justice.

Universal Jurisdiction: No More Impunity?

The two major war crimes tribunals held after the end of World War II demonstrated the need for transnational justice. The scale, visibility, and impact of these temporary institutions inspired the thinking of activists and innovators in international law. They began to see that one important path to justice for perpetrators of the most heinous war crimes and crimes against humanity was universal jurisdiction. This concept has spawned many transnational movements to expand the pursuit of historical transparency to the global arena. It was accepted in many countries after the Second World War, but recently it has become controversial. Many assume that universal jurisdiction is a very recent invention of "tyrannical" judges. Henry Kissinger, himself a master of secret diplomacy, in 2001 called it a great risk:

In less than a decade, an unprecedented movement has emerged to submit international politics to judicial procedures. It has spread with extraordinary speed and has not been subjected to systematic debate, partly because of the intimidating passion of its advocates. To be sure, human rights violations, war crimes, genocide, and torture have so disgraced the modern age and in such a variety of places that the effort to interpose legal norms to prevent or punish such outrages does credit to its advocates. The danger lies in pushing the effort to extremes that risk substituting the tyranny of judges for that of governments; historically, the dictatorship of the virtuous has often led to inquisitions and even witch-hunts.[51]

In reply, Kenneth Roth of Human Rights Watch finds Kissinger's accusation exaggerated and misplaced: "Behind much of the savagery of modern history lies impunity. Tyrants commit atrocities, including genocide, when they calculate they can get away with them. Too often, dictators use violence and intimidation to shut down any prospect of domestic prosecution. Over the past decade, however, a slowly emerging system of international justice has begun to break this pattern of impunity in national courts."[52] It is important to remember the signal role played by scandals in promoting the emergence of transparency. Revelations from scandals are wedges that disclose rifts, disagreements, or more seriously, outright violations of norms and values. They cry out for redemptive action. In politics, a scandal can engender new voting procedures or laws regulating political behavior. In the business world, scandals have resulted—after periods of reflection and recrimination—in codes of conduct and other regulatory policies.

In the case of transgressions long buried in the past, whose revelation creates perhaps the most serious forms of scandal, the response, when it comes, is equally serious and profound. The demand for historical transparency has resulted from new discoveries about slavery, genocide, false imprisonment, and torture that expose the depth of these abuses against humanity. These crimes are of such magnitude that nothing less than society's admission of guilt, shame, and eventual retribution can salve the conscience. The early twenty-first century has seen a multitude of these scandals of global import.

The efforts to bring transparency to the violations of human rights on a global scale are novel and forceful. A nation's sovereignty is no longer enough to assure impunity for crimes committed by people in high position. The campaign for universal jurisdiction is one form taken by this movement. Amnesty International (AI) has published a detailed report on this concept. AI is one of the largest and most distinguished worldwide volunteer movements, with a membership of more than 1.8 million people in

150 countries. Its purpose is to defend the Universal Declaration of Human Rights and to "undertake research and action focused on preventing and ending grave abuses of the rights to physical and mental integrity, freedom of conscience and expression, and freedom of discrimination within the context of its work to promote all human rights."[53] AI's report on universal jurisdiction is a comprehensive account of this idea.

There is a long history to the concept of universal jurisdiction. Heinous crimes that went unpunished because they occurred outside a functioning legal jurisdiction could be prosecuted by other powers as early as in the sixth century under the Code of Justinian. In the Middle Ages robbers committing crimes outside the jurisdiction of established city-states or principalities could be prosecuted and punished by other powers. For example, the disruption of trade by brigands robbing wagon trains was a grave threat to medieval commerce. It was a matter of concern not only for the authorities in the sending or receiving cities; there was a strong public interest in the security of roads. Anyone having the power to do so was expected to seize and punish such roving robbers. Rules about especially hideous war crimes in international conflicts already existed in medieval Europe and at times led to punishment. Such crimes could be punished under international rules as early as the fourteenth century. Of course, these acts of retaliation were often spontaneous (and possibly mistaken) and were not very similar to a modern, systematic, and regulated form of justice. Indeed, the contemporary global system of justice is still not systematic or well regulated.

The oldest and most obvious use of universal jurisdiction is the punishment of pirates on the high seas. Piracy was dealt with by states as a crime of international concern, but each state had its own definition of justice. The concept of universal jurisdiction on the high seas over piracy is now defined by the 1982 Convention of the Law of the Sea as the duty of all nations to cooperate in repressing piracy. A warship of any nation is duty-bound to arrest a ship that can be credibly suspected of being a pirate. Similarly, there is a rule that applies to slavery and the slave trade. This rule simply requires that every effective measure must be taken to stop the transport of slaves and that "any slave taking refuge on board any ship, whatever its flag, shall ipso facto be free."[54]

Before the Second World War a growing number of states had passed legislation providing for universal jurisdiction over ordinary crimes, not merely slavery and piracy, with certain restrictions. These laws began to be implemented, albeit to the discomfort of the United States, the United Kingdom, and France. The use of the concept of universal jurisdiction in cases of crimes in noninternational conflicts (crimes against humanity within a state that are not brought to justice by that state) is a recent development—it essentially developed toward the end of the twentieth century, as Henry Kissinger says. Of course, it would be rejected by the rulers whose citizens perpetrated these crimes. Quite obviously, this enlargement of the reach of courts beyond the nation in which the crimes occurred is a deliberate infringement of the sovereignty of that state. That, however, is part of the growing transnational process to redefine the very meaning and limitations of national sovereignty in the era of global transformations.

Recent interest in universal jurisdiction arose as part of the long-term legacy of the war crimes tribunals of 1945. The tribunals themselves had been defined in terms of international law, but it was expected that other trials would be conducted to consider war crimes committed in any nation. These certainly came under the rubric of universal jurisdiction. Further, according to Amnesty International,

> Some of the more than 1,000 trials conducted by Allied national tribunals after the Second World War under the authority of the Allied Control Council Law No. 10 of persons accused of crimes against peace, war crimes or against humanity in Europe, were based, at least in part, on universal jurisdiction. There were also many trials by national military courts and commissions for such crimes committed in Asia during that war. Indeed, several of these national tribunals expressly stated that they were asserting the universal jurisdiction in cases where the accused were convicted of crimes against humanity or war crimes.[55]

Soon after these trials had imposed penalties on convicted perpetrators, many governments stopped the further prosecution of World War II war criminals. This was at the beginning of the cold war. Germany did not take this course—it ultimately even abandoned the statute of limitations in such cases; Israel acted similarly. In 1961 Israel tried and convicted Adolf Eichmann, then living in Argentina, for war crimes and crimes against humanity. Germany tried cases of such crimes by its own nationals.

After the 1970s the moral framework had shifted in many countries. The idea of human rights had become widely accepted. World War II criminals had been discovered living in exile, and trials were carried out in Australia, Canada, the United Kingdom, Italy, France, and the United States. Many were outraged that some war criminals lived in impunity, hidden in far-distant places, and were even protected by some countries. Criminal investigations were resumed. In several countries legislation was necessary to give their courts universal jurisdiction over those accused of war crimes committed long ago.

At the same time, in the 1970s and 1980s, a wave of terrorist offenses occurred in several countries, mainly in Europe but also in the United States and other places. The reaction of states to these terrorist acts was to establish a new network of treaties on universal jurisdiction. They included certain "crimes of international concern," such as "hostage taking in peacetime, aircraft hijacking and sabotage, attacks on internationally protected persons, including diplomats, drug trafficking, attacks on ships and navigation, theft of nuclear materials, use of mercenaries and attacks on peace-keepers."[56] These treaties are significant because they built a strong foundation for universal jurisdiction for crimes that aroused shared international concern that such acts must not be tolerated.

Amnesty International's report sums up important legal consequences: The treaties have become important because they recognize that international law permits the exercise of universal jurisdiction with respect to ordinary crimes if they are matters of international concern. This justifies the concept of universal jurisdiction over such crimes. Some features of the treaties were included in the Convention against Torture, adopted in 1984 by the United Nations. They referred to the duty to apprehend, try, or extradite perpetrators. Finally, some of these treaties can be interpreted to supersede the idea of immunity for government officials who have gravely violated human rights.[57]

Clearly, after a long period of inactivity, by the 1970s the concept of universal jurisdiction was widening and applied to ever larger domains. Many further grave crimes of international concern have surfaced since the Second World War and caused intense outrage across the world, giving the concept of universal jurisdiction new significance. Many countries making the transition to democracy have had to deal with crimes against humanity committed by previous regimes. Such nations include Argentina, Chile, Germany, Poland, and, in a very special way, South Africa. After serious problems arose when Argentina changed from being a military dictatorship to a democracy, judges and prosecutors in other countries took action. In 1983 an Italian court started criminal investigations against the Argentine junta because of suspected murders. After the junta lost its power, prosecutions took place in Argentina against some of the worst perpetrators. Soon, however, President Alfonsín adopted a law of amnesty or impunity, whereupon Amnesty International and the court in Italy continued to press for the investigations. Italy, France, Sweden, Spain, and later Mexico became involved in investigating "disappearances." The struggles continue, since the Argentine government takes the position that crimes perpetrated in Argentina must be tried in an Argentine court. The case of Augusto Pinochet in Chile also gave rise to multiple efforts to bring this dictator to justice— with very ambivalent reactions by certain Western governments. Efforts of a Belgian court along these lines led to intense pressure by the United States to limit the use of universal jurisdiction, a limitation accepted by the Belgian government.

The widespread effort to bring violators of human rights to justice has run into problems because of conflicting conceptions of international justice and the protective interests of national governments (as well as nationalist sentiments among many in the population). However, the public demands of victims and their families and friends, as well as pressure from civil society groups, have led to international revulsion against such crimes, especially those perpetrated by high officials. Demands for justice based on the unearthing of secret information, given the move to historical transparency, have created worldwide support for punishing tyrants and torturers. With this call for transparency and justice also came the slow recognition that there had to be understandable, globally valid rules for how such justice should work.

An initiative to bring some order into the rules of universal jurisdiction was the Princeton Project on Universal Jurisdiction, known as the Princeton Principles. These are meant to be a contribution to the worldwide debate, not a complete doctrine. A distinguished group of organizations sponsored the effort. Mary Robinson, the former president of Ireland and the UN high commissioner on human rights from 1997 to 2002, wrote a passionate and detailed foreword to the published principles. The project is devoted to the idea that crimes of international concern cannot be tolerated anywhere in the world. National laws providing amnesty cannot be tolerated. The sovereign immunity defense for high officials, which also invites impunity, must therefore be limited. The heinous crimes of piracy, slavery, war atrocities, crimes against peace, crimes against humanity, genocide, and torture must be subject to universal jurisdiction. The Princeton Principles, of course, represents a valiant effort, but confusion and struggles persist.

International Tribunals: Yugoslavia, Rwanda, and Beyond

International tribunals offer a different path to assure "no impunity for evil!" The United Nations' ad hoc tribunals and special courts to investigate past crimes and to administer justice testify to the sense of outrage world-wide about the crimes perpetrated in vicious conflicts. Two tribunals are now in action: the International Criminal Tribunal for Yugoslavia and the International Criminal Tribunal for Rwanda. In both cases, the great powers in the Security Council hesitated for long periods before intervening in these horrendous conflicts. The war in the former Yugoslavia caused the death of more than 300,000 people. After much hesitation, NATO intervened, with prominent U.S. military participation. Even now Bosnia is patrolled by NATO troops. In Rwanda more than 500,000 Tutsis had been murdered, then millions of Hutus fled the country when a Tutsi army gained control over the country. The ferocity of the Rwandan genocide caused deep shock among global publics. Nevertheless, the great powers had procrastinated and failed to intervene as forcefully as they should have.[58]

The International Criminal Tribunal for Yugoslavia was established in 1993. A high point in its proceedings was the capture and extradition of Slobodan Milosevic, the main accused. A decade later, the trial is still in progress. The Security Council's decision to set up this tribunal was not a vigorous act of intervention. Aryeh Neier of Human Rights Watch and the ACLU was disappointed. He argues that the reason for establishing the Yugoslav tribunal was wrong. It was a decision made to avoid decisive action, merely to calm the outrage expressed by the countries represented on the Security Council. In his words, "Facing domestic criticism for allowing the slaughter to continue unchecked, some governments seemed to feel obliged to show that they were doing *something*. It was in this vacuum that the proposal for a tribunal advanced until its establishment was formally approved."[59] There is a multifaceted debate about this tribunal—it is slow, some Serbs claim that it is not fair to the Serbs, and some have criticized the procedures. Nevertheless, the tribunal has sentenced war criminals and is now proceeding to the central figure: Milosevic. It is true that the tribunal has very limited powers; it cannot arrest the accused but must rely on the cooperation of local government authorities and the influence of major powers. Even now some accused war criminals are free, and there is little the court can do directly. In Rwanda, the tribunal has thus far indicted a score of people, and some progress has been made, even though the Rwandan circumstances are particularly difficult and the root problems are likely to persist. Nevertheless, these two tribunals are valiant, if difficult and even faulty, path breakers in creating advanced forms of international justice. Amnesty International has issued a handbook to help governments understand precisely what needs to be done to enable the tribunals to function appropriate-

317

ly.[60] There is some hope for their success. Neier writes: "At every stage of the push to establish the [Yugoslavia] tribunal, partisans were conscious that its failure would severely set back the effort to hold accountable those responsible for great crimes. That fear has proved unfounded. What is surprising is not how little the tribunal has traveled but how far it has gone; even if governments of good conscience still have further to go to fulfill its mandate."[61]

The need for creating a functioning system of global justice continues to grow as general public awareness of horrendous evils in many parts of the world increases. In addition to the international tribunals, the UN, in cooperation with the governments of Sierra Leone, Cambodia, and East Timor, has made arrangements for special courts. All of these are cooperative efforts between each country and the UN. It is hoped that this judicial modality might be more efficient and less costly than the two major international tribunals.

Another special trial being set up is the Iraq Special Tribunal (IST). After Saddam Hussein was captured by U.S. military forces in December 2003, a trial for him and the major figures in the Baath party was obviously necessary, in view of his many crimes against the Iraqi people and in the war. Given the United States' tendency to limit its involvement in the United Nations, the tribunal is not based on the principles of Sierra Leone or the other courts in Cambodia or East Timor, nor any of the major tribunals. Planning for this tribunal is to some extent in the hands of the Iraqi interim government, obviously with direct guidance by the coalition forces, which means for all practical purposes the United States. The tribunal is described as an Iraqi court of justice, not an international one. Much may be learned from this special and risky effort. One problem will undoubtedly arise with regard to the United States' earlier support for Saddam Hussein in the war against Iran. Other problems include the demands by Iran and Kuwait to be part of the tribunal. Most of the challenges are practical difficulties that must be overcome.

The United States Institute of Peace is an independent, nonpartisan institution of the federal government, with a congressional mandate "to promote the prevention, management, and peaceful resolution of international conflicts."[62] It has been asked to assemble state-of-the-art knowledge about the experience of international tribunals to date. This can be useful for planning the Iraqi Special Tribunal (IST). To do this, the U.S. Institute of Peace has attempted to outline the challenges facing the creators of the special tribunal. For example, a sound information management system will be essential. According to an institute publication:

Dealing with documentary evidence will be a huge task in the Iraq context and therefore should begin promptly. However, it will be exceedingly important not to rush into putting evidence into a database before determining how the evidence and the database system will need to be used. The ICTY [International Criminal Tribunal for Yugoslavia], for instance, has changed its document management system several times, and each time has had to scan the documents into the new system and renumber millions of pages. Moreover, the ICTY did not develop a plan for systems for the whole tribunal, and only now is working to bring the office of the prosecutor, judges' chambers, and registry together into a single "enterprise" system.[63]

In addition to managerial issues, there are fundamental legal decisions to be made, such as what system of justice is most appropriate: "a civil law type system, in which investigative judges play the dominant role in investigating and preparing a case for trial, or a common law type system, in which prosecutors play the leading role."[64] Much work will have to go into the planning for this tribunal. In spite of its very special, indeed peculiar, political context among the United States, Iraq, the United Nations, and other nations, the work of the IST will contribute to the growing international capacity for transnational justice. It also will generate a new wave of political debates.

The International Criminal Court and the United Nations

The establishment of the plan for the International Criminal Court (ICC) in 1998 was by far the most ambitious and promising innovation in international justice since the war crimes tribunals of the late 1940s. It is the result of a major, almost comprehensive mobilization of an enormous worldwide coalition of supporters among both governments and civil society (and a small number of powerful detractors, led by the United States under the Bush administration). Other countries that are not members include the People's Republic of China, Israel, Iraq, and a number of dictatorships.

On July 17, 1998, the plan for the International Criminal Court was to establish the Rome Statute, the international agreement for creating the court.[65] One hundred twenty states participated in the process. The ICC was conceived as the first permanent, treaty-based, international criminal court to promote the rule of law and ensure that the gravest international crimes do not go unpunished. The court's role complements that of the national courts. Its mandate is defined by the Rome Statute, which went into effect on July 1, 2002. The court is now a fact. Currently, about 2,000 NGOs worldwide are supporting the International Criminal Court. A global coalition among these groups has been formed, with headquarters at the UN in New York and in The Hague. In the United States, a Washington Working Group on the International Criminal Court has been formed, coordinated by Citizens for Global Solutions in Washington, D.C.[66] The member organizations include thirty-seven major U.S. civil society groups.

Active supporters of the ICC in the United States include Advocates for Survivors of Torture and Trauma, the American Jewish Committee, the American Society of International Law, Amnesty International, and many religious organizations, such as the Cooperative Baptist Fellowship, the Lutheran Office for Governmental Affairs, Maryknoll Fathers, Brothers, Sisters and Lay Missioners, the National Council of the Churches of Christ, the Presbyterian Church USA, the United Church of Christ, the United Methodist Church, and the Unitarian Universalist Association of Congregations. There are also such professional groups as the National Association of Defense Lawyers, the Philadelphia Bar Association, the Lawyers' Committee for Human Rights, and the International Association of Women Judges. The coalition represents some of the major sectors of civil society, including some very influential groups. The worldwide support by the people of many nations and the even greater support by global NGOs are also impressive.[67]

The struggle over the ICC is a contemporary phenomenon that epitomizes the dramatic conflict over historical transparency and impunity for criminals in high positions of political responsibility. It also further illuminates the strong movement in the world to strengthen the global rule of law. The hope for an international court for war crimes goes far back in time. However, the immediate source of this idea goes back only to World War II and the trials in Nuremberg and Tokyo, which established the idea of international justice as a realistic possibility. By the end of the twentieth century, the need for transnational justice and the abolition of impunity for heinous crimes against humanity and war crimes had become even more urgent.

The Rome Statute that set up the ICC in 1998 was adopted by a UN Conference of Plenipotentiaries in Rome. Representatives of 160 states, 33 intergovernmental organizations, and 236 NGOs were there; 120 countries voted in favor of establishing the court, 7 voted against, and 21 abstained. The statute went into effect on July 1, 2002, after 60 countries had joined as members. Since then, the effort to make it into a functioning tribunal has progressed in The Hague.

The jurisdiction of the ICC extends only to states that are "a party to the statute." National courts are not replaced by the ICC. The court will come into action only if a state does not or cannot prosecute perpetrators of an especially egregious crime against the international community as a whole. Immunity for officials is not given; even a head of state is not exempt from criminal responsibility before the court.[68]

Transparency versus Secrecy and the Failure of the Bush Policy

Under these rules for the International Criminal Court, why is the United States campaigning so vigorously against the ICC? President Clinton had signed the statute for the ICC shortly before leaving office, albeit with reservations. Clinton hoped that the worry about exempting U.S. personnel from court jurisdiction could be resolved by negotiations. His concern was acute: the United States was deeply involved in military actions as peacekeepers and even peacemakers in many countries. Military officials feared that politically motivated charges would be brought against American troops for war crimes. Some form of exemption, Clinton hoped, could be approved. However, many states considered the idea of exemptions granted to one nation to be quite preposterous, especially since the various protections built into the court's mandate would make it extremely unlikely that Americans would be brought before the court. The ICC does not supersede national jurisdiction unless the nation concerned is unable or unwilling to prosecute perpetrators of serious war crimes or crimes against humanity.[69] It is very unlikely that U.S. courts would fail in this regard. Nevertheless, Congress adopted the American Service Members Protection Act that prohibits any form of U.S. cooperation with the ICC. George Bush "unsigned" Bill Clinton's signature and withdrew from the ICC.[70]

It is true that the United States is more often engaged in peacekeeping and enforcing missions than any other country. However, many European countries also serve extensively in these military missions, but they remain members of the "states parties" of the court. There is a visceral concern in the United States that foreign judges might pursue irresponsible accusations. Americans cherish their sovereignty. Further, among members of the extreme right, there are strong misgivings about the United Nations, which certainly has reinforced the antipathy against the ICC. Possibly most important, after the terrorist attack of September 11, 2001, the mood of America changed. President Bush was obsessed with the idea that he must undertake a drastic restructuring of American foreign policy and global posture as soon as he took office. He had already decided, even before September 11, to aggressively pursue the national interest, narrowly defined, and to abandon multilateral commitments wherever possible. He changed U.S. foreign policy from multilateral international approaches to "go-it-alone" unilateralism.[71] This policy decision was consistently applied, from the 2001 withdrawal from the Kyoto Protocol, to the United Nations Framework Convention on Climate Change, to the repeal in 2003 of the Spratt-Furse ban against the development of new, low-yield nuclear weapons.[72] This latter, partisan action by the Congress at the president's demand is particularly dangerous to American security because it threatens the nonproliferation treaty and undercuts the policy to limit the spread of nuclear weapons. Bush abandoned a significant part of America's role in the UN framework, treaties, and international institutions such as (especially) the International Criminal Court.

As the only superpower, the United States inevitably plays a crucial role in global change.[73] The Bush administration defined that role by showing its impatience at the slow and often bizarre policy making by multilateral bodies—for example, the UN Security Council. Instead, Bush saw U.S. military and economic strength to lie in quick and decisive action against threats to its own and global security. No other country or alliance would be allowed to match America's power—it must remain the arbiter of global affairs. The United States' posture would not be passive and defensive, but preemptive. Countries and terrorists that threatened America (and the world) must be struck before they attacked—preemption became the doctrine.

This doctrine posed a serious challenge to nations seeking to build a global system of shared norms and rules. The U.S. policy emphasized the creation of democracies worldwide, but it hoped that the movement toward electoral democracies would grow under U.S. tutelage. Americans have generally assumed that their national values are self-evident and should be compelling to reasonable people worldwide. If this does not happen, and it often does not, consternation and disappointment, at times even rage, are the result. The Bush policy in international affairs is thus caught in contradictions.

The results of Bush's decision to go to war against Iraq revealed these contradictions and the failure of the preemption doctrine. Without support by the UN Security Council, the United States invaded Iraq backed by Britain and a motley coalition of other nations. The assumptions were that the military campaign would be brief and would destroy Iraq's alleged weapons of mass destruction, that the people of Iraq would welcome the occupation as liberation from the oppression of Saddam Hussein, that a flourishing democracy would emerge in Iraq and influence all the Arab states in the region to move toward stable democracy. Finally, Bush asserted that this war would decisively increase U.S. security by destroying the terrorists' capacity for harm. The military campaign did succeed, but none of the other assumptions turned out to be true. In fact, the occupation turned out to be a chaotic nightmare, the tensions in the Near East grew, especially in the conflict between Israel and the Palestinians, and the number of terrorist volunteers grew enormously. The failures of U.S. leadership in the Iraq war have revealed how much the doctrine of preemption has alienated the world. The widely shared notion that preemption will provide security and open the path to democracy in the Near East is now beginning to crumble.[74]

The contradictions in President Bush's policy become very clear in his campaign against the International Criminal Court. His actions are not only passive withdrawal from the ICC, but also a passionate campaign against the court as such. This is an odd circumstance, since the court is a global innovation very much founded on American historic initiatives and values. The discrepancy between the nation's historical role and the current policy is particularly instructive regarding the dilemma the U.S. administration finds itself in. It has launched a campaign against an achievement in international justice that was created by American leaders after World War II. Now, unilateral preemption remains the U.S. strategy for spreading democracy around the world. Obviously, it defeats itself.

Nevertheless, following the commitment to unilateralism and American exceptionalism, the U.S. State Department in 2002 started a cynical pressure campaign against countries that had joined the court in favor of a bilateral exemption for Americans. This, of course, irritated various countries, especially those in the European Union. At the time, a compromise form of temporary exemption for Americans was actually obtained by the Security Council and grudgingly accepted by the administration. However, it did not remain that way. By 2004 it had become known worldwide that U.S. soldiers had tortured prisoners in both Iraq and Afghanistan, and probably in the Cuban detention center of Guantánamo as well. When photographs of tortured prisoners were published around the world, the scandal elicited outrage against the United States government.

The general belief abroad was that these torture methods must have been part of official U.S. policy. Secret memoranda gradually surfaced that strengthened this opinion. The government rejected these accusations, but President Bush had in fact denied the protection of the Geneva Conventions to certain detainees who were presumed to be terrorists or enemy combatants but not prisoners of war.[75] He later stated that the conventions were generally honored by the U.S. military, but the matter remained murky. Investigations were started and continue at this time. There was a consequence for the campaign against the ICC. When the United States asked the UN Security Council in the summer of 2004 to renew the American exemption from the International Criminal Court, it became clear that the council would not support the request. The torture scandal was too outrageous to the electoral publics in the member countries. The compromise was to postpone discussion of this topic indefinitely. This situation was obviously embarrassing to the Bush administration and to the United States.

The campaign against the ICC illuminates the struggle between transparency and secrecy within current U.S. policies and commitments. It is a painful dialectic. The Bush administration has created an unprecedented expansion of secrecy. This encompasses the treatment of people suspected to be terrorists or supporters of terrorists, but it also includes many government activities. The secrecy policy especially affects—obviously—the activities of organizations like the Central Intelligence Agency (CIA) and the Defense Department.

The recent performance of America's intelligence apparatus had been dismal.[76] The assumptions about the causes and outcomes of the preemptive war in Iraq proved to be wrong. The congressional assessment of the CIA's performance of intelligence gathering about Iraq and terrorism was extremely negative. The excessive reliance on secrecy apparently harmed the quality of research that was undertaken and presented, also in secret, to the executive branch. There was no chance for critique and reflection, and some results seemed tailored to the specific expectations of the leadership. This costly phenomenon is part of the secrecy syndrome and reveals the costs of secrecy. It has created multiple problems throughout the government, and the public demand for transparency by the news media and civil rights organizations is rising. The transparency process continues in America, in spite of the official policy of secrecy. Failures based on secrecy in the long run will inevitably become scandals and force a search for alternatives. We must rebalance the tension between transparency and secrecy in favor of openness, in spite of the threats of terrorism and the mistakes of a failing presidency.

Transitions to Democracy and Historical Transparency

The calamity of the two world wars in the last century finally set in motion a process of transnational justice that can present convincing evidence about crimes of great magnitude. Horrendous crimes are committed even now, and demands for evidence, justice, and a new social reality are rising in spite of resistance to change. Immunity from prosecution for persons in high office, or for citizens of powerful nations, will have to yield to a world under law for all its citizens. It will be a long road to travel. Establishing the truth about the past is not enough for these transitions; they also require a perspective into a future of democracy and reconciliation.

Pressures for historical transparency can be resisted for generations until truly colossal historical turning points force change. Transparency about the past is essential for justice and in certain ways also for security. Nevertheless, secrecy has also been important to make the process feasible, while at times distorting it. There are further aspects of historical transparency: the problems of transition and reconciliation, and the new perspectives on history and the politics of memory.

The transition from the oppressive regime of apartheid in South Africa to a state on the way to a modern democracy is a remarkable historical event. The political system of apartheid reflected extreme racism. Many white South Africans were convinced that the apartheid regime was not only just, but also necessary for all of Africa. The fight for reform was led by the African National Congress (ANC) under the towering leadership of Nelson Mandela, a member of the ANC since 1944. Seeing the regime's rigid defense of apartheid, he suggested creating a military wing of the ANC. As a revolutionary leader, he was anathema to the regime, and after various lengthy prison terms, in 1964 he was sentenced to life imprisonment. In spite of incarceration, he was able to sustain his dignity and his philosophy of democracy and reconciliation. Even in prison, he became a great symbol for the struggle for freedom in South Africa and in the world. In 1990 Mandela was released from prison and became president of the ANC. The years following this stirring event saw an improbable transformation of leadership. In 1993 Nelson Mandela and Frederik Willem de Klerk, president of South Africa, were jointly awarded the Nobel Peace Prize. In 1994 Mandela was elected president himself. The ANC's and Mandela's success was in part advanced by international opinion and sanctions against the country. The brutal racism of apartheid was simply unacceptable to the citizens of democratic countries, who communicated their displeasure by economic pressure. In the United States, Rev. Leon Sullivan announced the Sullivan Principles as a code of conduct for businesses that worked in South Africa. This initiative had the effect of a boycott against apartheid and also became an early initiative toward forcing corporations to accept social responsibility.

Mandela's most important strategy was to establish South Africa's Truth and Reconciliation Commission, designed to facilitate the transition from a nation troubled by racial violence and political tension to a functioning democratic state.[77] Truthful revelations of misdeeds could lead to amnesty for perpetrators, while the blame would remain with them. This strategy has had difficulty, but its wisdom in building a new society based on reconciliation has been recognized in many countries undergoing similar painful transitions. "Transitional justice" has become a global challenge in many countries wishing to avoid the costs of revenge as well as of granting amnesty without justice.

Today there are networks of major institutions that are devoted to solving the problems of nations in transition. In the foreword to the multivolume *Transitional Justice,* Nelson Mandela places the issue in a global framework:

> In recent years, particularly during the past decade, there has been a remarkable movement in various regions of the world away from undemocratic and repressive rule towards the establishment of constitutional democracies. In nearly all instances, the displaced regimes were characterized by massive violations of human rights and undemocratic systems of governance. In their attempt to combat real or perceived opposition, they exercised authority with very little regard to accountability.[78]

These transitions pose enormous challenges. Difficult choices have to be made, with difficult outcomes. In South Africa the transition highlighted the deep divisions within society. Mandela writes:

> As all these countries recover from the trauma and wounds of the past, they have had to devise mechanisms not only for handling past human rights violations, but also to ensure that the dignity of victims, survivors, and relatives are restored. In the context of this relentless search for appropriate equilibria, profound issues of policy and law have emerged. They have arisen out of the question of how a country in transition should respond to allegations of gross human rights violations by individuals of either the predecessor or extant authority. The issue that has concerned the international community is the problem created by the incompatibility of such amnesties with a state's international obligations.[79]

In 2001 the International Center for Transitional Justice was established in New York, with help from the Ford Foundation. Its initial president was Alex Boraine, one of the designers of the South African Truth and Reconciliation Commission. The president in 2004 was Juan E. Mendez, who was arrested and tortured in Argentina and named by Amnesty International "Prisoner of Conscience" in the 1970s. Mendez is also the UN special advisor for the prevention of genocide. By now, truth and reconciliation commissions have been created in many countries, communities, and even organizations. A veritable industry has emerged to help balance the revelation of painful truths with reconciliation and the creation of new solidarities. The International Center for Transitional Justice is a major resource for those seeking to build a viable future for traumatized countries.

Transitional justice requires new perspectives for the future as well as a new idea of the past, a reconstruction of history. It is not just a political process; it is also a task for the social sciences—and especially for historians. Debate is necessary for professional researchers, intellectuals, and political leaders. Criticisms of accounts of a nation's history in light of global events is now under way. It is the intellectual and even philosophical side of historical transparency.

Debates about history have become major issues for history textbooks, which are for most countries officially sanctioned versions of patriotic narratives; the goal is not only to communicate factual knowledge about history, but to encourage a civic and national spirit. This makes the history textbook an important political tool. As we have seen, many states insist on officially approved history textbooks that do not withstand scholarly scrutiny. This is a battle between Japanese historians and the right wing about how to describe Japan's role in World War II. It is also an issue in India. K. N. Panikkar wrote in 2001:

> Since coming to power three years ago, India's ruling Bharatiya Janata Party (BJP) has actively sought to impose a new history curriculum. This attempt has nothing to do with new trends or methodology within this discipline. By restructuring educational institutions, rewriting curricula and textbooks, and making major personnel changes, the government is attempting to recast the past by giving it a strongly Hindu religious orientation. The right-wing party now controls the Ministry of Human Resource Development and the National Council for Educational Research and Training (NCERT) which produces most school texts.[80]

As a consequence, Panikkar writes, the professional historians in these institutions have lost their academic freedom and are being replaced by people who are prepared to follow the political line. The rewriting of Indian history is actually an effort at changing the secular nature of India's educational and cultural policies so as to make India a Hindu nation:

> To inculcate a sense of national pride, Indian history is seen through stereotypes rooted in religious identity. No aspect of history has been spared, be it social tensions, political battles or cultural differences. The achievements of ancient Indi-

an civilization are identified only with Hinduism and are grossly exaggerated. The BJP would have us believe that humankind and all scientific discoveries, from bronze-casting to printing and aeronautics, originated in northern India, the original home of the Aryans. The period of the Rig Veda [a religious treatise] has been pushed back to 500 B.C. against the general scholarly consensus of 1500 B.C. in order to associate the Aryans with the Indus Valley civilization which flourished in Harappa and Mohenjodaro, now in Pakistan.[81]

Of course, other countries have suffered similar pressures to adjust the facts of history to fit political, ideological purposes. In 2002 a ferocious debate broke out in Italy about history textbooks. The Italian parliament was considering an initiative to give the Ministry of Education direct control over history books to be used in schools. The right-wing initiative wanted to make sure that leftist deviations were removed from the texts. The outbreak of fury among Italy's intellectuals, led by Umberto Eco and reinforced by thousands of people who criticized the initiative via the Internet, with protests being filed from Britain and other countries, led the government to distance itself from such proposals of censorship.[82]

UNESCO has played a very active role in monitoring the preparation of textbooks in many regions of the world. There is a Mediterranean program, as well as programs to raise the standard of history teaching in many other regions. Germany has had a strong incentive to compare its textbooks with those of neighboring countries. The Georg Eckert Institute for International Textbook Research sponsors a Franco-German project, a German-Russian textbook project, an Israeli-Palestinian textbook project, a program on Holocaust education, and an ambitious United States and Germany project about teaching world history.

It is highly likely that many school texts reflect a religious or political bias. This is certainly the case with U.S. textbooks—at least to some extent. Dana Lindeman and Hyle Ward have studied how U.S. history is presented in textbooks used in other countries, and they conclude that the picture is very different from what American students learn. A reviewer called their book "shocking and fascinating," while including occasional lapses into their own, U.S.-centered bias. While true objectivity can never be achieved, such studies make an approach toward bringing greater transparency to events of the past, joining the efforts of UNESCO, the Eckert Institute, and the global discourse on historical transparency.

Conclusions

Calls for historical transparency are growing, demanding the disclosure of facts that many would like to suppress. This is also not just one nation's discussion with itself, but a transnational phenomenon that may entail harsh debates across national borders. Our starting point had to be—as with so many aspects of transparency—the end of World War II, when a demand for transnational justice in a serious and enforceable manner began to emerge.

Public scandals of a global scope have aroused fresh demands for justice and human rights. We are now in the process of national and transnational value changes and therefore virulent value clashes. Historical transparency has been required as three defeated states, the Federal Republic of Germany, the German Democratic Republic, and Japan, set about rebuilding themselves. The legacy of U.S. jurisprudence played a role in the war tribunals in Nuremberg and Tokyo, but the political frameworks were different. The cold war and realpolitik soon changed the picture, and the outcomes in the three states were very dissimilar because of different historical traditions. The remarkable war tribunals in Nuremberg and Tokyo had a lasting legacy. Movements evolved around the world to seek remedies for the atrocious crimes of the past. NGOs like Amnesty International, Human Rights Watch and thousands of others have become a force in the world. The idea of universal jurisdiction emerged as a reality of sorts. In the new international tribunals established by the United Nations, the struggle between transparency and secrecy, between building multilateral rules and unilateral preemption, became very clear. The U.S. strategy to destroy the ICC is of course ironic, since it is based on the democratic tradition of the rule of law.

Transitional justice is not only a matter of adjudicating the past. It requires building a future of recreated solidarities without cheap amnesties. History is not only a matter of past events; it touches the present. Historical transparency affects the mindsets of people. There is a need to work on valid history, after serious debate. History textbooks are very dangerous tools in the hands of corrupt governments or ideologically blinded politicians, but they can be liberating by opening society to multiple perspectives and a cultivated sense of what is actually true. The movement to historical transparency has to struggle with entrenched powers and the narrowness of nationalist, religious, and ideological blinders for understanding the past, thus limiting the potential for the future. However, inescapably, the movement for global historical transparency is on its way.

10

GLOBAL CHANGE AND THE OPEN SOCIETY

We have established that the rise of transparency—from its slow historical beginnings and its current steep ascent—is likely to bring about major changes in social relations of global scope. It is indeed a startling historical phenomenon. Only a few periods in history have seen anything like such a swift and extensive change in information cultures. The increased demand and supply of information disclosed by centers of power is growing, fitting precisely into Durkheim's category of social facts. It is part of both the transformations in global change and of the emergence of claims for personal rights. Across many disparate domains of institutions, markets, and fields of knowledge, the demand for transparency and information flows has increased dramatically in recent decades. It reflects not only demands for valid information, but also the legal duty to disclose it. The growth trend of transparency continues.

To restate the definition of transparency: it is the social value of open, public and/or individual access to information held and disclosed by centers of authority. These centers include governments, corporations, professions, or other influential bodies such as civil society organizations, foundations, regulatory agencies, transnational, supranational or global authorities such as the United Nations, the European Union, the OECD, and others. The transparency syndrome of values also encompasses kindred values such as accountability and countervalues such as secrecy. These values create a context for the expansion or limitation of transparency.

Clearly, transparency does not stand by itself. The conceptual architecture of information values is much more complex than previously assumed. Transparency and secrecy are not always hostile to each other, but may form a calibrated balance. Other values such as the rights of privacy and the right to conduct surveillance, the rights to accountability and autonomy, enter into this architecture. The entire configuration can be rigidly stark in quiet times and in flux at times of change and reform. Authorities tend toward secrecy in times of insecurity, wars, and terrorism. Nevertheless, there is a broad shift to transparency because there is a powerful current toward openness due to global change, the acknowledgment of citizens' rights, and the need for information and trust at a distance. Yet distortions of information by special interest groups, or calls for secrecy for fear of enemies, are among the sources that fight against transparency.

Transparency remains ascendant (but not necessarily dominant) in most social institutions. It is embedded in a constellation of other values that inspire a culture and the structures providing the "glue" for a new phase of modern social life. New solidarities are emerging as the need for trust at a distance requires transparency and as the reliance on trust up close must be supplemented and in part replaced. In all likelihood, the responses to continuing global change will rely on these solidarities and especially on transparency.

Most people are unaware of the real global risks that are on the horizon of the world. These risks will increase, and recognition of their dangers will inevitably grow. We need to change our perspective and attempt to see what new shapes transparency might take in the future. Thus far, we have established transparency as a social fact, as a result of global change and the factors of changes in values. We have focused on what brought this development about. Now we need to ask, how might transparency affect the possibilities of open societies? How effective might be the enemies of the open society in the future? How might centers of power succeed in hiding behind secrecy? What is the effect of nationalism against the search for global problem solving?

Many major changes in global conditions pose serious dangers for human society. Still, debates continue to rage about what specifically to do. One factor causing global change is the growth in the world's population and the rising intensity of human activities in all regions of the earth. Above all, social and economic inequality among the peoples of the world must be confronted. The quest for security has had unintended, dangerous consequences, such as the proliferation of nuclear weapons in several countries, the growth of militarism in some nations, the destruction of natural resources by special economic interests. We do need to examine how our emerging global society might deal with these risks and what transparency and the open society can do to reduce them.

Emerging Global Risks

Scientists and scholars have identified the global risks and a range of responses, but as yet there is little agreement about action. Many feel a sense of alarm about the condition of the planet we inhabit. The present may indeed be "a special moment in history." We quoted Bill McKibben in chapter 6 on this theme. He sees the next decades as a very stressful period. And that seems very likely true. There are planetary dangers resulting from present massive human activities that pose threats that must be dealt with.

In addition to the deteriorating conditions of the planetary habitat, there are violent man-made disasters. This calls for dramatic action to reduce environmental risks: the risk of damage caused by global warming, the depletion of water in many regions, the pollution of the oceans, and the loss of animal and plant species. The problems of creating sustainable energy supplies without producing huge amounts of carbon dioxide and other harmful gases are not even near solution. These changes in the physical conditions of the planet are daunting enough. In addition, new health risks have suddenly emerged, and some seem to be stubbornly resistant to medical intervention, as in the current epidemic of AIDS.

In addition, political violence and man-made disasters must be resolved. All weapons of mass destruction should be eliminated, but in fact they are proliferating. Mass killings still occur with worrisome frequency. Outbreaks of appalling hatred and extreme violence mark the ethnic conflicts in the former Yugoslavia, in parts of Africa, in the Near East, and in the bizarre and murderous rule of the Khmer Rouge in Cambodia. The rise of terrorism poses a grave worldwide threat.

A major threat to global security is the conduct of the war in Iraq, begun in 2002. It was intended by the United States and Britain as a venture to create democracy there quickly, but it has become an example of unintended, dangerous consequences. U.S. and British leaders believed in a rapid military victory, convinced that the Iraqis' enthusiasm for liberty would make the task easy. Indeed, they assumed that democracy would spread in the Near East as a result. It did not happen that way. Instead, there is now a factual record of appalling mistakes, especially by American leaders. It is a war that has aroused anger about U.S. unilateralism among most world countries. It reflects the misperceptions that flow from the structure of American nationalism. As Minxin Pei writes:

> Americans not only take enormous pride in their values but also regard them as universally applicable. According to the Pew Global Attitudes survey, 79 percent

of the Americans polled agreed that "it is good that American ideas and customs are spreading around the world"; 70 percent said they "like American ideas about democracy." These views, however, are not widely shared, even in Western Europe, another bastion of liberalism and democracy.[1]

The United States adopted a doctrine of unilateral military action against nations that are suspected of facilitating terrorist violence. This doctrine and the U.S. administration's tactics for dealing with global terrorism have not strengthened, but weakened existing global institutions. Even before the attack on the World Trade Center on September 11, 2001, the idea of a U.S. "empire" as a military power capable of confronting rogue nations had already gained attention in U.S. security circles. Some found this notion even more attractive when an organized terror assault did occur. Thinking in terms of "empire" and of U.S. military intervention gained appeal among part of the U.S. public, but certainly was the attitude of the Bush government. It buttressed the notion that the United States should intervene in those nation-states that were suspected of harboring terrorists, such as Afghanistan and Iraq.

A particularly worrisome development in the U.S. defense strategy is the increasing reliance on private military firms that provide "surrogate soldiers and private mercenaries."[2] Chalmers Johnson gives a detailed picture of this rapidly expanding "industry" of nonstate, private military violence in many parts of the world. It is a threat to any form of legitimate political globalization. The private military enterprises used by the United States are surrounded by secrecy and are increasingly vulnerable to the abuses invited by lack of accountability.[3]

The belief that raw military power should be the primary focus of American security policy came from the so-called neocons, or neoconservatives, in the Bush administration who were extremely impatient with the painfully slow progress made by multilateral networks in building global security and who totally opposed the creation of supranational institutions. These ideologues encouraged policies for war that created a serious political impasse between the United States and most of the world. The Bush administration's adoption of extreme secrecy in government and especially in security programs did not improve the global situation; this strategy remains at odds with the global trend toward transparency and has aroused widespread criticism. Melvyn Leffler contends that the Bush strategy to win the "war on terror" will fail because it pursues conflicting means and ends. "Strategy links means to ends, designing tactics capable of achieving goals.

Bush's foreign policy is vulnerable to criticism not because it departs radically from previous administrations, but because it cannot succeed. The goals are unachievable because the means and ends are out of sync."[4] Fareed Zakaria points out that part of the rise of anti-American sentiment is due to the enormous, hegemonic power of the United States. However, he also emphasizes,

> The wave of anti-Americanism is, of course, partly a product of the current Bush administration's policies and, as important, its style. Support for the United States has dropped dramatically since Bush rode into town. In 2000, for example, 75 percent of Indonesians identified themselves as pro-American. Today, more than 80 percent are hostile to Uncle Sam. When asked why they dislike the United States, people in other countries consistently cite Bush and his policies.[5]

In brief, U.S. leaders have not only failed to face the problems of global risks, but have increased their dangers and especially those of terrorism. It remains for the generation of the future to remedy this additional, man-made problem.

In the future, these global constellations of power will inevitably shift. The effects of educational globalization and economic development in certain large countries have opened economic and even political growth that even a few years ago was not thought to be possible. Large developing countries, especially China, India, and Brazil, will likely graduate large numbers of competent scientists, mathematicians, and engineers, expanding the professional expertise in these countries. Many professional tasks are even now "outsourced" to these countries from the West. Enormous economic growth, especially in China, gives certain developing countries considerable weight in world politics. Military advances are also taking place, and new power configurations will emerge in the world, with different positions for today's great powers, the United States, the European Union, and Japan.

The world faces truly daunting problems, although many world movements, global NGOs, some UN and government initiatives, civil society organizations, and activists hope to bring change. Transparency, obviously, is the key to awareness of the dangers that must soon be confronted.

Does Transparency Create the Open Society?

Although transparency contributes to openness, it is limited and many questions will arise in the future. Demands for transparency may succeed in one social domain, while lagging in others. Further, there are many different versions of the open society, even though they have certain traits in common. To be called an open society, a country has to meet certain minimal criteria. It must be an electoral democracy that protects freedom of information and expression, as well as civil liberties. It must subscribe to the UN charter on human rights. It must enforce the rule of law and guarantee domestic security. Many democracies meet these general criteria, ranging from egalitarian Sweden to the United States, with its steep inequalities, or from the grassroots democracy of Switzerland to the representative democracy in the EU parliament. However, none of these open societies is without flaws. To meet the policy demands of the global era, one needs to apply higher standards, to think about the "challenged open society." The higher standards for an open society demand that truthful information reaches the public in a clear, comprehensible format. It would demand the end of corruption in all its forms, including especially political corruption. It would demand that freedom of speech and civil rights be valued and vigorously defended. These standards would raise questions about how information from centers of power is presented to the public, and how the public is able to absorb the information that transparency yields. An uneducated public can hardly be expected to understand or evaluate technical information offered by the media. An uneducated public cannot constitute the citizenry of an open society.

A serious problem is that the media often are in the hands of ruling political powers and distribute propaganda rather than facts. In spite of transparency norms and rules, even educated publics may believe assertions that are clearly false. Understanding global realities is difficult for most people, and especially difficult for politicians who represent narrow constituencies and fight for their special interests. The concept of the illiberal democracy comes to mind.

To meet the enormous challenges posed by current global risks, extensive changes in daily routines of citizens will become necessary. Thinking in new ways is always difficult, and calls for transparency have encountered resistance and long delays before transparency rules are adopted. Demographic changes, military conflicts or terrorist activity, migrations, cultural clashes, drastic structural changes in the world economy, environmental threats, and health problems have brought much instability. We need an open society able to deal with uncertainty and capable of adaptive learning—an "experimenting society." When information is claimed to be true, it must be validated. Competent "brokers" such as academies of science, evaluators, and responsible media organizations are needed to create valid public learning. And even when the open society is a learning society, there may still be fatal mistakes. This is also true of emerging global networks and solidarities. These challenges pose a tall order for the idea of the open society, and we cannot readily think of any current society fully meeting it. Certainly, dictatorships, theocracies, and other authoritarian societies are likely to founder in the maelstrom of the global transformations of the future. They most likely will be havens of misery, conflicts, and threats to international and economic security.

Today, opacity still limits information on many frontiers, including the rich countries of North America, the European Union, and Japan. It is of much more harm to the poor countries and emerging new powers. Opacity rules in vast areas in spite of the growth of transparency. Yes, we live in the era of the information revolution, with the increasing spread of communications technology that has hugely expanded the flow of information. Yet there is still a stark absence of accessible vital information in many places, especially in poor countries. For example, in many countries there are no systems for registering ownership of land and buildings, no functioning systems for public health surveillance, and little disclosure of government projects because there is no effective information infrastructure. These conditions may change, but they exist in many areas ranging from the countryside of China to the many states of Central Asia, Africa, Latin America, and even some places in Europe and in North America.

Transparency is growing, but it is still surrounded by an ocean of opacity. Where there is such opacity, there is also likely to be corruption. This does not simply mean the appropriation of public goods for private gain; it is also a source of dangerous distortions in policy decisions. Corrupt governments undermine public policy and harm their citizens, in many cases catastrophically. Corruption in high places is a major source of a nation's poverty, as is the grossly unequal distribution of resources. Until recently, fighting corruption was made difficult by the protective walls of opacity and privilege. Inquisitive journalism was, at times, able to expose crimes of corruption. Now, demands for transparency can be systematically deployed to discourage corruption. Transparency International has made remarkable progress, yet much of the world is still harmed by corruption. The fact of growing transparency does show that it is a vanguard of the open society. It can open the eyes of citizens to the enormous damage done to them by a corrupt elite, but difficulties still lie ahead.

Constitutions, Laws, and Transparency

Transparency has been shown to be an effective tool against corruption. Dishonest public officials, insufficient vigilance, power concentrated in the hands of the wealthy elite, as well as lack of education, are serious handicaps. One approach is to examine the historical growth of democracies, which can provide important guidelines for improving social systems. Over several centuries, citizens of democratic nations have learned from each other the importance of constitutions and the rule of law. Basic provisions must guarantee civil rights, including freedom of expression, honest elections, and lawful governance. The rule of law means the exclusion of arbitrary and unpredictable exercise of power. Nevertheless, to meet coming challenges, social systems must be improved. An open society will have to be far more than a nominally electoral democracy.

Essential tools for achieving the open society are laws giving access to government information, protecting free speech, and limiting undue influence of special interests over the media. There has to be an incorruptible judiciary and a legal basis for the profession of the ombudsman. Each of these objectives is pursued by global civil society organizations such as Transparency International, the ACLU, Article 19, Freedom House, Amnesty International, and others. The conscientious monitoring of the state of freedom in the world is a powerful counterbalance to the forces resisting liberty.

Civil society must be a healthy and transparent component of all social systems if they are to function well. Transparency International has made strategic contributions to the integrity of democracies, relying on its accumulated knowledge and local activists, as well as governments and corporate enterprises. The *TI Sourcebook* builds upon the idea of a national integrity system that is designed to encourage constructive responsibility, not punitive confrontation. Corruption cannot be fought in an environment of secrecy and intrigues. The *Sourcebook* reflects a process of continuous learning on the basis of practical experience. The process involves step-by-step efforts to create social systems that build integrity into everyday culture. It has become an effective tool both in developing countries and in industrial states.

Education and Access to Valid Knowledge

The challenged open society will have to have decisions made by an informed citizenry. Right now, the electorates of large democracies find it difficult to learn about the decisions and policies they need to address, and

337

what their consequences are likely to be. In modern societies the utilization of knowledge constitutes an elaborate (and often opaque) system. Specialists learn a great deal about a narrow field, while the general public has less and less understanding of that knowledge. Few voters have a frame of reference for knowledge about global change.

Increasing transparency requires that the public be literate and capable of reasoning. Too often demands for transparency may be avoided because no one is able to verify the accuracy of a truth claim. Even the most developed countries share the problem. If the public does not read and is little acquainted with science and mathematics, then unscrupulous politicians, business leaders, and others will exploit that vacuum for their own purposes.

The challenged open society must provide access to knowledge that can be used. Gathering knowledge, understanding it, developing a frame of reference enable one to evaluate a particular piece of information and determine whether it is true or false. However, there are other elements in forming opinions. Some are not based on rationality but on faith. Faith—whether in religion or in ideology—can override even the best scientific findings. Here the ethics of transparency, accountability, and responsibility must play a role for the challenged open society.

In many domains—business, medicine, public health, law, and others—there is a new concern with ethics as a buttress for conduct. Ethical codes are designed to govern the actions of caregivers, researchers, investment brokers, financial advisors, and sales personnel. Ethicists have formed a profession of their own, and courses in ethical standards are offered to students in business schools, medical schools, and even to undergraduates. Like so many things that are connected with the transparency phenomenon, this is an entirely novel phenomenon. This could develop into a publicly shared moral framework, but it is not likely to succeed without a growth of global awareness.

The ethics of truth and the power of "truth tests" have been mentioned in the discussion of transparency in political and military treaties. The maxim "Trust, but verify," which President Ronald Reagan used regarding nuclear armaments in other nations, reflects the significance of the truth/trust nexus associated with transparency. But "Trust, but verify" has a much wider application in business, quality assessments, and evaluation studies in nearly all imaginable fields. We have spoken of brokers in the medium of influence by which nongovernmental organizations establish their credibility or its opposite.

The issue of legitimacy for governments, international agencies, and

NGOs hinges on the establishment of truth tests. This, of course, increasingly requires high levels of expertise in the establishment of trust at a distance in transnational transactions and communications. The ethic of truth tests is a matter of great importance for the challenged open society. People must be able to form judgments about frames of reference, ranging from the narrow perspective of an individual's special interests to the encompassing frames of the global public good. We in the United States do have think tanks, foundations that sponsor inquiries, investigative commissions, expert panels, and libraries full of books, but we have not solved the problem of carrying the needed insights into the reality of a democratic election campaign. Campaign financing, the force of special interests, the power of private loyalties and faiths, all may undermine the capacity of an electorate to determine the truth about issues of vital consequence. The ethics of truth tests, however, is beginning to make a real beginning in the emerging movement of codes of conduct. How will new frameworks of ethics become a live reality? It will take events to mobilize the public for such a shift in the moral framework. But there have been such events.

Sources of the Demand for Transparency

As we view the circumstances that accompanied breakthroughs in the advance of transparency, again and again the historical turning points are the result of colossal, shattering conflicts. It took the Civil War to end slavery and to complete the core of the U.S. Constitution. It brought a new wave of freedom of expression to the American public and a new reality in the world. The current wave of transparency may be traced to the devastation of the battlefields and the crimes of the twentieth century's world wars.

The moral outrage against the crimes of World War II called for drastic change. A new moral framework began to take shape. "Never again!" was then the cry. The experience of catastrophe became the motive to search for ways to make such wars impossible. It spawned many innovations of new and hopeful institutions and many movements for change. Since 1945 new measures have been adopted: the creation of the UN with its mission for peace, the Marshall Plan for reconstruction, the gradual growth of the EU, and NATO. The cold war became a new danger, and all these early efforts were given new limits, as nations sought security and self-defense. Calls for transparency began only slowly in the era that ended colonialism. Many new states built their political systems on a colonial heritage. Some still suffer from some of that legacy, but some, like India, made the transition to some form of democracy. Some, like South Africa, invented important strategies for historical transparency. Decolonization was one element in the rise of global transformations.

The cataclysm and genocide of World War II created a new moral framework articulated in the UN charter. It remains an aspiration, never fully realized, yet it has added to the energies for human rights and transparency. It was the colossal catastrophe of war that caused the turn to new moral aspirations beyond nationalism. Now we can only hope that no further social catastrophes of that scope are needed to promote transparency and the challenged open society.

The social movements of the second half of the twentieth century advanced the values of equity and fairness in the fight for civil rights in the United States. Martin Luther King's landmark "I have a dream" speech resonated across the nation and the world. The movements for women's rights and civil liberties grew in vigor and prominence. Opposition to the Vietnam War in the United States and Western Europe raised a whole generation of critics of power and authority. New conceptions of family structure and child rearing promoted the values of autonomy and antiauthoritarianism. Patients' rights and consumers' rights have become enshrined in most modern democracies, and supporters have formed active global networks and civil society organizations. All have adopted, in one way or another, a strategy of transparency to attain their goals.

Scandals have often triggered decisive changes in governments, professions, and business corporations. Examples abound: one is the rise of celebrity CEOs who have appropriated corporate property for themselves; other scandals involve outright criminal fraud. Legislation such as the Sarbanes-Oxley Act imposed drastic punishments for failings in transparency. However, while many U.S. corporations have adopted codes of conduct, some are pressed by their leaders to return to the old ways: they continue to fight for excessive compensation for executives and for keeping stock options off their earnings statements. Further, the political system is corrupted by money. Donations to a political party are often rewarded by advantages granted by politicians. Corporate interests are often satisfied by carefully tailored deregulation or special rules that result in outrageous legal maneuvers. Some reforms are emerging. The reform of accounting systems through the International Accounting Standards Board, for example, brings a new and higher standard to accounting worldwide. Nevertheless, there continue to be efforts to circumvent transparency requirements.

After the Nazis' medical crimes were uncovered by the war crimes tribunal, rules requiring informed consent and carefully defined research plans were created. These value changes also came to the United States, but legal change did not occur until the 1970s. In Germany, many leaders of the medical profession maintained an attitude of denial and some even kept their professional positions until the early 1990s. These lag times are of considerable importance for understanding the slow patterns of adopting transparency rules as components of reform. The resistance to change has several causes; obviously, one reason is the defense that elites put up to preserve their privileges.

Other, seemingly harmless, obstacles are commonly shared professional practices. New daily routines and ethical practices often take a generation to adopt. The lag time for the adoption of informed consent rules in medical research with human subjects is one such example. On the other hand, the legally enacted norms for patient privacy (the HIPAA law in the United States) were imposed with considerable speed. However, the problems of implementing these rules revealed another kind of resistance to change: the creation of mountains of paperwork required to assure enforcement. There are many ways to resist long-term reforms. There always is at least some conflict and resistance against transparency.

In many cases, resistance can take on the appearance of a social movement opposed to reform. Demands for not expensing stock options are actually defended with considerable fervor by corporations and their friends in Silicon Valley and elsewhere as essential to capitalism itself. "Expensing" here means listing the actual value of the stock options to the investors and shareholders in financial statements, not just in footnotes. In fact, the cost to shareholders of giving stock options to CEOs can be enormous and can reduce corporate earnings by millions. The energy source in this movement is the defense of appropriations for private privilege.

The opposition to historical transparency can be even more passionate and filled with fear and hatred. The defense of silent taboos in Japan has created a whole literature creating a heroic image of Japan's role in World War II. Silent taboos protected some former Nazi party officials in the early postwar period. The defense of silence can be passionate as well. Indeed, patriotism can be the most vigorous source of resistance to historical transparency. Invariably, it also contains a strong element of self-interest, protection of privilege, and defense of a questionable identity claim.

However, there are many purely pragmatic reasons why governments, corporations, and professions adopt voluntary transparency programs. Ann Florini regards them as the special hallmark of transparency.[6] But transparency cannot be achieved merely by voluntary action; it must also be enforced by law, by investigations, by enforced codes of conduct in professional and corporate associations, and by the pressure of social movements. But there is a voluntary element in energizing transparency as well. It is often a matter of common sense adapted to the information needs of global transformations. The pragmatic approach to presenting transparency programs focuses on two things: first, establishing trust (for example, in the quality of products, services, and policies) among the public and across great distances; second, building and enhancing legitimacy (of a government, of the World Bank, of a global NGO). Advertising well-documented "truth tests" can establish the credibility of commercial products, procedures, codes of conduct, and benefits to the public, to buyers, to clients, and to patients.

Pragmatic considerations play a major role in the adoption of transparency in global transactions and networks. This is where transparency becomes a matter of everyday routine and common sense, in many cases aided by legal requirements, by codes of conduct, by competitively evaluated truth claims and assessments. Agencies with little or no direct power or authority still have influence. Civil society organizations and global NGOs operate in the medium of exchange called influence that generates its own trends toward long-term structures, operating in what we called competitive quasi-markets. The work of global NGOs in quasi-markets establishes their credibility and thereby their effectiveness, validating knowledge for the challenged open society.

Freedom of Information Past and Present

The idea of information freedom as an essential condition of democracy—in Lincoln's terms "government of the people, by the people, for the people"—arose in the Enlightenment. The vanguard of this movement started in Sweden and, later in the eighteenth century, in the newly created United States. Clearly, the idea of transparency, a product of Western civilization, has now reached much further into countries with very different cultural roots. It is remarkable how many countries in Latin America and in Asia have espoused democratic constitutions, with considerable struggle, and how widespread today is the specific movement for transparency, including South Africa. There are however still dictatorships and corrupt theocracies.

The city-states of Singapore and Hong Kong were poor and developing even after World War II and into the 1960s, but transparency in the business sector has blossomed. It was a movement to end corrupt relations between business and government. Today, both Singapore and Hong Kong are proud of their record of transparency in the business world and in public health. Hong Kong's efforts to become an open society included bringing historical transparency to knowledge of the past. In 2004 the Hong Kong Education Policy Concern Organization introduced new textbooks of Chinese and world history that include the 1989 Tiananmen Square demonstration in Beijing and its violent repression by the Chinese military. This is certainly an important step, given the Chinese government's reluctance even to discuss this historic event. The case of Singapore also illustrates that transparency is not necessarily accompanied by democracy.

Transparency International has helped vigorous movements for fighting corruption in countries in Latin America, Central Europe, Africa, and in parts of Asia. In India the grassroots movement of Mazdoor Kisan Shakti Sangathan was founded in 1991 and has become both a local and national force in its fight against corruption and for democracy. It has made political inroads that just a few years ago would not have been thought possible. Other movements of this kind are mobilizing in other developing countries.

This rise of transparency in developing countries may be attributed to economic globalization and the premium placed on transparency in economic transactions. Surely, both Hong Kong and Singapore are now modern, world-open business centers where the force of economic transparency is powerful. Second, grassroots domestic movements in many developing countries are awakening to the rights of citizens and to the need to limit government powers. The dictatorial military regimes in Latin America were bitterly resented and resisted by such movements. A third force is the redefinition of the sovereignty of governments in order to limit their immunity from crimes. Since the early 1990s Transparency International and other global NGOs have struggled against the notion that corruption may be protected by a nation's sovereignty. Today there is a worldwide consensus among international agencies—the World Bank, the OECD, and other powerful agencies in the global arena—that corruption must be curbed. Intervention in corruption of governments by international groups has become quite frequent.

The idea of information freedom thus has gained a foothold in civilizations other than those of the West. It is a worldwide trend, and much of it is based on very practical and common-sense necessity in the gradual move toward global governance. The sources of energy that press for more transparency are real and moving forward.

Global Transformations and Transparency

Many governments and organizations are attempting to create some mechanisms for global problem solving. We have proposed that there are ten dimensions of globalization that are causes for concern. Each has a strong link to transparency, or access to information.

One of these issues is the problem of subsidies to agriculture by the rich economies. The developing countries are disadvantaged by these policies, since they undermine the functioning of their own agriculture. The role for transparency in this debate is to document the actual facts of the consequences of these subsidies in contributing to global inequality. Global civil society organizations have played that role in addition to the diplomatic efforts of governments and global institutions. In this case, the World Bank became active in this matter, as did the World Trade Organization, in cooperation with an influential coalition of nongovernmental organizations that includes Greenpeace, Oxfam, and Friends of the Earth. There is a gradual change toward reducing the imbalance. NGOs engaging in documentation and lobbying helped decisively. The debate and efforts at resolution continue in the WTO as the practical forum.

There are similar worrisome issues in other dimensions of globalization, such as calls for reform in the structure of the United Nations and questions about the legitimacy of major supranational authorities (as in the recent treaty negotiations for the EU constitution), that require careful attention to transparency. All of these reform efforts are extremely complex. The creation of the EU constitution treaty is still in flux and treads on entirely new terrain. Reforming the UN to improve its capacities for action will also cover new terrain. Obviously, movements for reform are mobilized and hard at work, but national states very often go slowly with proposals for reform. Innovations at the supranational level obviously need to be linked to innovations in the single nations as well.

The quest for historical transparency has been extended worldwide. The tensions between China and Japan illustrate a transnational debate about how to view the past. Historical transparency can be an incentive for movements toward the challenged open society.

Today there is still no formal structure for effective global problem solving. Surely, the UN system could provide such governance, but it is strongly in need of structural reform. However, changes can be achieved by those who use the medium of influence to building transnational solidarities. These are efforts to move toward global solutions, even if there is little progress in controlling the global trade in weapons or terrorism. Yet there is now a process in motion in which transparency is increasingly demanded, despite barriers.

Transparency Infrastructures and Their Politics

Strategies for reform through transparency require infrastructures of information. Building these infrastructures can be a serious problem for poor countries—important information may simply not be recorded or unavailable. Information infrastructures in rich countries, on the other hand, have a long history, but they too may have significant shortcomings and flaws. Corporate accounting procedures have been much influenced by the single indicator of corporate performance in the "number," the quarterly earnings reports, which became an instrument of manipulation for less scrupulous corporate leaders. The fight over many other indicators in the business world burdens the reform efforts of the International Accounting Standards Board. The diversity of measurements in different countries makes it difficult to assess comparative performances in many areas such as health care, academic degrees, and environmental conditions.

The problem of comparability cannot be taken lightly by those evaluating different policies or assessing facts in different countries. Managing information infrastructures requires crews of professional experts, as do law, accounting, evaluation research, and other areas of expertise. The fact that China has joined the WTO, for example, means that it will have to create the professional infrastructure for economic performance and planning, as well as for reporting requirements. It is a massive undertaking that, in turn, will promote the significance of what we call educational globalization.

Information infrastructures can be extremely vulnerable. The information systems for an election have been sometimes rigged for political advantages. Similarly, business information systems can be influenced to show economic growth when the opposite is true. Even universities may measure the performance of faculty in ways that make them look more productive than they are. The list is almost endless. There are interprofessional wars that can mobilize national governments and transnational agencies to settle conflicts around information systems.

The Formalization of Transparency in Accounting and Law

In many different domains, like economic information infrastructures or health records, transparency requires standardized information and prescriptions for formalization. Because the Sarbanes-Oxley Act in the United

States requires very specific ways of reporting corporate data, there rapidly emerged a whole army of accountants and lawyers needed to help clients negotiate the new formal procedures. Accountants and lawyers often confront conflicts of interest, as in cases where the external professional becomes not only an advisor, but also a consultant who implements business strategies. Similar problems can arise in the health professions between physicians and pharmaceutical firms. The demand for transparency is a demand for accountability, in part a source of identifying ethical problems. This leads to far-reaching codes of conduct. There is a rapidly spreading movement to formalize rules of conduct and responsibility in business transactions as well as in governments and professions. However, formalization may also have a restraining effect on patterns of communication and work. Thus, this emerging formalization goes far beyond the important role assigned to formal contracts in the era of the industrial revolution. It is a blueprint for many activities that hitherto were left to individual discretion.

The Global Learning Process of Communicative Rationality

To repeat, transparency has become a social fact, but it faces many threats. It also has much quirky vulnerability as in the special problems of information infrastructures, the uncertain context of attempts to create global solutions to problems, the strengths and limitations of social movements, and the constraints of formalization. Poor countries do not have solid information infrastructures. Opacity is still a fact in many places.

Beyond these shortcomings, threats to transparency come from active enemies of the open society. In the "roaring 1990s," transparency and freedom of information laws made enormous progress, especially in the global business world, in spite of and even because of business scandals. But the beginning of the new millennium saw real threats to these values. Terrorism created an atmosphere of fear. Militarism and nationalism became America's answer to the danger. Religious fervor, which has often fueled fanatical conflicts over the centuries, has reappeared among violent Islamic extremists. Religious divisions have also arisen in the West. The fear of terror creates a search for refuge in national security. Geographical boundaries are tightened, suspicions are spread, and military forces are deployed. Policy making is shrouded in secrecy. Trust in the future is based on the hope of military victory. Most likely it will not happen that way.

The world faces very real threats, and the open society has enemies. These threats will not be overcome by authoritarian politicians acting in secret, nor by cults of faith. Authoritarianism and withholding knowledge inevitably lead to failure. The global challenges of our time will be overcome by deliberation and insight into reality. What is needed is communicative rationality, the ability to think clearly, to assess facts and to persuade societies to solve their problems. Communicative rationality depends on transparency, the free flow of information. It is the basis for the learning process in today's world. Communicative rationality has built on transparency in the many historical turning points toward openness we have encountered. The achievements of transparency have often required long periods of struggle. Establishing historical truth is one of the most powerful forces in global change. In many cases the demands for transparency about the past broke through taboos and secrets held by governments for decades. Many countries still have not experienced the force of historical transparency. Painful recognition of the evils of the past will likely catch up with them in time. This is part of a slow learning process.

People are capable of improving their social systems. For that, they need open flows of information. They can make attempts to establish better moral frameworks, to assess the validity of information, and to set up codes of ethics. Questions will have to be raised about the many different kinds of social system change. Such questioning accelerates the process of improving the openness of societies. There are sources of strength in the supporters of transparency—we have encountered many of them. There are also multiple rewards for transparency in all the domains of professions, business and government that we have examined. The benefits of transparency are large and powerful, but no one can assume that success is assured. People can still make wrong decisions that can lead to catastrophe. History has a sad record of such failures, usually based on ignorance. The absence of transparency is likely one source of failure. And ignorance and authoritarianism are the greatest threats to our future. But through learning, education, and the rational pursuit of the most good for the most people, transparency may yet be a prevailing value.

NOTES

1. The Culture Shift to Transparency

1. Karl R. Popper, *The Open Society and Its Enemies* (Princeton, N.J.: Princeton University Press, 1950), 463.

2. Ibid., 379.

3. Robert Kagan and William Kristol, eds., *Present Dangers: Crisis and Opportunity in American Foreign and Defense Policy* (San Francisco: Encounter Books, 2000), 3–4.

4. Ibid., 3–5.

5. Chalmers Johnson, *Blowback: The Costs and Consequences of American Empire* (New York: Henry Holt, 2004), ix.

6. Chalmers Johnson, *The Sorrows of Empire: Militarism, Secrecy, and the End of the Republic* (New York: Henry Holt, 2004), 311–12.

7. Ibid., 312.

8. Max Weber, *Economy and Society: An Outline of Interpretive Sociology,* ed. Guenther Roth and Claus Wittich (New York: Bedminster Press, 1968), 3:992.

9. Burkart Holzner, *Reality Construction in Society* (Cambridge, Mass.: Schenkman, 1968), ix.

10. See Daniel A. Bell, David Brown, Kanishka Jayasurita, and David Martin Jones, *Towards Illiberal Democracy in Pacific Asia* (New York: St. Martin's, 1995).

2. The Rise of Transparency

1. Max Weber, *Economy and Society,* 3 vols., ed. G. Roth and C. Wittich (Totowa, N.J.: Rowman and Littlefield, 1968), 3:1212f.

2. Ibid., 3:1239.

3. Ibid., 3:1322–39.

4. Benjamin Nelson, *On the Roads to Modernity: Conscience, Science, and Civilizations: Selected Writings by Benjamin Nelson,* ed. Toby E. Huff (Totowa, N.J.: Rowman and Littlefield, 1981), 178.

5. Ibid., 179.

349

6. Ibid., 179–83.

7. Ibid., 179.

8. Ibid., 183.

9. David Brin, *The Transparent Society: Will Technology Force Us to Choose Between Privacy and Freedom?* (Reading, Mass.: Perseus, 1998), 40.

10. R. R. Palmer and Joel Colton, *A History of the Modern World* (New York: Alfred A. Knopf, 1965), 131.

11. Robert K. Merton, "The Puritan Spur to Science," in *The Sociology of Science: Theoretical and Empirical Investigations,* ed. Norman W. Storer (Chicago: University of Chicago Press, 1973), 228; see also Robert K. Merton, *Science, Technology, and Society in Seventeenth-Century England* (Bruges: Saint Catherine Press, 1938).

12. Merton, "The Puritan Spur to Science," 252–53.

13. H. Floris Cohen, *The Scientific Revolution: A Historicographical Inquiry* (Chicago: University of Chicago Press, 1994), 510f.

14. Ibid., 516.

15. Donald T. Campbell, *Methodology and Epistemology for Social Science: Selected Papers,* ed. Samuel Overman (Chicago: University of Chicago Press, 1988).

16. Burkart Holzner, "Cultural Dimensions of the Experimenting Society," in *The Experimenting Society, Essays in Honor of Donald T. Campbell,* ed. William N. Dunn (New Brunswick, N.J.: Transaction Publishers, 1998), 171–88.

17. John Markoff, *The Great Wave of Democracy in Historical Perspective* (Ithaca, N.Y.: Cornell Studies in International Affairs, 1995), 3.

18. See Garry Wills, *A Necessary Evil: A History of American Distrust of Government* (New York: Simon and Schuster, 1999), 104ff.

19. See Leonard W. Levy, *Origins of the Bill of Rights* (New Haven: Yale University Press, 1999).

20. Garry Wills, *"Negro President": Jefferson and the Slave Power* (New York: Houghton Mifflin, 2003), 2.

21. Ibid., 5. The "gag rule" was the effort of representatives of the southern states to prevent petitions against slavery from being even introduced or at least from being discussed in Congress in any way. Some of them actually labeled such petitions as treason. The Kansas-Nebraska Act of 1854 was a compromise that gave the southern states an advantage. It determined that the issue of slavery should be decided by the settlers themselves. The resulting tensions were a prelude to the Civil War.

22. See Wills, *A Necessary Evil,* 104ff.

23. Ibid., 105.

24. Ibid., 23.

25. Talcott Parsons, *The Social System* (Glencoe, Ill.: Free Press, 1951), 58ff.

26. John Markoff, *The Abolition of Feudalism* (University Park: Pennsylvania State University Press, 1996), 427.

27. Palmer and Colton, *A History of the Modern World,* 343ff.

28. John Markoff notes that the French Revolution created a major change in gov-

ernment information capacities: the modern archive. See "Archival Methods," in *International Encyclopedia of the Social and Behavioral Sciences,* ed. Neil J. Smelser and Paul B. Baltes (Amsterdam: Pergamon, 2001).

29. Markoff, *The Abolition of Feudalism;* and private communications.

30. John Markoff, *Waves of Democracy* (Thousand Oaks, Calif.: Russell Sage, 1996), 3-4.

31. Robert K. Merton, *Sociological Ambivalence and Other Essays* (New York: Free Press, 1976), 157.

32. For information about Sweden, we are indebted to a personal communication from Michael F. Metcalf. See *The Riksdag: A History of the Swedish Parliament,* ed. Michael F. Metcalf (New York: St. Martin's Press), 1987. We are also grateful to Andrew Becker for his seminar paper, "Groundbreaking Legislation in Sweden: The 1766 Freedom of the Press Act and the 1809 Constitutional establishment of the Ombudsman Office."

33. Becker, "Groundbreaking Legislation in Sweden."

34. Peter N. Stearns, ed., *The Encyclopedia of World History,* 6th ed. (New York: Houghton Mifflin, 2001), 340-41.

35. Ruth R. Faden and Tom L. Beauchamp, with Nancy M. P. King, *A History and Theory of Informed Consent* (New York: Oxford University Press, 1986), 154.

36. Karl R. Popper, *The Open Society and Its Enemies* (Princeton: Princeton University Press, 1950), 5.

37. See Nicholas Rescher, *The Limits of Science* (Pittsburgh: University of Pittsburgh Press, 1999); and Robert Wright, *Non Zero: The Logic of Human Destiny* (New York: Pantheon Books, 2000).

38. See Daniel Patrick Moynihan, *Secrecy: The American Experience* (New Haven: Yale University Press, 1998).

39. Markoff, *Waves of Democracy,* 3-4.

40. "Article 19" is a London-based NGO advocating freedom of expression, based on the UN Charter on Universal Rights, article 19. Information derived from Article 19 publications are from its Web site, www.article19.org. We visited Andrew Puddephat, its executive director, in July 2002. Ken Bhattachargee and Toby Mendel, "Global Trends on the Right to Information: Survey of South Asia," is based on a project supported by Article 19, the Global Campaign for Free Expression, London; Centre for Policy Alternatives, Colombo; Commonwealth Human Rights Initiative, New Delhi; Human Rights Commission of Pakistan, Lahore, and distributed by the Article 19 Web site.

41. UN Charter on Universal Rights, article 19.

42. Interview with Heinrich Schneider, Munich, 2002.

43. Daniel A. Bell, David Brown, Kanishka Jayasuriya, and David Martin Jones, *Toward Illiberal Democracy in Pacific Asia* (New York: St. Martin's Press, 1995).

44. Freedom House, *Freedom in the World 2000-2001,* "Survey Methodology," www.freedomhouse.org/research/freeworld/2001.

45. Bell et al., *Toward Illiberal Democracy in Pacific Asia,* 8.

46. Fareed Zakaria, *The Future of Freedom: Illiberal Democracy at Home and Abroad* (New York: Norton, 2003), 159.

47. Data about the adoption of laws on access to government-held information are found in Bhattachargee and Mendel, "Global Trends on the Right to Information"; see also David Banisar, "Global Trends on the Right to Information," www.freedominfo .org. See also www.privacyinternational.org/issues/foia.

48. Charles L. Davis and Sigmund L. Splichal, eds., *Access Denied: Freedom of Information in the Information Age* (Ames: Iowa State University Press, 2000); Daniel Patrick Moynihan, *Secrecy: The American Experience* (New Haven: Yale University Press, 1998).

49. "Promoting Open Government: Commonwealth Principles and Guidelines on the Right to Know," Commonwealth Expert Group Meeting on the Right to Know and the Promotion of Democracy and Development, March 1999, distributed by Article 19.

50. Ken Bhattachargee and Toby Mendel, *Global Trends on the Right to Information: A Survey of South Asia, 2001,* www.article19.org.

51. Germany has a Parliamentary Committee that has taken the role of a freedom of information agency. Transparency International is proposing a more comprehensive law, to be discussed later.

52. David Banisar, "Freedom of Information and Access to Government Record Laws Around the World 2003," www.freedomofinformation.org; see also the Privacy International Web site, www.privacyinternational.org/issues/foia, an annual publication.

53. See the Web site of the International Ombudsman Institute at the University of Alberta, Canada: www.law.alberta.ca/centre/ioi.

54. Telephone interview with Sir Brian Elwood, October 11, 2002.

55. Paul Felix Lazarsfeld and Jeffrey G. Reitz, *An Introduction to Applied Social Research* (New York: Elsevier, 1975).

56. Edward Allen Suchman, *Evaluative Research: Principles and Practice in Public Service and Social Action Programs* (Thousand Oaks, Calif.: Russell Sage, 1967).

57. Eleanor Chelimsky and William R. Shadish, eds., *Evaluation for the 21st Century: A Handbook* (Thousand Oaks, Calif.: Russell Sage, 1997).

58. Catherine A. Callow-Heusser, *Digital Resources for Evaluators,* www. resources4evaluators .info/OrganizationsAssociationsFoundatiionsAgencies.htm.

3. Perspectives on Transparency

1. See Roland Robertson, *Globalization: Social Theory and Global Culture* (London: Newbury Park, 1992).

2. Martin Albrow, *The Global Age: State and Society beyond Modernity* (Stanford, Calif.: Stanford University Press, 1997). See also Jared Diamond, *Guns, Germs and Steel* (New York: Norton, 1997; Robert P. Clark, *Global Life Systems: Population, Food and Disease in the Process of Globalization* (Blue Ridge Summit, Pa.: Rowman and Littlefield,

2001); William H. McNeil, *Plagues and Peoples* (Garden City, N.Y.: Doubleday, 1998); Robert Wright, *Non Zero: The Logic of Human Destiny* (New York: Pantheon, 2000).

3. David Held, Anthony McGrew, David Goldblatt, Jonathan Perraton, *Global Transformations: Politics, Economics, and Culture* (Stanford, Calif.: Stanford University Press, 1999), 7.

4. Ibid., 444.

5. See, for example, Hedley Bull and Adam Watson, eds., *The Expansion of Global Society* (Oxford: Clarendon Press, 1984); Thomas L. Friedman, *The Lexus and the Olive Tree: Understanding Globalization* (New York: Farrar, Straus, Giroux, 1999); John Micklethwait and Adrian Wooldridge, *A Future Perfect: The Essentials of Globalization* (New York: Crown Publishers, 2000); but see Michael Hardt and Antonio Negri, *Empire* (Cambridge: Harvard University Press, 2000).

6. See Ann M. Florini, ed., *The Third Force: The Rise of Transnational Civil Society* (Washington, D.C.: Carnegie Endowment for International Peace, 2000).

7. World Bank, *World Development Report 2000/2001* (New York: Oxford University Press, 2001), 3.

8. Dieter Senghaas, "Die Konstitution der Welt—Eine Analyse in Friedenspolitischer Absicht," *Leviathan* 31 (2003): 117–52.

9. Joseph Stiglitz, *Globalization and Its Discontents* (New York: Norton, 2002), 195ff.

10. Held et al., *Global Transformations*, 235.

11. Ibid., 282.

12. Friedman, *The Lexus and the Olive Tree*, 93ff.

13. See Stiglitz, *Globalization and Its Discontents*.

14. See David C. Korten, *When Corporations Rule the World* (Bloomfield, Conn.: Kumarian Press and Berrett-Koehler Publishers, 1995).

15. See Bernard I. Finel and Kristin M. Lord, eds., *Power and Conflict in the Age of Transparency* (New York: Palgrave, 2000).

16. Robertson, *Globalization;* James N. Rosenau, "Diplomacy, Proof and Authority in the Information Age," in *Power and Conflict*, ed. Finel and Lord, 315–17.

17. Heinrich Schneider, in a personal communication, clarifies "quasi-market" as a field of interactions in which demand and supply meet each other, but without commercial or monetary characteristics (which are the core of "genuine markets").

18. See Stephen D. Krasner, *International Regimes* (Ithaca, N.Y.: Cornell University Press, 1983).

19. Held et al., *Global Transformations*, 65.

20. Stiglitz, *Globalization and Its Discontents*.

21. See International Monetary Fund, Independent Evaluation Office, IEO of the IMF, Oct. 19, 2001, www.imf.org/external/np/ieo/tra.htm.

22. Held et al., *Global Transformations*, 87–148.

23. Stefan Mair, "The New World of Privatized Violence," *Internationale Politik und Gesellschaft*, ed. Friedrich Ebert Stiftung (2003): 11–28.

24. John C. Baker and Ray A. Williams, "The Implications of Emerging Satellite

Information Technologies for Global Transparency and International Security," in *Power and Conflict,* ed. Finel and Lord, 221–55.

25. Michael Mandelbaum, *The Ideas That Conquered the World: Peace, Democracy, and Free Markets in the Twenty-first Century* (Reading, Mass.: Perseus, 2002), 108–9.

26. Ibid., 108.

27. John W. Meyer, David H. Kamens, Aaron Benavot, with Yun-Kyung Cha and Suk-Ying Wong, *School Knowledge for the Masses: World Models and National Primary Curricular Categories in the Twentieth Century* (Washington, D.C.: Falmer Press, 1992).

28. Alexandra Kaniasty, "The European Higher Education Area: Convergence Through Increased Transparency," presented at the annual meeting of the AIEA, 2003.

29. World Bank, *Constructing Knowledge Societies: New Challenges for Tertiary Education* (Washington, D.C.: World Bank, 2002).

30. Ann Florini, "The End of Secrecy," in *Power and Conflict,* ed. Finel and Lord, 13.

31. Ann Florini, *The Coming Democracy: New Rules for Running a New World* (Washington, D.C.: Island Press, 2003), 15.

32. Ibid., 59.

33. Ibid., 168.

34. Ibid., 209.

35. Finel and Lord, eds., *Power and Conflict,* 3.

36. James N. Rosenau, "Diplomacy, Proof, and Authority in the Information Age," in ibid., 330.

37. Finel and Lord, eds., *Power and Conflict,* 359–60.

38. Thomas Blanton, "The World's Right to Know," *Foreign Policy,* July–Aug. 2002, 50ff. The following paragraphs are taken from this source.

39. David Brin, *The Transparent Society* (Reading, Mass.: Perseus, 1998), ii.

40. Ibid., 321.

41. Ibid., 301.

42. Ibid., 334.

43. "The World's 20 Most Global Nations: The Fourth Annual Globalization Index," *Foreign Policy,* Mar.–Apr. 2004.

44. "Measuring Globalization: Economic Reversals, Forward Momentum," *Foreign Policy,* Mar.–Apr. 2004, 55–69.

45. Ibid., 59.

46. Transparency International, "1993–2003: Ten Years Fighting Corruption," Annual Report 2003, 20. The CPI index for 2003 lists 133 countries. "Seven out of ten countries score less than 5 out of a clean score of 10 . . . while five out of ten developing countries score less than 3 out of 10. But it is not only in poor countries where corruption thrives: levels of corruption are worryingly high in European countries such as Greece and Italy, and in oil-rich countries such as Nigeria, Angola, Azerbaijan, Kazakhstan, Libya, Venezuela, and Iraq."

47. Ibid., 57.

48. Ibid., 20–21.

49. Ibid.

50. "Measuring Globalization."

51. *Transparency International Global Corruption Report 2004,* 20–21.

52. Robin Hodess, "Where Did the Money Go?" *Transparency International Global Corruption Report 2004,* 13.

53. Emile Durkheim, *The Rules of the Sociological Method* (New York: Free Press, 1966), 13.

54. Ferdinand Toennies, *Gemeinschaft und Gesellschaft, Grundbegriffe der reinen Soziologie, vierte und fünfte Auflage* (Berlin: Verlag Karl Curtius, 1922), 201.

55. Patrick Doreian and Thomas Fararo, eds., *The Problem of Solidarity: Theories and Models* (Reading, Berkshire: Gordon and Breach, 1998), vii and passim.

56. Works by Emile Durkheim include *The Division of Labor in Society* (New York: Free Press, 1947); *The Rules of Sociological Method* (New York: Free Press, 1938); *Suicide: A Study in Sociology* (New York: Free Press, 1951); *The Elementary Forms of the Religious Life* (New York: Free Press, 1947).

57. Auguste Comte, *The Positive Philosophy of Auguste Comte,* ed. Harriet Martineau (London: George Bell, 1896).

58. Georg Simmel, "The Lie," in *The Sociology of Georg Simmel,* trans. Kurt H. Wolff (New York: Free Press, 1950).

59. A. Javier Trevino, ed., *Talcott Parsons Today: His History and Legacy in Contemporary Sociology* (New York: Rowman and Littlefield, 2001).

60. Uta Gerhardt, "Parsons's Analysis of the Societal Community," in ibid., 177–222.

61. Neil Smelser, foreword to ibid., xii–xiii.

4. Information Cultures in Transition

1. See "International Studies in Human Rights," in *Secrecy and Liberty: National Security, Freedom of Expression and Access to Information,* ed. Sandra Coliver, Paul Hoffman, Joan Fitzpatrick, and Stephen Bowen (The Hague: Martinus Nijhoff, 1999).

2. See Burkart Holzner, William N. Dunn, and Muhammad Shahidullah, "An Accounting Scheme for Designing Science Impact Indicators: The Knowledge System Perspective," *Knowledge: Creation-Diffusion-Utilization* 9 (Dec. 1987), 173–204; and Burkart Holzner and John Marx, *Knowledge Application: The Knowledge System in Society* (Boston: Allyn and Bacon, 1979).

3. In *The Sociology of Georg Simmel,* ed. and trans. Kurt H. Wolff (New York: Free Press, 1950), 330, emphasis added.

4. Ibid., 331.

5. Ibid., 15.

6. Ibid., 16.

7. Clark R. Mollenhoff, *Washington Cover-up* (Garden City, N.Y.: Doubleday, 1962), 21–23.

8. Mark J. Rozell, *Executive Privilege: The Dilemma of Secrecy and Democratic Accountability* (Baltimore: Johns Hopkins University Press, 1994), xi–xii.

9. Richard Gid Powers, *Secrecy and Power: The Life of J. Edgar Hoover* (New York: Free Press, 1987), 1–2.

10. Ibid., 2.

11. Ibid., 3–4.

12. Ibid., 492.

13. David Weir, foreword to Angus Mackenzie, *Secrets: The CIA's War at Home* (Berkeley and Los Angeles: University of California Press, 1997), xiii.

14. Daniel Patrick Moynihan, *Secrecy: The American Experience* (New Haven: Yale University Press, 1998).

15. Mackenzie, *Secrets: The CIA's War at Home,* 201–2.

16. *Secrecy: Report of the Commission on Protecting and Reducing Government Secrecy* (Washington, D.C.: GPO, 1997), xxi.

17. Daniel Patrick Moynihan, "The Science of Secrecy," presented at the Massachusetts Institute of Technology, March 29, 1999, www.aaas.org/sppp/secrecy/Presents/Moynihan.htm.

18. Joseph Stiglitz, Amnesty International Lecture, presented at Oxford University, January 1999, in *Globalizing Rights: 1999 Oxford Amnesty Lectures,* ed. Matthew Gibney (New York: Oxford University Press).

19. Lionel Cliffe, Maureen Ramsay, and Dave Barnett, *The Politics of Lying: Implications for Democracy* (New York: Macmillan, 2000), 207.

20. Elizabeth Evatt, "The International Covenant on Civil and Political Rights: Freedom of Expression and State Security," in *Secrecy and Liberty,* ed. Coliver et al., 83.

21. Robert K. Merton, *Sociological Ambivalence and Other Essays* (New York: Free Press, 1976), 6.

22. See Reg Whitaker, *The End of Privacy: How Total Surveillance Is Becoming a Reality* (New York: Free Press, 1999).

23. Erwin K. Scheuch, "Societies, Corporations, and the Nation State," *Annals of the International Institute of Sociology,* n.s. 7 (2000): 1–23.

24. Ronald A. Brand, "Comment on Chapter 2," in *Welfare States in Transition: East and West,* ed. Irwin Collier, Herwig Roggemann, Oliver Scholz, and Horst Tomann (New York: Macmillan, 1999), 41–49.

25. Interview with Nikiforos Diamandouros, Strasbourg, 2003.

26. Interview with Nikiforos Diamandouros, Athens, 2001.

27. See Burkart Holzner, *Reality Construction in Society* (Cambridge, Mass.: Schenkman, 1968); and Burkart Holzner and John Marx, *The Knowledge System in Society* (Boston: Allyn and Bacon, 1979).

28. See Nicholas Rescher, *Communicative Pragmatism and Other Philosophical Essays on Language* (Lanham, Md.: Rowman and Littlefield, 1998), 3–48.

29. Ibid., 3–4.

30. Ibid., 6–8.

31. Jürgen Habermas, *Between Facts and Norms: Contributions to a Discourse Theory of Law and Democracy,* trans. William Rehg (Cambridge, Mass.: MIT Press, 1996), 299.

32. Ibid.

33. Donald T. Campbell, "The Experimenting Society," in *Methodology and Epistemology for Social Science: Selected Papers,* ed. E. Samuel Overman (Chicago: University of Chicago Press, 1988), 290-314.

34. Eleanor Chelimsky and William R. Shadish, eds., *Evaluation for the Twenty-first Century, A Handbook* (Thousand Oaks, Calif.: Sage Publications, 1997).

35. Ibid., xiii.

36. "A Survey of the Internet Society," *Economist,* Jan. 25-31, 2003, 52ff.

37. David Brin, *The Transparent Society: Will Technology Force Us to Choose Between Privacy and Freedom?* (Reading, Mass.: Perseus, 1998).

38. See Ann Florini, *The End of Secrecy* (Washington, D.C.: Carnegie Endowment for International Peace, 2000); and Yahya A. Dehqansada and Ann Florini, *Secrets for Sale: How Commercial Satellite Imagery Will Change the World* (Washington, D.C.: Carnegie Endowment for International Peace, 2000).

39. Max Weber, *Economy and Society: An Outline of Interpretive Sociology,* ed. Guenther Roth and Claus Wittich (New York: Bedminster Press, 1968), 956-1005; cf. Arthur L. Stinchcomb, *Information and Organizations* (Berkeley and Los Angeles: University of California Press, 1990).

40. See, for example, Paul S. Appelbaum, Charles W. Lidz, and Alan Meisel, *Informed Consent: Legal Theory and Clinical Practice* (New York: Oxford University Press, 1987).

41. Ulrich Beck, *World Risk Society* (Cambridge: Polity Press, 1999).

5. Transparency in the World

1. See World Bank, *World Development Report 2000/2001;* and *Constructing Knowledge Societies: A World Bank Report* (Washington, D.C.: World Bank, 2000).

2. See Helmut Anheier, Marlies Glasius, Mary Kaldor, eds., *Global Civil Society, 2001* (New York: Oxford University Press, 2001); *Global Civil Society, 2002,* ed. Anheier et al. (New York: Oxford University Press, 2002).

3. See Albert Fried, *McCarthyism: The Great American Red Scare: A Documentary History* (New York: Oxford University Press, 1997).

4. Freedom House, *Freedom in the World: The Annual Survey of Political Rights and Civil Liberties 2001-2002,* ed. Adrian Karatnycky et al. (New Brunswick, N.J.: Transaction Publishers, 2002).

5. Pew Research Center for the People and the Press, "The 2004 Political Landscape; Evenly Divided and Increasingly Polarized," Nov. 5, 2003, www.people-press .org/reports.

6. Bernard Bailyn, *To Begin the World Anew: The Genius and Ambiguities of the American Founders* (New York: Alfred A. Knopf, 2003).

7. See Michael Mandelbaum, *The Ideas That Conquered the World: Peace, Democracy, and Free Markets in the Twenty-first Century* (New York: Public Affairs, 2002).

8. Pew Research Center for the People and the Press, "Bush Unpopular in Europe," Aug. 15, 2001, www.people-press.org/reports (2001); "America's Image Further Erodes, Europeans Want Weaker Ties," Mar. 18, 2003, www.people-press.org/reports (2003).

9. Citizens for Tax Justice and the Children's Defense Fund conducted the study of the effects of the 2001 tax cuts of President Bush and published it on June 12, 2002, www. children's.org.

10. Minxin Pei, "The Paradoxes of American Nationalism," *Foreign Policy,* May–June 2003, 31.

11. Anheier et al., eds., *Global Civil Society 2001,* 162.

12. David Banisar, *Freedom of Information and Access to Government Records Around the World* (London: Privacy International Reports, July 2002), freedominfo.org.

13. See *Privacy and Human Rights 2002: An International Survey of Privacy Laws and Developments* (London: Privacy International, 2002).

14. Ibid., 382–93.

15. Ibid., 386.

16. David Brin, *The Transparent Society: Will Technology Force Us to Choose Between Privacy and Freedom?* (Reading, Mass.: Perseus Books, 1998).

17. Ibid., 94.

18. Reg Whitaker, *The End of Privacy: How Total Surveillance Is Becoming a Reality* (New York: Free Press, 1999), 124.

19. Ibid., 126, emphasis in original.

20. Editorial, *Economist,* Mar. 8–16, 2003, 14.

21. Heinrich Schneider, *Leitbilder der Europapolitik: Der Weg zur Integration Europa Union* (Frankfurt: Europa Union Verlag, 1977).

22. Ibid., 57.

23. Ibid., 75.

24. Ibid., 76.

25. See *Handbuch der Judenfrage: Die wichtigsten Tatsachen zur Beurteilung des jüdischen Volkes,* ed. Theodor Fritsch (Bremen: Faksimile-Verlag, 1933), 231.

26. Frank Niess, *Die europäische Idee: Aus dem Geist des Widerstands* (Frankfurt am Main: Suhrkamp, 2001), 62–63.

27. Ibid., 30.

28. Francesca Lacaita, "Building Europe," review of ibid., www.transnational -perspectives.org/transnational/articles92.

29. Interview with Nikiforos Diamandorous, Strasbourg, 2003.

30. Heinrich Schneider, personal communication, 2004.

31. Interview with Bernhard Friedmann and Erich Haenelt, Luxembourg, 2000.

32. Deirdre Curtin, "The European Commission's White Paper on Governance: A Vista of Unbearable Democratic Lightness in the EU?" *Statewatch Bulletin* 11 (Nov.–Dec. 2001).

33. "European Governance: A White Paper," Commission of the European Communities, Brussels, 25.7.2001, COM (2001) 428 final.

34. Interview with Andrea Ulrike Kämpf, Brussels, 2001.

35. The EU Web site is www.europa.eu.int.

36. "European Governance: A White Paper," Commission of the European Communities, Brussels, 25.7.2002, P.11.

37. "Comments on the White Paper," 2002, www.statewatch.org.

38. Christian Jörges, Yves Meny, and J. H. H. Weiler, eds., *Mountain or Molehill? A Critical Appraisal of the Commission White Paper on Governance* (Florence: European University Institute, 2001); see also Christian Jörges, "'Economic Order'—'Technical Realisation'—'The Hour of the Executive': Some Legal Historical Observations on the Commission White Paper on Governance," in ibid., 127.

39. Ibid., 141.

40. "Treaties," Europa Web site, Mar. 16, 2003, wysiwyg://21/http://europa.eu.int/abc-en.htm.

41. Interview with Jean-Luc Dehaene, Brussels, 2002.

42. "Fundamental rights," Europa Web site, Mar. 19, 2003, http://europa.eu.int/abc/cit1_en.htm.

43. Ibid.

44. Tony Bunyan, "Secrecy and Openness in the European Union: The Ongoing Struggle for Freedom of Information," *Statewatch*, Oct. 1, 2002, www.freedominfo.org/case/eustudy.htm.

45. Ibid.

46. "Open and Shut Case: Access to Information in Sweden and the EU," Jan. 15, 2002, www.cfoi.org.uk/sweden1.html.

47. Bunyan, "Secrecy and Openness in the European Union."

48. Larry Gostin, ed., *Civil Liberties in Conflict* (London: Routledge, 1988), 118.

49. *Privacy and Human Rights, 2002,* 11–12.

50. Ibid., 15.

51. *Privacy and Human Rights, 2002.*

52. Ibid.; interview with Wim Prud'homme, Luxembourg, 2001.

53. *Privacy and Human Rights, 2002,* 347.

54. Ibid., 344.

55. *The Corruption Perceptions Index 2001* (Paris: Transparency International, June 27, 2001), www.transparency.org/cpi/2001/cpi2001.html.

56. Banisar, *Freedom of Information and Access to Government Records Around the World.*

57. *Privacy and Human Rights, 2001,* 190–91, 195.

58. Ibid., 192–93.

59. Interview with Virginia Tsoudereou, Athens, 2001. The following statements are taken from this interview, which included a group of volunteers from Transparency International Greece.

60. Interview with Demosthenes Agrafiotis, Athens, 2001.

61. Demetrios Constantelos, "The Historical Development of Greek Orthodoxy," in *Understanding the Greek Orthodox Church* (Boston: Hellenic College Press, 1990).

62. Interview with Christos Yannaris, Athens, 2001.

63. "The Holy Synod: Statement of the Orthodox Church of Greece on the Future of Europe," Apr. 5, 2003, www.ecclesia.gr/English/EnHolySynod/messages/europe .html.

64. Robert W. Compton Jr., *East Asian Democratization: Impact of Globalization, Culture, and Economy* (Westport, Conn.: Praeger, 2000), 109.

65. Ibid.

66. Interview with Ellen E. Mashiko, Tokyo, 2000.

67. Interview with Hiroshi Matsumoto, Tokyo, 2000.

68. Interview with Robert Grondine, Tokyo, 2000.

69. *Privacy and Human Rights, 2002,* 234.

70. "Japan. Breaking Down the Walls of Secrecy: The Story of the Citizen's Movement for an Information Disclosure Law," Information Clearinghouse Japan, July 26, 2002, www.freedominfo.org/case/japan1.htm.

71. Ibid., 3.

72. Ibid., 4.

73. Ibid., 7.

74. "Fighting Terrorism," *Economist,* July 12–18, 2003, 6.

75. Toby J. McIntosh, "News About Access to Information in International Financial and Trade Institutions," May 22, 2003, www.tmcintosh@bna.com.

76. Ibid.

77. Ibid.

78. Peter Eigen, *Das Netz der Korruption: Wie eine weltweite Bewegung gegen Bestechung kämpft* (Frankfurt: Campus Verlag, 2003).

79. Ann Florini, *The Coming Democracy: New Rules for Running a New World* (Washington, D.C.: Island Press, 2003), 195–209.

6. Global Civil Society, Transparency, and Social System Change

1. Michael Walzer, ed., *Toward a Global Civil Society* (Providence, R.I.: Berghahn Books, 1995).

2. Thomas L. Friedman, *The Lexus and the Olive Tree* (New York: Farrar, Straus, and Giroux, 1999), 322.

3. Moises Naim, "Devour and Conquer: How the White House Got Its Termite Problem," *Foreign Policy,* Nov.–Dec. 2004, 95.

4. Neera Chandhoke, "The Limits of Global Civil Society," in *Global Civil Society 2002,* ed. Marlies Glasius, Mary Kaldor, and Helmut Anheier (Oxford: Oxford University Press, 2002), 40.

5. Joseph E. Stiglitz, *Globalization and Its Discontents* (New York and London: Norton, 2002), 3.

6. Ibid., 4.

7. "Globalisation and Its Critics: A Survey of Globalization," *Economist,* Sept. 29, 2001.

8. See *Global Civil Society 2002,* ed. Glasius et al., chaps. 1–2.

9. Patrick Mulvany, UK abc Noticeboard, Jan. 2003, www.ukabc.org/wsf2003 .htm#c. The following quoted passages are taken from this source.

10. Bridget Anderson, "Porto Alegre: 'A Worm's Eye View,'" *Global Networks* 3 (Apr. 2003): 197–204.

11. Helmut Anheier, Marlies Glasius, and Mary Kaldor, eds., *Global Civil Society 2001* (Oxford: Oxford University Press, 2001), 16.

12. Union of International Associations, *Yearbook of International Organizations: Guide to Global Civil Society Networks 2002–2003* (Munich: K. G. Saur, 2004).

13. *Global Civil Society 2001,* ed. Anheier et al., 19.

14. Ibid., 3.

15. Ibid., 17.

16. Nancy Bermeo and Philip Nord, *Civil Society before Democracy: Lessons from Nineteenth-Century Europe* (Lanham, Md.: Rowman and Littlefield, 2000), xiv.

17. Sudipta Kaviraj and Sunil Khilnani, eds., *Civil Society: History and Possibilities* (Cambridge: Cambridge University Press, 2001).

18. Antony Black, in ibid., 38.

19. Kaviraj and Khilnani, eds., *Civil Society,* 12–13.

20. John Keane, *Global Civil Society?* (Cambridge: Cambridge University Press, 2003), 8.

21. Bill McKibben, "A Special Moment in History," *Atlantic Monthly,* May 1998, 78.

22. See American Enterprise Institute for Public Policy Research and the Federalist Society for Law and Public Policy Studies, www.ngowatch.org.

23. Kaviraj and Khilnani, eds., *Civil Society,* 12–13.

24. Union of International Organizations, Aug. 2003, www.uia.org.

25. *Global Civil Society 2001,* ed. Anheier et al., 195, table 8.1.

26. The UN's Web site for NGOs is www.NGO-INFO.org.

27. Global Reporting Initiative (GRI), Aug. 2003, www.globalreporting.org.

28. See Burkart Holzner, *Reality Construction in Society* (Cambridge, Mass.: Schenkman, 1968), chap. 4; Burkart Holzner and John Marx, *Knowledge Application: The Knowledge System in Society* (Boston: Allyn and Bacon, 1979).

29. See, for example, Stiglitz, *Globalization and Its Discontents.*

30. Melanie Beth Oliviero and Adele Simmons, "Global Civil Society and Corporate Responsibility," in *Global Civil Society 2002,* ed. Glasius et al., 84.

31. Platform of ATTAC, an organization for democratic control of fiscal markets worldwide, www.webmaster@attac.org.

32. See Helmut Anheier and Nuno Themudo, "Organizational Forms of Global Civil Society," in *Global Civil Society 2002,* ed. Glasius et al.

33. "Total Net Resource Flows from DAC Member Countries and Multilateral Aid

Agencies to Aid Recipients," *2002 Development Cooperation Report,* table 1, OECD, Development Cooperation Directorate (DAC), www.oecd.org/dac.

34. Ibid.

35. *Global Civil Society 2002,* ed. Glasius et al., 6, 322.

36. Bertelsmann Foundation, *Transparency: A Basis for Responsibility and Cooperation: Results of the International Survey Carl Bertelsmann Prize 2002* (Gütersloh: Bertelsmann Foundation, 2002).

37. From the Bertelsmann Foundation Web site, Aug. 23, 2003, www.bertelsmannstiftung.de.

38. Bertelsmann Foundation, *Transparency,* 7–8.

39. Web site of Joan Bavaria, founder of the Coalition for Environmental Responsible Economies (CERES), Aug. 29, 2003.

40. Bertelsmann Foundation, *Transparency,* 61–70.

41. See Stephan Schmidheiny and Lloyd Timberlake, *Changing Course: A Global Business Perspective on Development and the Environment* (Cambridge, Mass.: MIT Press, 1992); Stephan Schmidheiny and Federico J. Zorraquin, *Financing Change: The Financial Community, Eco-Efficiency, and Sustainable Development* (Cambridge, Mass.: MIT Press, 1998).

42. Bertelsmann Foundation, *Transparency,* 94.

43. See "Sustainable Mobility Project," at www.pladsen@wbcsd.org, and www.sustainablemobility.org.

44. The description of WBCSD is based on Bertelsmann Foundation, *Transparency,* 94–106; Globalist Web site, www.theglobalist.com/DBWeb.

45. Bertelsmann Foundation, *Transparency,* 74.

46. Report on the Gordon E. and Betty L. Moore Foundation, San Francisco *Business Times,* Feb. 5, 2001, in ibid., 76.

47. Bertelsmann Foundation, *Transparency,* 20.

48. Fredrik Galtung, "A Global Network to Curb Corruption: The Experience of Transparency International," in *The Third Force: The Rise of Transnational Civil Society,* ed. Ann Florini (Tokyo: Japan Center for International Exchange, 2000), 17–47; Eigen, *Das Netz Der Korruption,* 20, our translation. Information about TI in the following paragraphs is taken from these sources.

49. Eigen, *Das Netz Der Korruption,* 33.

50. Galtung, "A Global Network to Curb Corruption," 23, emphasis added.

51. Eigen, *Das Netz Der Korruption,* 238.

52. Galtung, "A Global Network to Curb Corruption," 23–24.

53. Interview with Virginia Tsouderou, Athens, Apr. 25, 2001.

54. Galtung, "A Global Network to Curb Corruption," 24f.

55. TI Web site on the Corruption Perceptions Index, www.transparency.org/cpi/index.html#cpi.

56. Johann Graf Lambsdorff, "Measuring the Dark Side of Human Nature: The

Birth of the Corruption Perceptions Index," Internet Corruption Research Center Web site, www.user.gwdg.de/~uwvw.

57. TI press release, www.transparency.org.

58. Business Information Service for the Newly Independent States (BISNIS), Sept. 9, 2003, supported by the U.S. Department of Commerce, International Trade Administration.

59. Transparency International, *The National Integrity Systems: TI Source Book* was created by Jeremy Pope in 1995 and published by TI; see also *TI Source Book 2000, Confronting Corruption: The Elements of a National Integrity System* (London: Transparency International, 2000).

60. Jeremy Pope, "Author's note," ibid., vii.

61. Interview with Jeremy Pope, May 17, 2002, London.

62. Oscar Arias, "Foreword," *TI Source Book 2000,* ix.

63. Ibid., 8.

64. Ibid., 25.

65. Ibid., 26.

66. Ibid., 135.

67. Robin Hodess, Tania Inowlocki, and Toby Wolfe, eds., *Global Corruption Report 2003* (London: Profile Books Ltd., 2003).

68. Interview with Michael Wiehen, Munich, July 8, 2003.

69. Eigen, *Das Netz Der Korruption,* 193–205; the following paragraphs are taken from this source.

70. *Transparency International Strategic Framework,* January 12, 2004, 2.

71. Ibid., 9.

72. Ibid., 12–13.

73. Interview with Jeremy Pope, London, May 17, 2002.

74. Peter Eigen, "Chasing Corruption around the World: How Civil Society Strengthens Global Governance," presented at Stanford University, Oct. 4, 2004; press release: *Transparency International Corruption Perceptions Index 2004,* 11, 17, 2004.

75. Peter Eigen, "Moving In and Cleaning House," *TI Q [Quarterly Newsletter],* Mar. 2004, 1.

7. Corporate Governance and Transparency

1. The idea behind the stock options was that CEOs would identify their own interests with those of their company. There are many different types of these options, but they have in common the idea that as a company's stock value rises, shares can be bought by the holder of options at a lower than market value. Of course, if the stock value declines, they might become worthless. Thus the options provide an incentive to managers to increase shareholder value. It is actually an intriguing strategy to deal with the perennial worry about the "hired manager" who is not an owner and who may not be bound to the firm as strongly as a full property owner and boss is. The

problem with options lies in the specifics that can allow mischief, not in the idea itself.

2. Paul Starr, "The New Life of the Liberal State: Privatization and the Restructuring of State-Society Relations," in *Public Enterprise and Privatization,* ed. John Waterbury and Ezra Suleiman (Boulder, Colo.: Westview, 1999), 22–44.

3. Max Weber, *Economy and Society: An Outline of Interpretive Sociology,* ed. Guenther Roth and Claus Wittich (New York: Bedminster Press, 1968), vol. I, 144–50, 341–43.

4. Ibid., 144–45.

5. Ibid., 342.

6. Arthur Levitt, interview by Hedrick Smith, *Frontline,* PBS, Mar. 12, 2002, in *Frontline: Bigger than Enron: Congress and the Accounting Wars,* www.pbs.org. The following passages are taken from this source.

7. Lynn Turner, interview by Hedrick Smith, *Frontline,* PBS, Apr. 5, 2002, in ibid. The following passages are taken from this source.

8. Alex Berenson, *The Number: How the Drive for Quarterly Earnings Corrupted Wall Street and Corporate America* (New York: Random House, 2003), xviii.

9. Ibid., 210.

10. Jeffrey E. Garten, *The Mind of the CEO* (New York: Basic Books, 2001), 277–78.

11. From AFL-CIO Web site, Oct. 8, 2003, www.aflcio.org/corporateamerica/paywatch/ceou/database.cfm.

12. Takao Kato, "Chief Executive Compensation and Corporate Groups in Japan: New Evidence from Micro Data," *International Journal of Industrial Organization* 15 (1997): 455–67. *Keiretsu* is the Japanese term for a loosely linked group of companies connected to a single bank. They cooperate with each other and may own each other's shares. Examples are the Mitsubishi, Mitsui, and Sumitomo groups.

13. Darrell Taft and Gangaram Singh, *Executive Compensation: Compensation and Benefits Review* (Thousand Oaks, Calif.: Sage Publications, 2003), 68–78.

14. Takao Kato and Katsuyuki Kubo, "CEO Compensation and Firm Performance in Japan: Evidence from New Panel Data on Individual CEO Pay," Apr. 2003, www.2.gsb.columbia.edu/japan/pdf/WP210.pdf.

15. Garten, *The Mind of the CEO,* 2–3.

16. See the Courtroom Television Network's summary of compensation and benefits for Jack Welch, 2001–2002, www.thesmokinggun.com/archive/gewelch1.html, Oct. 13, 2003.

17. James B. Stewart, "Spend! Spend! Spend! Where Did Tyco's Money Go?" *New Yorker,* Feb. 17–24, 2003.

18. Roger Lowenstein, "Heads I Win, Tails I Win: The Bull Market Is Gone, but Executive Compensation Keeps Climbing," *New York Times Magazine,* June 9, 2002, 102ff. Quotations in the following paragraphs are taken from this source.

19. Berenson, *The Number,* 123–24.

20. "Ex-Flow-Tex-Chef widerruft Geständnis," *Die Welt,* July 29, 2003.

21. Berenson, *The Number,* 193–204.

22. Bethany McLean, quoted in ibid., 195–96.

23. Berenson, *The Number,* 199.

24. Peter Behr and April Witt, "The Fall of Enron: Catastrophe Hidden Debts, Deals Scuttle Last Chance," *Washington Post,* Aug. 1, 2002, A1; Hedrick Smith and Marc Shaffer, *Frontline,* PBS, June 20, 2002, in *Frontline: Bigger than Enron*; Berenson, *The Number.*

25. Lynn E. Turner, "Just a Few Rotten Apples? Better Audit Those Books," *Washington Post,* July 14, 2002, B1.

26. Ronald Fink, "The Fear of All Sums (Survey: 17% of CFOs Have Been Pressured)," *CFO Magazine,* Aug. 1, 2002.

27. Frank Vogl, "The U.S. Business Scandals: Perspectives on Ethics and Culture at Home and Abroad," presented at the Transatlantic Business Ethics Conference, Sept. 27, 2002, Georgetown University. The following paragraphs are taken from this source.

28. Berenson, *The Number,* xii.

29. *The Transparency International Global Corruption Barometer: A 2002 Pilot Survey of International Attitudes, Expectations and Priorities on Corruption* (Berlin: Transparency International, July 3, 2003).

30. "Enron Everywhere," *Atlantic Monthly,* Nov. 2003, 53.

31. "Fallen Idols," *Economist,* May 4–10, 2002, 11.

32. "Fixing a Tarnished Market," *New York Times,* Sept. 21, 2003.

33. "Leaders: Where's the Stick? Something Has Gone Wrong with Bosses' Pay," *Economist,* Oct. 11, 2003, 13.

34. Diane E. Ambler and Kristen L. Stewart, *Sarbanes-Oxley Planning and Compliance* (Washington, D.C.: Thompson Publishing, 2003), 1–8, 213–46; see also information about the Sarbanes-Oxley Act distributed by the American Institute of Certified Public Accountants (AICPA), www.aicpa.org.

35. "Wide Range of Tax Shelters Attracts a Senate Inquiry," *New York Times,* Oct. 22, 2003, C7.

36. Nicholas G. Terris and Jeffrey B. Maletta, "The Sarbanes-Oxley Act and the New Order of Corporate Disclosure," in *K&L Alert: Securities and Securities Enforcement* (Kirkpatrick and Lockhart, LLP, Aug. 2, 2002), 1–6.

37. Ibid.

38. Ibid.

39. Jonathan D. Glater and David Leonhardt, "Both Sides Say Bill Addressing Business Fraud Is a First Step," *New York Times,* July 25, 2002, C1, C4.

40. "Enron: The Twister Hits," *Economist,* Jan. 19, 2002, 59.

41. Frederick D. S. Choi, Carol Ann Frost, and Gary K. Meek, *International Accounting* (Upper Saddle River, N.J.: Prentice-Hall, 2002), 3.

42. Mark E. Haskins, Kenneth Ferris, and Thomas I. Selling, *International Financial Accounting and Analyses* (Boston: Irwin, 2000), 26.

43. Günther Gebhardt, "The Evolution of Global Standards in Accounting," in *Brookings-Wharton Papers on Financial Services 2000,* ed. Robert E. Litan and Anthony M. Santomero (Washington, D.C.: Brookings, 2000), 352.

44. Helen Morsicato Gernon, Roland E. Dukes, and Gary K. Meek, *Accounting: An International Perspective* (Boston: Irwin, 2001), 31.

45. Ibid., 25–26.

46. Ibid., 32.

47. See the history of the IASB and the restructuring of the IASC, www.iasb.org.uk.

48. Gebhardt, "The Evolution of Global Standards in Accounting," 358.

49. Interview with Sir David Tweedie, London, May 16, 2002.

50. Interview with Kevin Stevenson, London, May 16, 2002. The following quoted passages are taken from this source.

51. Phone interview with Sir David Tweedie, July 29, 2002.

52. "Financial Reporting: Commission Adopts Regulation Endorsing International Accounting Standards," IASB press release, Sept. 29, 2003.

53. Norbert Elias, *The Civilizing Process: The Development of Manners,* trans. Edmund Jephcott (New York: Urizen Books, 1978).

54. "Our Credo History," the Johnson and Johnson code of conduct, is prominently displayed on its Web site, www.jnj.com.

55. "Global Sullivan Principles of Social Responsibility," www.globalsullivanprinciples .org/index.htm.htm.

56. Ethics Officer Association Web site, www.eoa.org/home.asp.

57. Ethical Trading Initiative Web site, www.eti.org.uk/pub/home/welcome/main/ index.shtml.

58. "Codes of Conduct sind ein Geschäft," Informationsstelle Lateinamerika Web site, www.ila-web.de.

59. Interview with Michael Bleier, Pittsburgh, Apr. 3, 2003.

60. John P. Friel, address presented to the Pittsburgh International Trade Executives' Club, Apr. 2003.

61. Business and Human Rights Resource Center, Amnesty International Business Groups, www.business-humanrights.org/Home.

62. Peter Eigen, *Das Netz der Korruption: Wie eine weltweite Bewegung gegen Bestechung kämpft* (Frankfurt: Campus Verlag, 2003), 67.

63. *The OECD Guidelines for Multinational Enterprises: A Key Corporate Responsibility Instrument,* OECD Policy Brief, June 24, 2003.

64. OECD Directorate for Financial, Fiscal, and Enterprise Affairs, "OECD Codes of Corporate Conduct: Expanded Review of Their Contents," in *Corporate Responsibility: Private Initiatives and Public Goals* (OECD: May 2, 2001).

65. The UN Global Compact, "The Nine Principles," www.unglobalcompact.org/ Portal.

66. *Norms on the Responsibilities of Transnational Corporations and Other Business Enterprises with Regard to Human Rights,* UN Doc. E/CN.4/Sub.2/2003/12/Rev.2 (2003), 3, 5.

67. Transparency International–USA, *Corporate Governance: Code of Conduct/Compliance Programs—Leading Practices Survey,* Feb. 2003, 2, emphasis in original.

68. David Litvin, "Memorandum to U.N. Secretary-General Kofi Annan: Needed: A Global Business Code of Conduct," *Foreign Policy,* Nov.–Dec. 2003, 68.

69. Don Tapscott and David Ticoll, *The Naked Corporation: How the Age of Transparency Will Revolutionize Business* (New York: Free Press, 2003).

8. The Changing Architecture of Information Values in Health Systems

1. "Health Care," *Charter of Fundamental Rights of the European Union,* Article 35, adopted by the EU Commission's Committee of Citizens' Freedoms and Rights, Justice, and Home Affairs, June 2002.

2. "Why 'Rekindling Reform'?" *American Journal of Public Health* 93 (2003): 15.

3. Ibid., 16.

4. Lotta Westerhäll and Charles Phillips, eds., *Patients' Rights—Informed Consent, Access and Equality* (Stockholm: Nerenus and Santerus, 1994).

5. "International Perspectives Forum," *American Journal of Public Health* 93 (2003): 20–24.

6. Beatrix Hoffman, "Health Care Reform and Social Movements in the United States," *American Journal of Public Health* 93 (2003), 75–81.

7. Peter Eigen, *Das Netz der Korruption: Wie eine weltweite Bewegung gegen Bestechung kämpft* (Frankfurt: Campus Verlag, 2003), 162; authors' translation.

8. Interview with Virginia Tsouderou, Athens, Apr. 25, 2001.

9. Interview with Dr. Michael Wiehen, Munich, May 3, 2002.

10. Marcia Angell, *The Truth About the Drug Companies: How They Deceive Us and What to Do About It* (New York: Random House, 2004).

11. Ruth R. Faden, Tom L. Beauchamp, and M. P. King, *A History and Theory of Informed Consent* (New York: Oxford University Press, 1986), chap. 1.

12. Dieter Giesen, "From Paternalism to Self-Determination to Shared Decision Making in the Field of Medical Law and Ethics," in *Patients' Rights,* ed. Westerhäll and Phillips, 20.

13. Ibid., 21.

14. Faden et al., *A History and Theory of Informed Consent,* 74.

15. Ibid., 75.

16. Ibid., 3.

17. Robert Jay Lifton, *The Nazi Doctors: Medical Killing and the Psychology of Genocide* (New York: Basic Books, 1986).

18. Ibid., 22–44.

19. Robert Proctor, *Racial Hygiene: Medicine under the Nazis* (Cambridge: Harvard University Press, 1988), chap. 2.

20. Wilton H. Bunch, "Informed Consent," *Clinical Orthopedics and Related Research* 378 (Sept. 2000), 74; see also Faden et al., *A History and Theory of Informed Consent,* 154.

21. Lifton, *The Nazi Doctors,* 46.

22. Proctor, *Racial Hygiene,* 69.

23. Ibid., 153.

24. Ibid., 69.

25. Ibid., xiii.

26. Götz Aly, Peter Chroust, and Christian Pross, *Cleansing the Fatherland: Nazi Medicine and Racial Hygiene,* trans. Belinda Cooper (Baltimore: Johns Hopkins University Press, 1994); see also Angelika Birck, Christian Pross, Johan Lansen (Hrsg.), *Das Unsagbare. Die Arbeit mit Traumatisierten im Behandlungszentrum für Folteropfer Berlin* (Berlin: Springer-Verlag, 2002).

27. Christian Pross, introduction to *Cleansing the Fatherland,* ed. Aly et al., 5–6.

28. In 1949 Mitscherlich established the psychosomatic department at the University of Heidelberg, which later became the Psychosomatische Klinik, of which he was the director. In 1966 he became the director of the Frankfurt Sigmund Freud Institut. He was awarded the Peace Prize of the German Book Trade (1969), the Goldene Wilhelm-Bölsche-Medaille (1972), and the Cultural Honor Prize of the City of Munich (1973). See Alexander Mitscherlich and Fred Mielke, *Doctors of Infamy: The Story of the Nazi Medical Crimes* (New York: Henry Schuman, 1949). Biography of Alexander Mitscherlich from www.dhm.de/lemo/html/biografien/MitscherlichAlexander; and Heinrich Schneider, personal communication.

29. Pross, introduction to *Cleansing the Fatherland,* ed. Aly et al., 6.

30. Ibid.

31. Ibid., 7–8.

32. Ibid., 8.

33. Ibid., 21.

34. Ibid., 11–12.

35. In Faden et al., *A History and Theory of Informed Consent,* 28.

36. Ibid., chap. 4.

37. Ibid.

38. The Nuremberg Code, in *The Ethics of Research Involving Human Subjects: Facing the 21st Century,* ed. Harold Y. Vanderpool (Frederick, Md.: University Publishing Group, 1996), 431–32.

39. Ibid.

40. Ibid.

41. Henry K. Beecher, *Experimentation in Man* (Springfield, Ill.: Thomas, 1959).

42. D. J. Rothman, *Strangers at the Bedside* (New York: Basic Books, 1991), quoted in *The Ethics of Research Involving Human Subjects,* ed. Vanderpool, 9.

43. Ibid., 162.

44. Ibid., 163ff.

45. Thomas Parran, *Shadow on the Land: Syphilis* (New York: Reynal and Hitchcock, 1937), 3.

46. See James H. Jones, *Bad Blood: The Tuskegee Syphilis Experiment* (New York: Free Press, 1981); Stephen B. Thomas and Sandra Crouse Quinn, "Public Health Then and

Now: The Tuskegee Syphilis Study, 1932 to 1972: Implications for HIV Education and AIDS Risk Education Programs in the Black Community," *American Journal of Public Health* 81 (1991): 1498–1505.

47. Charles Johnson, *Shadow of the Plantation* (Chicago: Julius Rosenwald Fund, 1931).

48. Jones, *Bad Blood,* 93.

49. Ibid.

50. Ibid., 178.

51. Ibid., 179.

52. Ibid., 180.

53. Ibid., 190.

54. Ibid., 196.

55. Faden et al., *A History and Theory of Informed Consent,* 10.

56. Thomas and Quinn, "Public Health Then and Now," 1498.

57. According to its Web site, the Center for Public Environmental Oversight CPEO) promotes and facilitates public participation in the oversight of environmental activities at federal facilities, private Superfund sites, and brownfields.

58. *The Belmont Report* (1979), in *The Ethics of Research Involving Human Subjects,* ed. Vanderpool, 10. The following paragraphs are also taken from this source.

59. See *Guidebook for Institutional Review Boards* (Washington, D.C.: U.S. Dept. of Health and Human Services, Office of Human Research Protections, 1993 and updates).

60. World Medical Association Web site, Dec. 24, 2003, www.wma.net/e/ethicsunit/index.htm.

61. The Web site for the medical ethics Syllabus Exchange Catalogue is www.georgetown.edu/research/nrcbl/syllabus/sylbcat.htm.

62. Major directives are the EUR-Lex Directive 95/46/EC of Oct. 24, 1995, and Directive 2002/58/EC of July 12, 2002, concerning privacy and electronic communications; see also EU Institutions press releases: "Data protection: Commission report shows that EU law is achieving its main aims," May 16, 2003; "Review of Directive 95/46/EC, IMS Health, July 2002."

63. The complexity of the HIPAA legislation is reflected in the enormous number of comments, summaries, and advisory pamphlets. See, for example, "The Health Insurance Portability and Accountability Act of 1996 (HIPAA)," modified Oct. 16, 2002; and "HIPAA Insurance Reform," modified Aug. 5, 2002, Centers for Medicare and Medicaid Services; "HIPAA Consumer Questions," modified Oct. 30, 2002, and "Summary of the HIPAA Privacy Rule," U.S. Department of Health and Human Services; Margret Amatayakul, *HIPAA Made Simple: A Guide to Fast-Tracking Compliance* (Marblehead, Mass.: Opus Communications, 2003); "Health Care Facility Records: Confidentiality, Computerization and Security," Monograph 3, American Bar Association Forum on Health Law, July 1995; *Privacy Under HIPAA With Tools,* Allegheny County

Bar Association, Philadelphia Bar Education Center, and Pennsylvania Bar Institute, 2001; *Fall HIPAA Round-Up,* Pennsylvania Bar Institute, 2002; and *The HIPAA Privacy Deadline Has Passed: Now What?* Pennsylvania Bar Institute, 2003.

64. Dibya Sarker, "HIPAA gives health industry a queasy feeling," *Federal Computer Week,* June 16, 2003.

65. Jeff Goldsmith, David Blumenthal, and Wes Rishel, "Federal Health Information Policy: A Case of Arrested Development," *Health Affairs* 22 (2003): 44-55.

66. U.S. Department of Health and Human Services, "Summary of the HIPAA Privacy Rule."

67. Laura Parker, "Medical-Privacy Law Creates Wide Confusion," *USA Today,* Oct. 17, 2003.

68. "Health Policy as It Happens," Dec. 10, 2003, Kaisernetwork.org; "WSJ Examines Lawsuit Challenging HIPAA Medical Privacy Rule," *Wall Street Journal,* Dec. 10, 2003.

69. Bruce Steele, "Researchers Seek Cure for HIPAA-Induced Ills," *University* [of Pittsburgh] *Times,* Dec. 4, 2003.

70. Laurie Garrett, *The Coming Plague: Newly Emerging Diseases and a World out of Balance* (New York: Farrar, Straus, and Giroux, 1994); and Laurie Garrett, *Betrayal of Trust: The Collapse of Global Public Health* (New York: Hyperion, 2000).

71. Garrett, *Betrayal of Trust,* 11.

72. Ibid.

73. Ibid., 8.

74. Ilan H. Meyer and Sharon Schwartz, "Social Issues as Public Health: Promise and Peril," *American Journal of Public Health* 90 (2000): 1189-91.

75. Alfred Sommer and Mohammad N. Akhter, "It's Time We Became a Profession," *American Journal of Public Health* 90 (2000): 845-46.

76. Ibid., 846.

77. Christopher Keane, John Marx, and Edmund Ricci, "Managerial and Professional Beliefs Influencing Public Health Privatization," *Journal of Health and Social Behavior* 44 (2003): 108.

78. Tommy Koh, Aileen Plant, and Eng Hin Lee, *The New Global Threat: Severe Acute Respiratory Syndrome and Its Impacts* (Singapore: World Scientific, 2003).

79. "WHO: At the Forefront of Combating SARS," May 12, 2003, in ibid., 11.

80. Ibid., 31.

81. Ibid., 32.

82. Resolutions proposed at the annual meeting of the World Federation of Public Health Associations, May 14, 2001, www.apha.org/wfpha/globalisation.htm.

83. Ibid.

84. Proposal on debt relief, WFPHA, May 17, 1999, www.apha.org/wfpha/international _debt_relief.htm.

85. "Global Tobacco Control," WFPHA, 1998, www.apha.org/wfphaa/tob.htm.

86. "International Trade Agreements: Priorities for Health," WFPHA, 2003, www.apha.org/wfpha/intl_trade_pol.htm.

87. "Declaration on Public Health, Peace and Human Rights," WFPHA, May 2003, www.apha.org/wfpha/skopje.htm.

88. Ilona Kickbusch, "The Contribution of the World Health Organization to a New Public Health and Health Promotion," *American Journal of Public Health* 93 (2003): 383.

89. Ibid., 383.

90. Ibid.

91. Ibid.

92. The American Public Health Association worked for some time to create a code of ethics, producing the "Public Health Code of Ethics, Principles of the Ethical Practice of Public Health" in 2003; see www.apha.org/codeof ethics/ethics.htm.

93. Ibid.

94. Nancy E. Kass, "An Ethics Framework for Public Health," *American Journal of Public Health* 91 (2001): 1776.

95. Ibid., 1779.

96. Ibid., 1780.

97. "Support for a New Campaign for Universal Health Care," American Public Health Association, policy no. 20007, adopted Jan. 1, 2000.

9. Historical Transparency

1. Leopold von Ranke, *Geschichte der Romanischen und Germanischen Völker von 1492 bis 1535,* in *Bartlett's Familiar Quotations* (Boston: Little, Brown, 1992), 418.

2. Jeffrey Herf, *Divided Memory: The Nazi Past in the Two Germanys* (Cambridge: Harvard University Press, 1997), 206.

3. Ibid.

4. Ibid.

5. Jeffrey Herf, "The Holocaust and the Competition of Memories in Germany, 1945–1999," in *Remembering the Holocaust in Germany, 1945–2000,* ed. Dan Michman (New York: Peter Lang, 2002), 9–30.

6. See Herf, *Divided Memory;* and Aryeh Neier, *War Crimes: Brutality, Genocide, Terror, and the Struggle for Justice* (New York: Random House, 1998).

7. See Herf, *Divided Memory,* 209–26.

8. Hans-Peter Schwarz, *Konrad Adenauer: A German Politician and Statesman in a Period of War, Revolution and Reconstruction,* trans. Louise Willmot (Providence, R.I.: Berghahn Books, 1995), 1:475.

9. Ibid., 1:503–4.

10. See *Biographie: Konrad Adenauer, 1876–1967,* www.dhm.de/lemo/html/ biografien/ AdenauerKonrad, presented by LeMO (Lebendiges virtuelles Museum Online); and Hans-Peter Schwarz, *Konrad Adenauer,* trans. by Geoffrey Penny (Providence, R.I.: Beghahn Books, 1997), 2:3–176, 2:249f.

11. Schwarz, *Konrad Adenauer,* 2:429f.

12. Ibid., 2:430.

13. Ibid., 2:431.

14. Herf, "The Holocaust and the Competition of Memories," 10.

15. Ibid.

16. Heinrich Schneider, personal communication.

17. Benjamin Ferencz, in *Facing History and Ourselves,* www.facing.org/facing/ fhao2.nsf/scholars/Benjamin+Ferencz. Ferencz was a prosecutor at the Nuremberg War Crimes Court, then became the director of the postwar restitutions programs that helped to formulate and implement the laws providing compensation to survivors of Nazi persecution.

18. Heinrich Schneider, personal communication.

19. Herf, *Divided Memory,* 337.

20. Interview with Karsten Voigt, Berlin, July 9, 2001.

21. Herf, "The Holocaust and the Competition of Memories," 20.

22. Ibid., 22.

23. Ibid., 23.

24. Heinrich Schneider, personal communication, Nov. 2004.

25. See Mike Dennis and Eva Kolinsky, eds., *United and Divided Germany since 1990* (New York: Berghahn Books, 2004).

26. Mike Dennis, "Constructing East Germany," in ibid., 14–15.

27. Ibid., 32.

28. "Holocaust Education in Germany," a publication of the German Information Center, 950 Third Ave., New York, N.Y., 10022.

29. Herf, *Divided Memory,* 394.

30. Herbert P. Bix, *Hirohito and the Making of Modern Japan* (New York: Harper Collins, 2001), 585.

31. From the Canadian Commission of Inquiry into War Criminals Report, Part I: Public 27, in Amnesty International, *Universal Jurisdiction,* AI Index IOR, Sept. 1, 2001 (Ottawa: Minister of Supply and Services, 1986), chap 2.

32. Bix, *Hirohito,* 610.

33. Tim Maga, *Judgment at Tokyo: The Japanese War Crimes Trials* (Lexington: University of Kentucky Press, 2001), 138–51.

34. Bix, *Hirohito,* 611.

35. Herf, *Divided Memory,* 374.

36. This refers to the Meiji Restoration that ended with the death of the emperor in 1912 and the Showa emperor Hirohito.

37. Bix, *Hirohito,* 688.

38. John Nathan, *Japan Unbound: A Volatile Nation's Quest for Pride and Purpose* (New York: Houghton Mifflin, 2004), 43.

39. Makoto Watanabe, "History Textbooks and Government Policy, Japan," www.fps.chuo-u.ac.jp/~jon/adv96/group2/group2c.html4.

40. Howard W. French, "Japan's Resurgent Far Right Tinkers With History," *New York Times,* Mar. 25, 2001.

41. Watanabe, "History Textbooks and Government Policy."

42. Akiko Hashimoto, "Japanese and German Projects of Moral Recovery: Toward a New Understanding of War Memories in Defeated Nations," Occasional Papers in Japanese Studies, Edwin O. Reischauer Institute of Japanese Studies, Harvard University, 1999.

43. Ibid., 4–5.

44. Ibid., 10.

45. "Franco's Legacy," *All Things Considered,* NPR, Jan. 2, 2003.

46. Telford Taylor, in *Facing History and Ourselves,* www.facinghistory.org. This is a large civic education organization that originated in the United States, but now international, fostering the history education of teachers.

47. Benjamin Ferencz, in ibid.

48. Henry T. King was a Nuremberg prosecutor and is now professor of law at the Canada/U.S. Law Institute.

49. Maga, *Judgment at Tokyo,* 140.

50. Ibid., 141.

51. Henry Kissinger, "The Pitfalls of Universal Jurisdiction: Risking Judicial Tyranny," *Foreign Affairs,* July–Aug. 2001.

52. Kennedy Roth, "The Case for Universal Jurisdiction," *Foreign Affairs,* Sept.–Oct. 2001.

53. Amnesty International, *Universal Jurisdiction,* AI Index: IOR 53/004/2001, Sept. 1, 2001; July 9, 2004, chap. 2, web.amnesty.org/pages/aboutai-index-eng.

54. Ibid., pts. C–D.

55. Ibid., chap. 3, pt. A.

56. Ibid., chap. 4, pt. B.

57. Ibid., chap. 5.

58. Global Policy Forum, *International Criminal Tribunals and Special Courts,* www.globalpolicy.org/intljustice/tribindx.htm.

59. Neier, *War Crimes,* 112.

60. Amnesty International, *International Criminal Tribunals: A Handbook for Governments,* AI Index: IOR 40/07/96.

61. Neier, *War Crimes,* 251.

62. United States Institute of Peace, "Building the Iraqi Special Tribunal," www.usip.org.

63. "Lessons Learned," in ibid.

64. "Coordination Between Investigative Judges and Prosecutors," in ibid.

65. International Criminal Court, www.icc-cpi.int/ataglance.html.

66. Washington Working Group on the International Criminal Court, "WICC Members and Observers," www.wfa.org/issues/wicc/memberlist.html.

67. Ibid.

68. International Criminal Court, Rome Statute, www.icc-cpi.int/romestatute.html.

69. Ibid., pt. III.

70. American Service Members Protection Act of 2001, a U.S. law to exempt U.S. military personnel from ICC jurisdiction.

71. President Bush's "National Security Strategy of the United States of America" was released on Sept. 17, 2002, by the White House. See John Lewis Gaddis, "A Grand Strategy," *Foreign Policy,* Nov.–Dec. 2002, 50–57.

72. Ritt Goldstein, "Preemption and an Arms Race with Itself," *Asia Times,* May 6, 2004.

73. P. Melvyn Leffler, "Bush's Foreign Policy," *Foreign Policy,* Sept.–Oct. 2004, 22–28.

74. Javier Solana, "Rules with Teeth," *Foreign Policy,* Sept.–Oct. 2004, 74–75.

75. Seymor M. Hersh, "Torture at Abu Ghraib," *New Yorker,* Nov. 23, 2004.

76. "Panel to probe CIA failure to predict extent of insurgency," *USA Today,* June 10, 2004. This is one of hundreds of similar articles. Most of the criticism focuses on the failure to avoid the terrorist acts of Sept. 11, 2001.

77. "South Africa's Truth and Reconciliation Commission," official Truth and Reconciliation Commission Web site, www.doj.gov.2a/trc.

78. Neil J. Kritz, ed., *Transitional Justice: How Emerging Democracies Reckon with Former Regimes* (Washington, D.C.: U.S. Institute of Peace Press, 1995), xi.

79. Nelson Mandela, in ibid., xi.

80. K. N. Panikkar, in *The Courier,* the cultural newsletter of UNESCO, Nov. 2001.

81. An editor's note to Panikkar's essay observes that the Indian government defended their textbooks, claiming that they were the product of "the most democratic manner" (ibid.).

82. "Italian MPs threaten to censor textbooks," *Guardian,* Dec. 18, 2002.

10. Global Change and the Open Society

1. Minxin Pei, "The Paradoxes of American Nationalism," *Foreign Policy,* May–June 2003, 32.

2. Chalmers Johnson, *The Sorrows of Empire: Militarism, Secrecy, and the End of the Republic* (New York: Henry Holt, 2004), 140–49.

3. Ibid.

4. Melvyn P. Leffler, "Bush's Foreign Policy," *Foreign Policy,* Sept.–Oct. 2004, 22–28.

5. Fareed Zakaria, "Hating America," *Foreign Policy,* Sept.–Oct. 2004, 47–49.

6. Ann M. Florini, "The End of Secrecy," in *Power and Conflict in the Age of Transparency,* ed. Bernard I. Finel and Kristin M. Lord (New York: Palgrave, 2000), 13; and Ann Florini, *The Coming Democracy: New Rules for Running a New World* (Washington, D.C.: Island Press, 2003).

CONSULTATIONS

Agrafiotis, Professor of Sociology, National School of Public Health, Athens, Apr. 25, 2001.

Albrow, Martin, Professor and Scholar in Residence, Woodrow Wilson Center for International Scholars, Washington, D.C., Nov. 2001.

Altinkilic, Oya, Assistant Professor, Katz School of Business, University of Pittsburgh, Nov. 11, 2001.

Barents, René, Expert on the Autonomy of Community Law, Court of Justice, Luxemburg, May 14, 2002.

Beck, Ulrich, Professor, University of Munich, Munich, Germany, Oct. 9, 2000.

Berns, Jessica, Program Officer, Transparency International, Berlin, May 6, 2002.

Birnberg, Jacob, Professor, Katz School of Business, University of Pittsburgh, 2000–2003.

Bleier, Michael, Chief Legal Counsel, Mellon Financial Corporation, Pittsburgh, Apr. 2, 2003.

Bonnenberg, Elena, Entrepreneur, Info-Verbo, Berlin, Apr. 2001.

Bonnenberg, Heinrich, Dr. Ing., Director of Treuhand, later Representative of the German Government to Ukraine, Member of the UCIS Board of Visitors, University of Pittsburgh, Berlin, 1990–2005.

Burkoff, John, Professor, School of Law, University of Pittsburgh, Nov. 26, 2001.

Cabral, Pedro, Councilor, Court of Justice, Luxemburg, May 3, 2001; May 13, 2002.

Carius, Alexander, Director, Ecologic, Center for International and European Environmental Research, Berlin, Oct. 11, 2000; Apr. 29, 2002.

Cheung, T. S., Professor of Sociology, Chinese University of Hong Kong, Dec. 8, 2000.

da Cunha, Miguel Mesquita, Member, Forward Studies Unit, European Union Commission, Brussels, Feb. 21, 2001; Apr. 30, 2001.

Daina, Luciano, Professor of Sociology, LUISS Guido Carli University, Rome, Apr. 19, 2001.

De Swardt, Corbus, Global Programmes Director, Transparency International, Berlin, Oct. 4, 2004.

De Vivanco, Wedigo, Dean of International Studies, Free University of Berlin, Berlin, May 6, 2002.

Dehaene, Jean-Luc, Former Prime Minister of Belgium, Member, European Parliament, Brussels, May 10, 2002; July 3, 2003; Sept. 29, 2004.

DeMucci, Raffaele, Professor of Political Science, LUISS Guido Carli University, Rome, Apr. 19, 2001.

Desai, Meghnad Lord, Director, Center for Global Governance, Professor of Economics, London School of Economics, London, Oct. 3, 2000.

Diamandouros, Nikiforos, Ombudsman, Greece; Ombudsman, Europe, Athens, Apr. 27, 2001; Strasbourg, July 10, 2003.

Elshorst, Hansjörg, Managing Director, International Secretariat, Transparency International, Berlin, July 9, 2002; May 6, 2002.

Elwood, Sir Brian, Chief Ombudsman of New Zealand, President, International Ombudsman Institute, Oct. 7, 2002, by telephone.

Epitropoulos, Mike Frank, Visiting Lecturer, Department of Sociology, University of Pittsburgh, Dec. 14, 2001.

Florini, Ann, Resident Associate, Carnegie Endowment for International Peace, Washington, D.C., 2002, 2003.

Friedmann, Bernhard, President of the European Court of Auditors, Jan. 18, 1996–Jan. 17, 1999, May 26, 1998.

Fujishima, Makoto, Planning and Coordination Division, International Communication Department, Japan External Trade Organization, Tokyo, Dec. 11, 2000.

Godano, Giuseppe, Director of Banking and Financial Supervision, Bank of Italy, Rome, Apr. 18, 2001.

Goulard, Sylvie, Group of Political Counselors, European Commission, Brussels, Belgium, May 8, 2002; July 3, 2003; Sept. 29, 2004.

Grondine, Robert, President, American Chamber of Commerce, Tokyo, Dec. 15, 2000.

Haenelt, Erich, Chief of the Cabinet of the President, European Court of Auditors, May 3, 2001.

Hahn, Heinz, Diplom Psychologe, Munich, Apr. 30, 2002.

Hänelt, Eric, Cabinet Member, European Court of Auditors, Luxemburg, May 3, 2001.

Hashimoto, Akiko, Associate Professor, Department of Sociology, University of Pittsburgh, 2000.

Hatzidimitriou, Zafiris, Secretary-General, Transparency International–Greece, Athens, Apr. 25, 2001.

Hodess, Robin, Project Manager, Global Corruption Report, Transparency International, Berlin, May 6, 2002; Oct. 4, 2004.

Infantius, Lorenzo, Professor of Economic Sociology, LUISS Guido Carli University, Rome, Apr. 19, 2001.

Iwinski, David, Managing Director, China and South East Asia, Respironics, Hong Kong, Dec. 5, 2000.

Jörges, Christian, Professor of Law, European University Institute, San Domenico di Fiesole, Italy, Apr. 23, 2001.

Kämpf, Andrea Ulrike, Intern, European Union Commission, Brussels, Apr. 30, 2001.

Kao, Charles, Chairman and CEO, Transtech, Hong Kong, Dec. 4, 2000.

Karlsson, Jan O., President, European Court of Auditors, Luxemburg, May 4, 2001.

Kazuhiko Kawamura, Vice-Chair of Council, Secretary-General, World Federalist Movement of Japan, Tokyo, Dec. 12, 2000.

Kiep, Walther Leisler, Chairman Emeritus of Atlantik-Brücke, Consultant Frankfurt, Apr. 29, 2002; June 9, 2003, by telephone; July 30, 2004, by telephone.

Kirsch, Leon, Cabinet Member, European Court of Auditors, Luxemburg, May 3, 2001.

Kohn, Diane, Program Director, Transparency International USA, Washington, D.C., Sept. 23, 2003.

Kraff, Manfred, Principal Administrator, Regional Sector and Cohesion Fund, European Court of Auditors, Luxemburg, May 3, 2001; May 13, 2002.

Kroger, Martin, Coordination II, Secretariat-General, European Commission, Brussels, Belgium, May 2, 2001; May 8, 2002; July 2, 2003.

Kurihasi, Takashi, Secretary, World Federalist Movement of Japan, Tokyo, Dec. 12, 2000.

Lau, Siu-Kai, Professor of Sociology, Chinese University of Hong Kong, Dec. 5, 2000.

Lechner, Frank, Professor, Department of Sociology, Emory University, Atlanta, 2002.

Lo, Charles, Partner, Deloitte-Touche Asia, Pittsburgh, Oct. 6, 2003; Hong Kong, Apr. 30, 2004.

Lockhart, Alec, Accountant, Court of Auditors, Luxemburg, May 14, 2002

Maffetone, Sebastiano, Professor of Political Philosophy, LUISS Guido Carli University, Rome, Apr. 19, 2001.

Marx, John, Professor of Sociology and Public Health, University of Pittsburgh, 2000–2005.

Mashiko, Ellen E., Executive Director for Scholarship, Tokyo Foundation, Tokyo, Dec. 12, 2000.

Matsudaira, Yoshifumi, Expert, Japan External Trade Organization, Tokyo, Dec. 11, 2000.

Matsumoto, Hiroshi, Senior Executive Director, International House of Japan, Inc., Tokyo, Dec. 13, 2000.

Meny, Yves, Director, Robert Schuman Centre, European University Institute, San Domenico di Fiesole, Italy, Apr. 23, 2001.

Metcalf, Michael, Professor and Director, Croft Institute for International Studies, University of Mississippi, Feb. 2000.

Millett, Timothy, Referee in the Cabinet of Judge Rodrigues, Court of Justice, Luxemburg, May 14, 2002.

Mouzelis, Nikos, Professor of Sociology, London School of Economics, Athens, Apr. 27, 2001.

Murakami, Teruyasu, Executive Managing Director, Nomura Research Institute, Tokyo, Dec. 13, 2000.

Myoshi, Masaya, President, JOAV- FM, Tokyo, Dec. 11, 2000.

Nakai, Kunihiko, Statistical and Econometric Analysis Division; Economic, Research and Analysis Department, Japan External Trade Organization, Tokyo, Dec. 11, 2000.

Panucci, Marcella, Representative to the EU, CONFINDUSTRIA, Rome, Apr. 19, 2001.

Pope, Jeremy, Executive Director, Transparency International, London, Oct. 4, 2000; May 17, 2002.

Preston, Lee, Professor Emeritus, University of Maryland, Nov. 7, 2001, by telephone.

Pross, Christian, Founder, Berlin Center for the Treatment of Torture Victims, 2000.

Prud'Homme, Wim, Head of Cabinet, Cabinet of the President, European Court of Auditors, Luxemburg, May 4, 2001.

Psomopolous, Panayotis, Director, World Ekistics Society, Athens, Apr. 25, 2001.

Pudephatt, Andrew, Executive Director, Article 19, London, May 16, 2002.

Riechenberg, Kurt, Councilor, European Court of Justice, Pittsburgh, Feb. 20, 2002.

Saccomanni, Fabrizio, General Director for International Affairs, Bank of Italy, Rome, Apr. 18, 2001.

Schaber, Gaston, Director, CEPS/Instead, Luxemburg, Oct. 6, 2000.

Schauss, Marc, Judicial Counselor for Administrative Affairs, European Court of Justice, Luxemburg, May 3, 2001.

Schneider, Heinrich, Professor Emeritus of Political Science, University of Vienna; Chairman, Institut für Europäische Politik, Berlin; Representative of the Vatican to the Organization for Security and Cooperation in Europe, Munich, May 2, 2002.

Schröder, Dagmar, Program Officer, Transparency International Germany, Berlin, Oct. 4, 2004.

Simon, Hugh, Investment Manager, Hamon Asset Management Ltd., Hong Kong, Dec. 6, 2000.

Stevenson, Kevin, Senior Manager, International Accounting Standards Board, London, May 16, 2002; June 22, 2002, by telephone.

Syrigos, Angelos, Vice President, Transparency International–Greece, Athens, Apr. 25, 2001.

Takagi, Akira, WFM Council Member, WFMJ Executive Council Member, Chair, International Relations Commission, Deputy President, Yokohama Chapter, World Federalist Movement of Japan, Tokyo, Dec. 12, 2000.

Tanami, Tatsuya, Director for International Relations and Special Projects, Department of International Affairs, Nippon Foundation, Tokyo, Dec. 14, 2000.

Thiel, Reinold, Board Member, Transparency International, Frankfurt, July 14, 2003.

Tiryakian, Edward A., Professor of Sociology, Duke University, 1990–2004.

Tsouderou, Virginia, Chairperson, Transparency International–Greece, Athens, Apr. 25, 2001.

Tülp, Walter, Cabinet Member, European Court of Auditors, Luxemburg, May 3, 2001; May 13, 2002.

Tweedie, Sir David, Chairman, International Accounting Standards Board, London, May 16, 2002; July 24, 2002 by telephone.

Umbach, Gaby, Wissenschaftliche Mitarbeiterin, Institute for Political Science and European Affairs, University of Cologne, Oct. 1, 2004.

Voigt, Karsten, Coordinator for German/American Cooperation, German Foreign Office, Berlin, July 9, 2001.

Von Weizsäcker, Ernst Ulrich, Member, German Bundestag, Berlin, Oct. 12, 2000.

Washio, Tomoharu, Special Coordinator, North American Affairs, Planning and Coordination Division, Japan External Trade Organization, Tokyo, Dec. 11, 2000; Pittsburgh, Dec. 2004.

Wiehen, Michael, Board Member, Transparency International–Germany, Munich, May 3, 2002; July 8, 2003.

Williams, Phil, Director, Ridgeway Center for Security Studies, University of Pittsburgh, Apr. 3, 2001.

Wong, Albert, Chief Operating Officer, Transtech, Hong Kong, Dec. 4, 2000.

Wu, Tsong-Ho, CEO and President, Transtech, Hong Kong, Dec. 4, 2000.

Yannaras, Christo, Professor of Philosophy, Department of International and European Studies, Panteion University, Athens, Apr. 26, 2001.

Hong Kong consultations with the Sociology Department of the Chinese University of Hong Kong, arranged in the form of a seminar by Prof. T. S. Cheung, May 3, 2004, followed by a large meeting with the Central Policy Unit of the Hong Kong government, headed by Professor S. K. Lau, with ninety-six senior officials, May 5, 2004.

INDEX

A. T. Kearney/Foreign Policy Globalization
Index (GI), 70–73
Abelard, Peter, 17–18
accountability, 69; in conceptual architecture of information value syndromes,
330–31; corporate, 54, 209–10, 215,
222–24; demands for, 44, 54, 109, 161,
193–94; democracy and, 64, 132; as EU
value, 142–43; in historical transparency, 63; India trying to increase, 159; lack
of, 60, 73, 215; of NGOs, 178, 200; penalties for deception and, 105; as principle
of good governance, 133–34; transparency and, 102, 155, 346; as U.S. value, 124–
25; as value of transparency, 84, 97,
100–101, 114
accountability perspective, in evaluation
research, 106–7
accounting, 230, 341; attempts to standard-
ize, 226–28; diversity of systems for,
225–26, 304, 345–46; needed for transparency, 224–27
Adenauer, Konrad, 131, 286, 288–92, 298
Africa: corruption in, 193, 245; democracy
in, 38, 310; Eigen working with, 186–87;
privatized violence in, 58–59
African Americans, Tuskegee syphilis study
on, 258–62
agencies, 185; government, carrying out
Freedom of Information Act, 123–24;

international, 243, 344; legitimacy of,
338–39, 342; UN, as authority in global
politics, 56–58. *See also* civil society
organizations; NGOs
Agrafiotis, Demosthenes, 148
agriculture: globalization and, 344; subsi-
dies to, 115, 156
AIDS, 243, 261–62, 274
Akhter, Mohammad N., 272–73
Alfonsín, President, 315–16
American Civil Liberties Union (ACLU):
defense of free speech by, 118, 124, 142;
resisting increased government powers,
128
Americas, extent of democracy in, 38
Amnesty International, 190, 235, 312–13;
Nobel Peace Prize awarded to, 176; on
treaties for universal jurisdiction, 315;
on war crimes tribunals, 314, 317–18
Angell, Marcia, 246
Annan, Kofi, 176, 178, 184, 236
Anti-Ballistic Missile (ABM) Treaty of 1972,
59
apartheid, ending, 325–26
appropriation, of property, 206–8, 211
Arab world, lack of democracy in, 38
archives, demand for access to, 28
Argentina, transitioning to democracy,
315–16
Asia, 59, 122, 305; extent of democracy in,

medical abuses by, 33, 246–55; resistance to, 294–95; resistance to historical transparency about, 252–54, 342; restitution to victims of, 290, 292; war crimes tribunals for, 286–88, 293

Neier, Aryeh, 317–18

Nelson, Benjamin, 17–18

neoconservatives, U.S., 157–58, 333

"new economy" era, 205–6

newspapers/journalists, 29, 32, 124, 337

New Zealand, 41

NGOs, 157, 198, 239; competition among, 175–77, 201–2; founders of, 183–86; International Criminal Court and, 319–20; legitimacy of, 338–39, 342; models for social change among, 183; power of, 163, 177–78, 342; public health initiatives by, 276–77; range of issues of, 178–79; relations among, 160, 185, 196–97; transparency of, 177–78, 200. *See also* civil society organizations; Transparency International

Nigeria, 203

Nixon, Richard M., 92, 118

Nobel Peace Prize, 176, 202, 325

Nuremberg Code, on medical experimentation, 33, 249, 256–57, 260

Nuremberg war crimes tribunals, 283–88, 310–11

obedience, in secrecy syndrome, 96

ombudsmen, 143, 148; accountability and, 100–101; rise of, 37, 41–44, 131–32; Swedish, 32, 119

opacity, 7, 86; effects of, 84, 336–37; extent of, 123, 336; secrecy vs., 90

open society, 1–2; definition of, 335; requirements for, 335–39; resistance to, 346–47; transparency compared to, 3

Open Society Institute, 3

oppression, 34, 51

Organization for Economic Cooperation and Development (OECD), 45, 54, 235; fighting corruption, 147, 160, 192, 344;

Transparency International working with, 195–96

Pan-Europa movement, 129–30

Panikkar, K. N., 327–28, 374n81

parliaments, elected, 30

Parran, Thomas, 258–60

Parsons, Talcott, 79–81, 176

participation, in government, 133–34, 136–37, 145

particularism and diffuseness, vs. universalism and specificity, 27

patent laws, 125–26

Patriot Act (U.S.), 117–18, 127–28

peace: efforts to unite Europe for, 128, 130–31; treaties promoting, 59–60

Pei, Minxin, 122, 332

Perraton, Jonathan, 49–50

Personal Data Act (Sweden), 145

philosophy, 17, 35

Poland, 41, 138, 315

political culture, America's, 23–26

political parties, in growth of democracy, 30

political rights, in democracy, 38

politics, 32; around health care, 242–43; business and, 199–200; corruption in, 188, 200, 341; in debates about history, 327–28; drug companies and, 246; global, 54–56, 56–58, 136–37, 139, 274; information cultures and, 108, 111, 125, 345–46; memory, 285

Pope, Jeremy, 192–93, 202

Popper, Karl R., 1–2, 35

population, increasing, 331

populists, in government value syndrome, 27

poverty: effects of, 114–15; efforts to overcome, 156–57; global inequalities in, 50–52

power, 77; isolation used to maintain, 109–10; as media of exchange, 81, 176; opacity as technique in, 90; secrecy as technique in, 78, 89–90, 92–93

Powers, Richard Gid, 92–93

DATE DUE